STORMS IN
HER HEAD

STORMS IN HER HEAD

FREUD AND THE CONSTRUCTION OF HYSTERIA

edited by

Muriel Dimen and
Adrienne Harris

OTHER

OTHER PRESS
New York

Production Editor: Robert D. Hack

This book was set in 11 pt. Veljovic by Alpha Graphics of Pittsfield, New Hampshire.

10 9 8 7 6 5 4 3 2 1

Library of Congress Cataloging-in-Publication Data

Storms in her head: Freud and the construction of hysteria / Muriel Dimen and Adrienne Harris, eds.

    p. cm.

    Includes bibliographical references and index.

    ISBN 1-892746-23-9

    1. Breuer, Josef, 1842–1925. Studien èber Hysterie 2. Hysteria—Case studies. 3. Psychoanalysis—Case studies. 4. Freud, Sigmund, 1856–1939. 5. Psychoanalysis and feminism. I. Dimen, Muriel. II. Harris, Adrienne.

RC532 .S58 2000

616.89'17—dc21

                                       00–035689

In memory of
Donald Kaplan
and
Stephen A. Mitchell

Contents

Preface
John Kerr

An odd habit, reading prefaces. By convention, the reader of the preface hopes to be informed somehow of what lies ahead, perhaps even of how to read it. And yet, by turning a page or two, the reader can get to where he or she is going anyway. Why, then, does a reader start a book with a preface, simply to encounter someone pointing ahead and saying, "Go to Chapter One. I'm behind you all the way"?

Of course, the reader will say, it is a literary convention. Books are written before they are published. And since the book won't change, except tendentiously through various acts of the reader's imagination somewhere down the road, it seems reasonable to begin reading a book by hearing out another reader who has already become acquainted with it. Ordinarily this will be the author or the editors; occasionally, as in the present case, an interloper will have to do. But whoever writes the preface, perhaps we will get lucky and find out in a few quick pages something essential about the book that lies before us. It won't change, after all.

The reader who rejoins in this way is, of course, being reasonable, but only in a literate sort of way. That is to say, the reader is taking something for granted—the existence of books and the psychic structures and mental habits formed by writing and reading books—that need not exist at all. And by taking that something for granted, by adopting what is an essentially literate mentality, the reader is committing himself or herself to a stance on the nature of the self, on its relation to imagination, and on the therapeutics needed to keep both in good working order that may actually deceive in an important way.

Consider that in the present instance the reader holds in his or her hand a book about another book. That other book describes a heuristic rationale for understanding the formation of symptoms in hysterical patients and offers a therapeutic strategy for alleviating them. *Studies on Hysteria* (1893-1895) is over a hundred years old. It was written by two nineteenth-century Viennese physicians, one already quite distinguished at the time and the other then largely unknown, Josef Breuer and Sigmund Freud. Of course, the great likelihood is that the reader has already read that older book, which not incidentally has a preface of its own, a perfectly good one in fact, that collegially announces a slight but unavoidable degree of dissonance in the two authors' views and a regrettable but equally inevitable degree of circumspection in not reporting more fully on sexual details.

How much really can that other book, more than a hundred years old, have changed? In terms of the reader's imagination, one could say that it has potentially changed a great deal, especially in the last few decades. Thanks to the published researches of Andersson (1979), Ellenberger (1972, 1977), Hirschmüller (1977), Fichtner (with Hirschmüller 1989), and Swales (1986, 1988), the reader can compare what is written in that book with historical information, at times revelatory, that brings alive the cultural context and the nature of the caseload. The existential encounter in the case of Katharina now reads quite differently, for example. So does the case of Frau Cäcilie M., which is discreetly broken up in the footnotes for reasons that become obvious when one grasps that she was arguably the richest woman in Vienna. She was not as rich, however, as another patient, Emmy von N., who could command a housecall from the junior physician in the collaboration, Freud, in faraway Zurich. The new historical information also challenges the optimistic assessment of the two doctors about their therapy. The cathartic cure of Anna O. is now known to be a fiction (see especially Borch-Jacobsen 1996); ditto the seemingly successful treatment of Elisabeth von R. Indeed, of all the cases, only that of Lucy R. remains known solely through the sympathetic account in the extant text, itinerant British governesses having the advantage over wealthy women in that they do not leave enough clues in the historical record for even the most diligent historian to track them down. But apart from Lucy's story, the reader can use the existence of the new historical information to set his or her imagination free and begin changing the text as he or she reads.

The text potentially reads differently in another way, too. Where once "hypnoid states" and "retention hysteria" (either or both could be triggered by nursing a dying relative, according to the authors) had gone so far out of fashion that commentaries were required to explain their presence in the text at all, today's clinician is inclined to go back to the particulars of the case reports and see illumined therein concepts and observations that, if they cannot be called modern except through the most determined misreading, nonetheless now seem far more prescient and more suggestive of some of today's latest therapeutic theorems than they did a scant twenty years ago. The universe of clinical understanding is changing profoundly at century's end. As the reader will see, this generates new readings of the old cases.

But in a strict sense, the cases themselves and the clinical observations of the two celebrated authors concerning them, like the book itself, have not changed. There everything still is, in the same steadfast prose, as it was more than a hundred years ago. The text is a permanent object; it connects the reader with an actual point of view and an actual past that can no longer be changed. To be sure, unless it is a first edition in the original German, the text of *Studies on Hysteria* is not quite on the same artifactual order as the bed that Washington slept in, or the gun that killed McKinley. But it is workably close. And for the literate mind, it is more than close. It is as exact as one needs it to be. Indeed, it is this degree of exactness, this permanence intrinsic to a book, that makes it possible for both the clinician and the historian to generate new readings, at first working alone, then by sharing their ideas, and ultimately by writing new books. It is this degree of exactness, in other words, that allows knowledge to advance in a systematic way. Similarly, it is this degree of exactness that makes revised readings, and imagination generally, safe. The literate world is a world peopled by literate selves, selves who feel themselves to be as permanent and as singular as the texts they write and read. It is also—quite paradoxically given the sustained psychic vigor of the selves who have produced it—a materialist world, a world whose permanence speaks for itself yet whose vitality has been reduced to a mindless machination of its parts through the systematic comparisons of causes and effects made possible by books. Finally, it is a historical world, a world with a past felt to be actual, not mythic. For all these reasons, it is a world where imagination is a relief, not a danger.

How different is the preliterate world. In the preliterate world there are no books and there are no prefaces. In the preliterate world only the spoken word and the memory of the group can be relied on. These are both fragile. In the preliterate world a sentence is uttered and immediately lost, the sound of it dissolved quite literally into the air that once bore its meaning, gone in an instant unless the collective memory saves it in some version that will allow another equally ephemeral but scarcely identical utterance to occur again.

Such a world is quite different from ours. Nineteenth-century anthropology looked at the preliterate world and saw primitivity. That is not the same thing. The preliterate mind does not lack for technical competence. Nor is it without philosophy. Nor art. Nor most of the things that an overconfident young science of man once equated with being civilized. Indeed, the great and general distinction between primitive and civilized, which in the late nineteenth century informed a range of sciences beyond anthropology, including psychoanalysis once it got started, has since been discarded as an unfortunate and misleading notion.

But a world without books, a world dependent on the spoken word, a truly preliterate world—this is something else again. Not primitive, but not the same as a literate world either. Twentieth-century commentators from a host of disciplines have begun to tease out the lineaments of the preliterate world. What they find can only be sketched lightly here.[1] It is a world that is alive in a way difficult for the purely literate mind to comprehend, at least outside of poetry. It is a world organized by myth, peopled by spirits. It is communal in its logic, not individualistic. In the preliterate world the self itself is a plurivocal affair, scarcely a self at all by the standards of the nineteenth century (if not the late twentieth).

1. I would like to thank Professor Nancy Reale of New York University and Peter Dimock of Vintage Books for their assistance in appreciating the relations between the literate and preliterate worlds. The reader who is interested in further pursuit of this distinction, which to repeat is not the same as between civilized and primitive, might consult the works of Ong (1982), Havelock (1986), Snell (1953), Luria (1976), Sanders (1994), and Illich and Sanders (1988).

In the preliterate world, further, unconscious mental states are taken for granted, and illnesses caused by unconscious states seen as the regular routine. The boundary between the physical, the psychical, and the spiritual is permeable in every direction. Indeed, it is not a boundary at all, but a membrane, one so elastic that it can stretch to cover the village and the cosmos, an ache in the heart and the afterlife, an accident down by the river and an insult to someone's ancestors, and yet somehow never lose its shape. In such a world, imagination, if it is not immediately reined in by ritual, is an essential danger. For, by virtue of the very permeability that makes the world of meaning immanent in every direction, imagination sets loose forces that go far beyond the self.

In the preliterate world diseases, even what we would consider diseases of clearly physical origin are seen not only as latently interpersonal, but also, and far more dangerously, as imaginative. Quite properly, the therapeutics of the preliterate world are based on ritual and trance, gratification and prohibition: anything to turn imagination back onto its proper course. Magic stones, magic places, magic potions, and magic spells all have their place in the preliterate pharmacy. Combined with these, no less shockingly to the literate mind, so do presents, feasts, sex, praise, and also reprimand and prescriptions of abstinence. And often enough, in the right combination, these devices work, the magical no less enduringly than the practical. But only for those who—"believe" is too weak a word—are immersed in their meanings and persuaded of the good will of those who minister to them. In a world without books and prefaces, therapeutics are based on suggestion.

It is not usually considered good intellectual manners to observe how truly proximal the preliterate world is to our own. To be sure, classicists remind us that the preliterate world was once universally the only world that existed, and that this universality obtained in a period historically closer to us than we like to remember—the first and therefore enduringly critical transition in the West occurred in ancient Greece—while anthropologists tell us that, broken into fragments around the globe, such a world still continues to exist today in many societies. But, accustomed as we are to being literate, we don't really believe them. Even less do we like to think that such a world could really have survived, nay flourished, in an important domain during the century just before our own, a century whose muscular sensibility is of a piece with our own.

It is the unrecognized nearness of the preliterate world to ours that perhaps best explains why the book the reader holds in hand concerns *Studies on Hysteria* by Breuer and Freud, and not some other meritorious work from the same period. For at the end of the nineteenth century, the preliterate world, though everywhere in retreat, still held on indomitably and most disconcertingly in an increasingly prominent realm. This realm lay between the latest conceptual frontier of medical therapeutics and the daily painful scenes being played out in the parlors and bedrooms of the unhappy. Nosologically, this realm was known as hysteria, but (as was not totally unrecognized at the time) under that general rubric one had also to include the devices and stratagems that were being used to treat it. Hysteria and its treatment formed a dismayingly intractible anachronism: a preliterate one.

But it was there nonetheless. The campaign whereby the literate mind finally conquered and annexed this last preliterate stronghold took almost the entire nineteenth century to complete. Such a long campaign could not have been predicted, given how extraordinary were the relevant advances at the very beginning of the century. At least since Wordsworth, the Western world already understood that a text could contain resonances and intuitions that could express unconscious processes, and could therefore give voice to the residuals of childhood and dreams and heartache, while remaining a text. In this, the literate world had already staked a very important claim. Among other things, the new literature meant that one could hope to own one's own biography in a way quite different from what any Renaissance writer could have ever foreseen, provided of course one was a poet—a proviso that guaranteed that poets would be envied throughout the century, even when they went famously mad.

Also recognized by the literate mind, ever since Mesmer's famous triumph over the renowned German exorcist Father Gasser in 1775, was that in understanding illnesses caused by the imagination one could substitute materialistic causes—even so flimsy cause as the magnetic fluid would do—over spiritual ones and lose nothing. This meant that physicians could finally replace priests and other kinds of healers on principle, and books could now supplant initiations and investitures. These substitutions became progressively more important as the nineteenth century rolled forward and evolved two new kinds of text, the detective story and the medical case history. In time, the magnetic fluid was gradually replaced by ever more recondite speculations about the functioning of the nervous system. Yoked to the new narrative forms, these speculations, premature though they might be, became progressively more informative, generating fresh clinical observations about family trees, about childhood, and about trauma, though now it was the physician, not the poet, who wielded authorial power.

But therapeutics lagged behind. Causes might be understood materialistically, but treatment still relied on suggestion. And it was this lag in therapeutics that was so embarrassing. Here we can pass by truly absurd instances like the use of metals and magnets to literally pull the symptom away from the body of the patient and put it into someone else, a practice more recent in historical time than the American Civil War. Let us consider only the otherwise sterling example of Pierre Janet at the century's end. Janet was the preeminent medical and psychological authority on hysteria in the world at the time Breuer's and Freud's book first appeared, a thinker of such sufficient power that his own works are now enjoying a long overdue reconsideration. Janet did many, many things only a literate man would do. He carefully and laboriously wrote down everything: his self-bemused "fountain pen method." He thereby accumulated extraordinarily detailed case histories, narratives that not only extended back into childhood but also encompassed, albeit under a dubious hereditary rationale, discussions of the families of the afflicted. Further, he compared cases systematically to discover which antecedent causes were essential, which accidental, in any given case, another possibility accessible only to the literate. Janet even instructed his patients to write. To be sure, on most occasions this was for the purpose of training the mind and thereby strengthening a hereditarily or traumatically weakened nervous system. But on some occasions, this was to be done while the patient was in a distracted state and the purpose was no less than to unlock the morbid secrets of the imagination—the phenomenon of "automatic writing." Yet automatic writing, like the "automatic talking" that Janet also used, was solely for purposes of reconnaissance. When it came time to combat the hysterical symptom directly and intimately, time for the therapeutically decisive confrontation with what Janet convinced his contemporaries was the crucial pathogen—the dissociated fixed idea or memory—the good doctor had nothing better than hypnotism and suggestion. He put his patients in a trance.

Thus, while Janet's understanding of the essentials of hysterical symptomatology was literate, he was still using an essentially preliterate means for its amelioration. He was not much different from a mesmerist, or for that matter an exorcist. To his credit, Janet knew this. But what else could he do? For the literate mind, the net result was an intellectual and narrative scandal, one that is still freshly felt to be shocking by today's readers. Rather than release the patient from the pathogenic memories and imaginings by recognizing them as part of a new kind of potentially healthy narrative, Janet was reduced to writing over them by suggesting—under hypnosis—that they were unreal or had never happened. This worked, but it meant that in the midst of literacy, an island of preliterate magic remained. The cure might be preferable to the symptom, but it was not finally a literate cure. It could never really be intellectually respectable for the growing middle classes, who after all were now universally literate themselves.

This brings us to why the book that the reader holds in hand is about that book by Breuer and Freud, and not about some other respected book of the time by Binet, Moebius, Janet, Benedikt, Schrenck-Notzing, or whomever. Breuer and Freud hit on a literate form of treatment. Inspired by the intricate hysterical caprices of Anna O., who would truly find peace of mind only a decade later when she herself became a writer, and misreading Aristotle (or rather Bernays on Aristotle) Breuer and Freud elaborated a rationale whereby the patient could become the author of her own story in a way that could express her imagination, not suppress it. This was a privilege heretofore reserved for the poet. It meant that hysteria could now be contained, not just by a text, but in a text. The patient could join the physician as author. The reconnaissance had become the cure.

How self-consciously did Breuer and Freud fashion their new therapy, the first therapy for diseases of the imagination truly acceptable to the literate mind? One can find here and there in their text metaphors of a picture book to represent the imagination and of a perfectly preserved archive to represent unconscious memory, as well as the admission that the cases read more like short stories than not. But it would seem hard to believe that the authors fully intended what they accomplished. Some fifteen years later, no less a person than that scion of a then famous psychiatric family (his uncle treated Nietzsche) and later founder of existential psychiatry, Ludwig Binswanger (1957), would note pointedly that this was the first "rational" form of treatment. But even Binswanger, already pondering the recent history of nervous disease and its cures, did not see that it was rational because it was literate.

More importantly, how well is the new literate form of cure enduring? A century has been spent with people eagerly pursuing this form of treatment. But, interestingly, the same century has also seen a growing distrust of the text, any text, as final arbiter of the imagination. To be sure, postmodernism is itself a literate enterprise—texts are still required to deconstruct other texts—largely confined to the intellectual class. But deconstructionism is no longer reserved just for matters literary. In the consulting room, too, we now honor a new intellectual freedom that seems destined to question and confront more than it confirms. This freedom, in turn, seems to be most valuable when we treat patients, be they children or traumatized and dissociated adults who are anything but intellectual. Moreover, beyond the recent turn to a dialogical narrative constructivism as practically a therapeutic rationale in and of itself, we also now begin to detect in the consulting room actual phenomena that truly defy our old text-driven understanding. All of a sudden, there now seem to be strange influences at work, contagions of self in the other and of other in the self (see especially Bromberg 1998), distortions in the warp and woof of time, confusions between memories of fantasies and fantasies of memories, all of which harken back to the preliterate imagination and to the preliterate world. Yet how shall we survive, as therapists and as patients, if we begin to think that we cannot fully trust texts as a vehicle for understanding, while at the same time we also know that we must inevitably still make use of texts if we are to communicate with one another, and hopefully not only advance knowledge but also get better ourselves?

Here, I suggest turning the page.

REFERENCES

Anderson, O. (1979). A supplement to Freud's case history of "Frau Emmy von N." in *Studies on Hysteria. Scandinavian Psychoanalytic Review* 2:5–16.

Binswanger, L. (1957). *Sigmund Freud: Reminiscences of a Friendship.* New York: Grune and Stratton.

Borch-Jacobsen, M. (1996). *Remembering Anna O.: A Century of Mystification.* New York: Routledge.

Breuer, J. and Freud, S. (1895). Studies on hysteria. *Standard Edition* 2.

Bromberg, P. (1998). *Standing in the Spaces: Essays on Clinical Process, Trauma and Dissociation.* Hillsdale, NJ: Analytic Press.

Ellenberger, H. (1972). The story of "Anna O.": A critical review with new data. In *Beyond the Unconscious: Essays of Henri F. Ellenberger in the History of Psychiatry,* ed. M. Micale, pp. 254–272. Princeton, NJ: Princeton University Press, 1993.

——(1977). The story of "Emmy von N.": A critical study with new documents. In *Beyond the Unconscious: Essays of Henri F. Ellenberger in the History of Psychiatry,* ed. M. Micale, pp. 273–290. Princeton, NJ: Princeton University Press, 1993.

Fichtner, G. and Hirschmüller, A. (1985). Freud's "Katharina"—Hintergrund, Entstehungsgeschicte und Bedeutung einer fruhen psychoanalytischen Krankengeschicte. *Psyche* 39:220–240.

Havelock, E. (1986). *The Muse Learns to Write: Reflections on Orality and Literacy from Antiquity to the Present.* New Haven, CT: Yale University Press.

Hirschmüller, A. (1989). *The Life and Work of Josef Breuer: Physiology and Psychoanalysis.* New York: New York University Press.

Illich, I. and Sanders, B. (1988). *ABC: The Alphabetization of the Popular Mind.* San Francisco: North Point Press.

Luria A. R. (1976). *Cognitive Development: Its Cultural and Social Foundation.* Cambridge, MA: Harvard University Press.

Ong, W. (1982). *Orality and Literacy: The Technologizing of the Word.* London and New York: Methuen.

Sanders, B. (1994). *A Is for Ox: Violence, Electronic Media, and the Silencing of the Written Word.* New York: Pantheon.

Snell, B. (1953). *The Discovery of the Mind: The Greek Origins of European Thought.* Cambridge, MA: Harvard University Press.

Swales, P. (1986). Freud, his teacher, and the birth of psychoanalysis. In *Freud Appraisals and Reappraisals: Contributions to Freud Studies, vol. 1,* ed. P. Stepansky, pp. 2–82. Hillsdale, NJ: Analytic Press.

——(1988). Freud, Katharina, and the first "Wild Analysis." In *Freud Appraisals and Reappraisals: Contributions to Freud Studies, vol. 3,* ed. P. Stepansky, pp. 81–164. Hillsdale, NJ: Analytic Press.

Acknowledgments

We would like to express our gratitude to the New York University Postdoctoral Program in Psychotherapy and Psychoanalysis for its sponsorship of a conference, "The Psychoanalytic Century," celebrating the centennial of the publication of *Studies on Hysteria*. The conference, at which many of these papers were first presented, was held May 4–6, 1995.

Thanks also to Maureen McGrogran for her early encouragement in developing this project for publication, and to Michael Moskowitz, Susan Fairfield, and Bob Hack at Other Press for all the tasks in shepherding this book into the world.

On a personal note, Muriel Dimen would like to thank Sue Shapiro for shelter from the storm. Adrienne Harris thanks Robert Sklar and Katherine Tentler for such steady love and support.

Introduction

Muriel Dimen and

Adrienne Harris

PATIENT AND ANALYST

Is it conventional wisdom or mere rhetorical flourish that psycho-analytic authors often demur that it is patients who instruct their analysts? Winnicott (1971) dedicated a book to the patients who had paid to teach him. Free association as a method of psychic investigation and mutation seems at least a collaborative venture of Freud and Anna O. She certainly gave the method its intriguing epithet, "the talking cure." In this sense, a centennial that marks authorship is almost controversial. To identify psychoanalysis now so exclusively with Freud does seem more rhetorical than substantive, and a careful consideration of *Studies on Hysteria* (Breuer and Freud 1893–1895) reveals that the analyst's collaboration with the patient has been a factor in psychoanalysis from the beginning. Therefore, when we began this project to mark the centennial of the publication of *Studies on Hysteria*, we set our authors the task of reacting to any one of the six women whose characters and histories and symptoms inhabit the pages of that volume. Reconfiguring the work for the edification and interest of a modern audience, we de-emphasize the authorial voice of the doctors and privilege instead the spectacle of the analytic pairs, moving in such amazing and stately form through the pages of *Studies on Hysteria*. We foreground the tension between the figures of patients and analysts in an attempt to dislodge the hegemonic and patriarchal aspect of the story.

Six women. Five essays. Like the buddy cohort in a World War II film, they represent a diverse set of characters and types, women set in distinct generations, social formations, and family circumstances. Anna O. was 21, a "markedly intelligent" young woman whose appetite for vital mental work—"solid mental pabulum"—remained unsatisfied. "Poetic" and "willful," "her willpower was energetic, tenacious, and persistent" and "completely unsuggestible" (p. 121). In his initial sketch of Anna O., Freud notes the discrepancy between lively mind and empty, monotonous life. Emmy von N., 40 years old, first appears resting on a sofa, frowning, enervated, speaking in a low voice, her speech disrupted by stam-

mers and strange cries. She is prone to somnambulism and to hypnoid states. Katharina ____, "a sulky looking" 18-year-old, is a peasant girl encountered on a mountain vacation. By her accent, setting, class, and situation Freud positions the trauma of incest as
the experience of a girl unmistakably outsider and Other. Miss
Lucy, an Englishwoman of 30, is living as a governess. Low spir-
ited and fatigued, she complains of heaviness in the head and diminished appetite, a woman "of delicate constitution" trapped and
symptomatic precisely because of the impossibility of her fierce
longings for mobility and love. Miss Lucy seems sometimes to have
stepped from the pages of a Brontë novel. Given the presence of
both Katharina ____ and Miss Lucy in this foundational text, it
seems important to note that hysteria was never solely positioned
as a disaffection of the idle bourgeoisie. Elisabeth von R., at 24,
exhibits one of the hallmarks of hysteria, "la belle indifférance,"
despite a family history of loss and bereavement. Although her
presentation of her body is as an odd, undifferentiated sea of pains,
Freud notes that, when he touched her, he "could not help thinking that it was as though she was having a voluptuous tickling sensation—her face flushed, she threw back her head and shut her eyes
and her body bent backward" (p. 137): the hysteric's body as an
imaginary erotic anatomy, a roadmap of pleasure, danger, and
prohibition. The sixth patient, Frau Cäcilie, is scattered across the
essays and into the footnotes, disguised, protected, fragmented.
Frau Cäcilie, is described by Freud as a woman whose history and
reputation must be protected, but whose distinct and often wildly
discordant mental capacities sharpened his sense of the mysterious power of psychic experience to shape and structure mental
life.

These six women, and a handful of others who appear in brief
clinical vignettes, live in our imagination, strange and exotic on
the one hand, deeply familiar and human on the other. They seem
to be in command of language. Their unique and evocative phrases
provoked four of the six thematic subtitles of this introduction and
the title of this volume. They taught their therapists, but they also
submitted to them. Words and speech could fail and desert them.
Their bodies, too, could speak eloquently but also collapse under
the weight of anguish and anxiety.

THEMES

In this introduction we put into play the metaphor of the kaleidoscope. Shake it up once and you get the scholarly meeting at which most of the essays presented here made their first appearance: "The Psychoanalytic Century: An International and Interdisciplinary Conference Celebrating the Centennial of Breuer and Freud's *Studies on Hysteria*," held at New York University on May 4–6, 1995. Each interdisciplinary panel at the conference crystallized around a single case. Shake the kaleidoscope again and you get this book. We have selected several papers from the conference (publishing constraints prohibited the inclusion of all) and added one more (Paola Mieli's) and a Preface from one of the original participants (John Kerr). We have asked the writers in this collection to address one of these women and the text(s) she inhabits in any way they wished. They might read closely and clinically, attending to the patient's suffering, or the treatment issues, or the theory of mind and trauma illuminated by the case. Or they could jump from the text to wide-ranging intellectual matters of mind and culture at which interdisciplinary deployments of psychoanalysis meet. The stances and choices and voices of these authors are variable and rich.

Here you will find the six women patients and their cases not as focus but as stimulus for several principal themes organizing the book. The themes of this collection web psychoanalytic thought and practice from one end of the century to the next. Some of them have been with psychoanalysis from the beginning. Others are new. Some have been prominent; others are untended threads of thought, picked up now for the first time. Sections are entitled with the words of a patient to her doctor or those of her doctor about her, words resonating in each of the cases as well as in the psychoanalytic past, present, and future. These titles introduce several critical themes: the relationship of doctor and patient, the question of hierarchy in clinical practice and the recent questioning of the doctor's authority, the importance of speech in psychoanalysis, the vitality of both doctor's and patient's voices, the very personal quality of expression that marks the particularity of each clinical treatment.

"You Can Say Anything to a Doctor": The History of Psychoanalytic Technique and the Birth of the Clinic

Or can you? It is Katharina _____ who speaks these words to Freud, and her situation calls up in many ways the question of power in psychoanalysis. We may imagine her, a peasant girl of 18, kin to the family that runs the guest house at which Freud is vacationing, looking up at him with eyes full of trust. Is it too difficult, at this point in the century, to imagine such trust? Perhaps. We are now accustomed to the critique of authority: doctors do not know everything, nor do they always follow the Hippocratic oath; science no longer corners the market on truth; never trust anyone over 30. Katharina, however, needs to talk to the great doctor. She has run across him, perhaps even set out to find him, on one of his morning walks in the mountains. She wants to tell him about her shortness of breath, so short she fears she might suffocate. And as she discloses to him her concerns, we discover that behind her suffering lies a history of what we would today call sexual abuse at the hands of an uncle.

Psychoanalysis is deeply implicated in the critique of power animating recent intellectual and political history. At once part of the problem and part of the solution, it walks a tightrope between freedom and constraint. As clinical practice, it is, as Benjamin Wolstein insists in his re-evaluation of Breuer's work with Anna O., a venture into the unknown, offering the exhilaration of discovery. At the same time, psychoanalysis as a discipline and profession is snug in prevailing cultural mores. This tension, between the institutional embeddedness of the field and its daringly radical insight about human possibility, laces the contributions to this volume. For Martin Bergmann, Freud and Breuer led the critique of authority in psychoanalysis: "Breuer and Freud demanded from the physician . . . that he listen to the patient. To convert an autocratic physician into a person who had to learn the biography of each patient . . . was a major step forward" (p. 344). Roy Schafer, in contrast, finds that very autocracy enacted in the case of Elisabeth von R. There is, he says, "a clear picture of [Freud's] determination to dominate the treatment" (p. 329). Schafer voices another major theme in this collection, the patriarchal core of this domination: "enacting the unilateral paternalistic authority of the physician" (p. 336), Freud does not clear a space to examine his patient's questioning of the conventional social goals prescribed for her.

The psychoanalyst is a powerful figure in the eyes of both patients and culture, a power patients began to contest from the moment they were inscribed in the writings of the field. How interesting that Anna O. and Frau Emmy insist on their analysts listening to them, as we are told by Benjamin Wolstein and Rita Frankiel. How interesting that Elisabeth von R. is cheeky, "masculine," asserting an independence of which, Roy Schafer says, Freud could make no clinical use. How intriguing that Freud referred to Frau Cäcilie as his teacher. Is it a matter of class that Miss Lucy and Katharina ___, governess and peasant, employees both, are the two who do not rebel?

These days no discussion of technique can proceed without an excavation of power: power in the consulting room, power in society. The question of freedom and constraint in psychoanalysis is imbricated with the power and authority of the analyst, and its history is at one with shifts in intellectual and political life that run across the twentieth century. Whether Breuer and Freud got it or not—and the essayists in this volume disagree—their case studies are riddled with patients' attempts to secure equality of power and recognition in relation to their therapists. The essayists notice what for Freud and Breuer was barely perceptible: that the quality of the relationship is key to the treatment, as Philip Bromberg argues in his essay about Frau Emmy von N. regarding the necessity of "treating symptoms with patience while treating patients with symptoms" (p. 131).

Most contributors argue that we can see in the *Studies* how patients upended the good doctors, thereby bringing about great changes in technique if not the birth of psychoanalysis itself. The women in these cases ask for recognition. Some patients are heard poorly, if at all. Working with the theme of women's desire in patriarchal culture, Schafer, as we have seen, does not feel that Elisabeth was at all recognized in her particularity and needs as a woman or coparticipant. Jan Goldstein's account extends our range. She tells us of a young French peasant woman, Nanette Leroux, whose symptoms of convulsions, lethargy, and hysterical catalepsy, brought on by having seen a man exposing himself to her, are markedly similar to those of the women in the *Studies*.

Goldstein argues in the end that Nanette did not get what she wanted: "her symptomatology . . . speaks of her desire . . . for . . . some freedom from society's demands on and close scrutiny of her biological performance" (p. 165), some freedom to name her symptoms and find her own cure.

Other patients are heard more clearly, although, as Philip Bromberg ruefully notes in regard to Frau Emmy, not always in time to get the help they needed. Certainly they have an aftereffect, their *Nachträglichkeit*, which Paola Mieli explains so clearly in her essay on trauma, nearly making psychoanalysis look as though it were always already there, all of a piece. When patients are heard, the hearing they receive sometimes reciprocally influences the therapist who hears them. Wolstein especially praises Breuer for recognizing Anna O.'s need for what interpersonal theory calls a co-participant relationship with her therapist when she invents "the talking cure." The patient may also, as Michael Roth writes, set "a limit, or at least a context, for [the analyst's] authority" (p. 180). In a contribution that appreciates the ironies of power, he depicts the way Frau Emmy von N., one of the richest women in Europe, submits to the ambitious but not yet world-historical Freud as he anxiously plays "the role of the powerful physician wielding the latest tool of science, hypnosis, to direct the mind of his patient" (p. 178).

There ensue clinical advances that will make psychoanalysis what it would later come to be. In the dialectics of psychoanalytic technique, with which contemporary psychoanalytic theory has caught up, the patients, in struggling with their doctors, force their doctors to change, and, in changing, they change what psychoanalysis is and has become. When hypnosis fails, Freud applies direct suggestion. Emmy's response to his maneuvers makes both hypnosis and suggestion give way in the end to a new model of the psychoanalytic relationship in which the hierarchy of doctor over patient will ultimately never be secure again. While this powerful woman at first becomes docile, she later complains "about Freud's eagerness to erase her memories before she has had the chance to recount them for him" (p. 180). She wants to tell him what she has on her mind, not to have her thoughts directed by his questions about their origins. Finally, Roth recounts, Freud falls in with what she wants, no longer giving definitive explanations or wiping away that past by means of hypnotic suggestion. Thus he falls into psychoanalysis, for there is born (again) not only the talking cure but the transferential relationship through which psychoanalytic change regularly takes place.

The technical focus, even in what Bromberg (p. 131) and Green (p. 89) call this "preanalytic" prehistory of psychoanalysis, is, the essayists argue, already shifting from the medical model of knowing doctor curing helpless patient to a more complicated and active dialogue between them. The seeds of transference, for example, are already here: Emmy, Bromberg points out, worries that her anger has offended her doctor, a worry that not only prompts Freud to begin listening to her but serves as "a relational act that allows Emmy to experience her own impact in shaping the process that Anna O. had called 'chimney sweeping'" (p. 132). Freud's healing profession is leaving physiology and becoming a psychology. Lewis Aron marks the year 1892–1893, when Freud was treating Miss Lucy, as a turning point in the evolution of his clinical work, because it was during this period that he became a psychotherapist, shifting "from hypnotism to a rudimentary form of free association" (p. 226). He argues that Freud's interest in the psychological foundations and dynamics of hypnosis dovetailed with his search for the psychological origins of hysteria. Recognizing the deep psychology of hypnosis, he could drop the belief that he had to put a patient into trance to cure her. He found out he could talk to her, find the meaning that she gave her symptoms, and thereby unearth their origins, a process leading to cure. "The reconnaissance," in John Kerr's words, "had become the cure" (p. xvi).

"Private Theater": Trauma, Spectacle, Crisis of Affect

With this evocative phrase, Anna O. described an inner world of daydreams and fantasy split off from "an extremely monotonous existence in her puritanically minded family" (Breuer and Freud 1893–1895, p. 22). The phrase conjures up certain pervasive features of hysteria: the power of image, dream, and daydream; hysteria's theatricality; its mimetic reproduction in action of the symptom of desire and thwarted desire; hysteria's status as wordless enactment. Theater and theatricality also imply a performer, an audience, and the interchangeable roles of watcher and watched. As much as it is an altered or distorted form of communication, hysteria is a performance, a spectacle produced in a complex paradoxical state of involuntary yet inexorable manipulation. And, as Roth argues, the hysteric in analysis is performing in duet, the inherent and theatrical illness in transference and countertransference scenes being still a much feared and anxiously defended feature of psychoanalysts' professional lives.

Anna O.'s "private theatre" was an inner world inhabited as a refuge from a quotidian enervation and boredom, an inner world living and running in parallel to more conventional forms of consciousness and self-consciousness. So in this term we examine the force and power of dissociation and splits in consciousness, both as particular and powerful defenses under conditions of trauma and conflict and as intrinsic aspects of human consciousness. A number of the authors in this volume (Brennan, Bromberg, Davies) draw on models of mind already in play in these early psychoanalytic texts, noting in particular the theoretical fork in the road at which Freud, after these early studies, approached repression and a metaphor of mind as archeological layering, and therapy as excavation. Bromberg, Brennan, and, in a different strategy, Green use the *Studies* to propose different models of mental life, in which multiplicity, heterochronicity, and dynamic shifts in psychic state are featured. In addition, a quite complex model of performance and the interrelation of soma and psyche is drawn out, a model illuminated by the clinical details of these cases.

In these early foundational cases, the hysteric's body is believed to register her history, and in particular the history of her relationships and her fantasies about them. Symptom read as though bodily state was a metaphor that could be tightly predicted from history. To read the cases now is to be caught up in all the debates within contemporary psychoanalysis about the power and scope of symbolization, the nature of representation, and the meaning of silences and somatization. We also see the successes and defeats in psychoanalytic attempts to decode the body. The tormented sexual history of the hysterical patient was represented wordlessly in a mimesis of sexual activity and motility (or its opposite, paralysis). Body was icon and text to be read as if by some anatomical dictionary that psychoanalysis was producing.

The spectacle of hysteria and its narrative record are also sites of power and control. The anorexic, apparently longing to disappear, is nonetheless, in her skeletal haggard state, completely riveting. In some of these cases one feels the impact and the tyranny of symptoms, the aggressivity in suffering. Certainly Goldstein's attention to the details and communication of Nanette Leroux's symptoms suggests a young woman excited and defeated by the surrounding social response to her. Power struggles and the status of bodily symptoms and enactments that express the hopelessness and the necessity of control are lived in this preanalytic case. Our authors read the *Studies* with very contemporary eyes, eyes attuned to the sadism in masochism, the effort to control in transference phenomena even of the most idealizing sorts, and the theatricality of the power struggle in the consulting-room dyad.

Teresa Brennan posits the hysteric and the hysterical body as caught up in the paradox of sight and touch, always also a paradox of passive/active. Brennan is proposing a return to an older theory of vision, of seeing as an act, and she connects this older theory both to the way Freud conceptualizes sight in hysteria and to Lacan's much later theory of the gaze, a highly potent form of phallic mastery. Her intention is to reclaim not a theory of extramission and vision as material activity but a theory of the psychic as material and a theory of body/mind integration. The hysteric's movements, the kinaesthetic and visual images, and her movements provide in the viewer the preoccupation with an imaginary anatomy that is not simply a physiology nor a conventionally erotized body, reflecting an insoluble dilemma of passivity/activity. This dilemma has intrapsychic as well as intersubjective dimensions. In a private theater, Brennan argues the hysteric's vision is almost prehensile, an act of touching that may inflame and frighten, a refusal of passivity through anguished motion. Here Brennan contends that Freud situated hysteria as a material phenomenon and certainly connected seeing and touching. Brennan links "the inward turning imagery of hysteria (the archetype of femininity) and the aggressiveness of the gaze" (p. 289). But she also extends this analysis to what we might call a hysteria of gender, in which the fantasies of autonomy, the male terrors of passification, wreak their particular psychic havoc in cultural as well as individual life.

Brennan also notes the presence in these early theoretical works of Freud of a view of consciousness and mental life as a double vision. From the phenomenon of hysterical blindness, a blindness that also sees "in their unconscious," Brennan argues for a model of the mental apparatus as multivisioned, multiconscious, with at least an experience that is both subject centered and other centered. In her view, both activity and passivity are constructed, and both mastery and introspection (too usually defaulted to masculinity and femininity) are historically specific "foundational fantasies": "This dialectic of passification and aggression intensifies as the foundational fantasy makes itself materially true" (p. 297). In a way, Brennan is outlining a kind of hysteria at the level of theory or epistemology. The aggressivity of projection (in the visual and intrapsychic senses of that term), with its inevitable return through paranoia and illusions of mastery and control, is counterposed to a constructed passivity too closely corralled as the feminine and distinct from what Brennan terms "the receptive." We might understand this as a dual or plural vision of subject who is also an object in an act of a mutual recognition with another subject. This perspective is at the core of Jessica Benjamin's essay.

Goldstein's fascinating account of Nanette Leroux, a Savoyard peasant who was the subject of and subjected to extensive medical writing in the 1820s, raises many intriguing problems as well as parallels with the women Freud and Breuer treated. Certainly there is the obvious erotism cathected in motility and immobility, both of which contribute to the spectacular quality of her symptoms: hysterical convulsions and catalepsy, a state of mind and body so frightening as to afford Nanette priestly confession and last rites. An aspect of the curative experience of Nanette is public, a spectacle in which her community quite theatrically participates. One wonders, then, about the spectacle in transference, the theatricality captured but buried in the term "enactment." Loewald (1980) has certainly elaborated these ideas in what one might call a performance theory of treatment, viewing transference as an action that repeats an action.

Bromberg's reading of Freud's treatment of Emmy takes up the theatricality of her symptoms and enactments as evidence of dissociated self-states. In describing Anna O.'s divided mind, Freud notes the ongoing, surreptitious presence of the private theater while the patient continues to function reliably in social settings and in daily life. It is this powerful and often pervasive mental characteristic, these splits in mental life, the autohypnosis and the multiple self states alive in parallel in the mind that engage

Bromberg's reading of Emmy's symptoms and her treatment. He describes the mind as a "configuration of discontinuous, shifting states of consciousness with varying degrees of access to perception and cognition" (p. 125). Bromberg rereads paralysis as "an intrinsic outcome of dissociation. . . . The ability to act purposefully . . . is repackaged in unlinked states of mind. . . . From this perspective, inhibition of action and hysterical outbursts of action are opposite sides of the same coin, and as Emmy demonstrated when she was in her unruly state, action was not only possible but was relentless in its power" (p. 133).

Bromberg highlights a number of important features: Freud's use of hypnosis, Emmy's powerful immersion in hypnoid states, her splits in consciousness, her own dim understanding of the dynamics of her mind and conversation. He argues that present-day clinical psychoanalysis is reconnecting to these earlier modes of treatment because the model of mind they are underwritten by conforms to the clinical situation so much better than the model of repression. Bromberg sees the enactment of dissociated states less as performance than as "a hypnoidally discontinuous domain of self with its dominant affect, its own selectively structured perceptual field, its own range of memories, and its own mode of interpersonal relatedness" (p. 129).

These cases and the commentary they have inspired raise an essential and difficult mystery in psychoanalysis, a provocative question now reemerging in the current debates on technique. How close to repetition, an action that repeats an action, must the private theater of psychoanalytic treatment come in order to do its work? What are the limits, the potency, and the dangers of the performed reliving of scenes and plays from the past?

The question of a past that continues to live and is revivified or disowned in the present is taken up in a different way by André Green, whose paper explores the structure of the hysterical symptom, its intermingling of fantasy and reality, and the complex infiltrating of mental life that affectively charged experience constitutes. Green uses the cases as the site to explore problems in metapsychology and then to propose a heterochronic model of time: "Freud is always willing to define two sources of the symptoms: the traumatic event arising out of the subject's will and the pathogenic idea born in his imaginative mind" (p. 77), but he is also promoting a model of divided consciousness, of the constitutive power of affect and of drive, a term he uses very differently from the ego psychologists. Drive, he says, is "born" at the border between the somatic and psychic," so "it can fall on one or the other side. Falling within the body, we have hysteria; falling on the most abstract aspects of the intellect (the cognitive), we may have obsessional neurosis just as well" (p. 79).

Making an important and intriguing distinction between psychosis and madness, Green finally diagnoses these women as mad, suffering from "madness as a vicissitude of Eros. . . . What was their madness about? They just wanted to live and love" (p. 88). What many of our authors emphasize is the impact of these wishes and wills on mental life and on the interrelation of levels of consciousness and bodily life. Thus both Green and Bromberg, inhabiting quite different vocabularies, insist on the dynamic shifts in states of mind, each with its own unique affective and relational configuration and geography.

"A Smell of Burnt Pudding": Class, Culture, and Illness

Miss Lucy was not a cook; she was a governess, but she was haunted —even, Freud wrote, "attacked"—by a smell of burnt pudding that, as it were, floated above and obscured another persecutory smell, that of cigars. As they unlayered these symptoms, patient and analyst were led backward through the recent past into the flowering and death of Miss Lucy's love for her employer. Her body memory had turned her psychic conflict into flesh: how could she love a man who was, she saw, so cold not only to his two little girls, whom she loved, but to her, his loyal employee who adored him? She did not want to know what she knew, she told Freud. She tried to put it out of her mind and, of course, failed.

Jane Gallop (1982) has remarked that it is through the governess that class enters Freud's case histories. Though always brimming over with social relevance and implication, psychoanalysis has been notoriously reticent in welcoming contributions from social thought. How often one hears the dismissive phrase brought out to still some challenge from other disciplines or some observation about the social bases for clinical and theoretical practice: "But that's not psychoanalysis." Psychoanalysis has customarily entertained only two legitimate bases for speech, the biological and the psychical. It has excluded, in other words, the social, which nevertheless sneaks back into discourse in the service of the normative or, what is effectively the same thing, the universal. It is almost as though the only good psychoanalysis is a pure psychoanalysis.

Yet, as Gallop has argued, the social has always been present; it simply has not been noticed until recently. The governess, after all, is hired by a paterfamilias to take care of his children; receiving remuneration, she is in financial need in a way that her employer is not. She is of a different class. Class thus becomes an unspoken but very powerful force structuring not only the population of analysts and patients, but the way psychoanalysis is practiced and the way treatment was discursively represented. Lewis Aron suggests, for example, that one reason for Freud's delay in beginning to use hypnosis, about which he was very excited upon his return from France where he had been studying with Charcot, was a concern for his reputation and economic chances in the market of bourgeois society, from which he was drawing his clientele. He wished to avoid controversy, having just been married and begun his private practice.

Given the class positioning of psychoanalysis itself in high bourgeois culture, it is extremely interesting that, of the six patients appearing in the *Studies*, two are outside that class. Frau Cäcilie and Frau Emmy von N. were the first and second richest women in Europe; Peter Swales, another original participant in this conference (whose contribution could unfortunately not be included here), suspects that it was Freud's dependence on Frau Cäcilie's wealth that inclined him to refrain from writing up a proper clinical account, leaving her identity disguised and scattered in sundry footnotes across all five case histories. Elisabeth and Anna O., in turn, were daughters of the upper middle class. Katharina ____, as we have seen, was a peasant. The position of Miss Lucy, a *petite bourgoise*, was perhaps the most ambiguous and therefore uneasy. Stephen Mitchell, writing in this volume about her, takes the measure of her longings to go beyond her class, noting that they appear in the form of a passion for her employer: "We might say that in 'falling in love' with her employer, Miss Lucy had fallen out of her everyday sense of self, securely nestled in its 'place' within a well defined socioeconomic status system" (p. 204). Lucy's aspirations for what the mid-twentieth century would call upward mobility are not unusual for members of her class, nor is her fantasy about how she would achieve this out of the ordinary: a woman, she will move up by marrying up, and so she falls in love with her employer. Mitchell ends with a wish that she could find avenues for personal growth other than impossible loves. That such a route would have been difficult to carve out for herself is attested by the hard row undertaken by Bertha Pappenheim, who, Rita Frankiel observes, seems to have traded in heterosexual desire for what was for her a safer solution of "motherhood without sexuality, and being a rescuer" (p. 102); others elsewhere have suggested that her asexuality disguised her lesbian desire.

As Mitchell's essay, like others in this collection, shows, the psychoanalytic refusal of the social is on its last legs. Every contributor to this volume refers tacitly or overtly, in some measure or other, to the social theory most germane to the psychoanalytic project: feminism. The seventy-fifth anniversary of the *Studies*, Jessica Benjamin points out, was also the rebirth of the feminist movement, a renaissance bringing "the dialectical poles of psychoanalysis and feminism into violent contradiction, seemingly . . . . between the acknowledgment of social oppression and the awareness of internal repression" (p. 33). Benjamin goes on to recall that, in this clash, hysteria was one of the first psychoanalytic problems subjected to feminist critique, producing "the idea of the hysteric as an antecedent form of woman's protest against the constraints of the patriarchal family" (p. 33).

These events in intellectual history position the family in psychoanalysis in a way appropriate to the evolution of psychoanalysis itself. The advent of object-relations theory, whose historical emergence converges not coincidentally with the second wave of feminism (as Benjamin observes), throws the family into the psychoanalytic limelight. We notice today what was taken for granted then. If there is no such thing as an infant but only the mother–infant surround, then implicitly predicated is a family structure. We could push this point further: systems of kinship vary culturally. The mother–child relationship is socially constructed as well as psychodynamically constructing. Several of the essays here make sure to think of the family constellations from which the patients come, especially those by Davies, D'Ercole and Waxenberg, Frankiel, Mieli, and Schafer. Most contributors pay special attention to the early relationship with the mother. In keeping with one of the most important metatheoretical advances in psychoanalytic thinking, one that we may call "the maternal turn," they tend at least to revise, if not to criticize, Freud for this crucial lacuna. Schafer, for example, regrets that Freud did not find out when Elisabeth's mother became sickly, so that we might better understand many of her difficulties, whether having to do with separation or with sexuality. In detailing Anna O.'s family history, Frankiel views her hysterical pregnancy as a reparative gesture toward her mother: sensing her mother's vulnerability to loss, she wished to provide her with a child to replace her next older sibling, dead three years before her own birth. Nor, Bergmann suggests, is the nanny to be ignored here. If a child may lose a mother, a child may, like Freud, also lose a nanny, and object loss, we have come to understand, is critical in development. Behind Freud's idea of the Oedipus complex lies a memory of a lost, significant figure in his childhood: his own nanny. "Was," Bergmann wonders, "one discovery made at the expense of the other?" (p. 356).

The family, it turns out, may be responsible for the similarity of symptoms that cross the lines of class. We note that, while Nanette Leroux and Frau Emmy von N. come from opposite ends of the social spectrum (and different countries), their symptoms are two sides of a coin. "Emmy's 'clacking,'" writes Goldstein, "has its counterpart not only in Nanette's bouts of mutism but in her periods of speaking in falsetto and in her occasional recourse to nonsense syllables" (p. 163). Shared between them, she thinks, is a protest at aspects of women's lot, whose structure forms in the crucible of normative arrangements for marriage and family. Certainly their family structures were not identical, Frau Emmy's having probably included a governess among its members. Yet a common set of representations of the family, itself dialectically dependent on the very same notion of gender complementarity that makes for psychoanalytic participation in normativity and the regulation of sexuality, would have connected these two women of widely disparate social fortunes.

What causes mental illness? At this point in the century, we have complexified the answer. If Freud moved from theories of hereditary degeneracy to theories of unconscious conflict, we now

think, as does Frankiel, in terms of "multiply determined hysterical symptoms" (p. 99). The psychoanalytic metabolization of the
social has explanatory power. Here, then, we should note another
thread running through this volume and across the century: the
relation between the psychological and the social in the matter of
illness and its origins, symptoms and their causes. André Green's
stance in "The Psychotherapy of Hysteria, 1995" exemplifies the
multiple possibilities these essays implicitly or explicitly consider.
The theory of repression, he argues, is still valid, but we cannot
ignore the social context of hysterical symptoms.

"I Shall Have to Swallow This": Trauma, Soma, Symbolization

We have to search out Frau Cäcilie in the interstices and footnotes
of Freud's texts. She inspires our voyeurism, our curiosity, a woman
too powerful to have the searchlight focus on her own case history but powerful enough to have provoked extensive theorizing
in Freud. Frau Cäcilie is an avowed inspiration to his work on
hysterical communication and on the decoding of trauma through
reading the somatic as symbol. In the descriptions and clinical
vignettes about her, we find a woman whose use of metaphor was
always slightly more than just metaphoric. What panic has dis-
placed itself into the mouth, what trauma has produced a mind in
pieces and a woman who sometimes cannot stay in the symbolic,
whose body and images must speak for her? For Frau Cäcilie, the
symbolic fails in certain circumstances of overwhelming affect and
agitation. Language and speech give way to a concrete representation of psychic pain. She and Freud read her symptoms as almost
straightforward conversions of action and event.

Frau Cäcilie's is a mind fractured by trauma, the effort of living
through and processing overwhelming experiences having distorted
not simply the contents of thought but the function of thinking.
Capable of "some poems of great perfection," she also lives in states
where language's capacity to conjure and represent gives way to
flatfooted concrete voice and where the body speaks a direct, unmediated translation of an emotional and affective anguish. One
might say that Frau Cäcilie both shapes and misleads Freud with
regard to symbolization and somatic life. The body and speech about

the body hold a kind of mystery, a disguise and conversion of word to psyche to soma and back. The case history as detective story or as scientific mystery unraveled by the doctor/sleuth: this genre and way of thinking in Freud's own work owes much to Frau Cäcilie. Yet while we would certainly not be so confident of an inevitable equation of body states and speech states, the power of Frau Cäcilie's anguish to distort her mind and her body was a crucial aspect of Freud's theory of hysteria's etiology in trauma.

This centennial falls at a moment in history when it is impossible to revisit these cases and these essays without acrimony. The battle over the reality and the sequelae of sexual abuse and trauma of many kinds has been waged over the entire century. In the footnote appended to the case of Katharina ____, the disguise is pulled away from her experience: not an uncle but her father. Despite developments in his psychoanalytic theorizing, incest and trauma continue to play a role in Freud's understanding of symptoms, as the date of the footnote (1924) evocatively suggests.

Papers in this volume take up the question of trauma, widening its parameters and meanings. There is the trauma in all sexual development (Mieli), the trauma in subjectivity itself. There is the trauma of abuse (Davies, Goldstein) in one case within the family, in another within a traditional and intimately connected community. There is the trauma of loss (Frankiel), with the sequelae of guilt, converted rage, and compromise. There are papers that address the powerful processes through which pain and loss are managed (Bromberg, Davies, Roth).

Rita Frankiel integrates the case of Anna O. with scholarly material on the life of Bertha Pappenheim and on Breuer's reaction to her during and after treatment, developing a convincing and compelling account of the role of traumatic loss and aborted and blocked mourning both in Anna O.'s symptoms and in the distortions and compromises with which she continued to live and work. Most interestingly, Frankiel locates ungrieved traumatic loss in both analyst and patient and shows how these traumas were reenacted in the treatment though horrifyingly left unprocessed when Breuer abandoned his patient. In interpreting Anna O.'s hysterical pregnancy as an aspect of the hysteric's reaction to loss, maternal bereavement, and transference, Frankiel commits us to an understanding of symptom as "infiltrated" (Green's term) with unconscious fantasy that stains the actual experience of events of loss and mourning. In writing of Pappenheim's work choices and the meaning and symbolization she produced in and through her work, Frankiel shows the lifelong shadow of trauma, the degree to which unworked-through symptoms and sadnesses, formed in development and reactivated and iatrogenically produced in treatment, fix and spoil an entire life. Frankiel evocatively describes a lifetime of asexual, disciplined service, a life lived intensely and productively but in a state of profound abandonment and aloneness. Poignantly, Frankiel suggests the power of a psychoanalytic treatment not invented in time for Pappenheim but a power explosively alive in Anna O.'s experience with Breuer.

Goldstein's account of Nanette Leroux's symptoms, symptom relief, and their traumatizing trigger draws out the connections between sexual abuse and hysterical reactivity. Interestingly, although a modern reader hears and feels the sexuality in Nanette's bath experience, the massage, and the interplay of touch and talk by her doctor, this element was apparently unseen by the doctors and community of the period. Nonetheless, sexual abuse, in this case repeated exposure by a field warden, was easily understood as a terrifying event for this virginal girl.

Bromberg draws on a telling clinical detail from Emmy's treatment to illustrate the "continual readiness of the dissociative vigilance" (p. 130), her panicky use of a protective formula that kept her in a highly aroused, hypervigilant state which as Bromberg ruefully notes, does not prevent harm from occurring. Quite the contrary: harm and danger are consistently, repetitively evoked, reenacted, and reexperienced. But dissociated vigilance paradoxically produces repetition in such a way that harm never recurs unexpectedly. For a number of these authors (Green, Mieli, Davies), no simple dichotomy of reality/fantasy, abuse/conflict, or internal/external is really sufficient. Trauma, as Mieli and Davies argue from quite different vantage points, is always multiple trauma and one that reorganizes the past as well as the ongoing present and future.

Paola Mieli uses the cases of Katharina _____ and Rosalie (a good-looking and unusually intelligent girl, a 23-year-old singer) to argue for the analyst's grounding his/her own observation into a more general conception of the role played by trauma in transference. This project acknowledges the violent power of certain traumatic events and the specificity of their consequences, situates the clinical questions in two cases of incest, and also carefully works out the more general perspective on trauma in which sexual abuse must be understood. Human immaturity, the nature of sexuality itself, primary repression, and the complex double-phased development of human sexuality all contribute to the trauma in human subjectivity. Much like André Green, Mieli discusses how symptomatic experiences that signal trauma are constructed through the action of events upon prior scenes that are then reconstituted: "An event that, in the very act of positing itself, reinvests a past inscription and takes on the status of a revelation. That which occurs 'after' turns what has preceded it into an occasion" (p. 268). "The constitution of trauma is logical, not linear, structural and not developmental" (p. 268). Analysis is the time not only of recognition and return but also of the "construction of the original myth," the moment of reckoning with the limits of symbolization. Mieli connects trauma to the original seduction through which the parent inducts the child as a desiring subject, cathecting various sites of the body "where a privileged exchange with the Other, the mother or caretaker, occurs" (p. 273). The inevitability of trauma as the realization of fantasy is beautifully worked out in Mieli's account of how Freud treats the appearance of fresh hysterical symptoms, when Rosalie becomes both the object of attentions and the object of scrutiny during the course of the analysis. The re-enactment of trauma in the transference through fascination, sadism, or desire in the analyst is, by many modern analysts' reckoning, inevitable, and in Mieli's account it defines the web of traumas. "The trauma that sets off the symptoms gives voice *nachträglich*, a posteriori, to the traumatic experiences of the past" (p. 279).

Davies's essay on Katharina ____ traces the roots, in early analytic work, of contemporary understandings of trauma, including the use of concepts like dissociation, shifting states of consciousness, constructed memory, and enactments, all features strongly influenced by Janet. Dissociation, more than the classical concept of repression, conveys the complex shifting states of consciousness, the shifts in affective schemes, and their unique history in internal object worlds. It describes the internal psychic states of the women in these case studies and certainly the present-day traumatized subject. Dissociation, Davies argues, must also be deployed in experiences of trauma that require the management of massive interpersonal contradiction like that occasioned by sexual abuse within the primary family (Katharina _____'s situation). These perspectives on mind in extremis, both historically in the *Studies on Hysteria* and in the current psychoanalytic literature, depend on and elaborate a particular model of mind and a model of traumatized mind.

Davies gave us the kaleidoscope metaphor, our image for this introduction. In considering the nature of mind, she suggests we envision "[N]ot an onion or an archeological site, but a child's kaleidoscope in which each glance through the pinhole of a moment in time provides a unique view: a complex organization in which a fixed set of colored, shaped, and textured components rearrange themselves in unique crystalline structures determined via infinite pathways of interconnectedness" (p. 253). What better conceptual grid to capture the astonishing play of mental and affective life in Freud's daily visits to Emmy and Emmy's stunning shifts in state, from hypnoid, to fugue state, to agitated enactment, to thoughtful commentary.

As Davies points out, work on trauma is subject to dramatic vicissitudes. The discourse on trauma throughout the century, and certainly today, is waged in a bitterly argued, often misleading dichotomization of psychoanalytic theories and in social and political quarrels. In this volume, the questions of trauma's reality, the mystery of memory, the impact of harm and overpowering experience on the mind and body, and the inevitable mixture of reminiscence, construction, history, and fantasy are kept in play. It is in so many ways a tragic history: damaged people helped and mishandled, understood too well and not at all. Hysteria as a response to trauma requires both a clinical and a theoretical eye and touch, and in a number of the essays in this volume that combination is employed.

"She Has Married Someone Unknown to Me": Countertransference, Transference, Cure

Imagining ourselves today into Freud's mind as he wrote this sentence, we think about countertransference. These are the words with which he concludes his case history of Elisabeth von R. The treatment having been terminated about a half year earlier, he has seen her at a ball, whirling past him. In the same social class and cultural milieu, they had found themselves in the same place. Did he dance with her? We do not know. We do know, however, that he later hears about her wedding, which he offers to us readers as, in Schafer's words, "the conventional comfort of a happy bourgeois ending" (p. 330). Schafer's language intentionally leaves us with some doubt, a doubt Freud did not, at this point, want to entertain, although, in the period of what Schafer considers his best work, the 1920s and 1930s, he might very well have wondered more openly whether and in what way his assertive young patient had in fact gotten better, and what role both his unconscious and his person might have played. That he would not have noticed the patriarchal streak in his coda is a given, as D'Ercole and Waxenberg observe. Ideologically at least, the man, the father, who chooses the mate for the girl was a structure of society and mind so deeply buried in Freud's countertransference that he could have no more noticed it than he could his routine obscuring of the mother's significance in the early object world.

At this centennial point in psychoanalytic history, we are invigorated by an extremely fresh interest in countertransference. One of the least developed regions of Freud's clinical thought, it was left to those taking other forks in the psychoanalytic road to give it its proper prominence. The work of Ferenczi and then much later of interpersonal theorists, like Wolstein in this volume, is a step forward that permits us now to look back and see not only what Freud but Breuer saw—for they included it in their narratives—but what they could not see: the role (as we would put it today) of the analysts' subjectivity and the power of their own participation in clinical process.

Roth writes in this volume that "the problem of suggestion . . . is a version of the problem of epistemological contamination: there is no pure place from which one can know the past" (p. 171). The same may be said about countertransference. Its recognition is our loss of innocence: the analyst is always part of the analysis. Schafer criticizes the Freud of the *Studies* for his commitment to positivism: the analyst, for the Freud of that early work, was the neutral observer recording and measuring "process and materials in the physical uni-

verse" (p. 92). The Freud of twenty years later was beginning to know
better and was moving toward a hermeneutics, even though he
would not have thus labeled his method of interpreting symptoms
ranging from the conversion manifestations of hysteria, to the slips
of the tongue of daily life, to the dreams of nightly existence.

Considerations of countertransference unfurled in tandem with
theories of the pre-Mycenean inner object world. Not only the
patient's representations of the analyst are at stake in illness, treatment, and cure. Analysts, we now see, must take up their contribution, their subjectivity, their fantasies about their patients, their
actions toward them, and their enactments with them. Frankiel
argues that Breuer's countertransference was implicated in
Anna O.'s embodied fantasy of having his baby. He misrecognized
not only his sexual feelings for her, but also how in tune were their
experiences of early object loss. She had lost her father at age 5,
he had lost his mother between the ages of 3 and 4. Perhaps she
embodied for him an unbearable pain he could not accommodate.
This entanglement produced in him a passionate love and violent
hatred for her so deep that he could, breathtakingly, remark upon
her subsequent rehospitalization, "Would she not be better off dead
and spared further suffering?" (p. 100). Unrecognized, countertransference is a key ingredient in iatrogenesis. Recognizing, interpreting, and articulating such feelings to oneself and perhaps
to one's patient, many analysts hold today, safeguards the Hippocratic Oath: "First, do no harm." Acknowledged, such passions need
not drive us to act out damagingly, causing patients to act out in
turn, as Breuer did Anna O.

Did the hysterics get well? It is noteworthy that, refusing either to idealize or to demonize Freud and the entire field of psychoanalysis, the contributors to this volume are willing to voice
their dissatisfaction with the conclusions of these treatments. Not
only Elisabeth's fate but that of others is open to question. Frankiel
argues persuasively and movingly a strong contemporary view of
cure, namely that we think of Anna O.'s life as Bertha Pappenheim
as a creative solution to great problems. We know less about the
others. Mitchell fears that he wants for Miss Lucy more out of life
than she could have envisioned for herself. Could Freud have
helped her to want more? Or did he imagine that greater desire
meant only greater suffering?

Bromberg's essay on Frau Emmy von N. is devoted to understanding why Emmy's cure did not last. In Freud's clinical model of treating the effects of repression, she was to be helped to remember and thus really to forget and thereby to move on. In Bromberg's model of alleviating dissociation, she would be helped instead to hold it all, to occupy the spaces of her divided mind. Here we think of Margo Rivera's (1989) contemporary contribution to the dialectical ebb and flow of integration and dissociation in the treatment of mutiple personality disorder: integration does not require choosing one *alter* as the dominant personality. Instead, it "prescribes . . . the growing ability to call all those voices 'I,' to disidentify with any one of them as the whole story, and to recognize that the construction of personal identity is a complex, continuing affair in which we are inscribed in culture in a myriad of contradictory ways" (p. 28). Davies says of Katharina . . . Frau Cäcilie? . . .

Writing from what we may think of as the depressive position psychoanalysis has lately achieved, these commentators are more in tune with the mood of the Freud of "Analysis Terminable and Interminable" (1937). Theories of treatment and of cure have unrolled in fascinating ways in the course of the psychoanalytic century. We began with the chimney-sweeping of catharsis insisted on by Anna O., Frau Emmy von N., and, "in a conflicted, delinguisticized way" (Schafer, p. 328) by Elisabeth von R. From there we moved to interpreting symptoms, as Bromberg tells us, and dreams, which, according to Bergmann, marks the real beginning of psychoanalysis. And now we find ourselves in the toils and coils of countertransference analysis, the recognition of the analyst's subjectivity, and the enigmatic riches of enactment and embodiment.

No contributor to this volume believes any longer that a pure health replaces an equally identifiable illness. That the well and the ill have more in common than is ordinarily thought is a thread running from Freud through Sullivan right up to the psychoanalytic present. Ten years after the *Studies*, the *Three Essays on the Theory of Sexuality* (Freud 1905) argues that, all sexual proclivities being at home in the human heart, the line between health and pathology begins to be hard to draw. That we are all more simply human than otherwise, as Sullivan famously put it, prefigures the hermeneutic move. Well or ill, life is a search to create meaning. Problems engage less the struggle to get rid of them than the effort to understand them. They are "acts of meaning," says Bromberg (p. 131, quoting Jerome Bruner), a "groping toward a true dialogue about the inner and outer worlds" of both patient and analyst, as Schafer puts it (p. 338). Psychoanalysis here catches up with the twentieth-century paradigm shift, just in time for the twenty-first century.

"Storms in Her Head": Sex, Gender, Feminism

Emmy von N. used this metaphoric term to describe confusional states to which she was extremely susceptible. Freud repeats her phrase towards the end of the case report, a report that is really almost a blow-by-blow account of these powerful scenes of panic and agitation, altered states of awareness, and suspended hallucinatory scenes. The weather in Emmy's head is violent and unpredictable, and Freud describes the scenes of hypnosis and trance through which he tried to drive these clouds and violent images away.

No account of the historical placement and meaning of hysteria is separate from the situation and historical position of women. Hysteria, hysterics, and psychoanalytic treatment were crucial in the development of feminism and feminist theory. The hysteric was in certain ways an early heroine of feminism; iatrogenically pathologized, hysteria was political or social protest in the only form available to women. Hysterical illness could be construed as a kind of work stoppage or strike. The scene of hypnotizing doctor and fainting hysteric could be the cartoon derivative of patriarchal control and female victimization. But beneath such a stereotyped vision lurks a deep critique of the gender inequalities that affect scientific theory, intellectual practice, healing, and internal conscious and unconscious life.

Feminist theory took a quantum leap in sophistication and power when psychoanalysis could be creatively and powerfully enaged with. The past two decades have occasioned an explosion of theoretical and clinical writing, an explosion that can be said to have reconfigured the psychoanalytic landscape and, without question, the understanding of this foundational text, the *Studies*. Jacqueline Rose (1978), in a well-known essay on the case of Dora, points out that the theorizing of the feminine in psychoanalysis begins with a theory of hysteria. One defaults to the other. This is one explanation for the impossible position Freud and psychoanalysis got into with regard to female desire and agency. Feminine sexuality was either absent, replaced by illness and symptom, or present but masculinized.

In these essays the problem of femininity is not solely a problem of sexuality. One way of reading behind the question of hysterical symptomatology in relation to impossible and forbidden desires is to see the conflict of freedom, of agency, in the world in general, with its explosive and depressing results. Green and Mitchell, from quite different vantage points, see the women in the cases as suffering from love and longing for romance. Other contributors, for example D'Ercole and Waxenberg, see the hysterics in the *Studies* as caught up in extreme reactions to powerlessness, which is enraging, terrifying, or dangerous. Frankiel traces Anna O.'s accommodation of passions, guilty torments, and despair into the narrow possibilities shaped by women's limited prospects.

Feminist readings of these cases, discernible in the essays of Benjamin, Schafer, Frankiel, Bromberg, Goldstein, and Schwartz, focus on the power of culture in the distortion of personality and wish, distortions in reaction to prohibited forms of sexuality and identity. Thus Bromberg says of Emmy that "she was a woman locked in by time, place, and social role to an identity defined by the power of men—in real life, an identity defined by widowhood and by what her husband's family said about her—and, under her pseudonym, an identity defined by patienthood and by what Freud said about her" (p. 124).

It is interesting to note that, although psychoanalysis is considered the bourgeois science, and the conventional picture of the early hysterics is one of enervated, reclining, bored bourgeoises (or even in its feminist version, middle-class women on strike), these cases include Miss Lucy, a woman caught in the cycle of genteel poverty, whose hopes for love are helpless in the face of conventions of class.

Jessica Benjamin's essay inaugurated the conference and explicitly marked the connection between the rise of feminism within psychoanalysis and an intensification of the interest in object relations. Feminism has been one prism through which to see a missing element in many of the cases, and Benjamin deepens the traditional feminist version of tracing the political dimension of these women's distress, reading, particularly in Anna O., the political and social dimension of living, working, and loving for women. But for Benjamin, feminism must penetrate a psychoanalytic understanding at the level of technique and transference. The admixture of the political and the personal suffuses transference and countertransference phenomena, in such a way that we can now see that Freud and Breuer's immersion in gender conventions and gender polarities distorted the forms of mutual identification possible in treatment. Benjamin illuminates the dilemmas of identification, recognition, and agency often disguised within psychoanalytic theory as toxic forms of feminine passivity and envy.

Goldstein deploys a Foucauldian reading of her preanalytic case to comment on the discursive categories used to understand Nanette Leroux and to note the absent sexuality. Nanette's withdrawal from the regularities of female bodily life, her amenorrhea, her childlike falsetto voice, and her demand for and experience of her gold watch are read by Goldstein as the young woman's attempt to wrest control from the social forces arrayed around her. And, Goldstein reminds us, this array includes her doctor, whose act of restoring the functioning of her watch and becoming invested in the restoration and regularity of Nanette's menstrual cycle constitutes the kind of transference/countertransference power struggle that feminism has taught us to read and inquire about.

In his layered reading of Elisabeth von R.'s treatment, Schafer marks the way feminism, as social theory and in its engagement with psychoanalytic theory, now influences both analyses of gender and clinical technique. Schafer notes the patriarchy in Freud's unilateral assumption of authority to know and to diagnose, as well as in the lacunae in Freud's perspective on Elisabeth, his inability to attend to the role of her mother in her situation and symptoms, and even the bourgeois happy end envisoned for this patient. In his imaginative and creative reading of Elisabeth in treatment with a later Freud, Schafer argues that even with more sophisticated theories of identification, Elisabeth's "masculinity" would have remained a problematic choice.

Schwartz reads the essay on Emmy as a place to trace a shift from question to prescription, to note the subtle but unmistakable way that normative biases, like heterosexism, and a positivist view of psychoanalysis as natural science replace the local, particular clinical query. The influence of an evolutionary perspective begins to stain through Freud's texts, changing the pristine radicalism in his theory of sexuality. In the context of the missing presence of the pre-oedipal, the shadow lurking over these cases dominated by various fathers, real and imaginary, it is tempting to wonder about the role and space for more transgressive forms of sexuality. In most of these case histories features that have become commonplace concerns in feminist and queer-theory readings of psychoanalysis are silent untheorized presences: the women's bisexuality or their homosexuality, their pre-oedipal life, the power and conflict in maternal relations, the powerlessness of some of their social and intrapsychic situations, and the constraints on woman's agency and desire.

CONCLUSION: DISTURBING PSYCHOANALYSIS

There are a number of layers to this organization. Throughout this volume, we can see the conversation between psychoanalysis and cultural life. Much of the history of psychoanalysis' relationship to other disciplines has been in the name of a rather imperialistic colonizing action: the discipline that knows even what its objects of inquiry do not about their own mind and souls establishes claims to deeper truths. We hope here for a different, more braided, and interdependent model. This project was always imagined as an interdisciplinary undertaking. Analysts, historians, philosophers, and literary critics participated in this venture, and from outside psychoanalysis critical questions and new interventions appear.

Within psychoanalysis we tried to be eclectic and wide reaching. What we believe this has produced is a wonderful tension between the idealized and the devalued Freud, and all the continua between. As Roth puts it, the tendency is to be either whiggish or demonizing. We have both Freuds here. In some essays, there is a single-seeming Freud who overarches his work and the work of psychoanalysis. In others, Freud is located at a particular moment in his intellectual and professional life, poised to figure out some puzzles but to be stymied by others. A set of binaries appears and reappears in the book: mind/body, psyche/

society, domination/submission, male/female, analyst/patient, soma/word, interpretation/suggestion, universal/local. What we aspire to is to produce a contradictory relationship to the text *Studies on Hysteria*. We are remembering, refinding, creating, deconstructing, and contextualizing.

A risky business, returning to a classic. You return to the roots of your field, and in doing so, you disturb them. Settled for a century, they are well established, a landmark of cultural and medical history. But unanswered questions lie at the root of any field. There are dividing points, forks in the practical and theoretical roads that, had they been taken, might have made for a different psychoanalysis. What seem to be certainties turn into questions in the course of examination. Doubt returns. Does psychoanalysis tell the truth? Do its methods work? Does it cure? What is cure? What is psychoanalysis, for that matter? These doubts and questions are, in fact, occupational hazards. They are experienced daily for clinicians committed to their craft. And they are questions the public asks, and has a right to ask. They voice some of the deep and ramifying matters taken up by the essays in this book. Perhaps it is a good thing to disturb the roots. If you aerate the soil, the plant grows better.

REFERENCES

Breuer, J. and Freud, S. (1893–1895). Studies on hysteria. *Standard Edition* 2.

Gallop, J. (1982). *The Daughter's Seduction*. Ithaca, NY: Cornell University Press.

Loewald, H. (1980). Psychoanalysis as an art and the fantasy character of the psychoanalytic situation. In *Papers on Psychoanalysis*, pp. 277–299. New Haven, CT: Yale University Press.

Rivera, M. (1989). Linking to psychological and the social: feminism post structuralism and multiple personality. *Dissociation* 2:24–31.

Rose, J. (1978). Dora—fragment of an analysis. *m/f* 5–21.

Winnicott, D. W. (1971). *Playing and Reality*. London: Tavistock.

The Primal Leap* of Psychoanalysis, from Body to Speech: Freud, Feminism, and the Vicissitudes of the Transference

Jessica Benjamin

1

---

*Origin = *Ursprung* in German, literally "primal leap."

In reflecting on the one-hundredth anniversary of the *Studies on Hysteria*, I felt impelled to remember an earlier point, the seventy-fifth anniversary, in which the rebirth of the feminist movement occurred—a movement that had at least equal importance for the inventor of the "talking cure," Anna O., a movement that has been shadowing psychoanalysis since its inception and has, in our time, called for and led to a massive revision in how we view ourselves and the subjects of those original studies. The inception of the women's movement brought the dialectical poles of psychoanalysis and feminism into violent contradiction, seemingly the contradiction between the acknowledgement of social oppression and the awareness of internal repression. The notion of rebellion opposed the notion of illness, making heroines, or at least protesters, out of patients. Not surprisingly, hysteria was among the first issues explored by feminist criticism, and the idea of hysteria as an antecedent form of woman's protest against the constraints of the patriarchal family (Cixous and Clement 1975; see also Bernheimer and Kahane 1985, Showalter 1985) was among the earliest revisions proposed by feminist scholarship.

Although we remember her primarily as Anna O., the patient of Freud's older colleague Breuer on whose treatment Freud based much of what he wrote in the *Studies*, this is not the only way she is remembered in Germany today. Anna O., known to her world as Bertha Pappenheim, settled in Frankfurt after her recovery from hysterical illness in the 1890s. While we are all familiar with the story of her intense attachment to Breuer, which led to a precipitous end to the treatment by the frightened physician and so inspired the founding myth of transference love as Freud conveyed it to us, Pappenheim's reaction to this experience is also significant. She became the founder of the first feminist Jewish Women's Organization and a leader in the nascent field of social work, rescuing children and young women who might fall victim to the slave trade (Hillmann 1992; see also Appignanesi and Forrester 1992).

In recalling Pappenheim's history it is not my intention here to create a countermyth of the feminist heroine or to take an uncriti-

cal feminist revisionist version of hysteria at face value. Both as she
appears to us in Breuer's recorded recollection and in the later histories that value her as the founder of the German Jewish women's
movement and a forerunner of modern social work, Pappenheim is
surely a difficult figure with whom to identify. A woman who saw
the straight lines of needlepoint as a metaphor for the well lived,
socially useful life (Hillmann 1992), who renounced sexual freedom
in favor of social agency, she was a woman guided by an incredibly
powerful superego. Nonetheless, it was she who became a rebel
against the role of women prescribed by her religion and family, who
did not finally remain paralyzed by unexpressed anger and desire,
who strove valiantly to express them through her body and her
speech. One could say that she overcame her incapacity by developing a position of active mastery in the world—a reversal which,
in Freud's thought, would count as the characteristic masculine strategy for overcoming hysteria (Freud 1896).

The reversal of passivity and the overcoming of the feminine
position will turn out to be quite important, indeed fateful, to psychoanalysis. Pappenheim herself promulgated a feminism that
founded women's active position in the virtues of maternal care
as well as in economic independence and self expression, the right
to which she defended eloquently along with the right to freedom
from sexual exploitation. Appignanesi and Forrester (1992) term
this transformation from illness to health an "inexplicable discon-
tinuity." In fact, one could easily see her effort to forget her past,
to repudiate her identity as patient and assume that of an activist
social worker, as a kind of defensive reaction. Then again, one could
say that it reflects an identification with the other side of the analytic couple, the position of healer and helper, an identification
Freud himself would later propose as a means of cure.

As historical figures, Pappenheim and Freud inhabit the same
discursive world, the tradition of German enlightenment and hu-
manism that secularized Judaism had made its own. In one respect
their assessment of women's condition matched: even as Pappenheim saw the one possibility for equal self-expression and agency
in the maternal, Freud too defined the maternal position as the
one in which women are active rather than passive. However, the
gap between their positions becomes evident when we consider
Pappenheim's (1912) declaration, in her address to the German

Women's Congress in Berlin, that the only commandment that gives women a position equal to that of men in the Jewish community is the one that constitutes the main tenet of the Jewish religion, "Love thy neighbor as thyself," the very commandment that Freud (1930) uses to illustrate the naiveté of religion and the nature of reaction formation. The disjunction between Pappenheim and Freud marks the site of a tension between psychoanalysis and feminism regarding love and femininity: for Freud, love is to be deconstructed, revealing the terms of sexuality or libido—yet this endeavor will be fraught with the contradiction between the effort to identify woman's hidden desire and his relegation of her desire to passivity; for Pappenheim, altruistic love is to be liberated from a desire associated with sexual passivity and exploitation into a protective identification with the vulnerable Other. If you like, the tension between these positions may be seen as constituting an unfortunate kind of choice, between equally valid directions: on the one hand, Freud's attempt to liberate us from the ideal, on the other, a feminist effort to reinhabit and so revalue the position of the cast-off other.

Observing these pulls and counterpulls in the history of feminist thought, one might well ask: what does it mean, in light of Pappenheim's trajectory, to found feminism in a flight from the primary leap into the arms of the male healer, from the unanalyzed, unworked-through erotic transference? But my focus will be on psychoanalysis, its founding in a particular constellation in which femininity becomes imbricated with passivity. Does this not also reflect a flight from the erotic, from the confrontation with female sexuality? This essay, therefore, will query psychoanalysis, concentrating on the ambivalent legacy Freud bequeathed us, a kind of liberation, freedom from religious and moral strictures, from grand ideals, from the temptation to save and redeem—but liberation at a price: denial of the analyst's subjectivity and desire, which might mirror those of the patient, and distance from the helpless, the passive, and for that matter, the feminine Other, identification with whom did not always come easily to Freud, did not fit with his notion of objectivity and science. (It will follow from his own thinking, however, that such identification is ineluctable and can be prevented only by acting against it in some intrapsychic way.) Thus I shall ask: how has the history of psychoanalysis been marked by the move from passivity to activity, and how is this move fundamental to the problems of the transference, especially the transference between unequal persons—doctor and patient, male authority and female rebel? How did Freud's way of formulating that move reflect his ambivalence about attributing activity, especially sexual activity, to women and incorporate defensive aspects that the psychoanalytic project must continually bring to consciousness?

Beginning with the *Studies*, the issue of passsivity versus activity—along with other complementarities such as identification or distance, empathy or objectivity—can be seen as gender underliners of the themes that recurrently trouble the evolution of psychoanalysis. The effort to clarify those themes, to overcome an old and shallow opposition between feminism and psychoanalysis, might be seen as the work of producing a more creative tension between the seemingly disparate personas, Anna and Bertha. So if psychoanalysis asks of femininism that it interrogate a founding gesture of liberation that denies the truth of dependency and desire, feminism asks of psychoanalysis that it reconsider its historical positioning of its Other, the one who is not yet able to speak for herself. Let us remind ourselves that in front of the Salpêtrière, where Charcot paraded his hysterics as a spectacle for popular audiences, stands a statue of Pinel freeing the mad from their chains; indeed, Freud noted at the time that this scene was painted on the wall of that very lecture theater (Showalter 1985). Doesn't that irony necessitate such a reconsideration?

In our time, this reconsideration has led to a concern with the radical effects of perspective, the necessity of struggling to grasp the viewpoint of another, and of straining our own view through the critical filter of analysis. Easily said, but not easily done. Seeking to grasp the real process involved in attaining an approximation of another's viewpoint (or even glimpses of it), as well as awareness of our own subjective view, is central to our current efforts to elaborate an intersubjective psychoanalysis. Hopefully, we shall reach some clarification of what this means by the end of this essay. I will say provisionally that grasping the other's viewpoint means striving to dissolve the complementary opposition of subject and object that inevitably appeared, and reappears, in the practice and theory of psychoanalysis. As I shall try to show, Freud's work, beginning with the *Studies,* aspired to move beyond the evident constraints of this complementarity but was nevertheless continually drawn back into that opposition because of the confluence of scientific rationalism and gender hierarchy.

If we, in hindsight, are more aware of what pulls us back into that complementarity, we are also more inclined to identify with Bertha's position in the story. This is not only because our theory of the unconscious teaches us that we cannot prevent such identification, that we can only split it off, repudiate it, in effect dislocate it and thus create a dangerous form of complementarity (one that, indeed, allows only a choice between immediate, unthinking, "hysterical" identification or repudiation). It is also because of the contribution both contemporary feminism and psychoanalysis have made to our awareness of the necessity of taking in the position of the other. As a result, we recognize that the only choice is to develop this identification, that the (re)admission of what was rejected is central to evolving the analyst's position as well as the patient's. The dialectic by which we undo repudiation is as important to psychoanalysis as it has been to the project of women's liberation, as it has been to each of the successive demands for recognition articulated in this century by the silenced or excluded.

The process by which demands are raised against those who already claim to be empowered as rational, speaking subjects is not identical with psychoanalysis. Nonetheless, the movement of psychoanalysis has a certain parallel with this project, which requires the self-conscious consideration of how to develop its forms of identification. As we see in social movements that found new identities, demands for recognition have their problematic side— a kind of entitlement or moral absolutism that is always inextricable from and fueled by the power it opposes (Benjamin 1998). It therefore always draws the other into the relationship of reversable complementarity. In many ways, as I shall try to show, Freud's journey through the transference is an allegory of learning to traverse the unmapped and surprising (though oddly familiar) paths of such complementary relationships.

Lest the comparisons I have drawn between the movement of psychoanalysis and that of feminism seem forced, let me delay consideration of the history of the transference a moment and consider the background of psychoanalysis in relation to European thought. Our consciousness of who we are today should take into account the history of psychoanalysis as a practice indebted to the project of liberation rooted in the Enlightenment. And Freud, despite all his political skepticism, surely did see psychoanalysis as an activity thinkable only through and because of the Enlightenment project of personal freedom, rational autonomy, and being for oneself. This project, as Kant (1784) described in "What is Enlightenment," is that of freedom from tutelage, in German *Umündigkeit*. Usually translated as "having attained majority, adulthood," the term *mündig* refers to speaking for oneself. To be *mündig* is to be entitled, empowered to speak, the opposite term to the one so often used today: silenced. It may thus fairly be understood as the antithesis of hysterical passivity, speechlessness. For the better part of the twentieth century this project of freedom from authority has been questioned precisely because—so the poststructural, postmodern critique goes—the subject of speech was never intended to be all inclusive, was always predicated on the exclusion of an other, an abject, a disenfranchised one, or an object of speech. And yet, precisely this critique of exclusion and objectification operates by referring back to a demand for inclusive recognition of subjectivity that the Enlightenment project formulated (Benjamin 1998).

Now this contradiction, between rejecting and calling upon the categories of the Enlightenment, makes for a particular uneasiness regarding the place of psychoanalysis. For the twentieth-century theory that rejects the Enlightenment has invoked Freud himself in its efforts to show that the figure of the autonomous, coherent, rational subject is a deceptive appearance, that serves to deny the reality of a fragmented, chaotic, incoherent self whose active efforts to articulate and make meaning are ultimately defensive. And yet the advocacy of meaning over chaos, thought over suffering, integration over splitting, symbolization over symptom, consciousness over unconsciousness remains essential to psychoanalysis. Finally, we can cite one more contradiction, one that arises regarding the psychoanalytic relationship: the achievement of autonomy is revealed to be the product of a discourse that situates the subject in the oppositional complementarities—subject and object, mind and body, active and passive, autonomously rational and "irrational"—that worked historically by splitting off the devalued side of the opposition from the subject. And, of course, by associating femininity with the devalued side. Psychoanalysis has thus continually reenacted these oppositions, which are in fact reiterations of gender hierarchy, even as it offers the possibility of uncovering their meanings. As with Freud's frequent rehearsals and disclaimers of the association between passivity and femininity, psychoanalysis reproduces the splits it aims to analyze.

Thus, to pick up where I left off, it is useful to explore the identification with Anna O./Bertha Pappenheim, because she incarnates for the first time and in a most compelling way that dual identity that each psychoanalyst–patient pair, separately and together, must embody. The contradictions of Anna/Bertha, which appear through the split image of the helpless, fragmented patient and the articulate, stalwart feminist who defends the helpless, reflect the split in every analyst, who is her/himself subject to, and subject of, the analytic process. In Freud's own evolution, as well as in psychoanalysis in general, we can see the problem of constructing the encounter as one between the analyst/subject who already speaks and the patient/Other who does not yet speak for herself. This suffering Other requires recognition by the subject who does speak. But this recognition will be effective only if it incorporates a moment of identification, and so disrupts the enclosed identity of the subject. Likewise, the Other's attainment of speech can proceed only by her identification with the speaking subject, by which she is in danger of losing her own "identity" as Other. If the patient must "become" the analyst, the analyst must also "become" the patient.

Thus both analyst and patient have reason to resist the identifications that result from their encounter, for eventually the doubleness of identification leads to a breakdown of the rationalistic complementarities between knower and known, active and helpless, subject and object. And while this identification may in theory be laudably subversive of heirarchy, it is in practice a "most dangerous method" (Kerr 1993), generating a muddle of boundaries, mystification, anxiety, and old defenses against it. To this analytic heart of darkness we will turn shortly. For now, speaking of theory, let us say that psychoanalysis and feminism can join in the project of inspiring this inevitable breakdown to assume a creative rather

than destructive form—to challenge the valorization of the autonomous, active, "masculine" side of the gender polarity without re-
actively elevating its opposite.

I am highlighting this paradoxical movement in psychoanalytic
history: that even in the moment of breaking down those oppositions through which the masculine subject was constituted, the psychoanalytic project necessarily participated in the hierarchical opposition between activity and passivity with its gender implications.
This project, raising the symptom to articulation in the symbol, I
have designated here as the primary move from the body into
speech, referring to this founding form of psychoanalytic activity
as the "primal leap": a pun on the German word for origin, *Ursprung*,
sprung meaning leap and *ur* meaning original, primal, first, deepest. From body to speech. To make the inarticulate articulate, to
translate the symptomatic gestures of the body into language, is
incontrovertibly the first lesson of Freud and Breuer's work.

No sooner having said this, however, we must object, or at least
ask: whose speech? For the leap that is psychoanalysis consists,
properly speaking, in Freud's decision to give up hypnosis in favor of a more collaborative enterprise, one in which the patient
herself becomes the subject of speech—and if Freud chose to attribute this transition to his patients' resistance to hypnosis (Breuer
and Freud 1893-1895), perhaps in order to legitimate it as a necessity (or to occlude his fear of the erotic transference that hypnosis
unleashed, as his autobiography later revealed), this makes the
sharing of credit no less true.

How else could the value of collaboration be discovered, if not
through the patient's refusal of the passive position of being hypnotized, even if that refusal appeared to be a resistance? In effect,
the step out of passivity is framed as resistance. Subjected to her
own symptoms and captive in her own body, the patient can nonetheless mobilize against surrender of consciousness. And so the
origin of psychoanalysis, its decisive move, is ambiguous. I hope
here merely to underscore a certain paradox in the evolution of
psychoanalysis as a discipline, and in each individual analysis as
well: each fresh resistance of the patient drives the process forward. Resistance itself becomes the revelation, as in Freud's discovery of the function of erotic transference, or any acting in the
transference. But more of that later.

So far I have been constructing a leading argument here, suggesting that the move from the body that suffers itself to be an instrument of unconscious communication to the speaking subject who articulates insight seems to fit with a transition to active subjectivity as long defined by the Enlightenment tradition. Thus Freud framed his understanding of overcoming resistance and defense in the *Studies* in characteristic fashion:

> What means have we at our disposal for overcoming this continual resistance? . . . By explaining things to [the patient], by giving him information about the marvellous world of psychical processes into which we ourselves only gained insight by such analyses, we make him himself a collaborator, . . . for it is well to recognise this clearly: the patient gets free from the hysterical symptom by reproducing the pathogenic impressions that caused it and by giving utterance to them with an expression of affect, and thus the therapeutic task consists solely in inducing him to do so. [Breman and French 1895, pp. 282–283]

So, we see, the analyst has merely set the patient free, has in fact found a way to make him a collaborator (NB! when the patient is active, Freud uses the male pronoun; when the patient is simply ill, he uses the feminine). The patient is to identify with the analyst in the overcoming of resistance through self-reflection, a process of internalization that implies both tutelage and freedom from tutelage. He is to collaborate in an investigation. By contrast, Breuer's use of hypnosis with Anna O. seems of a piece with his medicating her, case managing her in the manner appropriate to the metaphor of an illness, still embedded in a discourse of subject and object, actor and acted upon. Such a discourse, sustained by the practice of hypnosis, could explore the patient's subjectivity only by vitiating it of the qualities that otherwise characterize it: agency and intentionality.

Of course, the transition from passivity to activity, from suffering symptoms to being the subject of speech, turned out to be not a one-time leap but a process that Freud evolved slowly, a process for which the giving up of hypnosis was only a beginning. Indeed, we can see Freud's subsequent elaboration of psychoanalytic practice as an ongoing effort to remove the analyst from the position of coercive authority and to enfranchise the patient.

But even as Freud reports his move away from hypnosis, he allows us to discern the way that the patient exerted her power to bring into being another force. This, the force of transference, is already discernible, already beginning to destabilize the main event of the *Studies*. This event was meant to be Freud's discovery of a formulaic equation: one symptom, one recollection. In any case, it is apparent in the first study that symptoms are not the only matter at hand. For it is not merely in her body that Anna O. offers up the encoded memories; equally important are the reliving of perceptions and feelings. These Freud will later figure as the main thing opposing language: "acting," a term that evokes not merely doing, but dramatizing, representing in deed. When Anna O. refuses to drink water because it reminds her of the despised dog who drank from the bowl, this is not a bodily symptom, but acting.

Where speech, symbolic articulation, would constitute the true activity of the subject, acting has been seen as merely another form of representing without knowing what is being represented, of evacuating or expelling, hence not an expression of subjectivity. This distinction between communicating and acting is still subscribed to by many analysts, for instance Green (1986). Yet acting has also been seen as a phase between discharge and full representation (Freedman 1985) that implicates the analyst in a new way. In fact, in contemporary relational analysis, acting and interacting are the indispensible medium through which the analytic work proceeds. At the very least, acting constitutes a new intermediate position between unconscious and conscious, a different kind of effort at representation, which at once reveals and resists; to paraphrase what Winnicott (1971) says about destruction, it is resistance only because of our liability not to understand it, to become caught up in it.

Freud was at first sanguine about siezing this new opportunity for mastery through understanding. For although the patient, Freud tells us, is "deceived afresh every time this is repeated . . . the whole process followed a law" (Breuer and Freud, 1895, pp. 303–304). The work follows a "law," the law of logic, the same law formulated for relieving symptoms through images or pictures produced under pressure: as soon as the images have been put into words, fully explicated, raised to the symbolic level, they disappear. In the same way, Freud contends, the illusion of the transference "melts away" once he makes the nature of the obstacle clear. Freud has not yet confronted the intersubjective aspect of the phenomenon, the bidirectionality of unconscious communication; he believes that transference can simply be observed from without. He remains reassuringly within the law, according to which words must replace action, symbol replace symptom, each proceeding in order. Once the activity of speech—language—substitutes for action of the body or of the transference, everything follows. Where before the patient's resistance was overcome by the pressure of the physician's hand, now the patient must be more consciously enlisted to overcome her own resistance.

Freud's move away from hypnosis is of a piece with a gradual process of lessening the doctor's grip on the patient's mental activity, of relinquishing coercion and control by the doctor, accompanied by a freeing of the analysand, whose autonomy should be realized within the analysis itself. Already we have glimpsed the contradictions within the discourse of autonomy, and it should not surprise us that Freud continues to struggle with them, that the new technique does not remove these contradictions *but displaces them in the transference.* In his writings on the transference more than a decade later, we will observe in new form the reinstituting of the hierarchical binaries that have been so readily exposed in the paradigm of male doctor, female hysteric. Indeed, the transference gathers these contradictions together in a way that led Freud to the apt metaphor of explosive chemicals.

In "Remembering, Repeating and Working Through" (1914), Freud looks back on the path he has followed in order to relinquish charismatic authority, hypnotism, and faith-healing. Freud's narrative constructs a consistent, logically proceeding evolution of his method and aims. Notwithstanding this coherence, there are some significant points of difference between these later writings on transference, and his earlier formulations in *The Interpretation of Dreams* (1900a). In particular, this is evident in his ideas regarding the surrender of the critical function of reason. In *The Interpretation of Dreams* Freud tells us that "we must aim at bringing about two changes in the patient, an increase in the attention he pays to his own psychical perceptions and the elimination of the criticism by which he normally sifts the thoughts that occur to him . . ." (p. 101).

Freud emphasizes the importance of *"the relaxation of a certain deliberate (and no doubt also critical) activity,"* of allowing ideas to emerge "of their own free will" (p. 102). And here, following a suggestion made by Rank, who was particularly identified with the tradition of Romanticism and its aesthetic reflections, he invokes Schiller, who explained to a friend that his inability to be creative probably lay

> in the constraint imposed by your reason upon your imagination. . . . it seems a bad thing and detrimental to the creative work of the mind if Reason makes too close an examination of the ideas as they come pouring in—at the very gateway, as it were. . . . [W]here there is a creative mind, Reason . . . relaxes its watch upon the gates, and the ideas rush in pell-mell, and only then does it look them through and examine them in a mass. . . . You [critics] reject too soon and discriminate too severely. [p. 103]

The relaxation described by Schiller "of the watch upon the gates of Reason" is not all that difficult, Freud avers. He then goes on to discuss the two psychic agencies or forces, first the wish expressed in the dream, which corresponds to the Imagination, then the censor, the gate, which corresponds to Reason.

This text expresses what might be considered the first of Freud's two, antithetical theories of mental freedom: the first proposal advocates a freedom from the critical faculty that creates resistance, allowing the real, in other words unconscious, thoughts to emerge. The second theory, which emerges in his later writings on transference, emphasizes the freedom that comes in reorienting the mind to the reality principle and relieving it of preoccupations with unconscious thoughts that hold it captive to the past and to the pleasure principle.

Now in the beginning, Freud intended that the patient abandon his critical faculty and, in effect, turn it over to the analyst, who retains a rational, organizing mentation, noting the logic of dream thoughts, following gaps and clues. In a sense, the division of labor here involves the alignment of the patient with the first psychic agency, imagination, and the doctor with the second, discriminating reason. But soon Freud came to recognize that deliberate attention is as problematic for the analyst as for the patient. It is after he has formulated his theory of dream interpretation that he comes to realize that inner, mental freedom is necessary for the analyst, to prevent him from controlling the patient and so losing the access to repressed material that would be gained from the patient's obeying the fundamental rule. We may speculate that Freud attained this realization through hard experience, his failure in Dora's case (Freud 1905).

The case of Dora, we know, was the one Freud hoped would actualize his dream theory, but which, instead, came to exemplify the transferential difficulties that ensue when the analyst tries to retain all logic and reason on his side. It is easy to read Dora as an object lesson in the catastrophic results of attacking the resistance in the way Freud originally and naively recommended, of controlling the locus of attention in order to create a seamless narrative of cause and effect. Freud was disappointed in his expectation that Dora would, as he wrote to Fliess, "smoothly open to the existing collection of picklocks" (1900b, p. 427).

Dora has been understood by a multitude of authors to encapsulate what is problematic in any simplified understanding of bringing the hysterical patient to speech. Unlike Anna O., Dora and the unnamed female homosexual (Freud 1920) both reveal, more than Freud seems to intend, a conflict in which Freud tries to penetrate woman's sexuality but the woman resists or rebels. If Freud (1905) thinks that he who disdains the key, which is sexuality, will never open the door to the patient's mind, then Dora, as Jane Gallop (1982) remarks, is there to let him know that no one wants to be opened by a skeleton key. Feminists and psychoanalysts alike have pointed out the way in which Freud pursued the unlocking of meaning, the mining of secrets, the connecting of event and symptom in a seamless narrative—without gaps and holes, or other feminine metaphors of incomplete knowledge (Moi 1985)—to the detriment of the analytic stance toward the patient.

In any event, the recognition of the transference, Dora's particularly "pointed" resistance, once again pushed Freud to reflect on his position and to abandon a certain form of control. He moved toward the model of evenly suspended attention, as he described in his own retrospective account. Nonetheless—and here we come to Freud's "second theory"—Freud seems to reproduce the conflict between reason and imagination on a new level in his writings on the transference between 1912 and 1915. The old refrain of the conflict between language and action can be heard in his discus-

sion of struggle between "intellect and instinct, recognition and
the striving for discharge" (1912, p. 108). Yet again the problem
emerges that action is indispensable, for "No one can be slain in
absentia, in effigy" (p. 108). Thus, in order to put an end to the
unconscious manipulation of the powerful forces, we must expand
our permission, invite the patient to take certain liberties—not just
the relaxation of judgment and freedom of thoughts, but now the
actual reenactment in the transference in the "intermediate region"
or "playground" of the analytic situation (Freud 1914, p. 154). At
the same time, the analyst must be able to go near the dark forces
without succumbing to them, protecting himself from the patient's
effort to assert "her irresistibility, to destroy the physicians's authority *by bringing him down to the level of the lover*" (1915 p. 163,
emphasis added). And "to overcome the pleasure principle . . . to
achieve this *mastery* of herself she must . . . (be led to) that greater
freedom, within the mind which distinguishes conscious mental
activity" (p. 170, emphasis added). As I've said elsewhere (Benjamin
1995), paradoxically the patient's autonomy emerges out of the
identification with the analyst's authority, which she accepts. *She*
makes the axiomatic move from loving him as an object to identification and puts him in place of her ego ideal.

But this is a dangerous project, and Freud (1915) must justify
his persistence in unleashing the explosive forces. As he does so
often, he looks for legitimation not in the freedom of imagination,
but in science, the discourse of objectivity, of reason over instinct.
He compares the analyst handling the transference to the chemist
who carefully handles the dangerous chemicals in the laboratory.
Of course, the problem with this analogy is that the chemist is not
the chemical, whereas the analyst does act as a force in the com-
bustion of the transference. The psychoanalytic doctor is less like
a chemist than like the priest who must encounter the demonic in
order to exorcise it. Indeed, it turns out that psychoanalysis can
refuse hypnotism and faith healing precisely because the same
force reappears in the transference; as Freud (1921) will say later,
it is only a step from being in love to being hypnotized. For that
matter, how could any German-speaker miss the connections between healing (*heilen*), holy (*heilig*), and redeemer (*Heiland*)?

What Freud's warnings scarcely conceal is the impossibility of
the very objectivity that he prescribes. As these connections sug-

gest, the psychoanalytic doctor is not able to heal without becoming implicated in the transference, and so in the illness itself. This could be the message to analysts offered by Kafka's story, "A Country Doctor," a story written as though in response to Freud, or perhaps a doctor's dream. The doctor is called out to a distant village at night, but he has no horses of his own to pull his wagon. Seemingly in exchange for the team of horses that mysteriously appears in his barnyard, he must leave at home his maid, Rosa, to be raped by the groom who appeared along with the horses. While he is objecting, the horses simply carry him off. In a moment he arrives at the village, is surrounded by the patient's family and neighbors, who press him toward the patient, a young boy lying in bed who hardly appears ill, perhaps a malingerer. But as the doctor would leave he looks closer and discovers the patient is truly ill; he has a gaping wound in his side, pink—that is to say Rosa—that is alive with little worms (maggots). The family grab him, undress him, and lay him in bed, while outside the school choir sings, "Unclothe him, unclothe him, then he will heal, and should he not heal, then kill him. He's only a doctor, only a doctor." But he, "thoroughly collected and above it all," simply looks at them. As he escapes naked, his coat hanging from his carriage, the villagers triumph; "Rejoice you patients, the doctor has been put in bed with you." Still, as he flees, he knows his practice will go to pieces, he will never recover, his Rosa is sacrificed, and the stable groom is still rampaging in his house.

We might consider this dream-story to evoke something of the danger Freud would have had in mind when he admonished the young physicians to heal by remaining covered, true to their cloth. To become unclothed, naked, is to be de-vested of one's authority, brought down to the patient's level. It is thus to have the parts of the self that have been split off into the patient—one's own dangerous instincts—exposed, unavoidably, to face the way in which one's authority has been created out of this very process of projection. To be clothed, in-vested, is to have this process remain invisible, and in a sense to protect the authority of the official, the clergyman, the father, the physician, from exposure (Santner 1996).

If the patient and the doctor speak a dialogue that is actually made of two voices within one mind, still they are in competition with each other for space (You're crowding my deathbed, says the boy) as well as recognition or pity (What should I do? believe me, it's not easy for me either, replies the doctor. I'm supposed to be satisfied with that excuse/apology? complains the boy.) The doctor consoles him by suggesting that his wound is something others never get to have: "Many offer their side, and never even hear the axe in the forest, let alone have it approach them." Then the doctor snaps out of it. Too late: his authority can never be recovered.

As the symmetry of their dialogue implies, the level of action here reflects a complementarity that, like the erotic transference, first requires and then risks the analyst's authority. We might better grasp this form of complementarity by referring to a distinction well known in the detective genre (Žižek 1991). In the *Studies*, Freud is still in the mode of Holmes, the investigator who is "collected and above it all," who has a collection of picklocks and an eagle eye for holes in others' stories, who intends to construct a seamless narrative to which he knows the culprit will surrender. She will be able to object no further, she will have to admit the truth of her desire. Then there is the noir detective, Marlowe or Spade for instance, who gets involved and is implicated in the whole story, and if he in the end places the guilt where it belongs and refuses to take the fall with the guilty one, still, like the country doctor, he is not untouched—indeed, he is never quite the same. This might be seen as the passage Freud has to suffer in the Dora case, from a complementarity that establishes well bounded opposites, to the reversible complementarity of "it takes one to know one," the one that takes you into bed with the patient.

Freud's difficulty in accepting his identification with the passive, helpless position of the young woman Dora, struggling against her reduction to the position of object, leads him into the reversible complementarity of the power struggle. He becomes the complementary other to Dora's resistance not only by identifying with Herr K., but by becoming invested in proving that he knows what is really going on. One of the most striking points in his narration is the way that his own observation in the text, that one always reproaches the other with that which one does oneself, applies to his own ending: he reproaches Dora with wishing only to take revenge, while one can hardly see his refusal to treat her on that ground as any less vengeful. Dora's resistance, her cool rejection of Freud's perfect interpretations that mimics the rhetorical position of the scientific authority with its object helpless before it—like his unnamed "female homosexual" (Harris 1991)—uncloaks his vestments of neutrality, provoking him to reveal his investment.

The patient who acts, rather than thinks or speaks, pulls the analyst into the complementary identification and away from both representation and empathy. The analyst who resists identification with the patient's position engages the complementary aspect of the relationship and unwittingly stimulates action. The patient's action then painfully becomes an inverted mirror of the action that aspires to achieve, through knowing or helping, a security-in-control. As Racker (1968) made clear, the complementary position can be countered by the identificatory position in the countertransference, the analyst's ability to be on both sides of the divide. By adopting the concordant position of identification with the patient's position, the analyst has the leverage to think about the patient. If the analyst does not identify with the patient in her or his own ego, "recognizing what belongs to the other as one's own," (p. 134), she or he will become identified with the patient's bad or good objects, and the split complementarity ensues: doer/done to, vengeful/victimized, and the like.

What does it mean to identify in one's own ego? In a sense, it means the opposite of hysterical identification, which involves a "mapping" (Mitchell 1995) of the self on to the other, an unmediated assimilation of other and self that Freud writes of in *The Interpretation of Dreams* (1900) and later classifies as a phenomenon like mass contagion (1921). Such hysterical identification—part of the inevitable "enmeshed" feeling evoked by the relationship with certain patients and which we can sometimes divest only by cloaking ourselves with our role—can be distinguished from those identifications that are mediated by representation and so eventually become useful sources of knowledge for us and the patient. Another way to formulate this is to say that, properly speaking, not the act of identification, which is unavoidable and unthought, but the act of representing identification, creates a point of freedom.

In practice, we also distinguish identification that retains contact with the patient's multiple and conflicting positions from the kind that appears in split complementarities, in which we take one side of a conflict. As we see in Dora, the notion that enemies re-

semble each other applies, perhaps because the patient is also identified with the bad objects in her ego. Following the unconscious
logic of "I could be you, and you could be me," complementarity
often involves symmetrical responses, tit for tat, I'm rubber, you're
glue. Thus the complementary countertransference recreates an
internal dialogue, as in Kafka's dream story, that captures both
participants. Insofar as the patient experiences the analyst's investment in being the one who "understands rather than the one who
is understood, who is needed rather than who needs" (Hoffman
1991), to be the master or Lacan's "subject supposed to know," the
analyst may find her- or himself pulled ever deeper into the power
struggle. In such a case, when the analyst is in-vested in omni-
science, the basic fault in the idea of the patient making the analyst into her/his ego ideal is exposed.

For this ego ideal of analytic understanding has, to varying
degrees, already been constituted through split complementary
structures that devalue the one who is speechless, passive, does
not know, is needy, the object of pity, and so forth. What it means
to pull ourselves out of such complementary power struggles by
immersing ourselves in a very specific way, learning to swim in
the countertransference rather than drown, can surely be seen as
the psychoanalytic project of the last few decades of the century.
Freud's notion that the patient could identify with the ideal side of
analytic authority did not encompass the equally plausible reaction of rejecting authority: that the patient would also attack the
analyst precisely in her or his effort to be a different kind of healer,
would call forth the hidden dimension of power in knowledge, that
which Freud thinks can win out against unreason without the usual
consequences of subjugating a binary opposite.

In drawing a line between hypnosis/suggestion and analysis
aimed at freeing the patient's subjectivity, Freud instituted a crucial paradigm for dealing with binaries. As we shall see, regarding
the idea of analyst as ego ideal, such simple opposites are likely to
conceal or obscure the contradictions that inevitably arise in our
practice. The strict equation of the analyst's distance and objectivity with the patient's freedom that Freud invoked seems to have
been more successful in providing legitimation for psychoanalysis than it was in working with patients. A case in point is Rivière,

whose reflections on the negative therapeutic reaction drew on her own experience with Jones and Freud and apparently inspired Freud's original discussion of that phenomenon (Kris 1994). In Freud's (1923) footnote on the negative therapeutic reaction in *The Ego and the Id,* he remarks that successful work with a patient whose unconscious guilt leads to narcissistic defenses may "depend on whether the personality of the analyst allows of the patient's putting him in the place of his ego ideal, and this involves a temptation for the analyst to play the part of prophet, savior and redeemer to the patient" (p. 50).

Kris (1994) believes this statement refers to Freud's decision to be more supportive in order to penetrate beneath the patient's critical attitude to the unconscious guilt, which Rivière herself saw as tied to depressive love for the lost, critical object. In other words, the supportive stance aims to steer clear of the inevitable complementarity that ensues when an attacking object is on the screen and either patient or analyst is impelled to play its part. To this aim the therapeutic move will be to achieve concordance, an identificatory position, what is commonly called empathy, and so steer clear of being attacker or attackee. But, Freud objects, this move will foster the patient's feeling that the analyst is now the savior from the critical object, will be loved in its place. What is to be done? In the very next sentence Freud objects to his suggestion that the analyst's personality can play a role in counteracting the negative therapeutic reaction, stating that "the rules of analysis are diametrically opposed to the physician making use of his personality in any such manner." Characteristically, he refers us again to the aim of giving "the patient's ego *freedom* to choose. This, not making pathological reactions impossible, is the goal of analysis" (p. 50, my italics).

It is noteworthy that Freud, in referring to what we now think of as the classical rules, does not distinguish between the analyst's countertransference fantasy of being a redeemer and the patient's fantasy of him as the savior in the transference. The countertransference fantasy reflects the analyst's disowned desire to be saved, which is projected onto the vulnerable, needy patient. It is this unconscious identification with the wish to be saved that stimulates and colludes with the idealization, sometimes leading to enactment of the erotic transference in a dynamic very like that between Breuer and Anna. But the analyst's reaction against the desire, the superego demand for abstinence, leads to other difficulties. For the idealization that devolves upon the abstaining analyst, who counters grandiosity and redemption with impersonal austerity, produces a formidable ego ideal. And are we to think that, because the patient is to identify with the analyst's abstinence, the analyst appears any less the "redeemer"? The history of sainthood in Christianity hardly supports such an assumption. This scenario produces the antierotic enactment in which the patient will have difficulties with the analyst's authority, will experience adherence to rules as withholding, critical of her needs, and so will reinstitute the analyst as a guilt-inducing object. We may question whether such withholding of subjective response makes the analyst less exalted (Menaker 1972), less a god, especially to himself. And for the patient, certainly, he may well appear to be the god who denies only this particular sinner the redemption she seeks.

Freud sets up a parallel between two sets of contrasting terms: between using one's own subjectivity and remaining objective/abstinent, and between falling into the temptation to be a redeemer/healer and giving the patient freedom. But setting up those contrasts leads Freud to an impasse—he should like his personality to make him available to the patient, but it would tempt him to be a redeemer—that he resolves not by analysis but by falling back on the rules. This paradigm of objectivity, with its conflation of subjectivity with idealization, held sway over analytic work for decades. As a guide to those ensnared in the complementary transference, this view of the rules of analysis may well have created the problems it claimed to solve.

Doubtless the clinical impracticality of holding the position of objective knower as well as the influence of postmodern challenges to objectivist epistemologies have led to the intersubjective and relational revisions in contemporary psychoanalytic thought (Aron 1996, Pizer 1998). The idea of analytic neutrality is increasingly challenged (Renik 1994) or subject to redefinition (Gerson 1996). The intersubjective analyst's idea of freedom—the analyst's freedom—is to make use of one's emotional responses, one's subjectivity, in a knowing way.

To refigure what it means to use one's subjectivity rather than accept the polarity of subjectivity and objectivity is an important aim of contemporary analysis (Aron 1996; Hoffman 1998; S. A. Mitchell 1993). We aim to formulate a space in between suggestion and objective distance, which encompasses the analyst's emotional response to the patient and takes account of her or his involvement in the complementarity transference action as well as being the means for extricating her- or himself from it. In the process, the distinction between speech and action necessarily breaks down (Greenberg 1996, Aron 1996), as we become aware that all speaking has the impact of an action and all action communicates "information" from a particular point of view. In other words, as we cease to privilege the analyst's perspective as objectively derived knowledge, we acknowledge the analyst's participation in an interaction of two subjects. The double action of intersubjectivity, recognizing the other's subjectivity and one's own, means that as the patient becomes less objectified, the analyst becomes a more "subjective" subject.

Such acknowledgement requires a different understanding both of mental structure—that is, symbolic representation—and of the intersubjectivity of the analytic situation, each understanding furthering the other. The principle that informs both is the idea of transforming complementarities into dialectical tension, into tolerable paradox, instead of into antinomies that compel dangerous choices. Opposites are to some extent unavoidable because of the inherent psychic tendency to split, because, in fact, they allow the mind to think; it is the capacity to hold them in tension and overcome splitting that is at stake. This inevitable movement through opposites is what we need to hold in mind both in our theory and in the clinical situation.

Likewise, we may accept that the split complementarity inevitably re-emerges time and again in the transference, and consider how we re-solve it in our minds, modify it by restoring the sense of separate subjectivities. Frequently this occurs not through distance, conventional objectivity, but through one person trying to know what the other is feeling, so that identification becomes a recognizable effort to break up the enclosure in the paranoid position. In this case, identification functions as a channel allowing the flow and processing of emotion (in self-psychological terms, through empathic introspection [Stolorow et al. 1987]). The ability to symbolize emerges via the analyst's ability to survive the inevitable involvement in complementarity by making use of of identificatory responses that bypass or dissolve it.

The analyst is always striving to represent both the patient's position and her or his own. Even if this representation is at best only an approximation of the other's meaning, and at worst a misrepresentation, it can nevertheless serve to create the two planes necessary for a third, a double-sided perspective that can support a third point of the triangle. It maintains a tension or space between self and other; it can be extended to the patient as an invitation to collaborative thinking. But since we also grant that knowing is intrapsychically filtered, we must tolerate the inevitable misrecognition that accompanies our efforts at recognition. To react to this inevitability by relinquishing the effort to know or recognize would simply reinstall the principle of objective knowledge as the only one worth having.

The psychoanalytic efforts to deconstruct the dominance of an objectively knowing subject in favor of a personal subjectivity parallel recent feminist efforts to disrupt the conventional oppositions and their encoding in gender hierarchies. The question of how we envision dissolving the ever-recurring complementarities, especially the idealizations intrinsic to binary hierarchies, is common to each. Some important overlaps can be found in the reassessment of the maternal function and the maternal transferences that psychoanalysis and feminism have undertaken in the last decades.

For example, we may now reverse the movement we followed in considering how psychoanalysis evolved its focus on symbolic function, which I have put in the shorthand "from body to speech." Current theorizing about the use of the analytic space as an extension of the maternal body container suggests that this container is what holds and gives coherence to the self, what first makes symbolic thinking possible (Bion 1962, 1967). The formulation of this aspect of the psychoanalytic process sprang from the observation that many people suffered from an inability to represent affect except through acting; they could not "use" the analyst (Winnicott 1971), that is, the intersubjective properties of the relationship.

Whereas Freud had articulated the means of interpreting unconscious symbolization, it now became necessary to theorize the conditions that foster development of symbolic capacity. The person who remains unable to process bodily tension except through motoric discharge or somatic symptoms could be described not as lacking speech or symbolic capacity, but as lacking a relationship that is a condition of that capacity.

This relationship in which subjectivity develops is predicated on certain kinds of activity by the other, variously described as recognition, attunement, holding. The mother acts as an outside other who is able to help the subject to process and tolerate internal states of tension (Beebe and Lachmann 1994). The evolution from a concrete to a metaphorical experience is contingent on some achievement of bodily regulation and its intersubjective quality of recognition, through which the body metaphorically becomes the mental container.

In sum, the early two-body experience is seen as crucial to the way that representation emerges intersubjectively. Because communicative speech establishes a space of dialogue potentially outside the mental control of either or both participants, it is a site of mediation, the "third term."[1] In the dialogic structure, mediated by symbolic expression, identification can become not a collapse of differentiation, but a basis for understanding the position of the other. The kind of separation that allows this symbolic development is predicated on a maternal subjectivity that is able to represent affect, specifically the pain of separation between herself and the child.

---

1. I have argued elsewhere (Benjamin 1995) that we can set the dialogue of the maternal dyad in the place of Lacan's third term that breaks the dyad, the symbolic father or phallus. This is significant because Lacanian feminists such as Juliet Mitchell took this point to mean that there was no escape from the "dyadic trap" (J. Mitchell 1974) other than the patriarchal form. Intersubjective space, I suggested more broadly (Benjamin 1988), could be understood in terms of the dialogue as creating a third, something like the dance that is distinct from the dancers yet cocreated by them. Ogden's (1995) idea of the analytic third, a cocreated yet independent relationship of two subjectivities, is similar to my idea of thirdness.

This view of the mother's mental work of representation or thinking[2] becomes an Archimedean point of the shift in the notion of the subject as active representer of the world. We can recast Freud's original splitting between active and passive that has played such a large role in psychoanalytic theory. The psyche's main work of representing and thereby digesting bodily/affective stimuli and tension may still be seen as the antidote or counterpole to passive subjection. But this ability is better understood as derivative of the other's response to one's acts and affects, thus requiring two subjects rather than a subject and an object. Maternal recognition fosters the overcoming of the active–passive polarity in the relation of two subjects.

Conceptually, this notion of recognition as activity indicates the basis for transcending the split complementarity in which the (traditionally female) other was, if not helplessly subjected to the subject's power, relegated to the position of passivity in order to mirror his activity, contain his unmanageable tension. Providing mirroring for the subject, being his container, would in effect compromise one's own subjectivity, disrupt one's own capacity for thinking (Brennan 1992), whereas, in the intersubjective conception of recognition, two active subjects may exchange, alternate, in expressing and receiving, cocreating a mutuality that allows for and presumes separateness. The arena for this catching and throwing is the intermediate, in-between space.

Historically, as long as the identificatory channel was blocked at the level of gender, as long as the intersubjective potential of the maternal dyad was insufficiently theorized, psychoanalytic theory could not really raise to the symbolic level this critique of complementarity. This insufficiency is intrinsically related to the inability to represent—in theory and in life—an identification with the mother as a subject: a desiring sexual subject, to be recognized as a a person in her own right. It could not formulate a mother who is more than a mirror or evolve an idea of active femininity. Insofar as these divisions reflected the basic paradigm of subject

---

2. Work, as the nineteenth-century metaphor for transformations of energy, seems an appropriate term, as does Ruddick's (1989) "maternal thinking."

and object, psychoanalysis remained captive to the active–passive binary in the analytic relationship.

In conclusion, I will briefly sketch how the prohibition on representing maternal identification perpetuates the active–passive complementarity so fateful for psychoanalysis. The child's attempt to reverse the complementarity by turning tables on the mother— by actively discharging into a controlled container as well as by controlling her—is an important (and, again, probably inevitable) piece of mental life. What *is* problematic is the institutionalization of this reversal as the predominant form of masculine activity. In accord with other feminist thinkers (see Chodorow 1980), I have theorized that this reversal is consolidated during the oedipal phase when the boy repudiates the identification with the mother, thus losing access to an important means of remaining in relation to her (Benjamin 1988, 1995). This, in turn, makes more dangerous the now sexualized stimulation that, in his mind at least, appears not as his own desire but as emanating from her—all the more so because he cannot identify with her as a container of his own feelings. The boy does not so much strive to contain as mother contains, as he projects or splits off the experience of being the passive, stimulated one, lodging this helplessness in the female and defining it as the feminine position. At the same time, the boy displaces the mother's envied activity onto the father with whom he identifies, rather than seeking to appropriate maternal activity directly as a form of power.

In the oedipal transformation, then, the aspect of passivity, which absorbs the experience of being the helpless baby and the overstimulated oedipal child, devolves onto the feminine position: it becomes "feminine passivity." This position becomes the structural basis for the figure of the daughter, as reflected in Freud's oedipal theory of the girl's passive sexuality in relation to the father. This creation of a "feminine" representation, which transmutes the boy's own position of dependency and powerlessness, is precisely represented in his idea of the oedipal daughter's switch from being identified with the active mother to being the father's passive object (Benjamin 1995). (As Horney [1926] contended, one could see the whole set of propositions about the female Oedipus complex as mirroring the view of the oedipal boy.)

We might well say that the *Studies* provide an allegory of the way in which the daughter's position, the renunciation of activity and absorption in passivity, leads to the speechlessness, the *Unmündigkeit* of hysteria. Combined with the cultural prohibition on female aggression, cutting off recourse to any form of defensive activity (the well-known reversal out of passivity), this position makes hysteria the daughter's disease (Showalter 1985). What is it in the daughter's passive position—the switch from mother to father—that dictates the form of her illness, even when the symptoms are not directly related to sexual passivity, to exploitation, or to sexual abuse?

I am implicitly suggesting a theory about the construction of femininity, one that overlaps in many essentials with ideas Brennan (1992) has formulated from a somewhat different perspective. The gist of my argument is that the oedipal switch to passivity should be understood not as a product of the girl's search for the penis, but as her compliance with the father's search for a passive object, represented in the cultural norm of femininity (though often put in the service of the mother). Here "father" is read as a cultural, structural position, not necessarily an individual one, produced in the oedipal boy's repudiation of his own passivity in the face of the exciting or abandoning maternal object, a move that sparks a fantasy of the daughter's passivity.

Consider briefly Freud's train of thought when he asserts, in a paper concurrent with the *Studies*, "The Neuro-psychoses of Defence" (1896), that a repressed feminine passivity lodges behind the male obsessional's use of defensive, aggressive activity. In other words, a certain kind of activity is necessary in order to overcome helplessness, and this kind of defensive activity structures the masculine position (Christiansen 1993). If father–daughter incest represents the most egregious encapsulation of this defense, it is made possible by the generalized complementary relationship between the sexes, in which the daughter functions not merely as the split-off embodiment of the passive object, but also as the missing maternal container into whom the father discharges and expels unmanageable tension. The dual function of embodying passivity and containing unmanageable projected tension gives form to femininity; this femininity takes the daughter, not the mother, as its defining figure. This structuring of the daughter position may be the missing link in explaining the equation of hysteria with femininity. It is worth noting here that both Anna and Dora nursed their fathers through long illnesses, clung to and identified with them, incorporated their symptoms. They became containers for the other, but were unable to contain themselves.

I have suggested that we understand the active–passive gender complementarity as an oedipal form, not merely repudiating identification with feminine passivity but actually shaping it in a reversal that negates the mother's activity. The masculine subjectivity that emerges from this move reflects both the absence of identification with a containing mother and the failure to represent the mother as a sexual subject.

For the moment it must suffice to suggest what might be recovered and represented beyond the dominance of the active–passive complementarity. I have elaborated elsewhere (Benjamin 1995) how it is possible to theorize a different position in relation to gendered oppositions, to formulate a different kind of complementarity than the one that emerges at the oedipal level, that of have or have not, phallus or no phallus (Birksted-Breen 1996). To go beyond the polarization of the oedipal level might mean to change the form of complementarity—perhaps a parallel move to the way that sustaining identification with different positions transforms complementarity in the countertransference.

From this standpoint, true activity does not take the defensive form of repudiating passivity. Activity predicated on the activity–passivity split, directed toward a passive object, is merely action; it lacks the intersubjective space of a potential other. Such space, as we have seen, is the very condition of symbolic activity; in other words, the counterpart to the representational activity of the subject is always a representation of the other subject (which need not be a real other, and could be nothing less than the world outside). Characteristically such activity can embrace receptivity to that other, responsive recognition of the other's impact on the self, and hence participation in the reality of two subjects. Of course, every psychoanalytic relationship has to work through oscillations between action and activity, split complementary and mutuality, and so we are always rededicating ourselves to finding a path toward intersubjective speech, learning from action.

Insofar as defensive repudiation of passivity helped to constitute the figure of ideal mastery that has burdened psychoanalysis,
psychoanalysis must go beyond the oedipal complementarity in
order to cure itself. The characteristic of the post-oedipal complementarity is that it can hold paradoxical rather than oppositional
formulations. It is this that gives rise to a third position that neither denies nor splits difference, but holds it in a paradoxical state
of being antagonistic and reconcilable at once. This is the position
that can tolerate the incessant reversals of opposites by weaving a
net from the attraction to both sides, a net that allows us to take
the primal leap of psychoanalysis, the leap into the space between
certain knowledge and unthinking action, the space of negative
capability that is thought.

To become disinvested in any one position, in this way, is close
to the goal of mental freedom Freud strove to formulate. To even
imagine such freedom, Freud knew, requires a consciousness of
our own investment; what we have added perhaps, is that this is
possible only by becoming aware of our inevitable participation
in the split complementarities that organize our lives and our
thought. Thus the reintegration of the missing half of the com-
plenientarity is always a necessary step to thinking through that
splitting. Toward this end, I have called upon the figure of Anna/
Bertha, alongside the figure of Freud, so that our imagination will
continue to include whoever, whatever, appears in the guise
of the complementary other, and so that we may view afresh the
reversal between analyser and analyzed. Such reversals mark
the dialogic encounter with those others, which is at the heart of
the psychoanalytic endeavor, calling forth our own reaction to
the action of the other, whose pain, passion and opposing other-
ness will inevitably unclothe us to ourselves, and tell us: Think
again!

REFERENCES

Appignanesi, L. and Forrester, J. (1992). *Freud's Women*. New York:
    Basic Books.
Aron, L. (1996). *A Meeting of Minds: Mutuality in Psychoanalysis*.
    Hillsdale, NJ: Analytic Press.

Beebe, B. and Lachmann, F. (1994). Representation and internalization in infancy: three principles of saliency. *Psychoanalytic Psychology* 11:127–165.

Benjamin, J. (1988). *The Bonds of Love: Psychoanalysis, Feminism and the Problem of Domination*. New York: Pantheon.

—— (1995). *Like Subjects, Love Objects: Essays on Recognition and Sexual Difference*. New Haven: Yale University Press.

—— (1998). The shadow of the other subject. In *Shadow of the Other*. New York: Routledge.

Bernheimer, C. and Kahane, C. (1985). *In Dora's Case: Freud–Hysteria–Femininism*. New York: Columbia University Press.

Bion, W. (1962). Learning from experience. In *Seven Servants*. New York: Jason Aronson, 1977.

—— (1967). *Second Thoughts*. New York: Jason Aronson.

Birksted-Breen, D. (1996). Phallus, penis and mental space. *International Journal of Psycho-Analysis*. 77:649–657.

Brennan, T. (1992). *The Interpretation of the Flesh: Freud and Femininity*. New York: Routledge.

Breuer, J. and Freud, S. (1893-1895). Studies on hysteria. *Standard Edition 2*.

Chodorow, N. (1980). Gender relation and difference in psychoanalytic perspective. In *Feminism and Psychoanalytic Theory*. New Haven, CT: Yale University Press, 1989.

Christiansen, A. (1993). Masculinity and its vicissitudes. Paper presented at Seminar on Psychoanalysis and Sexual Difference, New York Institute for the Humanities at New York University.

Cixous, H. and Clément, C. (1975). *La Jeune Née*. Paris: Union Générale d'Editions. English translation: *The Newly Born Woman*. Minneapolis, MN: University of Minnesota Press, 1986.

Freedman, N. (1985). The concept of transformation in psychoanalysis. *Psychoanalytic Psychology* 2(4): 17–39.

—— (1980). On splitting and its resolution. *Psychoanalysis and Contemporary Thought* 3:237–266.

Freud, S. (1896). Further remarks on the neuro-psychoses of defence. *Standard Edition* 3:162–185.

—— (1900a). The interpretation of dreams. *Standard Edition* 4/5: 1–626.

—— (1900b). Letter to Fliess, October 14. In *The Complete Letters of Sigmund Freud to Wihelm Fliess 1887–1904*, ed. J. M.

Masson, pp. 426–427. Cambridge, MA: Harvard University Press, 1985.

—— (1905). Fragment of an analysis of a case of hysteria. *Standard Edition* 7:3–124.

—— (1912). The dynamics of transference. *Standard Edition* 12.

—— (1914). Remembering, repeating and working through. *Standard Edition* 12.

—— (1915). Observations on transference-love. *Standard Edition* 12.

—— (1920). The psychogenesis of a case of homosexuality in a woman. *Standard Edition* 18:145–172.

—— (1921). Group psychology and the analysis of the ego. *Standard Edition* 18:67–144.

—— (1923). The ego and the id. *Standard Edition* 19:1–66.

Gallop, J. (1982). *The Daughter's Seduction: Feminism and Psychoanalysis.* Ithaca, NY: Cornell University Press.

Gerson, S. (1996). Neutrality, resistance and self-disclosure in an intersubjective psychoanalysis. *Psychoanalytic Dialogues* 6(5): 623–646.

Green, A. (1986). *On Private Madness.* Madison, CT: International Universities Press.

Greenberg, J. (1996). Psychoanalytic words and psychoanalytic acts: a brief history. *Contemporary Psychoanalysis* 32:177–184.

Harris, A. (1991). Gender as contradiction: a discussion of Freud's "The psychogenesis of a case of homosexuality in a woman." *Psychoanalytic Dialogues* 1(2):197–224.

Hillmann, U. (1992). Bertha Pappenheim: Psychoanalyse–Frauenbewegung–Sozialarbeit. In *Frauenstadtbuch*, pp. 50–56. Frankfurt: WEIBH.

Hoffman, I. (1991). Reply to Benjamin. *Psychoanalytic Dialogues* 1(4):535–544.

—— (1998). *Ritual and Spontaneity in Psychoanalytic Process.* Hillsdale, NJ: Analytic Press.

Horney, K. (1926). The flight from womanhood. In *Feminine Psychology.* New York: Norton, 1967.

Kerr, J. (1993). *A Most Dangerous Method: The Story of Jung, Freud and Sabina Spielrein.* New York: Random House.

Kris, A. (1994). Freud's treatment of a narcissistic patient. *International Journal of Psychoanalysis* 75:649–664.

Menaker, E. (1972). The masochistic factor in the psychoanalytic situation. In *Masochism and the Emergent Ego*. Northvale, NJ: Jason Aronson, 1996.

Mitchell, J. (1995). Unpublished colloquium, New York University, January.

Mitchell, S. A. (1993). *Hope and Dread in Psychoanalysis*. New York: Basic Books.

Moi, T. (1995). Representation of patriarchy: sexuality and epistemology in Freud's Dora. In *In Dora's Case: Freud–Hysteria–Feminism*, ed. C. Bernheimer and C. Kahane, pp. 181–199. New York: Columbia University Press.

Ogden, T. (1995). *Subjects of Analysis*. Northvale, NJ: Jason Aronson.

Pappenheim, B. (1912). Die Frau im kirchlichen und religiösen Leben. In Wagner, L., Mehrwald, S., Maierhof, G. and Jansen, M., *Aus dem Leben Jüdischer Frauen*. Kassel: Archiv der Deutschen Frauenbewegung, 1994.

Pizer, S. (1998). *Building Bridges: The Negotiation of Paradox in Psychoanalysis*. Hillsdale, NJ: Analytic Press.

Racker, H. (1968). *Transference and Countertransference*. London: Maresfield Library, Karnac, 1982.

Renik, O. (1994). The perils of neutrality. *Psychoanalytic Quarterly*. 63:495–517.

Ruddick, S. (1989). *Maternal Thinking*. Boston: Beacon.

Santner, E. (1996). *My Own Private Germany: Daniel Paul Schreber's Secret History of Modernity*. Princeton, NJ: Princeton University Press.

Showalter, E. (1985). *The Female Malady: Women, Madness and English Culture, 1893–1980*. New York: Penguin.

Stolorow, R., Brandschaft, B., and Atwood, G. (1987). *Psychoanalytic Treatment: An Intersubjective Approach*. Hillsdale, NJ: Analytic Press.

Winnicott, D. W. (1971). *Playing and Reality*. New York: Basic Books.

Žižek, S. (1991). *Looking Awry: An Introduction to Jacques Lacan through Popular Culture*. Cambridge, MA: MIT Press.

2

The Psychotherapy of Hysteria, 1995

André Green

One year after having finished with "The Psychotherapy of Hysteria" for the *Studies on Hysteria* (Breuer and Freud 1893–1895), Freud, writing to Fliess, confessed that he had always longed, in his youth, for philosophical knowledge and that now he had finally reached the moment to realize his aspiration by shifting from medicine to psychology.[1] It was against his will that he became a therapist. This statement seems to indicate that his association with Breuer had finally come to an end, freeing him from the limitations of a too narrow medical point of view. Writing the chapter on "The Psychotherapy of Hysteria" was a rather tedious task, performed without enthusiasm.[2] If 1895 was the year when the *Studies on Hysteria* were published, it was also the year when his most complex and sometimes obscure "Project for a Scientific Psychology" came out of his pen. Freud had really shifted now from medicine to psychology, understood and enlightened from a point of view close to what we would today call "neuroscience." His philosophy was to be a *Naturphilosophie*. His speculations of 1895 would pave the way to *The Interpretation of Dreams*, published five years later by Freud in 1900. So "The Psychotherapy of Hysteria" can be read as a farewell to Breuer. If one compares the "Preliminary Communication," published in 1893 when Freud endorses many of the views of his elder coauthor, and the final chapter of the *Studies on Hysteria*, published two years later, one easily realizes how far Freud has traveled from Breuer. Albrecht Hirschmüller (1978) clearly shows that the ambivalence in the relationship between the two men had started long before, even at the time of the "Preliminary Communication."[3]

I will not deal in detail with the differences between Breuer and Freud, since much has been written on the topic. Instead I shall

---

1. Letter to Wilhelm Fliess, April 2, 1896.
2. Letter to Wilhelm Fliess, March 4, 1895.
3. Hirschmüller, A. (1978). Physiologie und Psychoanalyse in Leben und Werk Josef Breuers. Bern: Hans Huber Verlag.

try to elaborate on an epistemological point. In a letter to Breuer
dated June 29, 1892, Freud writes to his honored friend: "The main
question, no doubt, is whether we should describe it [our theory
of hysteria] historically and lead off with all (or two of the best)
cases histories, or whether, on the other hand, we should start by
dogmatically stating the theories we have devised as an explanation."[4] Freud concludes: "I incline to the second suggestion" (1892,
p. 147). In other words, theory has to be stated first in terms of
theorems and ideas. Forty-six years later, a few months before
dying, Freud expresses the same dilemma in an unfinished draft
written in London in English, "Some Elementary Lessons in Psycho-
Analysis" (Freud 1938), a sort of British outline.[5] He calls the historical method "genetic," enabling the reader to participate in the
building up of a new theory. He opposes this method to another
one that he labels "dogmatic" and that begins straightaway by stating its conclusions. In 1938, Freud now decides to make use of one
and not the other. We can see that the problem was constantly in
Freud's mind: the historical-genetic versus the dogmatic. Are we
very far from our present debates on history and structure? I will
follow Freud's last statement using one or the other alternately.

The psychotherapy of hysteria is an elaboration of the cases
treated by Freud, each being set forth historically. Nevertheless,
Freud the thinker could not refrain from expressing his views on
theory. The "Project" (1895) is an extreme example of the dogmatic
method. Nevertheless, it included a marvelous clinical example
illustrating "The Hysterical Proton Pseudos." The second part of
the "Project," entitled "Psychopathology," is about hysteria. It is
striking to compare the last chapter of the *Studies on Hysteria* and
the second part of the "Project" written in the same year. Here
Freud is liberated from any obligation to accept Breuer's ideas.
Symbolization is now at the center of the theory. He concludes:
"the process of repression remains as the core of the riddle"[6]
(p. 352). Freud's enthusiasm and boldness is in writing the "Project"
for Fliess,[7] one month after ending "The Psychotherapy of Hyste-

---

4. *Standard Edition* 1:147.
5. *Standard Edition* 23:281.
6. *Standard Edition* 1:352.
7. Letter to Wilhelm Fliess, April 27, 1895.

ria." The whole thing is obvious: Freud is not anymore in "love" with Breuer, even if he is still affectionate to him.[8] His new "lover," for whom he writes that scientific poem, the "Project," is Fliess. Freud wants to convince Fliess just as he wanted to convince Breuer earlier. It was in vain—both love affairs will fail. Freud, in order to "become" Freud, had only one way: to give up the hope of being understood and to shut himself in with his own dreams. *The Interpretation of Dreams* could be called "Sigmund Freud's Correspondence with Sigmund Freud." But let us now come back to "The Psychotherapy of Hysteria." How are we to regard this chapter? The *Studies on Hysteria* were not the act of birth of psychoanalysis, because psychoanalysis was not born once and for all in 1895. For me, its childbirth started some years before the *Studies on Hysteria*. In 1905, with the *Three Essays on the Theory of Sexuality* and the book *Jokes and Their Relations to the Unconscious*, the labor and delivery ended. So, how do we read "The Psychotherapy of Hysteria"?

An immediate reaction is to sort out what belongs to each of the authors. Anzieu (1988) had examined Freud's findings of July 1895: his classification of psychic disorders (psychoneuroses of defense, actual neuroses, and psychoses), their sexual etiology (seduction, abstinence, or frustration), their specific mechanisms, and so on. Nearly sixty theoretical notions are presented. Twenty of them will be definitely accepted, twenty of them will be developed in the future to become part of psychoanalytic theory, ten of them will be abandoned, and the last ten were already part of the psychological or psychiatric terminology of the day.[9]

Hypnoid states were the main interest of disagreement between Breuer and Freud. The *Studies on Hysteria* contain few references to dreams. It is only when Freud dissociated himself from Breuer that he gave full attention to dreams. Even before deciding to write *The Interpretation of Dreams*, the "Project" devoted many sections to dreams. Freud linked primary processes with dreams, presented some views on dream analysis, and studied consciousness in dreams. It is as if not satisfied in staying halfway with the idea

---

8. Letter to Wilhelm Fliess, May 25, 1895.

9. Anzieu, D. (1988). *L'autoanalyse de Freud et la découverte de la psychanalyse*. Paris: Presses Universitaires de France, pp. 28–32.

of a hypnoid state and linking it with special mental states supposed to be created by some cloudy consciousness, Freud prefers
to immerse himself in the dark, in a state of complete sleep in order
to let the dream appear as a mental state in its own right, deserv-
ing an interpretation that will serve as a royal road to what he is
searching for.

One of the most striking differences between Freud's writing
in 1895 and our present thoughts is about hysteria itself. When
Freud writes on the topic, he omits to remind us that hysteria has
been known since the Greeks, who not only gave the first descriptions but also identified the sexual etiology of the disease. Freud
makes no reference to the prehistory of the disease. Neither does
he question the rather recent increase of patients suffering from
symptoms of hysteria. The influence of the Salpêtrière School, as
well as the memories of Charcot's presentations and conceptions,
are obviously detectable in the book. Oddly enough all the quota-
tions of Charcot are either in the "Preliminary Communication" or
in Breuer's contribution. Is this not an indication that Freud is also
on his way to free himself from the influence of the "Master of Paris"
and now has his own ideas? In any case, "The Psychotherapy of
Hysteria" still bears strong marks of a nosographic inspiration. If
he adheres to the distinction between different groups of clinical
entities such as actual neuroses, transference neuroses, narcissistic neuroses, and psychoses, as well as the different sorts of hysteria that are separated (hypnoid hysteria, defense hysteria, retention hysteria, traumatic hysteria, and conversion hysteria) will
progressively shrink. Only conversion hysteria will be saved from
oblivion. Later on Freud will add to it anxiety hysteria (phobias).
Finally a triptych will constitute the transference neuroses: conversion hysteria, phobias, and obsessional neurosis, all of them
having in common truly psychic structures related to object libido.
When Freud was in Paris in 1885, he could hear Charcot developing a psychological theory of hysteria, psychic traumas being the
real etiological factors rather than physical ones. It was thanks to
hypnosis that this conception was born. But the pathogenesis of
the symptom was very different from what Freud was up to discover. Charcot at the end of his life was convinced that hysteria
was for the most part a mental disease. Nevertheless his conception was based on the forgetting by the patient of the representa-

tion of motor patterns (Dantchev and Widlöcher 1994).[10] Of course, everybody knows that Freud overheard Charcot saying to one of his pupils that it was always the "genital thing" that was the cause of the illness, not understanding why he did not state that loudly. In fact Hirschmüller (1978) says that the sexual etiology of hysteria was not ignored at Freud's time, so it was less the fact in itself than how it was supposed to create the symptoms that was important. It is also well known that Breuer's disagreement with Freud was about the sexual origin of the symptoms.

Here we are, at the end of the century in Vienna with two highly gifted doctors belonging to the Jewish community, both of them in a close working relationship, trying to cure women of strange symptoms. They are having hypnotic sessions during which they talk of very intimate topics. At certain moments the doctor exerts pressure with his hand on the patient's forehead to force her to evoke indecent topics.

HYSTERIA'S NEUROLOGICAL SYMPTOMS IN 1995

What do we know, one century later, about conversion? A recent review from the Salpêtrière brings fresh news which I will have to summarize. Derouesné (1994) [11] notices that there is a great confusion in that field. One should distinguish conversion from hysteria. Both can appear separately, conversion without hysteria or hysteria without conversion, but they can be associated as well. Conversion symptoms can be classified as sensory-motor manifestations, seen as deficits, dissociation phenomena (amnesias, disturbances of consciousness, pseudo-epileptic fits) considered as psychic symptoms, and finally, as psychogenetic pains. All are considered as conversion accidents independently of the underlying psychopathological mechanisms. Contrary to general opinion, patients presenting conversion symptoms have not vanished from

---

10. Dantchev, N. and Widlöcher, D. (1994). Charcot et l'hystérie. *Neuro-psy*. 9:301–307.

11. Derouesné, C. (1994). Aspects neurologique de l'hystérie. *Neuro-psy*. 9:308–316.

hospitals and consulting rooms: the frequency is around 23 in 100,000 patients. The number of patients in psychiatric consultations is between 3.7 and 4.5 percent. It is lower in neurologic consultations. Of these, 60 to 70 percent of the patients are women. Male patients are frequently observed in military institutions or prisons—which is to say in constrained homosexual situations. As to age, the average seems to be around 37–41, the extremes varying from 9–15 to 70–82. In 30 to 40 of these cases a neurological disease is associated. Most of the time multiple symptoms are present. The diagnosis is twofold: absence of neurological pathology explaining the symptoms and presence of psychological factors considered as determinants of etiological value. Among these investigations, Derouesné and Lepastier underline the importance of *la belle indifférence* as a sign of repression and resistance, especially when motor paralysis is present. (On the contrary, when symptoms of dyskinesia or disturbances of sensibility are noticeable, they diminish if the patient's attention is diverted.) Emotional indifference is in the picture from 7 to 43 percent, hysteric personality from 9 to 50 percent, other psychopathology 22 to 50 percent, and disturbance of sexuality from 50 to 98 percent according to the different studies.

The psychical meaning of conversion symptoms, as it appears from psychological investigations, emphasizes, apart from the classical sexual etiology, the role of aggressive drives and the adaptive aims of the symptoms. It seems that the conclusions follow the theoretical choices of the investigators.

In conclusion, the neurophysiological findings are unable to shed light on the neurological symptoms of conversion. Complex models of explanation, including emotional and motivational factors, are needed.

This review, a century later, is rather reassuring for psychoanalysis. Contrary to what has been said, hysteria is not an artificial disease created with the compliance of Charcot and his pupils. It has not disappeared as some had predicted. The idea of a total explanation of conversion by neurophysiological findings has proved to be scientific wishful thinking—such things do not exist. The relative independence of conversion and hysteria is puzzling. Nevertheless the relationship of conversion to hysteria is light. No one will discuss the possibility of hysteria without conversion. But can one say that conversion, in itself, can be understood independent of hysteria? It seems more plausible to say that conversion is one of the ways that hysteria expresses itself. The feminine predominance is still observed in our day despite great changes in the condition of women. The concepts of repression and resistance are valid. The role of sexuality remains predominant. But other factors are now considered that have to be submitted to a close examination. To end with, it is indeniable that our models should improve in complexity.

The reevaluation of "The Psychotherapy of Hysteria," one century later, is twofold. On the one hand, we have to think of the technique of the therapy. As far as technique is concerned, so much has been written on the transition from the hypnocathartic method to psychoanalysis that I shall limit myself to brief remarks. In a case of conversion hysteria, indications for psychoanalysis are discussed today, not only according to the structure of patient's symptoms, but on more global considerations. Breuer and Freud's principles are still used; for instance, the analyst has to adopt a more active attitude towards the patient to obtain from him or her the communication of the repressed representations. The combination of an active struggle against the resistances and the use of the positive transference which endows the therapist with an important authority are factors of great help. This technique has been refined in Widlöcher's terms (Lepastier 1994).[12] It is amazing to realize how much we remain indebted to the *Studies on Hysteria* written a century ago.

Freud's contribution of 1895 is worth reading and commenting on in connection with the foundations of psychoanalytic theory. We will select some of the topics he wrote about. The most convenient way is to start with the model in which he organizes his findings and his thoughts, and then to turn to the concepts that derive from it.

---

12. Lepastier, S. (1994). Traitement de l'hystérie. *Neuro-psy.* 9:316–320.

THE MODEL

In spite of the fact that Freud's task was limited to an exposition of the hypnocathartic method, his speculative mind could not refrain from proposing to the reader a full picture of the "complicated structure" of the neurosis. Different strata can be described. First, a nucleus in the center consisting of memories of events or trains of thoughts "in which the traumatic factor has culminated or the pathogenic idea has found its purest manifestations" (Breuer and Freud 1893–1895, p. 288).[13] It is clear that the nucleus is of a purely psychical nature. Around the nucleus a profuse amount of mnemonic material, that is memories related to the nucleus, arranged in a threefold order. In the first place, we find a disposition organized along a linear chronological order within each of them: "It was as though we were examining a dossier that had been kept in good order."[14] The order is from surface from depth, that is from the freshest and newest to the oldest documents that are the best protected. A second kind of arrangement is found: "Each of them [the themes] is stratified concentrically round the pathogenic nucleus."[15] An equal degree of resistance is found for the contents of the same stratum. The deepest are those with the strongest resistances. Freud speaks of modification of consciousness, the different themes extending across these zones.

The third kind of arrangement, the most important one, and the most difficult to grasp concerns the thought content, "the linkage made by a logical thread which reaches the nucleus as far as possible and tends to take an irregular and twisting path, different in every case."[16] Freud insists that this arrangement has a *dynamic* character in contrast to the *morphological* one of the two strata mentioned previously. The model becomes complex. This last arrangement is different from the preceding ones, which can be represented by a continuous line, whether curved or straight. Here the course of what Freud calls the "logical chain" would

---

13. *Studies on Hysteria*, p. 288.
14. Ibid.
15. Ibid., p. 289.
16. Ibid.

follow a broken line going from surface to depths and back, trying to find its way to the nucleus and stopping at every halting place, in the manner of the Knight's move on a chessboard jumping over other pieces of the game. Freud emphasizes that the logical chain evokes a ramifying system of lines and more particularly a converging one. The symptom is overdetermined, as the picture suggests. As we have frequently to deal with more than one nucleus, corresponding to multiple traumas and confronted with other hysterical attacks, the degree of complexity is very high.

According to Freud, the pathological organizations behave like an infiltrate (and not as a foreign body that the therapist could or would extirpate). The whole system implies *"that it is quite hopeless to try to penetrate directly to the nucleus of the pathogenic organization."*[17] The progress has to overcome resistance. Freud observes that logical connections are sometimes lacking, and the reason for this is the "existence of hidden unconscious motives."[18] Lacunae in the patients' first descriptions are often covered by "false connections." It is no surprise now if Freud complains how complicated a work of this kind can become. In the end, after many steps and moves forward and backward, dropping threads and picking them up again or selecting others, we may at the end reach the nucleus. Here we have not finished the work; we still have to go back and take up other threads to exhaust the material by guessing the connections.

Freud will always insist later on that the unconscious can only be deduced. Solving a riddle once and for all could create in the therapist a feeling of omnipotence. On the contrary, Freud emphasizes that he is not *"in a position to force anything on the patient about the things of which he is ostensibly ignorant or to influence the products of the analysis by arousing an expectation."*[19] An important step since the time of hypnosis. These findings come to an important conclusion: "In all this . . . the hysterical symptoms is not behaving in any way differently for the memory-picture or the repro-

---

17. Ibid., p. 292.
18. Ibid., p. 293.
19. Ibid., p. 295 (emphasis in original).

duced thought which we conjure up under the pressure of our hand."[20] The two systems, symptoms and memories, are paralleled. *Mnemic resides* of affective experience, acts of thoughts take part in the hysterical symptoms that become the mnemic symbols of these experiences and thoughts. Such are the conclusions of Freud's thoughts upon his experiences with hysterical patients.

Commenting on such a construction one century later, we observe that neither the first nor the second topographical model of Freud's psychical apparatus has anything in common with this one. The reason is that what Freud has in mind here is not a picture of the psychic apparatus but a representation of the structure of the hysterical symptom and of the way the therapist influences it by understanding its disposal. If we wish to establish connections with the structures described by Freud, we could eventually find some analogies with the dream processes. The reference to the threads reminds us of Freud's quotation from Goethe's *Faust* in *The Interpretation of Dreams:*

> A thousand threads one treadle shows
> Where fly the shuttles hither and thither
> Unseen the threads are knit together,
> And an infinite combination grows.

The model is essentially a temporal one; it is focused on mnemic symbolization. When Freud gave his lectures at Clark University in 1909, he decided to choose the historical-genetic method starting with the *Studies on Hysteria* in order to present his discoveries. He came back to the idea of mnemic symbols. In the first of the five lectures Freud used a metaphor: the hysterical symptom in the patient plays a similar role to monuments in cities that celebrate historical events. [21] Hysteria was a secret commemoration of a private history. History is at the center of Freud's concern. But one easily notices that Freud's conception of history is not an orthodox one. He starts with the idea of a nucleus. Let us remark that he does not give any indication of time for that nucleus. For instance, he does not date it as the first event that took place. It is a mixture of memories of events or a train of thoughts. Sometimes

---

20. Ibid., p. 297.
21. *Standard Edition* 4:283.

these are linked with the traumatic factor born from external reality, sometimes with the pathogenic idea born from the patient's mind. Freud is always willing to define the two sources of the symptoms: the traumatic event arising out of the subject's will and the pathogenic idea born in his imaginative mind. The important thing is to understand that they combine their action to form a nucleus. Reality and fantasy are not opposed here; they act hand in hand. One could think, in the end, that the nucleus could be less determined by one single event but that it represents a sort of condensed structure containing the essential meaning of the secret and hidden motive born from several experiences that create the nucleus just as the mnemic symbol is related to the symptom.

But let's come now to the specific mnemic material. Here Freud adopts the classical orthodox view. What he describes is what we could call today the secondary processes concerning memory and their preconscious derivatives. Freud's terminology is clear: he speaks of linear chronological order, files of documents, archives. But these memories are also grouped according to their relationship to a theme. So there is a selection of mnemic facts according to a theme. The theme picks up memories and classifies them in an orderly manner that is respectful of the passage of time. The themes are grouped concentrically around the nucleus owing to the intensity of the resistance. One can consider that the themes agglutinate around the nucleus by some unknown linkage; or that the nucleus attracts the themes to itself; or that nucleus expands its ramifications catching the themes related to it. But the relationship of the nucleus to the theme is not only a dialectic one with an interaction of chronological thematic grouping (history and structure again). The concentric stratification of the pathogenic material opens up the possibility of the third kind of arrangement. Here the orderly chronological organization and the material concentrically disposed offer a new kind of connections, truly dynamic: the broken, zigzag line, discontinuous, nonrespectful of the chronological order as it progresses from the periphery to the center and back, advancing in the end in a ramifying form, converging toward the nucleus.

It is important to notice that Freud calls it the "logical chain." The logical chain has its own criteria of logic: the hidden unconscious motives. The logic of its chain obeys a causality that is not ruled by a logic of succession, since the links are established according to a "strangulated" affect in order to maintain repression and resistance. It is both *historical* and *structural*. The reference to infiltration is evocative of the way affect operates. We can now suppose that the third kind of arrangement with its logic of the broken line, is under the influence of affects which are reawakened in the processes of remembering and verbalization. The affects infiltrate the concentric model, they penetrate to recathect the places from which they have been chased and sent into the somatic. Some of them are fixed in the body, but the therapy, in favoring the circulation of the representations and their associations, also mobilizes the segregated affects which are caught in a conflict. The affects are attracted to regain the center of the nucleus, but, because of the defense, are kept away from it. As a consequence, the progression of the cathexis to the representations has to use trickery: stopping, changing the line on which they were advancing, jumping to another one or to another theme, forcing the resistance where they have enough strength to do so, receiving some additional quantity of impulse to move forward, receding because of the dangers associated with their possible discovery, and so on. The final reaching near the heart of the nucleus happens from time to time, giving intense satisfaction to the partners of the process. Freud speaking of his work with the patient defines it as introducing him to the "marvelous world of psychical processes."[22]

One important fact about Freud's model is that it can be seen either as a picture that describes the patient's mental functioning alone, or the combination of the patient's and the analyst's working together. It foreshadows the division between representation (memories, ideas, thoughts) and affects. The dynamic and quantitative factor are related to affects, the mnemic material to representation; in other words, both together constitute meaning. I dare to say that this model, in the fundamental lines of its construction, is still illuminating one century later, resisting all the assaults of so-called modern or even postmodern psychoanalytic conceptions.

_____

22. *Studies on Hysteria*, p. 282.

The importance of conversion, even today, in spite of its considerable decrease, is not only historical. A close examination of the concept of the drive, or instinct, is related to hysteria. Freud (1915) defines the instinct as a concept at the limit of the somatic and psychic, as the psychic representative of excitation born in the interior of the body and reaching the mind, and as a measure of the demand for work addressed to the mind because of its connection with the somatic. This intermediate situation and need for elaboration could end, in certain cases, because the impossibility of maintaining the psychic representative in the mind to its expulsion within the somatic, as far away as possible. What I mean is that if the drive is "born" at the border between the somatic and the psychic, it can fall on one or the other side. Falling within the body, we have hysteria; falling on the most abstract aspects of the intellect (the cognitive), we may have obsessional neurosis as well.

I will therefore plead for a very old-fashioned view: the division between body and mind. Of course, I agree with their unification de facto, but it is difficult to deny that these are two different modes of organization with different rules of functioning. We got rid of hysteria but we now have a worse case: psychosomatic illness, the modern version of Freud's actual neuroses.

THE MAKING OF A THEORY

What are the implications of this model? Freud makes no references here to the brain, as Breuer does when he mentions "intracerebral tonic excitation" (Breuer and Freud 1893–1895). Freud's description is a transposition in theoretical language of his experience with the patient. All his findings derive from this unique source. It is an entirely psychological model that can be interpreted either in *intrapsychical* terms or in *intersubjective* ones. We have already quoted his assertion that the hysterical symptom behaves exactly like the memory picture or the reproduced thought. This is consistent with Charcot's idea that hysteria is a disease of memory, which Freud translates beautifully by saying the patient suffers from reminiscences. This statement will be repeated until 1937 in "Construction in Analysis," extending the field of reminiscence far beyond the classical conceptions of memory. Freud's

imaginative thinking becomes extremely fruitful in the description
of the three kinds of arrangements of the nucleus, the mnemic
material, and the dynamic force that advances in a broken line,
transversely, overcoming the chronological order of the concentrically disposed memory. It could be said that the mental functioning has to disorganize the well-ordered succession of memories, uncovering the specific causality, shown by the logical chain.
This causality, which is based on a different structure of temporal
organization, is the one that will appear during the analysis. It
seems to be imprisoned in the nucleus as a holy of holies and protected by the concentric circles of the themes enrolled in the
mnemic guards. The only way to reach the nucleus is through the
infiltration of disguised commandos who would cross the lines of
the memory organization.

How to define the nucleus? Freud, once more, finds help in
metaphors: "A psychical group that has once been split off plays
the part of a 'provoking' crystal from which a crystallization which
would otherwise not have occurred will start with the greatest
facility."[23] Later on, Freud again took up the metaphor of the crystal. He remarks that when a crystal breaks up (experienced a
trauma in other words) its fragmentation respects its constitutive
line of forces. So does psychopathology in spite of the difference
between the mind and the mineral order. The crystallization, a
word also used by Stendhal to define the processes of falling in love,
can be a synonym for psychic work. In conversion hysteria in 1895,
another splitting is operating: the ideas or the thoughts associated
with a traumatic event, happening unexpectedly are split off from
the affects. The affect is "strangulated," that is immobilized and
encircled, isolated from the rest of psychical functioning. All its
energetic power is directed towards the body causing the conver-
sional symptom, performing that mysterious leap in the somatic.
The affect that is thus neutralized is not mastered in spite of the
belle indifférence. On the one hand, it seems to be longing to come
to light like the unhappy prisoners in Beethoven's Fidelio, on the
other hand, a repression forbids it to penetrate consciousness. We
arrive here at a point where psychic functioning is divided between

---

23. Ibid., p. 264.

two entities: ideas and thoughts that will be named representations and will be present as mnemic traces, and affects as processes of discharge through somatic innervation. We can now figure out how the prohibition of a cathected idea—that is a thought experienced emotionally—is not only submitted to repression by disappearing from consciousness, but is also dismembered, separating the ideational content from its corresponding affect.

Therefore it is comprehensible that the work of undoing, or of unbinding, will resist any attempts at reconstituting the initial entity, combining thoughts with emotion. Freud speaks here of resistance as a "psychical force."[24] It is also a force that has proceeded to splitting off and repression, and it is a *force* that opposes the attempts to become conscious, that is, to be remembered: resistance. But the reason to invoke such forces and not only meaning follows logically if one considers resistance as a counterwill against an invisible, strongly prohibited will: the sexual etiology. By reading the *Studies on Hysteria* carefully one notices that sexual fantasies are in fact nearly absent from the picture. In Katharina's case, the girl is submitted to the incestuous assaults of her father. The trauma comes massively from external reality, very little from the girl's reveries. In all the other cases, what Freud calls a "sexual etiology" are romance fantasies. It is no wonder that Freud, in starting his discussion of Elisabeth von R. observes that his case histories "lack the serious stamp of science" and that they should read as short stories. In fact Freud's findings were revolutionary, because for the first time "intimate connections between the story of the patient's sufferings and the symptoms of his illness"[25] could be established. In other words, to be ill was to suffer from the vicissitudes of love life. Of course, sexuality was banned from the "morally correct" desires, especially for women. But in 1895, erotic fantasies were of a very innocent type. So-called "sexual etiology" is an invention of Freud. Of course, he could find some evidence when one of his patients embraced him, putting her arms around his neck, but all the patients mentioned in the *Studies on Hysteria* would not dare behave this way. It is not always clearly stated that

---

24. Ibid., p. 268.
25. Ibid., pp. 160–161.

the field of sexuality encompasses a wide spectrum—orgasm is at one end and wishful thinking at the other. In other words, sexuality can unite thoughts devoid of any bodily expression, even when accompanied with feelings, or refer to overwhelming states of sensual excitement, the well-known "possession." Freud had discovered wishes, sentimental fantasies, and reveries in hysteria, and he concluded that all these indicated a longing for sexual satisfaction. Hence the conflict in terms of force and meaning.

Thus, forces are struggling in the mind of patient. Later on, sexuality will be included in a drive theory and repression will be understood as a psychological force mobilized in the ego. An important consequence of Freud's theory is that psychic work develops on many grounds. The sexual force will create symptoms through conversion, some of them quite strange. Frau Emmy von N. produces a "curious clacking" sound from her mouth which defies imitation. Freud probably tried to imitate it as he says that colleagues with sporting experience told him on hearing it, that its final notes resembled the "call of a capercaillie!"[26] Imagine Freud imitating that birdcall to Breuer! The symbolic meaning could be less obscure. Sometimes, it was clearly connected with sensation. A remark felt as an insult was the cause of a pain in the cheek, because it could be like a slap in the face. This process could be called "symbolic metaphorization." Freud's important discovery has been the fundamental role of association, which favor mechanisms such as displacement and substitution condensation, and so on. The greatest of all substitutions are those responsible for false connections,[27] the precursors of transference.

Freud recognizes the influence of the doctor's authority. Suggestion is still in the background. Nevertheless, there is an evolution in Freud's technique from Emmy von N. to Elisabeth von R. With Emmy, Freud is entirely under the power of medical ideology: a little science and a lot of moral coercion. It is the roughest form of struggle—the patient's bad will against the doctor's good will. When Freud starts to treat Elisabeth, he has become more

---

26. Ibid., p. 49.
27. Ibid., p. 302.

modest. He has understood that the patient's counterwill is always the stronger and that he cannot force the repressed thought to be remembered if the patient's counterwill is too powerful and if the patient's defense against the unconscious desire is to keep it hidden. Even in successful cases the truth will not appear naked as truth coming out of the well. In the end, it has to be guessed through its veils—more than seven, I think. Sometimes we can see a true chain of signifiers, as if Freud had read Lacan. Instead of being obsessed with visions, as it was most often the case, words arise abruptly in the patient. They seem silly: "concierge," is the initial one. Others follow: "night-gown," "bed," "town," "farm," and "cast."[28] Freud implicitly makes the comparison with the Pythia spelling oracles. Soon the words will find their place and meaning in a memory that takes the form of a story. Of course, the story is about a secret; the sexual assault on the patient's 12-year-old sister, when she herself was 10. Freud fights during the treatment to obtain logical connections. He does not believe that a neurosis can relax these. If one gets a different impression it is because of the existence of "hidden unconscious motives,"[29] in other words, secrets.

The chain of signifiers that arises here in oracular fashion is in no way given a special significance by Freud. The unconscious expresses itself through different channels: symptoms of conversion of course, of different kinds, affects, fantasies, memories, thoughts, and words. Today we would say that most of them belong to the preconscious. As far as the unconscious is concerned we see that the nucleus is and is nothing but, psychical. Analysis shows that mainly two types of material take part in the structure of unconscious representations, which include ideas, thoughts, memories, and fantasies on the one hand, and affects on the other hand. The specificity of conversion hysteria is the special treatment reserved to the affect, which is dissociated from the idea and blocked. What is left of affect is considerably weakened, harmless. We can understand that there are at least two ways of repression: the affective one, which consists in a sort of paralyzing effect, and the representational, which proceeds to displacement, substitution,

---

28. Ibid., pp. 275–276.
29. Ibid., p. 293.

condensation, and so on. Hence the need for abreaction of the affect because of its links with motion/emotion.

If an event is considered as a trauma, the restoration of the patient must bring back the memory of it with its corresponding affect, which has to be put into words. Only then does the traumatic effect stop. So it is not enough to relive the experience; it is necessary to verbalize it, to include it in a representational network. In other words, the affect must infiltrate the chain of words. Hallucinations, visions, and pictures frequently assault the mind of the patient and have to be worked through verbalization: *"The patient is, as it were, getting rid of it by turning it into words."*[30] Several remarks can be made at this point. First, that thing presentations, essentially visual, are closer to affects than to words, and second, we have here one of the first statements about the differences between thing presentations and word presentations (cf. Freud 1915). The unconscious does not contain any word presentation. It is not a language or "like a language," as Lacan says. The work of "becoming conscious" has to involve the transformation from thing presentations to word presentations—in other words, verbalization with the corresponding affect.

In the last lines of the case of Elisabeth von R., Freud writes:

> Hysteria is right in restoring the original meaning of the words in depicting its unusually strong innervation [pain in the cheek for a slap on the face in case of humiliation]. Indeed, it is perhaps wrong to say that hysteria creates these sensations by symbolization. It may be that it does not take linguistic usage as its model at all, but both hysteria and linguistic usage alike draw their material from a common source. [p. 181]

Is not Freud alluding here to the drives?

TO KNOW AND (NOT) TO KNOW AT THE SAME TIME

Understanding hysteria goes against simplifications and clear-cut statements. At first glance, the procedure of the "psychotherapy of hysteria" shows how verbalization sweeps the symptom away,

---

30. Ibid., p. 280 (emphasis in original).

leaving the mind free and lucid. What was supposed to be unknown has become known, similar to the way that a light that has been switched on in a dark room clears it up. That is what the reader may think. What one has to discover for the circumstance is much more enigmatic until everything becomes explainable.

Freud, in dealing with resistance, shows the splitting between the conscious expectancies of the patients and their deep thoughts that are against the unearthing of memories. The best condition would be to accept the loss of control, which will help the unconscious material to appear. But that is not easy to perform. Of course, part of us admits that they can't help it, but another part will suspect some opposition. When the therapist finally succeeds in being told something, the patient then adds, "I could have told you that the first time." "Why didn't you say it?" "I could not believe it could be that. It was only when it came back every time that I made up my mind to say it." Or else, "I hoped it wouldn't be that of all things. I could well do without saying that. It was only when it refused to be repressed that I saw I wouldn't be let off."[31] So truth does not walk from shade to sunlight witnessed by a neutral observer. It is seen, yet refused to be accounted for, without any obvious reason. It is denied: "It couldn't be that" and then actively rejected: "It should not be that" and finally accepted because its unpleasant effect is stronger than its warding off. The phantom of the disquieting memory comes back day and night to reawake the tormenting anxiety. We have here an early description of splitting: "I know it should be that, still I do not want to be aware of it, because I don't want it to be so."

Truth does not manifest itself as a revelation through which everything becomes rational. We do not accept its statements objectively. Because of the pleasurable or unpleasurable consequences, we cheat with our consciousness. Not blatantly, or overtly, but in a masked, dishonest way, mobilizing for the occasion the higher standards of morality. Let's not be confused: this is not simply lying; it is an original state which hysteria exemplifies, it is not limited to it. Philosophically we are speaking of a state of "knowledge of not knowing" (savoir de non savoir). This is not a Socratic

---

31. Ibid., p. 279.

condition; we could not say of the patients that they know that they do not know. More subtly it would be: "My knowledge is one of knowing not that I know." Freud is aware of the importance of what he has discovered. He states it again, differently: "It happens particularly often that, after we have laboriously forced some piece of knowledge on a patient, he will declare: 'I've always known that, I could have told you that before.'" [32] Freud explains the statement according to the material it is related to: more or less superficial, more or less unconscious. In that last instance many hesitations and doubts precede the acceptance of the thought when deeply unconscious. Freud decides to make his mind as independent as possible from the variation of the "psychical illuminations" of the patients.[33] He shall be guided mainly by the "logical consistency and interconnection between the various parts of the material."[34] To end with, he confesses not to be able to guess which part of the train of thoughts was recognized by the patient as a memory and which part was not.[35] A shared approximation, Bion would say, is possible.

One could think all that is described is due to the patient's illness. I would rather say that the cause of these contradictions is in getting closer and closer to the unconscious, a condition which has the capacity to blur the differences between real and imaginary, recognizable memories and fantasies, knowing and not knowing. A fruitful "negative capability."

In a footnote to the case of Lucy R., Freud finally guesses that the patient is concerned about the relationships with the servants because of her secret hope of taking the mother's place as the wife of the director, after the mother died. Lucy admits this is the truth. "But if you knew you loved your employer, why didn't you tell me?" Freud asks. "I didn't know, or rather, I didn't want to know. I wanted to drive it out of my head and to think of it again; and I believe latterly I have succeeded."[36] Freud comments in a footnote the "strange state of mind in which one knows and does not know a thing

---

32. Ibid., p. 299.
33. Ibid., p. 300.
34. Ibid.
35. Ibid., pp. 300–301.
36. Ibid., p. 117.

at the same time." Recalling a personal experience, he concludes: "I was afflicted by that blindness of the seeing eye which is so astonishing in the attitude of mothers to their daughters, husbands to their wives and rulers to their favorites."[37] No wonder that Freud, adding a note in 1924 to the story of Emmy von N., is ashamed to confess : "I am aware that no analyst can read this case history to-day without a smile of pity."[38] As far as I am concerned, it would rather be self-pity for our modern denials.

WORK OF THE NEGATIVE AND PRIVATE MADNESS

My last comments recall the inspiration that guided Freud in 1925 when he wrote his paper on "Negation." Lacan commented many times this paradoxical state of mind of knowing and not wanting to know. Georges Bataille, who was also influenced by Hegel, went in the same direction. In the end one will be forced to recognize, with Freud himself, that resistance is the main course of the *Studies on Hysteria*. Freud later stated, summarizing Breuer's ideas and his, that the *Studies on Hysteria* reflects a struggle of "hypnoid states" against "defense." As we know, "The Neuropsychoses of Defense" (Freud 1894), was written before "The Psychotherapy of Hysteria" in the *Studies on Hysteria*. One century later, reviewing the concept of defense in Freud's work with its different steps: repression, foreclosure, negation, and disavowal, we can see that throughout all of his life Freud was concerned about the unity, or the plurality, of the concept of defense, to which he came back in 1926, in *Inhibitions, Symptoms, and Anxiety* (1926). Its varieties call for specific descriptions for each of them with different sorts of mechanisms. I have called the assemblage of these different types of defense "the work of the negative" (Green 1999). There is no better example than the *Studies on Hysteria* to see the work of the negative in progress. Today, I believe that no analyst analyzing any patient of any kind can neglect the differences according to this viewpoint. Why is defense so important? Too many answers are

---

37. Ibid., p. 117.
38. Ibid., p. 105.

at hand: the bourgeois ideology, the slavery of the condition of women, male chauvinism, the imperialism of natural science, and so on. All these factors that combine to be part of the total picture are true. Still, the essential is missing, at least for me. More than one reader will be tempted to defend the idea that these women living in the capital of the Austro-Hungarian Empire, under the rule of Franz-Josef and Sissi (who could be one of Freud's patients) were in fact completely crazy. Not because of their fantasies, romances, secret love lives, or complicated relationships with their families. Literature has taught us a lot more than the *Studies on Hysteria* from that point of view. But because of the symptoms by which they expressed their unhappiness, uneasiness, anxieties, and despair, in other words, their passion. *That* made them look like mental patients with their pains, paralyses, visions, hallucinations, somnambulism, and so on.

I proposed, instead of seeing them as psychotics, to define them as "mad" (Green 1986). As far back as one goes in the history of humanity, men and women have always known that they were mad. They have been aware of their irrational behavior, of the importance of passions in their inclinations, their judgments, their choices, the changes of their moods, the conduct of their life. No need to quote Shakespeare here. Against their profound nature men and women have erected monuments to reason, to intellect, and to lucidity, that are periodically overthrown with lots of rationalization. What is the difference between madness and psychosis? I have proposed to consider madness as a vicissitude of Eros, of the erotic drives, which can always get hold of the mind of the wisest and the best adjusted with unforeseen consequences with its specific logics; on the other hand, psychosis is the disastrous fate of destructive drives, not only as an act of despair, but as to what enacts that the only valid motive is material omnipotence. Anna, Emmy, Lucy, Katharina, Elisabeth, Cäcilie, and so many others were mad. What was their madness about? They just wanted to live and to love.

I shall end with a quotation of Freud, from the case history of Elisabeth von R.:

> In the spring of 1849 [after the treatment ended] I heard she was going to a private ball for which I was able to get an invitation,

and I did not allow the opportunity to escape me of seeing my former patient whirl past in a lively dance. Since then, by her own inclination, she has married someone unknown to me.[39]

A happy end, isn't it? We shall never know if Freud danced with his former patient freed from her pains or with anybody else to whom he could have been attracted. After the marriage of his gifted hysteric, Freud started another Viennese waltz, wild and frenzied, with a woman that no one knew. Finally it was discovered that she bore a strange name, probably of foreign origin: psychoanalysis.

REFERENCES

Anzieu, D. (1988). *L'autoanalyse de Freud et la découverte de la psychanalyse.* Paris: Presses Universitaire de France.
Breuer, J. and Freud, S. (1893–1895). Studies on hysteria. *Standard Edition* 2.
Dantchev, N. and Widlöcher, D. (1994). Charcot et l'hystérie. *Neuropsy.* 9:301–307
Derouesné, C. (1994). Aspects neurologique de l'hysterie. *Neuropsy.* 9:308–316.
Freud, S. (1887–1902). *The Originis of Psycho-Analysis. Letters to Wilhelm Fliess, Drafts and Notes: 1887–1902,* ed. M. Bonaparte, A. Freud, and E. Kris, trans. E. Mosbacher and J. Strachey. New York: Basic Books.
—— (1895). Project for a scientific psychology. *Standard Edition* 1:281–397.
—— (1900). The interpretation of dreams. *Standard Edition* 4/5:1–626.
—— (1905a). Three essays on the theory of sexuality. *Standard Edition* 7.
—— (1905b). Jokes and their relations to the unconcious. *Standard Edition* 8.
—— (1909). Five lectures on psycho-analysis. *Standard Edition* 11:3–55.
—— (1915). Instincts and their vicissitudes. *Standard Edition* 14.

---

39. Ibid., p. 160.

—— (1925). Negation. *Standard Edition* 19.

—— (1926). Inhibitions, symptoms and anxiety. *Standard Edition* 20.

—— (1938). Some elementay lessons on psychoanalysis. *Standard Edition* 23.

Green, A. (1986). *On Private Madness*. London: Hogarth Press.

—— (1999). *The Work of the Negative*. A. Weller, trans. London: Free Association Books (originally published 1993).

Hirschmüller, A. (1978). *Physiologie und Psychoanalyse in Leben und Werk Josef Breuers*. Bern: Hans Huber Verlag.

Lepastier, S. (1994). Traitement de l'hystérie. *Neuro-psy.* 9:316–320.

3

Pregnancy, Death, and Loss in Anna O.'s Hysteria

Rita V. Frankiel

INTRODUCTION

Anna O. is compelling to us for many reasons: her terrible symptoms, so vividly and sympathetically described by Breuer, her beauty, her youth, her brilliance. Breuer's treatment of Anna O., as he describes it, gives us a look at a process of collaboration, invention, and discovery that is at times breathtaking in its sensitivity. Following Anna's lead, he shows that moments of trauma and/ or intense feeling, because they were intolerable to consciousness, were producing distortions of consciousness or physical functioning. He began to see that if one could trace each disturbance back to its source, one could restore the disrupted function. Ultimately, his personal obstacles to accepting Freud's ideas about infantile sexuality made it impossible for him to continue working with his patient or with Freud.

He withdrew abruptly from both. The ending with Anna was as dramatic as the treatment itself. In the morning session of the last day, as we now know Breuer pronounced his patient cured and discharged her. This was after eighteen months of work. Anna O. was walking, talking, and had the full use of her limbs, sight, and hearing. By dinner time, however, he was again summoned to her bedside. She was ill again, being now in the grip of the fantasized delivery of Breuer's child. This time Breuer did not try to understand the sources of this new set of symptoms. He hypnotized her, perhaps gave her some drugs, and turned her over to a colleague. His part in the work with her was over. She was left to fend for herself.

The extraordinariness of their collaboration grabs our imagination. They are the mythic pair that together conceived a basic part of the psychoanalytic method, a living, breathing entity, changeable and changing. The psychoanalytic method has had a far different life story from that of the child of Anna's fantasized union with Breuer, from which he had to flee, abandoning both her and their work together.

The fuller story of the treatment, which is not in the version in *Studies on Hysteria* (Breuer and Freud 1893–1895) or Jones' *Life and Work of Sigmund Freud* (1953) can, to a large extent, make Breuer's reluctance to publish the case or to go on with the work more understandable.

THE TREATMENT OF ANNA O.

Pollock (1968, 1972, 1973) has explored the influence of pathological mourning in the etiology of both her illness and Breuer's vulnerability to countertransference. In this paper, I plan to explore her fantasy that Breuer had impregnated her and her reaction to his inability to continue the treatment in the face of that fantasy. I believe that there is ample reason to understand the direction of her subsequent life, her preoccupations, accomplishments, frustrations, and strengths—all of them reconstructible from her own writings and the various biographical studies now available (Edinger 1968, Ellenberger 1972, Freeman 1972)—in the light of her complex and iatrogenically intensified difficulties with mourning.

Although I am not the first to posit the importance of pathological mourning in the Anlage and ultimate scenario of Anna O.'s illness and life, I plan to do here something that is my own: to show how pathological mourning is implicated in the hysterical pregnancy she revealed at the point of her termination from Breuer, and also how the fantasy that she had been abandoned, alone with her illegitimate baby, became a significant constituent of her later conflicts and achievements. Hers was a lonely life, but one filled with extraordinary accomplishment, determination, and perhaps some ideas of revenge.

Feminist critics have convincingly described Anna as the victim of the social restrictions and paternalistic control so characteristic of her era: a woman made ill by boredom and hopelessness and a total lack of outlets for her talents (e.g., Kaplan 1983, Micale 1995, Mitchell 1984, Smith-Rosenberg 1985). Later critics have seen hysteria as a gendered diagnosis, the consequence of a phallocentric view of femininity and female sexuality. My own view of the plight of Anna O. leads me to look to the contributing influence of loss and mourning, especially pathological mourning. I believe that her mourning's impacted rage and unrelenting self-punishment have been insufficiently recognized, etiologically significant factors in her illness, just as they have been in the illnesses of many others.

Modern views of the treatment process have it that Breuer was drawn to his patient in terms that transcend the clearly professional. He departed sharply from the approach to hysteria common in his day. In the text of *Studies on Hysteria*, there are marked differences in his approach to the work with these women and Freud's sometimes ambitious prodding and impatience. He saw Anna almost daily. At times he called in on her twice a day. Also, he was not judgmental and stigmatizing. His sympathy and concern seem to have won her confidence. Initially almost psychotically withdrawn, then cautiously testing him, she quickly began to trust him and allowed him to touch and spoon-feed her. She manifested intense separation reactions—often rages—when he was called to the side of another patient or went on vacation, or when she was taken away from him to the country because the danger of suicide complicated her care in Vienna. She refused to acknowledge the presence of the doctor meant to cover for Breuer's absence. These separation reactions were warnings that things were heating up in a potentially dramatic and destructive way. From today's perspective, we can say that unless her mounting feelings of attachment and demands for gratification were understood and taken up with her in some way, she and Breuer were headed for a big crash.

It is apparent that the inevitable separations that occur in any protracted treatment stimulated intense feelings of neglect. I believe that Anna O. began punishing her therapist for leaving her or being what she considered insufficiently attentive. Breuer describes this in several places; for example: "I was obliged to overcome her unwillingness [to talk] by urging and pleading and using devices such as repeating a formula. *But she would never begin to talk until she had satisfied herself of my identity by carefully feeling my hands*" (p. 30, my italics).

Breuer was not insensitive to the issue of loss, however. In his narrative of the treatment, his attentiveness to themes related to Anna's response to the loss of her father is striking. We know today, thanks to the work of Pollock and others, that Anna O. and Breuer shared a significant piece of personal history: both had suffered the loss of an indispensable person. Breuer's mother died giving birth to his brother when Breuer was between 3 and 4 years of age. That is a catastrophic time for such a loss. Oedipal fantasy would surely have had a powerful grip on his inner world, and it would have produced, among other possible outcomes, a longing for the mother he lost because of childbirth and also guilt about the fantasy of having wishfully caused the pregnancy that led to her death.

In Anna O.'s case, her overt illness began as she sat at her consciously beloved father's bedside. He was an intelligent and forceful man who had indulged and pampered his daughter and tied her to him with bonds of privilege and duty. It is my idea that he refused to modify his conventional ideas about the place of women, perhaps concealing an erotized wish to keep her tied to him by denying her his support of an intellectual life for this sublimely gifted girl; this is a not unknown situation between fathers and daughters, even today.

Bowlby (1980) has shown us much about bereavement. For some it can eventuate in compulsive caretaking of those who are similarly bereaved. It could have entered into Breuer's choice of his lifework in medicine, and, as we now know, it could have led Anna into her life-choice of care for unfortunate wayward girls and orphans.

Studies on Hysteria contains five major case studies; in three cases, the death of a loved one is the event that precipitates the illness. In a fourth case, too, there is a loss, though it is not a death but a disappointment in love. In approaching these patients, Breuer and Freud were on a mission. They wanted to demonstrate the incredible power of the mind to form symptoms out of repressed conflict and to employ the body to carry and express that conflict. They also wanted to demonstrate that one could use that understanding to remove these symptoms, first through hypnosis and later, after hypnosis had been abandoned, through abreaction. It has remained for modern feminist scholars to enumerate, in addition, the ways in which sex-role enclosure affected both patient and doctor. Patriarchy, social isolation, and restricted opportunity profoundly shaped the experiences and illness of the Victorian and post-Victorian hysterics.

Many psychoanalysts, standing on the shoulders of Breuer and especially of Freud with all his achievement of genius, imagination, and patience, have developed a perspective that includes what these two pioneers did not explore because they were so engaged in their single-minded and ambitious venture: demonstrating symptom removal through tracking associative processes and affects (cf. Karpe 1961, Meissner 1979, Stewart 1984). To comprehend the issues in contemporary analytic terms, I must retell, refocus, and reinterpret some of the family history as researched by Pollock (1968, 1972, 1973) and others (Edinger 1968, Ellenberger 1972, Freeman 1972, Karpe 1961, Schonbar and Beatus 1990).

Bertha Pappenheim, the real name of the patient Anna O., was born into an ultra-observant, Orthodox Jewish family. Her parents' marriage was an arranged one. Her mother came from Frankfurt, and it is likely that she and Bertha's father had seldom met and knew each other very slightly when they were married. Four children were born to this couple, three girls and a boy, the youngest. Two of the girls died in childhood. The firstborn girl died at 18, probably of tuberculosis, when Bertha was 8. The second girl was born four years after the first and lived only to the age of 2. She had been dead for three years when Bertha was conceived. Bertha's brother was born eighteen months after Bertha.

Several writers mention that Bertha's mother looks depressed in family photos and had the reputation in Vienna, her adopted home, of being a sad woman. Some have suggested that she felt she had married beneath herself—she was from a deeply cultured and eminent family that included Heinrich Heine. Another factor, not usually included, is that her own mother had died when she was 10, an event that would have made her especially vulnerable to profound reactions to the losses that were to be endured in her new family. In some texts, she is referred to as having become in later days an old dragon.

It was a bourgeois family that expected Anna to marry, found a good Jewish household, bring forth children, and be good to her parents. Anna, who was brilliant and imaginative, felt wasted in that too-limited, conformist life (Gay 1988, pp. 64–65). An excellent education was considered her brother's birthright; hers was considered completed when she reached 16. How puzzling and enraging it must have been to her to see him in the world of books and achievement, while she was to be focused on embroidery, lacemaking, and household matters. That must have added mightily to her envy and passionate dislike of her brother.

Much has been made of Bertha's powerful hatred of her brother, born so soon after her. He was the recipient of all the maternal attention; characteristically, in an Orthodox Jewish home, much pampering is bestowed on the first born, and in this case, only, son. Also, her own birth took on added significance because she was born after the death of a sib. The reality of the situation of the so-called replacement child is that he or she comes into a bereaved family, one that is either consciously or unconsciously preoccupied with the misfortune of the loss of the prior child. Usually, the family is idealizing the child that was lost. Replacement children are often dogged by especially intrusive parental restrictions that are based on guilt and anxiety. Having lost a child once, the parents feel that it is essential that all care be taken to make certain that catastrophe is never repeated. Idealizing fantasies about the lost child can often dominate the life of a family and then become a special burden in the inner world of the next child to be born. For Bertha's mother, the death of two of her children surely terrified her and revived her inner state after the death of her mother who had died when she was very young.

Among the fantasies common among replacement children is the idea that they must develop very special qualities—often altruistic, idealistic ones—in order to recompense the family for what they have lost. Survivor guilt is another significant ingredient in the psychic makeup of the next born in a context of child loss. What better gift for the new child than to imagine that she will bring the family a baby to replace the one that was lost, thereby allowing the child to feel that her debt of guilt has been paid in full? Hopefully, it would relieve guilt all around and also free the child to live a life of his or her own, rather than continue to be bound by the feeling that whoever or whatever they are, their needs are a burden to the still grieving family. And especially if her mother was still carrying the grief of the loss of her own mother, Anna O. could have had a special need to produce a child.

It has often been inferred that the false pregnancy that concluded Bertha and Breuer's work together expressed Bertha's inaccessible sexual passions belonging in all likelihood to phallic-oedipal phase fantasies and imperatives. Initially, the fantasized oedipal baby would have been the child of Bertha and her pampering and much loved and unconsciously hated father. Also, it would have been the vehicle for the bursting forth of her denied sexuality. I do not dispute that formulation or the others that derive from it, but I feel that it is an insufficient account of the multiply determined hysterical symptoms with which she unconsciously hoped to return Breuer to her side. The pregnancy came to light in the context of Breuer's abrupt termination of the treatment.

His withdrawal must have been a massive blow. During the treatment, she had repeatedly reacted sharply and deeply to separations from Breuer, becoming anorectic, inaccessible, violently disturbed at the times when he could not come to her side for a day or more. He laid hands on her in comforting ways, and when she was most seriously anorectic, she allowed him and him alone to feed her. I think we might safely say that having become fiercely possessive of him, she was traumatized by the way he ended the treatment.

Jones (1953) claims that Breuer, in panic, fled with his jealous wife to Venice on a second honeymoon, where his youngest child was conceived. Modern research into the birth records of the time shows that Jones' version of the ending of the treatment is untrue. Breuer's wife had *already* given birth to a little girl during the later part of his treatment of Bertha. In all likelihood Bertha knew about it. We know that the Jewish bourgeois and professional classes in Vienna were very closely connected. Martha Bernays (Freud's wife) and Bertha Pappenheim were well acquainted, and it seems very likely that the activities of the Breuer family would have been well known. The idea that Breuer had given his wife this most precious gift would have been yet another source of Bertha's rageful excitement.

Rey (1988) has observed that patients who cannot seem to bring their treatments to a successful close often have had a hidden agenda for undertaking the treatment in the first place: the wish that the treatment would repair or heal a damaged internal object. I suspect that in the case of Anna O., in addition to her need to bring her sexuality into integration with the rest of her brilliant, creative self, she needed to provide herself with the baby that would bring happiness to her own sad and unavailable mother. This baby would be a gift to the mother, and a way of restoring hopefulness in a situation in which she was sunk into despair and mourning once again following the death of her husband, an event preceded some years earlier by the death of her oldest daughter and her own mother as well. For Anna O., the baby would be a vehicle toward a more mature identity for herself, both as a mother and as no longer invalided, or she would have hoped.

Just as the discoverers of atomic energy were perhaps unaware of the power of what they were dealing with and so were unable to protect themselves or the ranchers in the southwestern desert from the awful consequences of radioactive fallout, so the unknown consequences of repressed sexuality exploding into an enormous wish for a baby at the point of separation in an intense transference–countertransference matrix was a psychic fallout that was almost fatal to the patient. The claims of a cure made in *Studies on Hysteria* did not give an accurate picture of Bertha's state at the end, and Breuer knew that. Addicted to morphine and chloral as another consequence of her treatment, she was hospitalized twice, once while Breuer was treating her and she became suicidal and was transferred to a hospital outside Vienna. Breuer, in the report of this, refers to it in a way that makes it sound like the family home in the country. It was, in fact a cottage that was part of the program of the sanitarium at Inzersdorf. When Breuer could not get to see her, she was followed and medicated by the physicians from the sanitarium. One month after Breuer terminated his treatment of her, she was again hospitalized for three months. She was then discharged as somewhat improved but iatrogenically addicted to morphine and chloral and still symptomatic. At the time he heard of this, Breuer made the shocking statement, "Would she not be better off dead and spared further suffering?" (Jones 1953, p. 225). In that moment, the death wish he harbored for her surfaced. She was a reproach, a memento of the outcome of a forbidden adventure into the dangerous and forbidden territory of oedipal desire mixed with fears of loss and painful mourning—his own, hers, and her mother's. He wished there were no trace of the dangerous game that they had played.

Breuer fled but Freud worked on, though not with Anna O. Ultimately, he would describe the sexual forces that we can now understand had played a big role in fracturing the Breuer–Anna

O. working affiance. As a demonstration that repressed emotions could cause bodily symptoms, and that retrieving those repressed emotions could lead to symptom removal, the treatment was an enormous success. As a therapeutic intervention, however, the treatment of Anna O., viewed from the perspective of today, was incomplete. When, later on, Freud supplanted symptom removal as a goal of treatment and gradually came to focus on the psyche and the tensions between psychic agencies plus the nature of the erotic and hostile relationship with the analyst as an obstacle to cure, psychoanalysis began to resemble the treatment we know today. It is a form of treatment that might have had a more complete and beneficial effect on Anna O's inner world. Even then, the role of loss would have remained to be analyzed as well.

We now know that at termination, symptoms often recur. The loss of Breuer, Pollock speculates, would have exacerbated her feelings about the loss of her father and led to the reappearance of her pathological mourning. Pollock generously recognizes that Breuer did not know about mourning work, termination-phase phenomena, and working through. I differ with his generous conclusion that "when Bertha Pappenheim had completed her mourning for Breuer and recovered from iatrogenic complication of her later treatments, she became the gracious and productive worker that the world recognized" (1973, p. 331).

It is my observation that her reaction to the abandonment did not dissipate but became an embedded rationale of her new life. She was enabled eventually to function on a very high level of organizational skill and relatedness to women and children in work tasks, but her bitterness toward men was vastly increased and her sense of herself as living a lonely and sexless life by personal necessity was confirmed. It was as if this were the price of her other accomplishments. In many respects, she was a driven and relentless woman, as Meissner (1979) has observed.

After her stay at the Sanitarium Bellevue, Bertha disappeared from view and surfaced again five years later in Frankfurt, where her mother was now living. There is no record of where or how she fared in this period. When she joined her mother, she accepted an invitation to volunteer in a home for orphans—at first reading to the thirty little Jewish girls. She ran out of fairy tales and began inventing stories, some of which have survived to this day; they have been collected in an anthology called *The Rummage Store*, that is, a place where abandoned objects are sent to wait to be bought. The store was run by a depressed man who had been abandoned by his wife but was reborn through the return of his daughter, who devoted herself to his care: an oedipal family romance and tale of rescue in which the rescued daughter is also the rescuer of her father. The orphans were children whose parents were dead or who were the illegitimate children of Jewish mothers who could not care for them (Freeman 1972).

Gradually, she was more and more drawn to the double pleasures of motherhood without sexuality and of being a rescuer. In 1895, the year of the publication of her case, she became the director of that home for orphans. In her spare time, she began to write more seriously. She wrote a play, *Women's Rights,* that explored the theme of abandoned women and their children as abused victims of exploitative and indifferent men. In this play, the abandoner's wife, upon learning of his infidelity and abandonment of his child, decides to continue the marriage but deny her husband sexual contact with her. This is her "woman's right." Certainly polemical, but also a true, bitter statement of her view of women in relation to men: men have the worldly power; woman's only power is to deny her own sexuality as a way of avenging herself on the man.

Reading feminist literature, Bertha discovered Mary Wollstonecraft and translated *The Vindication of the Rights of Women* into German a hundred years after it had been published in English. She published it with her own funds, under the assumed names "P." or "Paul Berthold." She was drawn both to the book's message— that the state should take responsibility for the education of women and that marriage should be based on the intellectual companionship of equals—and to the life story of this founder of feminism who earned her own way as a secretary and then a reporter, traveling alone to France and becoming involved in the French Revolution. Mary Wollstonecraft twice conceived children out of wedlock, the first liaison ending with her having been abandoned by her lover. She refused his offers of financial help. She married the father of the second daughter, Mary, who ultimately married Shelley.

From the vantage point of her job at the orphanage, Bertha became a powerful organizer of volunteerism in the Jewish community and eventually in all of Germany. She made the role of caregiver the center of her concern. "Care by Women" was the name of the volunteer group she started, and it flourished. Ultimately, she founded a national federation with the same goals. She was, however, an outspoken opponent of professional social work, feeling that it would lead to a devaluation of the accomplishments of volunteer women, and that others like herself whose feeling of worthwhileness was dependent on the rescue of others would be deprived of their entree to this life-saving occupation.

One of her most ambitious but least successful campaigns was to halt the sale of Jewish girls into white slavery by their parents. On this campaign, she traveled extensively and alone, to Galicia, Budapest, Turkey, Jerusalem, and Egypt, and even to the United States in an ultimately hopeless attempt to enlist the cooperation of eastern rabbis and power brokers in stemming the tide. In this project, she was indefatigable. On another front, she worked successfully to develop facilities for the education and training of the illegitimate children of prostitutes and abandoned women.

In her private writings, her *Gebete*, that is, prayer-like meditations on her life and times, and in her many communications with her followers, she expressed the profound frustration and sadness of her life. This *Gebet* was written after a visit to her mother's grave:

Wind blows over the graves, sunlight lies on the stones.
Drop by drop, memories trickle through my thoughts.
I lay a small stone on the beloved spot,
And I, childless, wish for myself
Small memorial stones placed on the rim of the red stone,
With the inscription: "She was very severe." [Freeman 1972, p. 167]

Bertha Pappenheim was a driven woman; she sought peace in discipline and endless work. Even her closest allies and admirers found her difficult to get along with as one who could not tolerate opposition and who insisted on total control. In one of her letters, she wrote, "I have often thought that if one has nothing to love, to hate something is a good substitute" (Freeman 1972, p. 110).

After her death, one of her colleagues wrote, "One wonders, where does this acrimony come from? . . . A volcano lived in the woman; it erupted when someone angered her. . . . Battle was her life element and the expression of her strength. She used a sharp rapier and did not spare the opponent, but she never misused the fight for small or personal reasons" (Cora Berliner, cited in Freeman 1972, pp. 174–175).

She filled her life with projects of all kinds. She was active, she was involved in a life of good works, and in that life she provided generously for many in need. She was important to many individuals whom she rescued from a horrible and uncompromising fate, but she herself remained a lonely person without any close ties to anyone. Her hatred and fear of men is apparent. She envied men their power, their prestige, and the status society provided for them, and she felt most betrayed because she could not get them to put their power at her disposal. Meissner (1979) has observed:

> Her zeal was single-minded and unwavering. It drove her to extremes of physical and emotional exertion, depriving her of many of the joys of human companionship and relaxation . . . but she had a cause, a crusade, a war which had to be fought and won, which required her most strenuous and unremitting dedication and effort. [p. 47]

How much better that she lived on instead of dying to ease Breuer's conscience! And yet we owe to Breuer a considerable debt for his part in the creation of the psychoanalytic method, and to Bertha Pappenheim our thanks for her having played a part in creating our method, while she searched for her own salvation.

REFERENCES

Bowlby, J. (1980). *Attachment and Loss,* vol. 3, *Loss: Sadness and Depression.* New York: Basic Books.

Breuer, J. and Freud, S. (1893–1895). Studies on hysteria. *Standard Edition* 2.

Edinger, D. (1968). *Bertha Pappenheim: Freud's Anna O.* Highland Park, Il: Congregation Solel.

Ellenberger, H. F. (1972). The story of "Anna O.": a critical review with new data. *Journal of History of the Behavioral Sciences* 8:267–279.

Freeman, L. (1972). *The Story of Anna O.* New York: Jason Aronson.

Gay, P. (1988). *Freud: A Life for Our Time.* New York: Norton.

Jensen, E. M. (1970). Anna O.: a study of her later life. *Psychoanalytic Quarterly* 39:269–293.

Jones, E. (1953). *The Life and Work of Sigmund Freud. Vol 1*. New York: Basic Books.

Kaplan, M. (1983). A woman's view of DSM III. *American Psychologist* 38:786–792.

Karpe, R. (1961). The rescue complex in Anna O's final identity. *Psychoanalytic Quarterly* 30:1–27.

Meissner, W. W. (1979). A study on hysteria: Anna O. rediviva. *Annual of Psychoanalysis* 7:17–52.

Micale, M. S. (1995). *Approaching Hysteria: Disease and Its Interpretations*. Princeton, NJ: Princeton University Press.

Mitchell, J. (1984). *Women: The Longest Revolution*. London: Virago.

Pollock, G. (1968). The possible significance of childhood object loss in the Josef Breuer–Bertha Pappenheim (Anna O.)–Sigmund Freud relationship. I. Josef Breuer. *Journal of the American Psychoanalytic Association* 16:711–739.

—— (1972). Bertha Pappenheim's pathological mourning: possible effects of childhood sibling loss. *Journal of the American Psychoanalytic Association* 20:476–493.

—— (1973). Bertha Pappenheim: addenda to her case history. *Journal of the American Psychoanalytic Association* 21:328–332.

Rey, J. H. (1988). What patients bring to analysis. *International Journal of Psycho-Analysis* 69:457–473.

Schonbar, R. A. and Beatus, H. R. (1990). The mysterious metamorphoses of Bertha Pappenheim: Anna O. revisited. *Psychoanalytic Psychology* 7:59–78.

Smith-Rosenberg, C. (1985). *Disorderly Conduct: Visions of Gender in Victorian America*. New York: Knopf.

Stewart, W. (1984). Analytic biography of Anna O. In *Anna O.: Fourteen Contemporary Reinterpretations*, ed. M. Rosenbaum and M. Muroff, pp. 47–51. New York: The Free Press.

A Psychology
of Unconscious
Experience
without Interpretive
Metapsychology

Benjamin Wolstein

4

Breuer and Anna O.'s genuinely new discovery of the hypnoid states in 1880–1882, it is becoming clearer in retrospect, inaugurated a scientific revolution in psychotherapy. As its latent historical implications are more clearly explored in that light, it is increasingly acknowledged as the clinical and conceptual starting point of psychoanalytic inquiry, with the theory of hypnoid states entering the vocabulary of psychoanalysis in terms of unconscious psychic experience. To put its meaning into critical perspective, however, took some equally fundamental clinical discoveries made since then, all built around this founding cornerstone of psychoanalytic therapy. I am referring, here, to such fundamental clinical discoveries as Freud's dawning observation of transference with Dora, and Ferenczi's experiments in the mutual analysis of transference and countertransference with RN and other patients, as well as the covariant observations of resistance and counterresistance first by Reich and later by Anna Freud, and anxiety and counteranxiety first by Rank and later by Sullivan, and, more recently, the psychic center of the ego–interpersonal self, both therapist's and patient's, all discovered directly within the experiential field of therapy. The clinical reality of these defined observations is basic and enduring. They gain empirical sense and systematic meaning, in turn, from being coordinated with the earlier theory of the relation of conscious and unconscious psychic experience, or, as Breuer originally termed it, the "theory of hypnoid states."

In my view, that is the distinguishing theory around which the evolving structure of psychoanalysis has become focused in practice. It is the sine qua non of all subsequent psychoanalytic therapy, setting psychoanalysis apart from the other modalities of psychotherapy across the board, done under the aegis of whatever perspective on interpretive metapsychology. Without it psychoanalysis has no empirical base, and without this empirical base psychoanalysis has no interpretive completion. About the substance of this theory, to paraphrase Breuer's statement of it: psychic processes and patterns are approached solely in terms of

psychology, that is to say, observed psychological conditions, responded to by psychological means, pointed toward psychological
language ends formulated in psychological language (Breuer and
Freud 1893–1895, p. 185). So it is psychological theory through and
through, a scientific development without clinical or conceptual
ties to the physiology, in which Breuer, interestingly enough, had
already established a solid measure of competence.

THE ORIGINALITY OF THE CLINICAL THEORY

Breuer and Anna O. saw—without precedent, as far as I know, in
direct psychological inquiry—that a patient may undergo uniquely
individual changes in response to a particular therapist during
their psychotherapeutic relationship, no matter the socially defined roles assigned to them as therapist and patient in accordance
with the conventional medical model. Anna O.'s deeply personal
changes, Breuer theorized, took the form of hypnoid (not hypnotic, take note, but hypnoid) states, which he then subsumed
under the rubric of unconscious psychic experience. It has the
enduring strength of true theory for the long haul, the reliable
core of psychoanalytic inquiry sought by a practically infinite
pluralism of metapsychologies.

If you have any residual doubts about the creative originality
of this new theory, it may be useful to recall, surprisingly enough,
Freud's clear recognition of it. In the 1890s, he had, I believe,
wrongly criticized Breuer for not treating the contents of hypnoid
states in accordance with Freud's own sexual point of view then
emerging. Breuer had, of course, dealt with sexual issues (Breuer
and Freud, 1893–1895, p. 246), without recourse, however, to any
single universal perspective about them. Yet in spite of that un-
warranted criticism, Freud expressed no reservation at all about
the paramount strength of the theory: Breuer's discovery, he declared in his 1915–1917 *Introductory Lectures* (Freud, p. 248), remains the foundation of psychoanalytic therapy. You may, of
course, disagree with this judgment. If so, you must then offer an
alternative source of the empirical and systematic base of psychoanalysis, equal in its pervasive explanatory power to that of un-

conscious psychic experience that Breuer had derived from hypnoid states by the abreactive means of catharsis. Apart from Breuer and Freud's differences in speculative interpretation, it is clear, they agreed on the substance of clinical observation. And that made it possible for them, finally, to co-author the founding text of psychoanalysis, built around Breuer and Anna O.'s new therapy of experience held beyond awareness. I comment on their co-authorship more fully below.

That new therapeutic discovery was not the result of any transcendental speculative scheme. It was, instead, the fortunate result of empirical observation made possible by the unique cooperation of a particular therapist and a particular patient. The talking cure, as Anna O. privately named it, opened up a fundamentally new approach to psychotherapeutic inquiry, a field of clinical observation and inference that made so much else explicable, using the theory of hypnoid states to explain the abreactive experience of the new cathartic therapy, first following his procedure, then hers. Breuer and Anna O. got into a cooperative venture initiated from both sides, and going both ways and that became part of their new discovery. For the first time, to my knowledge, a therapist and patient formed a unique two-way mode of therapeutic inquiry, in which they both carried out the cathartic abreaction of the patient's psychogenic symptoms. They were, clearly, both unaware of how complex and compenetrating their therapeutic experience had in fact become; unaware, indeed, of how strong and deep their interlocking connections would unconsciously grow; unaware, finally, of how to get through those unconscious connections to psychic freedom with each other.

Their therapeutic focus, especially from Breuer's side, dedicated empiricist that he was, dwelt on detailing the history of Anna O.'s psychogenic symptoms back to their first occurrence, by means of which they found it became possible for her to remove the current dysfunction through emotional catharsis, that is to say, by living through the abreactive emotion embedded in the patterning of her hypnoid states. From the standpoint of present-day practice, they set a rather narrow and limited therapeutic focus that ignored such primary observables as transference and countertransference, and so on, now central to the empirics of psychoanalytic inquiry and capable of being lived and worked through from both sides, under whatever umbrella of metapsychology, in whatever culture of beliefs and values.

Theirs, however, remains the landmark case study—in the matter of origins, certainly, the breakthrough study—of psychoanalysis. Its theory laid the cornerstone of direct inquiry for the later models of psychoanalytic practice that are, in my view, multiplying to cover the unbounded uniqueness of each dyad, indefinitely. That case is the first recorded effort at intensive psychotherapy in its modern sense and form: therapist and patient both working with the dynamic manifestations of unconscious psychic experience, under the deep personal conditions of direct psychotherapeutic inquiry. Not that the interlocking of unconscious psychic experience between therapist and patient, prior to their revolutionary effort, was completely beyond knowing in hypnotic psychotherapy. Others doubtless sensed its existence—such as Bernheim, Charcot, Janet, and Liédbault of the late nineteenth-century French schools, as well as Mesmer and Puységur of the nineteenth-century Viennese school. By the end of the nineteenth century, varieties of hypnosis were being rather widely practiced with a considerable degree of success, and the release from psychogenic symptoms—in Vienna with abreaction, in Paris without it—was also coming into its own. Yet Breuer and Anna O.'s breakthrough was unique and unprecedented, in addition, because theirs was a shared discovery of hypnoid states, first with him as hypnotist, later with her as autohypnotist. By that cooperative procedure, they found that the disturbing emotion embedded in her symptoms was abreacted, and each symptom, serially treated, disappeared in turn.

Hypnocathartic therapy provided direct clinical and empirical, as distinct from philosophical and interpretive, evidence for unconscious processes and patterns becoming conscious. The original evidence for the theory of hypnoid states was gathered under the unmediated conditions of direct psychological interview, unsupported by any schematic extension of its interpretable content, whether about sex or power, about transcendental archetypes or absolute will, about irrational dependency or identity crisis, or hostility and aggression, or love and fear, or mystical union, and so on: hence, in my view, the enduring originality of their root discovery of the major systematic theory of psychoanalytic inquiry, no matter the later interpretive school that grew up around it. From the fact that Breuer refrained from any strong hermeneutic adumbration of his theory, it may be inferred that its prospect for romantic self-expression escaped his vision. In 1880–1882, he was, instead, deeply engrossed in the clinical case at hand, seeking further empirical insight into it. He introduced Freud to its startling novelty and encouraged his younger colleague to study French hypnotism, especially with Charcot in Paris, in order to master hypnotic phenomena in general and perhaps learn something evidential about the hypnoid mystery in particular. Not before 1889, however, did Freud attempt any hypnocathartic therapy on his own. He first undertook it with Emmy von N., of course, using more of his direct suggestion with her than the emotional abreaction Breuer had used with Anna O. seven years earlier. How to understand this revision of approach? In my view, it is a matter of individually different therapists, individually different patients, and hence individually different dyads.

Still of some interest concerning the Breuer–Freud relationship is the question why that long a period of time elapsed before Freud attempted the new Breuer–Anna O. therapy of hypnoid states. Nothing in the historical record so far known (Hirschmüller 1989, p. 142) accounts for the belatedness of his decision, after first learning about it, to attempt this new therapy. Of equal historical interest, moreover, is the so far unanswered yet even more complex question why Freud, given his awareness of countertransference through self-analysis, never required of himself a direct personal experience of this new method. Nor, of course, did Breuer. It was not until the middle of the 1920s, when Ferenczi and Rank first suggested making that innovation standard for all practicing psychoanalysts, that students in training finally began to take seriously the personal value of a dynamic therapeutic experience as distinct from didactic instruction in the impersonal use of someone else's metapsychology.

THE BEGINNINGS OF THERAPEUTIC COPARTICIPATION

To this point, I have discussed Breuer and Anna O.'s therapy by means of hypnoid states in order to put their 1880–1882 discovery into perspective as the original, if often overlooked, clinical source of psychoanalytic therapy down to the present day. I want to note, here again, some other major elements of the emerging scope of psychoanalytic coparticipation. Nearly twenty-five years later, in a postscript to the published case of Dora, Freud (1905) became curious about the clinical fact of transference, even though it took him some ten years to learn how to work with its positive manifestations, in his own distinctly historio-genetic, interpretive, and suggestive way. His part of the therapy was, in sum, to interpret transference and overcome resistance, the patient's, in turn, to present historical data and receive the therapist's instinctual-libidinal insights about them.

The therapist's countertransference and counterresistance were quite another story, from its actual beginnings with Breuer to its later strict readings by Freud. On principle, at first implicit and later made explicit, they both kept countertransference outside their field of therapeutic inquiry, without awareness, in process, of the probable effects of counterresistance. And that was to remain the standard operating procedure until, in 1932, Ferenczi carried out his remarkable experiments with RN, among other patients, in the mutual analysis of transference and countertransference. During these rich, though risky, experiments, therapist and patient both discovered a fruitful way to work through the complexities of transference and countertransference interlocked in direct interpersonal relationship. They became aware of themselves living through a deeply interactive meeting of psyches, the unconscious side of each dovetailing into the other. This last factor of unconscious connectedness was not new, however, and that is why I bring it up in this context. It calls to mind Breuer and Anna O.'s deep therapeutic coparticipation some fifty years earlier, about which, undergoing it unawares, they could not do anything, finally, but part company. The knowledge of its psychoanalyzable conditions that existed in the early 1880s was hardly adequate to the task.

To sum up this brief sketch: Breuer and Anna O. began to explore unconscious psychic experience together; Freud became aware of Dora's transference in his postscript to the case study; and Ferenczi and RN learned to get through transference and countertransference *in medias res* under the direct conditions of intensive clinical inquiry. At the core of these discoveries in therapeutic coparticipation is unconscious experience becoming conscious, the medium through which each therapist uniquely sought a distinctly psychoanalytic inquiry with each patient.

One last historical point about Breuer and Anna O.'s new therapy that still has consequences for the coparticipant procedures of the present: Breuer and Anna O. limited their study of hypnoid states to abreactive catharsis, it is clear in retrospect, because he did not work with her in transference, nor she with him in countertransference, for the immediate purpose of exploring both their unconscious roots. Nor, of course, did his younger colleague and close critic, Freud, from Emmy von N. onward. He, too, did not explore the patient's transference intersecting with his countertransference as live issues. To the very end, one should recall, he kept direct inquiry into countertransference beyond the clinical reach of his patient, so he never learned how to work through it in a therapeutic context. As far as we know, Freud, again like Breuer, preferred not to do that in immediate experience with either a personal therapist or a private patient. Ferenczi, on the other hand, followed the lead of transference and countertransference interlocked, but a consideration of that effort extends beyond the scope of this paper.

Though Breuer never changed his mind about the adequacy of hypnocatharsis for Anna O., there is no report of his practicing it with other patients at the same level of therapeutic value. Nor, indeed, did he report cultivating the personal characteristics of openness, flexibility, and unattachment required in order to practice it with other patients at the same level of intensity. He could not, finally, resolve his disturbing experience in vivo with Anna O. because he, in my view, also lacked a clinical sense of self-aware individuality, his own as well as his patient's, in their coparticipant field of therapy. However, given the evaluation of their extraordinary breakthrough into new therapeutic ground, such limitations of his personal psychography are hardly relevant to the validity of the theory. Breuer obviously did not shirk his responsible presence in their therapeutic relationship; he could not, otherwise, have dealt so evenhandedly with a patient who, in spite of standard medical procedures, was treating herself psychotherapeutically. Their willingness to collaborate with each other openly—first with his hypnotic procedure, then with her autohypnotic procedure— is not only without recorded precedent in therapeutic conduct. Its implications are, in my view, still not fully exhausted.

Looking backward now, no therapist in practice would doubt the creative imagination Breuer released to envision the theory, or the enormous courage he found to remain in the therapy after Anna O. began to conduct the hypnotic therapy, in his presence, on her own. He himself may not have noticed the courage of his creativity as such, perhaps only that he saw the empirical value of following the lead of his patient into a new two-way mode of therapeutic inquiry. Given how far the two of them had already come together, each with a psyche of their own, he probably had no other choice of procedure, except, of course, to discharge her. And so, without looking to established Viennese medical authority for approval, he got on with it. Caught, as they say, between a rock and a hard place, he had nowhere to go in the therapy but forward. My point is that, in order to continue the work with Anna O., he faced a new therapeutic situation. His choices narrowed down either to working more closely with the hypnoid limitations of her unabreacted symptoms or to abandoning the intensive exploration of her psychopathology altogether. Breuer and Anna O. continued together as far as they could, and they jointly opened a new frontier in psychotherapy.

A THEORY OF THERAPEUTIC INQUIRY WITHOUT SCHEMATIC METAPSYCHOLOGY

Today, practicing psychoanalysts from all persuasions in all schools, no matter the political, cultural, or individual ax they may grind, invariably agree on the explanatory power of unconscious psychic experience in their therapeutic inquiries. It is this theory that denominates them psychoanalysts: they could not, otherwise, consider the psychodynamics of transference and resistance, countertransference and counterresistance, or anxiety and counteranxiety. Breuer and Anna O., then, carved out the central theory of observation and inference for the evolving psychoanalytic structure of inquiry from within the larger domain of her psychic life, thereby extending the field of clinical psychology beyond the conscious surface of her symptoms and into the unconscious underground of blocked affective and cognitive experience, both patterned and in process.

Given certain specific responses to each other, Breuer and Anna O. most probably sensed as well, even without direct clarification, that their closely shared two-way relationship had brought about a series of deep psychological changes unawares. It had, of course, struck deeply radiating roots into both their personal psychologies: she developed symptoms of false pregnancy, and he hurriedly left the therapeutic field. So while there may be dynamic psychological change, as Breuer and Anna O. most likely knew, outside a real relationship to others, there is no dynamic psychological relationship, they both learned the hard way, without real change in oneself.

The miracle of real change is, in fact, never painless, never without suffering. To digress: considering briefly, in this context, why interpretive metapsychologies have so widely proliferated in psychoanalysis since 1895, their conventional usage immediately comes to mind. That is to say, when carefully worked out and rigorously adhered to, however else they may function, they enable therapist and patient to defend themselves against free and unfettered experience, against spontaneous and unpredictable change. Even though the various models of therapy inevitably differ in perspective on myth and metaphor, they all exhibit one clinical feature in common: their frame promises the safety of containment, even the illusion of invulnerability, at the personal price of counterdefense behind a curtain of schematic consistency. Their therapeutic inquiry so modeled and framed, therapist and patient may move toward each other with, as Wilhelm Reich (1972) put it, their character armor in place. A well-framed model protects its makers against going over the psychoanalytic edge, so to speak. Yet, in the search for new self-knowledge, there is no way around it: you should have to go over the edge of the known in order to get into the unknown. A model of therapy does not give comfort against the unknown, nor does it confer safety against the unexplored, for it leaves both therapist and patient pushing and pulling beyond the edge of its frame. That, in my sense of it, is why some therapists report feeling so very tightly locked within the prison walls of their interpretive attitude. All they can do, so they strictly believe, is interpret. By itself, however, interpretation more often constricts than liberates. It makes the patient feel rather more conscious, even hyperconscious, of looking from the outside inward. In the dynamic movement of conscious and unconscious experience, the search for psychic change, looking from the inside outward, usually arouses the anxiety of freedom instead.

That Breuer and Anna O.'s originality was both procedural and conceptual rarely receives the critical attention it deserves in the psychoanalytic literature, mainly, I think, because the therapists of today, like the surgeons in Freud's analogy of yesteryear, generally believe they are to take charge of the therapeutic procedure and keep it focused in the direction of the patient. Breuer and Anna O., however, did something quite radical: they both—first one, then the other—codirected the course of the therapeutic procedure itself. That is to say, as already indicated, they tried something entirely new, and it worked. Not only did she follow the hypnotic procedure he first introduced; he also followed the auto-hypnotic procedure she later introduced; and they both geared their procedures to the elucidiation of hypnoid states, hers of course.

Contrary to the conventions of standard medical practice, then and now, they both shared responsibility for the conduct of her therapy. When they began working together, Breuer was, as expected, putting her under hypnosis, tracing back her symptoms in search of origins, and observing her abreaction of emotions once these were found locked into those origins. Then, without fanfare, she one day opened the session with her own procedure, put herself under a hypnotic-like state for the chimney sweeping, as she joked about it, and carried out the emotional catharsis in his presence, all on her own. Wherefore as they both conducted the therapy together, it is fair to say that they both created the new therapy together. Breuer later published a study of this new theory of therapy, covering the results of both their procedures, while Anna O. went on to other things.

UNITY IN OBSERVATION, PLURALISM IN INTERPRETATION

To summarize their accomplishment of the cornerstone theory of psychoanalytic therapy without interpretive metapsychology: crucial to their new therapeutic inquiry, especially to the procedures they innovated from both sides, is the basic distinction between unconscious psychic experience and its various interpretive metapsychologies. This distinction has had a rather curious history in psychoanalytic knowledge, often left obscure and undefined by the grand and greedy continental systems that sought to envelop all of psychic life in one fell swoop, each with the universal coverage of its own special brand of myth and metaphor. But the history of this distinction did not begin that way.

In 1880–1882, Breuer and Anna O. implicitly built the procedures of hypnocathartic therapy around it. And nearly fifteen years later, Breuer and Freud could finally coauthor *Studies on Hysteria* precisely because they concurred about making it explicit. Breuer and Anna O., in both their procedures, carried out the removal of psychogenic symptoms in a way that was adequate to their conceptual theory of inquiry, without, in addition, feeling compelled to make universal and unexceptionable interpretations of their hypnocathartic findings. And this earned Breuer, as students of psychoanalysis well know, Freud's rather sharp negative reaction, even smacking of disdain: Breuer couldn't face up to the sexual etiology of Anna O.'s symptoms, so Freud said, because he resisted the clinical merit of Freud's instinctual-libidinal vision of human nature then evolving. From the other side, it may also be said, with equal merit, that the romantic Freud got stuck in biological mythology because he could not face up to his direct clinical curiosity: he lacked Breuer's patient and even-handed discipline of empirical and systematic inquiry. What it comes down to, finally, is a matter of psychoanalytic judgment. If you believe Freud's singular perspective applies unreservedly in all cases, including that of Anna O., then, clearly, Breuer underreached; if, on the other hand, you accept the pluralism of their perspectives on metapsychology, then, of course, Freud overreached.

Breuer and Freud obviously saw different things in psychotherapeutic inquiry from the very outset, an inbuilt situation of radical pluralism that they, in fact, both accepted as unmodifiable in their joint preface to the first edition of *Studies on Hysteria*. There were, they wrote, "natural and justifiable differences between opinions of two observers who are agreed upon the facts and the basic reading of them, but who are not invariably at one in their interpretations and conjectures" (Breuer and Freud 1893–1895, pp. xxix–xxx). In context, this statement of agreement and difference between them needs no further commentary. They could both observe the therapeutic strength of hypnoid states, while they each took different approaches to their interpretation. They both came to realize, and we should not forget, that there is no necessary connection yet established between the psychology of observation and the metapsychology of interpretation: it is possible to agree about either one with, or without, agreeing about the other. Now Freud, it may be suggested, did not fully believe what he signed for; instead he expressed public support for this basic distinction between psychology and metapsychology here, even though he did not privately believe it, only to accomplish the publication of the *Studies on Hysteria* with a somewhat skittish and uncooperative Breuer. Still, carefully reread in context, that prefatory remark remains a straightforward statement of position, however else historians may find it plausible to construe its meaning from such other sources as biographies, correspondence among colleagues, collateral reports of friends, relatives, and patients, or simply from gossip. About Breuer and Freud on observation and interpretation here, I think the record is clear. And while they may not, either of them, have said all that they meant, they must be taken to have meant at least what they said. Whatever else may turn up in the historical archives, this piece of the record is plain to read: the psychology of unconscious experience is one thing, the metapsychology of its interpretive myth and metaphor something else. Breuer could, therefore, join the suffering Anna O. at the empirical and systematic orders of hypnocathartic therapy; he could not, however, join the imaginative Freud at its interpretive and speculative order for the myth and metaphor about Anna O. and his new therapy of hypnoid states.

REFERENCES

Breuer, J. and Freud, S. (1893–1895). Studies on hysteria. *Standard Edition* 2.

Freud, S. (1905). Fragment of an analysis of a case of hysteria. *Standard Edition* 7:1–123.

—— (1943). *A General Introduction to Psychoanalysis*. Garden City, NY: Garden City Publishing.

Hirschmüller, A. (1989). *The Life and Work of Josef Breuer*. New York: New York University Press.

Reich, W. (1972). *Character Analysis*. New York: Touchstone Press.

5

Hysteria, Dissociation, and Cure: Emmy von N. Revisited

Philip M. Bromberg

This chapter, with minor changes, was originally published in *Psychoanalytic Dialogues* 6:55–71 (1996).

"An hysteric," it has been said, "is someone who goes through life pretending to be who he really is."[1] I've never heard a diagnostic description of hysteria I liked better, except perhaps "an hysteric is like a glass of water without the glass." Each of these aphorisms, in its own imagery, points a finger directly at the hysteric's most pronounced interpersonal handicaps: his readiness to dramatize his feelings lest they not be taken as "real" by others, and his burden of chronic anxiety engendered by the mistrust that is indeed felt by others as to where they stand with him at any given moment. Whether male or female, the hysteric, in other words, suffers not only from reminiscences (Breuer and Freud 1893–1895, p. 7), but from a tragic inability to convince others of the authenticity of his or her own subjective experience. Comparing this to what Sullivan (1953) labeled "security operations," Laing (1962) suggested that "the hysteric is engaged in sincerity operations." He noted, however, that:

> It is usually others who complain of the hysteric's lack of genuineness or sincerity. In fact, it is regarded as pathognomonic of the hysteric that his or her actions should be false, that they should be histrionic, dramatized, etc. The hysteric, on the other hand, often insists that his feelings are real and genuine. It is we who feel that they are unreal. [p. 36]

This issue of the collision between the subjective reality of the patient and the subjective reality of the therapist is, of course, at the heart of every clinical psychoanalysis, and has probably never been portrayed as openly or in as pure a form as it was described in *Studies on Hysteria* (Breuer and Freud 1893–1895), in Freud's struggle with the use of hypnosis as a technique while attempting to treat Frau Emmy von N., first in 1889 for about seven weeks and then about one year later for an approximately equal length of time.

---

1. A slightly different version (possibly the original) can be found in Laing (1962, p. 34).

Friedman (1994) discussed the impact on the history of psychoanalysis of Emmy von N., who, under her actual name, Fanny Moser, was the widow of an affluent Swiss businessman (see Ellenberger 1977). She was a woman locked in by time, place, and social role to an identity defined by the power of men—in real life an identity defined by widowhood and by what her husband's family said about her;[2] and, under her pseudonym, an identity defined by "patienthood" and by what Freud said about her. Friedman (1994) writes that the great lesson of psychotherapy discovered by Freud was that "you cannot fail if you invite the patient to do what she wants to do," and Freud was thus "prepared to obey his patient, Emmy von N., when, in effect, she told him to stop pestering her about the cause of her symptoms and let her talk about whatever she pleased. Freud instantly made her rule his own—in fact, his Fundamental Rule" (pp. 8–9). He took the rule as a key to the storehouse of mental contents—the needed raw data—the ingredients to be placed into the crucible of psychoanalysis, which the analyst would then link together and transform into the substance of cure: objective truth. As Friedman puts it, Freud "saw that if he could himself make all the necessary connections among the data, then all he would need from the patient is what she was anyway inclined to give him," but he then encountered a new problem with patients. "Freud no longer had to solicit cooperation; but he now had to solicit belief ... since they could refuse to believe in Freud's inferences" (p. 9). This, as Friedman notes, led Freud to the concept of resistance (see also Bromberg 1995b) and led the psychoanalytic situation to be framed for close to 100 years as a struggle between ignorance and objective truth. The problem that psychoanalysis has faced since that time is that although Emmy was correct, and Freud's genius allowed him to recognize this, the human mind was not sufficiently understood to comprehend *why* the Fundamental Rule was useful, and that *Emmy's lesson was really a statement about*

---

2. According to Appignanesi and Forrester (1992), "Fanny's husband died of a heart attack a few days after the birth of her second daughter. Fanny was then twenty-six. Following his death, the children of the first marriage accused Fanny of having poisoned him. An exhumation found no evidence of murder, but his relatives kept up their campaign against her and the rumors persisted . . ." (p. 92).

the analytic relationship, not a lesson in analytic technique. I would argue that this, more than any other single misunderstanding, has slowed the subsequent evolution of psychoanalysis, clinically and conceptually.

Freud (Breuer and Freud 1893–1895) used the term "waking-state" to distinguish it from Emmy's state of consciousness when she was in a hypnotically induced trance. For example, he says that "in her waking-state she seemed, so far as possible, to, ignore the fact that she was undergoing hypnotic treatment" (p. 51) and that "during this hypnosis I convinced myself that she knew everything that happened in the last hypnosis, whereas in waking-life she knows nothing of it" (p. 55). Similar to the distinction that classical theory has made between dream-life versus waking-life as reflecting the difference between unconscious and conscious, the parallel division between consciousness as "healthy" versus unconsciousness as "regressive" (in the sense of involving—as in dreams—more "primitive" modes of functioning) has never been seriously questioned. Because of the increased attention now being paid to the normal multiplicity of states of consciousness, an important shift is taking place that is leading away from the unconscious-preconscious-conscious continuum per se, toward a view of the mind as a configuration of discontinuous, shifting states of consciousness with varying degrees of access to perception and cognition. Some of these self-states are hypnoidally unlinked from perception at any given moment of normal mental functioning—lending support to some of Freud's ideas in his *Project* (1895) and *The Interpretation of Dreams* (1900)—while other self-states are virtually foreclosed from such access because of their original lack of linguistic symbolization.

The major difference between Freud's early view and more recent findings about the nature of the mind is that what Freud called the "perceptual system" is now seen as circumvented or compromised not only during sleep and dreaming, but as a normal developmental response to trauma and as a person's most basic defense against its anticipated recurrance. From this frame of reference, dreaming may be simply the most familiar special case of the more general phenomenon of dissociation, the normal self-hypnotic capacity of the human mind—the voice of other "selves." It might, thereby, be fair to conclude that Freud's willingness to see hypnosis as a phenomenon worthy of his serious attention was startlingly ahead of its time in his treatment of Emmy, but that, in utilizing it, he went about things the wrong way. That is, the key he was looking for is not in hypnosis as a technique (something to be "applied" from outside), but in the fact that autohypnosis is an intrinsic aspect of mental functioning that shapes every human relationship, to one degree or another, without having to be induced.

There are always domains of dissociated self-experience that have weak or nonexistent links to the experience of "I" as a communicable entity, and this is particularly so with patients such as Emmy. Before these hypnoidally inaccessible self-states can be taken as objects of cognitive reflection and resolvable intrapsychic conflict, they require that the necessary conditions for cognitive resolution be available. That is, they must first become "thinkable" by becoming linguistically communicable through enactment in the therapeutic relationship. Until this happens, neither genuine repression nor the experience of intrapsychic conflict can take place, because each state of consciousness holds its own experientially encapsulated "truth" that is enacted over and over again (Bromberg 1993, 1994). The difficulty for psychoanalysts is that they have not had a strong theoretical model to deal with the implications of this, because Freud, in abandoning trauma theory, also dismissed the phenomenon of dissociation and formulated a conceptual system that led to the belief that, except for the most seriously disturbed patients, interpretation of "unconscious conflict" should be sufficient. This belief, as we know, began with his break with Josef Breuer over the issue of how to conceptualize the etiology of hysteria, and it is to one aspect of this controversy—the issue of hypnoid states and splitting of consciousness—that I would like to turn next.

HYSTERIA AND DISSOCIATION

Breuer, essentially agreeing with Charcot and Janet, stated in his theoretical chapter in *Studies on Hysteria* (pp. 185–251) that "what lies at the centre of hysteria is a splitting off of a portion of psychical activity" (p. 227), but he went even further by writing that this deserves "to be described as a splitting not merely of psychical activity but of consciousness" (p. 229).[3] In brief, Breuer was advancing the opinion that traumatic hysteria is mediated by a process that can "be classed with autohypnosis" and that "it seems desirable to adopt the expression 'hypnoid,' which lays stress on this internal similarity" (p. 220). The importance of autohypnosis in the genesis of hysterical phenomena, Breuer writes, "rests on the fact that it makes conversion easier and protects (by amnesia) the converted ideas from wearing-away—a protection which leads, ultimately, to an increase in psychical splitting" (p. 220). Almost parenthetically, Breuer adds an observation that in postclassical analytic thinking embodies the heart of our contemporary understanding of normal personality development, its pathology, and its treatment; he writes that in response to trauma, *"perception too— the psychical interpretation of sense impressions—is impaired"* (p. 201, italics added).

But, while Breuer asserted that the basis of hysteria was the existence of hypnoid states that had the power to create an amnesia, Freud rejected Breuer's concept of self-hypnosis and later contended that he had never encountered a self-hypnotic hysteria, only defense neuroses (Bliss 1988, p. 36).[4] After *Studies on Hysteria*, Freud was, for the most part, openly contemptuous about the possible usefulness of theorizing about dissociation, hypnoid states, or alterations in consciousness (Loewenstein and Ross 1992, pp. 31–

---

3. Baars (1992), among others, presents research data supporting the conclusion that there is so much evidence for the internal consistency of momentary conscious experience that we are now obliged to go beyond even the idea of divided or dissociated consciousness and must now accept the concept of dissociated aspects of *self*.

4. Eventually, Breuer halfheartedly supported Freud's concept of defense hysteria, "although not without adding that in his opinion defence alone would be hardly sufficient to produce a genuine splitting of the psyche" (Hirschmüller 1978, p. 167). "Auto-hypnosis," Breuer writes, "has, so to speak, created the space or region of unconscious psychical activity into which the ideas which are fended off are driven" (Breuer and Freud 1893–1895, p. 236). Thus, while Breuer seemed later to modify his earlier postion by including defense as an additional factor in hysteria, he also, "on the other hand, insisted openly that the greater importance should be attached to hypnoid states" (Hirschmüller 1978, p. 167).

32). Berman (1981) characterizes this as a "one-sided anti-Janet stand" (p. 285) that led psychoanalysis, for the next century, toward an "emphasis on repression at the expense of dissociation" (p. 297).

Freud (Breuer and Freud 1893–1895), who liked to use the term "delirium" to represent the switches from Emmy's "normal" state of consciousness, writes, in a brilliant piece of clinical observation, that:

> The transition from a normal state to a delirium often occurred quite imperceptibly. She would be talking quite rationally at one moment about matters of small emotional importance, and as her conversation passed on to ideas of a distressing kind I would notice, from her exaggerated gestures or the appearance of her regular formulas of speech, etc., that she was in a state of delirium. ... It was often only possible after the event to distinguish between what had happened in her normal state. For the two states were separated in her memory, and she would sometimes be highly astonished to hear of the things which the delirium had introduced piecemeal into her normal conversation. [pp. 96–97]

This anecdotal observation is, in fact, empirically supported by current research on dissociative disorders, which confirms that switches between self-states occur quite imperceptibly to the patient, who essentially has amnesia for the switching process itself. Putnam (1988) writes that "it is as if the 'self' that observes and remembers is state-dependent and is suspended during the moment of transition between states of consciousness" (p. 27). It is often also very difficult for the therapist to observe the transitions unless he knows what to look for.

Freud's observation is also, of course, right at the heart of the contemporary controversy about memory, and he is here taking an interesting stand about the reality of subjective experience and the issue of "lying." People with dissociative disorders frequently present with a lifelong history of having been accused of lying, not keeping their promises or, at best, unreliability—very much like Laing's observation about hysterics. Freud reports that "in her ordinary life, Frau von N. scrupulously avoided any untruthfulness, nor did she ever lie to me under hypnosis. Occasionally, however, she would give me incomplete answers and keep back part of her story until I insisted a second time on her completing it" (p. 98).

Freud's point of view implied that there was a conscious control by his patient over the incompleteness of her answers and that the characterological issue of veracity was somehow independent of the condition itself. From a contemporary vantage point, however, the "incompleteness" of Emmy's answers is consistent with the limited access she had to self-states that possessed additional memories that would have changed not only the content but the *meaning* of her narrative. Freud's "insisting" may have indeed sometimes enabled her to shift to another self-state, but what was missed in the "successful" result was quite important to the future of psychoanalysis. Freud discovered at this early point in his research that if he pushed hard enough he could get his patient to provide previously undisclosed data that he believed then created a more "complete" story. But, as Lionells (1986) has commented, "the mind of the hysteric shows a particular propensity for dissociation" (p. 587), and what Freud did not recognize was that his patient was already telling the "whole" truth[5] as structured by the dissociated view of reality held by a particular domain of self. In other words, a hysteric's dramatization of feelings is, most of the time, not a performance or an act, and, I might add, this includes many occasions in treatment when the patient herself may be insisting that it *is* an act. Emmy was always reporting not just the *information* held by a particular self-state, but a view of reality defined by the limited part of the self to which Freud was relating at that moment—a hypnoidally discontinuous domain of self with its own dominant affect, its own selectively structured perceptual field, its own range of memories, and its own mode of interpersonal relatedness, including relatedness to Freud.

If an analyst can access and personally engage the particular self-state that is there at a particular moment—what its individual "story" is and how his own here-and-now feelings about his patient are part of that story—he will get not only information (that is, "data"), but, as Rivera (1989) has eloquently put it, he will also facilitate "the erosion of dissociative barriers to a central conscious-

---

5. For an extended discussion of the issue of authenticity, dissociation, and self-states, see the dialogue between Goldberg (1995) and Bromberg (1995c).

ness that can handle the contradictions of the different voices—
not the silencing of different voices with different points of view—
but the growing ability to call those voices 'I,' to disidentify with
any one of them as the whole story " (p. 28). In other words, it might
be said that patients such as Emmy suffer mainly from an "I condition," and that the dissociative symptom Freud referred to as
"reminiscences" is just one of the more dramatic consequences of
what Rivera calls the contradictions between voices.

TRAUMA, ENACTMENT, AND THE "TALKING CURE"

This brings us to the subject of trauma. Freud (1910) described
hysteria as the result of having "been subjected to violent emotional
shocks" (p. 10), and, in this context, it is not difficult to see how
the ordinary experience of surprise becomes phobically associated
with traumatic "shock." (See also Reik 1936.) In Emmy's case, it
led to what Freud called her "constant fear of surprises" (Breuer
and Freud 1893–1895, p. 59), and Freud in fact proposed that the
root of her repetitive "Keep still! Don't say anything! Don't touch
me!" was a "protective formula...designed to safeguard her against
a recurrence of such experiences . . ." (p. 57). I would put it that
this type of "safeguard" takes the form of maintaining perpetual
readiness for harm by foreclosing any sustained experience of
safety. By repeating her formula, she reminds herself that danger
is always present and that she must stay on guard; by staying on
guard, she is prepared for the ambush she "knows" will come as
soon as she feels safe. It is the preparedness, (which the formula
reinforces) that is the safeguard, so that, if an unanticipated experience happens, it is less likely to be traumatic because her mind
is ready to process potential harm. Thus the continual readiness
of the dissociative vigilance is what serves as the protection. It
doesn't prevent a harmful event from occurring and, in fact, may
often increase its likelihood. It prevents it from occurring *unexpect-*
edly (Bromberg 1995c).
    Freud's technique, in treating Emmy, was an effort to wipe out
the memories of the various events that occurred by surprise—to
wipe out the memories of events that caused the shock to the
psyche and thus wipe out the negative affect associated with these

events. It was not the content of the events that was crucial, but rather their form or structure as something that took place unexpectedly, as with the friend who liked slipping into her room "very softly," or the strange man who opened the door of her compartment "suddenly" (Breuer and Freud 1893–1895, p. 59). Freud was trying to erase the negative affect being expressed through Emmy's symptoms, and he believed at the time that, if the memories could be rooted out hypnotically, there would be no need for the negative affect. Why did it not work?

Freud writes, "my therapy consists in wiping away these *pictures*, so that she is no longer able to see them before her. To give support to my suggestion, I stroked her several times over the eyes" (p. 53). He is saying that he was trying to influence the relationship between perception and cognition, but, because he was also attempting to discover, empirically, what would "work," he could not realize how close he had come to the genuine key (perception), and was inconsistent in his effort. Thus, at other times he tried to influence not perception, but thoughts, in the hope of changing their meaning directly, as for example, when he writes, "I tried to reduce the importance of this memory, by pointing out that after all nothing had happened to her daughter, and so on" (p. 54).

In what is probably the first instance of Freud's referring to the phenomenon that in later work would be described as "transference," he states that Emmy "declared that she was afraid she had offended me by something she had said during the massage yesterday which seemed to her to have been impolite" (p. 59). It is here, in the midst of his first preanalytic experiment, that Freud begins to acknowledge the importance of treating symptoms with patience while treating patients with symptoms. Emmy complained "in a definitely grumbling tone that I was not to keep on asking her where this and that came from, but to let her tell me what she had to say" (p. 63). "I saw," Freud states, "that my general prohibition had been ineffective, and that I should have to take her frightening impressions away from her one by one. I saw now that the cause of her ill-humour was that she had been suffering from the residues of this story which had been kept back" (pp. 62–63). Acting on this insight, Freud then responded to Emmy's description of her fear of worms by crediting its significance and asking her to tell him some more animal stories, here displaying his emerging recognition that it might be more therapeutic to attend to Emmy's perception of what was meaningful than to continue trying to "figure her out" on his own. Freud, as we know, was accurate, but the shift in his approach was more important than simply being a key to the storehouse of hidden memories. It was a relational act that allowed Emmy to experience her own impact in shaping the process that Anna O. (Bertha Pappenheim) had called "chimney sweeping" (Breuer and Freud, 1893–1895, p. 30). It might even be said that at this moment in Freud's treatment of Emmy von N., psychoanalysis was presented with its first piece of data that the "talking cure" is therapeutically effective only in a relational context, and is not in fact a catharsis but a negotiated "act of meaning" (Bruner 1990).

What Freud was unable to see at that time was that his failure was not a lack of patience with Emmy's symptoms as symptoms, but a lack of patience with her symptoms as representing her perceptual reality, and in this sense were more than "pieces of pathology" that should or could be "taken away," whether one by one or all at once. Freud writes that through hypnosis he "made it impossible for her to see any of these melancholy things again, not only by wiping out her memories of them ... but by removing her whole recollection of them, as though they had never been present in her mind. I promised her that this would lead to her being freed from the expectation of misfortune which perpetually tormented her" (p. 61). Ironically, it is this very promise, in its various forms, that I feel most accounts for Emmy's having reacted to Freud over and over in a way that I've referred to as "throwing rocks at the fireman" (Bromberg 1995b). Because the anticipation of misfortune is the principal way a traumatized person protects himself from future trauma, the promise of "cure" (which is always implied by a therapist, even if not explicitly stated) makes the process of attempting to "free" a traumatized patient from the expectation of misfortune probably the most complex treatment issue a psychoanalyst faces.

Freud (Breuer and Freud 1893–1895) states that, contrary to his expectations following this intervention, Emmy "slept badly and only for a short time" (p. 62). He expected her to be much better. She was not, of course, better, because his hypnotic suggestion simply addressed one self-state and left the others untouched and, more to the point, unheard. It is the unheard voices of these other dissociated states that, in Emmy's relationship with Freud, were having negative responses to his helpful "technique" and were not only upset but also angry.

Nevertheless, Emmy's angry complaint that she felt "unheard" had a powerful impact in making Freud sit up and take notice, and he subsequently realized he could not just attack symptoms as if hypnosis were an experiential eraser and expect it to have any positive effect. In talking about the origin of symptoms, Freud thus writes that, while pains can be determined organically, pains can also be *memories* of pains—"mnemic symbols," as he puts it (p. 90). He was here foreshadowing the issue of the dissociative split between the mind and what Winnicott (1949) called "psyche-soma," a split that prevents the linguistic symbolization of immediate experience by the use of conceptual perspective (Goldberg 1995, Bromberg 1995c), thus forcing the body to process experience physically, through symptoms.

The essence of dissociation is that the mind is disconnected from the psyche-soma to protect one's illusion of unitary selfhood from the potential threat of traumatically impinging experience it cannot process cognitively. This can frequently lead to symptoms such as, in Emmy's case, agoraphobia, and what Freud interpreted as her inhibition of will (abulia). On the basis of my own clinical observation, I would offer the view that a so-called loss of will can be most usefully understood as an intrinsic outcome of dissociation. Because self-agency is limited to whatever function is performed by the dissociated self-state that at that time has access to the mind, what is most frequently seen by a therapist treating a patient such as Emmy, represents a specfic mode of the patient's self-experience that has limited or no access to other aspects of reality, self-expression, or modes of relatedness. In this regard, the ability to act purposefully—what we call willpower—is not inhibited in the sense of a global suppresion of will, but is "repackaged" in unlinked states of mind, leading to a personality dynamic whereby certain self-states are dramatically willful while others are inhibited but are simultaneously "on alert" (Bromberg 1995c). From this perspective, inhibition of action and hysterical outbursts of action are opposite sides of the same coin, and, as Emmy demonstrated when she was in her unruly state, action not only was possible but was relentless in its power (e.g., her determination to act on her belief that eating and drinking water was harmful to her despite Freud's effort to make her more "reasonable" [Breuer and Freud 1893–1895, pp. 81–83]).

Using Emmy's anorexia as an example of an abulia, Freud concludes that "abulias are nothing other than a highly specialized ... kind of psychical paralysis" (p. 90), which, in Emmy's history, represent an escape from the fact that "it is impossible to eat with disgust and pleasure at the same time" (p. 89). This formulation speaks directly to the basic adaptational function of dissociation when one's overarching sense of self cannot hold two incompatible modes of relating to the same object at the same time. In its most general form, it protects the person from the felt impossibility of responding self-reflectively with feelings of fear and security toward the same object at the same moment. There is thus, inevitably, a "psychical paralysis" in anorexia simply because the psyche–soma is always disconnected from the mind with regard to the experience of eating.

A "TRUE LADY" OR A "WOMAN OF PARTS"?

Freud concludes the case history of Emmy with an extraordinary addendum that followed his final contact with her in May 1890. He had received, three years later:

> a short note from her asking my permission for her to be hypnotized by another doctor, since she was ill again and could not come to Vienna. At first I did not understand why my permission was necessary, till I remembered that in 1890 I had, at her own request, protected her against being hypnotized by anyone else, so that there should be no danger of her being distressed by coming under the control of a doctor who was antipathetic to her.... I accordingly renounced my exclusive perogative in writing. [p. 85]

Here one can feel the powerful effects of the hypnosis in having subdued Emmy's capacity for self-authorized assertiveness in a relational context. Claiming that to have a relationship with another doctor she first needed to be released from Freud, Emmy felt that she needed to have her paralysis undone by Freud in order to restore selfhood. Whether this was literally true is a matter for speculation, but I think a plausible case can be made for the possibility that this communication was her final effort to bring Freud's attention to bear (as it indeed did) on the fact that his technique of hypnotic suggestion itself evoked an iatrogenic "abulia," a paralysis of Emmy's experience of herself as a human being entitled to make her own choices. All in all, I agree with the observation made by Appignanesi and Forrester (1992), that "if we draw up the inventory of this early analytic episode, we are struck by Freud's attentiveness to the doctor–patient relationship, even when he is abusing it with tricks and his pride in the shaman-like power granted him over his patients" (p. 102).

Freud had recognized that there was a part of Emmy (the part he called "her unruly nature") that was angry at not being allowed to tell her version of what had happened to her in the past; but he was, of course, not aware of the importance of her immediate reality as material in itself—what she felt was happening to her right then in her relationship with Freud. It was not simply that Emmy needed more time to narrate her history, as Freud believed. She needed a cohesive temporal context that addressed both the past and the present—a context within which Freud would not only listen to and engage her multiple historical narratives, as told, but, equally importantly, would respond to, and engage, her enacted responses to his behavior with her in the here-and-now: that is, *her dissociated responses to both his messages and his massages.* From a present-day perspective, he might have thus comprehended that her formulaic "Keep still! Don't say anything! Don't touch me!" was not simply an echo from the past, but a warning to remain vigilant with regard to Freud himself.

An illustrative case in point can be drawn from my own work with a patient severely traumatized in childhood, who has described herself as having "a talking vagina." She experienced vaginal pain in situations with older men whom she "trusted," but who made her feel anxious in their efforts to help her. The pain, which sometimes occurred during analytic hours, was eventually connected to her father's overdetermined, overzealous, and frequently inappropriate efforts to teach her how to cope with life. Because she had no one but her father to rely on, she could not process the fact that his compulsive determination to teach her "the facts of life" was, simultaneously, an assault on her mind, and she thereby processed the pain of his disregard for her feelings as though it were an assault on her body. As she grew up, she was always ready to discover this kind of "father" in a man she relied on, and was always prepared to deal with his dark side through pain in her "talking vagina." She was thus typically able to forestall potential trauma while keeping the relationship intact by not making the "father" aware of anything about himself that seemed outside of his consciousness. Her vaginal pains were eventually eliminated by our processing this enactment as it played out between us over time. When the pains came during or after a session, our ability to address the phenomenon together was contingent on our being able to confront the dissociative process *in each of us* that prevented her, while she was with me, from recognizing that my efforts to explore her early memories (particularly sexual ones) during a session were felt as potentially traumatic to her. That is, what I was looking at as an "exploration"of the past, was for her an event that pulled her into a reliving of the original feelings in the here-and-now. She was thus always feeling at the edge of traumatic hyperarousal, but could not hold that experience in awareness. Because I was needed as someone on whom her security depended and who, she felt, was genuinely acting in good faith on her behalf, she could could not simultaneously hold that aspect of my behavior that was painful and frightening. She thereby dissociated this domain of reality, including the reality that I sometimes did indeed become impatient with her "distractions," leaving only her physical pain to testify to the experience. We arrived, little by little, at the understanding that her "talking vagina" was talking simultaneously about me and to me, and was not just a symbol of a memory of the past (a "mnemic symbol") but a representation of her present experience that could not be processed as such. In other words, the connection to her past could not be made real to her without authentic negotiation of the here-and-now intersubjective context being enacted with me, a context that paralleled its source in the relationship that caused the original pain. As Guntrip (1971) observes, "physical sexual symptoms mask a more broadly based and significant need for 'personal relationship' in its basic security-giving value" (p. 168).

Freud writes about Emmy: "She was afraid that I would lose patience with her on account of her recent relapse" (p. 75). I would say that she was *always* afraid that Freud would lose patience with her, because she felt, accurately, that Freud wished to silence her "unacceptable" voices. Even though she welcomed his trying to cure her, she didn't want him to "cure" her of being herself. She was "unruly" because she needed to get all of her selves into a human relationship and was afraid Freud was going to lose patience because she was insisting, through her symptoms, on her right to have him accept that her "crazy" (unruly) reactions to his therapeutic efforts had to do with him as well as with her. I think it is particularly interesting that Freud's own description of Emmy supports this idea quite dramatically. Apart from the "unruliness" of her symptoms, Freud held her to be totally restrained in her life and in the choices she made living it.[6]

She was, in fact, eulogized by Freud as a model of virtuous self-denial, the perfect Victorian widow, commended for "the moral seriousness with which she viewed her duties, her intelligence and energy, which were no less than a man's, and her high degree of education and love of truth" (p. 103). But most telling is his praise of her as the woman who, after her husband's death, refused to remarry, sacrificing her personal needs (sexual and otherwise) for the protection of her children, bearing forever the scars of unjust victimization by her husband's family. "[H]er benevolent care for the welfare of all her dependents," Freud states, "revealed her qualities as a true lady as well" (pp. 103–104). Small wonder that Emmy's most dramatic vehicle of self-expression with Freud was her "pathology." A case can in fact be reasonably argued that this "true lady" was "a woman of parts," and that Freud's problem was compounded by his powerful idealization of Emmy—an idealization that contributed to a dissociative process in his own thinking whereby he considered her symptoms as pathology but the woman herself as morally irreproachable. Freud's most imperative reason for the idealization, I would conjecture, was to preclude any possible Janet-like view of her as "degenerate"; but in addition, one might also speculate as to whether some part of Freud's need to place her on

---

6. That there was indeed another, more "alive" and sexually unrestrained, side to Emmy is documented by Appignanesi and Forrester (1992, pp. 97–99).

a pedestal was an unconscious effort to insulate himself from the kind of problem that Breuer had with Anna O.

Freud listened to Emmy, but for the most part he was listening, as he put it, so as to be able to "deliver maxims," and that stance, in my view, was the core of the problem. Emmy, limited by her dissociative mental structure in her capacity for relatedness, could only indirectly or symptomatically protest being treated simply as an object to be "cured" (see Bromberg 1995b) and was continually enacting, dramatically, her dissociated self-states. All through the treatment there was an underlying, unacknowledged, and unverbalized relationship between Freud and those parts of Emmy's self for whom her illness was an interpersonal reality to be taken seriously. I offer the view that, all told, her "relapses" represented dissociated enactments of self-states that were not authorized to express their existence in a "true lady"—a sane Victorian woman whose character, as depicted by Freud, was defined by "her humility of mind and the refinement of her manners" (p. 103)—someone who could not possibly be furious that, in her relationship with Freud, including her relationship to his therapeutic massages, she was allowed to exist only as either a highly moral person who had renounced her sexuality in the interest of motherhood or as a patient possessed by craziness that made her "unruly" or "delirious."

In his evaluation of Emmy's treatment outcome, Freud said, very honestly, that "the therapeutic success on the whole was considerable; but it was not a lasting one," and that "the patient's tendency to fall ill in a similar way under the impact of fresh traumas was not got rid of" (pp. 101–102). From my own perspective, the reason Emmy was still susceptible to falling ill was that her need to maintain the dissociative structure of her mind was her way of protecting herself against trauma that had already occurred: a protection against the future by plundering her life as if it were nothing but a replica of the past. In this context, her "illness" was a foreclosure of the "here-and-now" on behalf of the "there-and-then," effectively preventing her from living life with spontaneity, pleasure, or immediacy. To understand why Emmy's cure was not a lasting one is also to understand that we do not treat patients such as Emmy to cure them of something that was done to them in the past; rather, we are trying to cure them of what they still do to themselves and to others in order to *cope* with what was done to them in the past. As both Breuer[7] and Freud discovered, each in his own way, this is at times a messy undertaking (see also Bromberg 1991, 1995a), and were Freud alive today, it would probably not be difficult for him to appreciate the wry humor in the contemporary quip that "psychoanalysis is a good profession for someone who wants to do something dangerous without leaving the office."

REFERENCES

Appignanesi, L. and Forrester, J. (1992). *Freud's Women*. New York: Basic Books.
Baars, B. J. (1992). Divided consciousness or divided self. *Consciousness and Cognition* 1:59–60.
Berman, E. (1981). Multiple personality: psychoanalytic perspectives. *International Journal of Psycho-Analysis* 62:283–300.
Bliss, E. L. (1988). A reexamination of Freud's basic concepts from studies of multiple personality disorder. *Dissociation* 1:36–40.
Breuer, J. and Freud, S. (1893–1895). Studies on hysteria. *Standard Edition* 2.
Bromberg, P. M. (1991). On knowing one's patient inside out: the aesthetics of unconscious communication. In *Standing in the Spaces: Essays on Clinical Process, Trauma and Dissociation*, pp. 127–146. Hillsdale, NJ: The Analytic Press, 1998.
—— (1993). Shadow and substance: a relational perspective on clinical process. In *Standing in the Spaces: Essays on Clinical Process, Trauma and Dissociation*, pp. 165–187. Hillsdale, NJ: The Analytic Press, 1998.
—— (1994). "Speak!, that I may see you": some reflections on dissociation, reality, and psychoanalytic listening. In *Standing in the Spaces: Essays on Clinical Process, Trauma and Dissociation*, pp. 241–266. Hillsdale, NJ: The Analytic Press, 1998.

---

7. Hirschmüller (1978) comments that "if Breuer did not in fact treat any more patients by means of the cathartic method, one factor instrumental in bringing this about was probably the fact that he did not wish to become involved in any more doctor–patient relationships with such deep emotional content" (p. 202).

—— (1995a). A rose by any other name: commentary on Lerner's "Treatment issues in a case of possible multiple personality disorder." *Psychoanalytic Psychology* 12:143–149.

—— (1995b). Resistance, object-usage, and human relatedness. In *Standing in the Spaces: Essays on Clinical Process, Trauma and Dissociation*, pp. 205–222. Hillsdale, NJ: The Analytic Press, 1998.

—— (1995c). Psychoanalysis, dissociation, and personality organization. *Psychoanalytic Dialogues*, 5:511–528. In *Standing in the Spaces: Essays on Clinical Process, Trauma and Dissociation*, pp. 189–204. Hillsdale, NJ: The Analytic Press, 1998.

Bruner, J. (1990). *Acts of Meaning.* Cambridge, MA: Harvard University Press.

Ellenberger, H. F. (1977). L'histoire de 'Emmy von N.' *L'Évolution Psychiatrique* 42:519–540.

Freud, S. (1895). Project for a scientific psychology. *Standard Edition* 1:295–397.

—— (1900). The interpretation of dreams. *Standard Edition* 4/5:1–626.

—— (1910). Five lectures on psycho-analysis. *Standard Edition* 11:9–55.

Friedman, L. (1994). The objective truth controversy: how does it affect tomorrow's analysts? *International Federation of Psychoanalytic Education Newsletter* 3:7–14.

Goldberg, P. (1995). "Successful" dissociation, pseudovitality, and inauthentic use of the senses. *Psychoanalytic Dialogues* 5:493–510.

Guntrip, H.J.S. (1971). *Psychoanalytic Theory, Therapy, and the Self.* New York: Basic Books.

Hirschmüller, A. (1978). *The Life and Work of Josef Breuer.* New York: New York University Press.

Laing, R. D. (1962). *The Self and Others.* Chicago, IL: Quadrangle.

Lionells, M. (1986). A reevaluation of hysterical relatedness. *Contemporary Psychoanalysis* 22:570–597.

Loewenstein, R. J. and Ross, D. R. (1992). Multiple personality and psychoanalysis: an introduction. *Psychoanalytic Inquiry* 12:3–48.

Putnam, F. (1988). The switch process in multiple personality disorder and other state-change disorders. *Dissociation* 1:24–32.

Reik, T. (1936). *Surprise and the Psychoanalyst.* London: Kegan Paul.

Rivera, M. (1989). Linking the psychological and the social: feminism, poststructuralism, and multiple personality. *Dissociation* 2:24–31.

Sullivan, H. S. (1953). *The Interpersonal Theory of Psychiatry.* New York: Norton.

Winnicott, D. W. (1949). Mind and its relation to the psyche-soma. In *Collected Papers: Through Paediatrics to Psycho-Analysis,* pp. 243–254. London: Tavistock, 1958.

6

The Case History in Historical Perspective: Nanette Leroux and Emmy von N.

Jan Goldstein

In order to place Freud and Breuer's (1893–95) *fin-de-siècle* case studies of hysteria in historical perspective, this paper will attempt a loose comparison of Emmy von N. with a French case from the 1820s, one that bears the intriguing title "Observations of Nanette Leroux: Hysteria Complicated by Ecstasy."[1] I should confess at the outset that I chose this particular case for the wrong reasons—not after a thorough canvass of the competing possibilities and a weighing of their pros and cons, but because I stumbled upon it in manuscript in a Paris archive in the winter of 1989 and decided to microfilm it. Thus preserved, it lay untouched in my desk drawer for some five years, until the invitation to participate in the conference gave me the incentive to unearth, transcribe, and begin to interpret it.

My initial decision to microfilm the manuscript was not, of course, entirely arbitrary. As far as I can tell, the Leroux case is terra incognita: not only was it never published, it was never so much as reported in the French psychiatric literature. Even more significant is its length; it fills three notebooks and runs to nearly 150 manuscript pages. Although I have not systematically traced the development of the psychiatric case study as a genre, years of working with the French materials have given me an unmistakable impression of the overall developmental pattern. The case study began around 1800 with the "little stories" (*historiettes*) of Philippe Pinel, the founding father, occupying no more than a printed page.[2] Over the course of the nineteenth century it grew

---

1. "Observation Nanette Leroux: Hystérie compliquée d'extase." My examination of the manuscript for purposes of this article convinced me of its importance not only as a document in the history of psychiatry but also as a rich slice of early nineteenth-century European social life. I am currently preparing an English translation of the text and an extensive introduction to it that will be published as a book by Princeton University Press.

2. Pinel called his case studies "little stories (*historiettes*) [that are] the true results of observation"; see Pinel 1801, pp. 228, 231–232, and my discussion of Pinel's clinical method in Goldstein 1987, pp. 80–105.

steadily in length, artfulness, and narrative complexity, making the
Freudian version far more a culmination than a sharp rupture or
an appearance out of nowhere. Thus in 1887 one French psychiatrist noted with a touch of surprise that his protracted account of a
certain patient "savored of a novel," (Tissié 1887, p. 58) and another
remarked in the early 1890s that a full description of his patients
would more nearly approximate "a novel of manners and morals
than it would a clinical observation" (Janet 1894, 1:224–225).[3] In
this context the Leroux case caught my attention because of its
patently excessive length—excessive, that is, for its date of com-
position, the mid-1820s. I was interested in finding out why this
patient, described as a "peasant" (*paysanne*) or a "simple village girl"
(*simple villageoise*), inspired so much investment on the part of her
doctor that he departed from the scientific norms of his day and
lavished upon her a zeal for writing that even his most precocious
colleagues would not begin to display until sixty or seventy years
later.

In fact, length and intricacy of detail turned out to be only one
of the features that the Leroux case shares with the celebrated
Freud and Breuer cases. Other parallels include the use of hypnosis (here still called by its eighteenth-century name, animal magnetism) to treat hysteria, and the fact that two physicians, of whom
the younger is the more astute, take part in the case.[4] Unlike Freud
and Breuer, the two French physicians, Alexandre Bertrand and
Antoine Despine, were not exactly collaborators, nor did they even
live in the same city. The younger man, Bertrand, assumed the
actual task of writing the case study, using as his primary source
the journal of treatment kept by Despine. Thus part of the manu-

3. These comments are very similar in content and tone to the much-
quoted one that Freud would later make in the case of Elisabeth von R.:
"it still strikes me myself as strange that the case histories I write should
read like short stories. . . ." See Breuer and Freud 1893–1895, p. 160.

4. Although Emmy von N. is Freud's case, Breuer nonetheless figures
in it peripherally as another physician with whom the patient was acquainted and who helped her to break off treatment with Freud's prede-
cessor; see Breuer and Freud 1893–1895, pp. 54–55, 77.

script is in Bertrand's energetic hand, larded with the cross-outs and inserts that convey the self-critical and self-corrective activity of a mind at work; other parts are verbatim transcriptions of selected passages from Despine's journal, and these generally appear in the more regular, mechanical hands of secretaries. It is doubtful that Bertrand ever saw Nanette Leroux in the flesh (a situation that parallels Freud's sight-unseen analyses of little Hans and the German judge Schreber). There must have been considerable friendly rapport between Bertrand and Despine for the latter to have entrusted his case notes to the former. Yet the Bertrand who emerges in the manuscript is almost invariably critical of Despine's interpretations, so that in telling the story of Nanette Leroux's illness, he turns it into a curious polyphony of conflicting authorial voices. Bertrand's layered narrative is oddly similar to the one that Freud would eventually achieve in his cases, although the Frenchman's layering effect comes from the conscious scientific dispute between the two doctor-authors rather than from the intra- and inter-psychic conflicts of patient and analyst.

A sociological dimension of the disparity between the perspectives of Bertrand and Despine should be underscored: the former was very much the big-city doctor and savant, the latter very much the provincial. The recipient of a medical degree from the Paris Faculty of Medicine, Bertrand hobnobbed with some of the most important intellectuals in the capital, men like the future Prime Minister François Guizot. During the 1820s, he wrote for Guizot's encyclopedia an article (Bertrand 1826b) on "ecstasy"—a term that figures in his title for the Leroux case and a concept that was, as we will see, so closely identified with his scientific position as to be his virtual signature. Eighteen years Bertrand's senior, Despine had little contact with the glamorous life of the French capital. Born in the Alpine region of Savoy (which was incorporated into France from 1792–1815 and again after 1860 but was an independent duchy during the period covered by this case), he took his medical degree at Montpellier. Returning home, he followed in his father's footsteps by entering the medical administration of the state-run thermal baths at Aix-les-Bains. What drew Bertrand and Despine together was their passionate interest in animal magnetism as well as Despine's sense of his own intellectual limitations, which led him to seek out a more sophisticated and theoretically minded colleague to convert his voluminous case notes into coherent narratives.[5] Despine may not, however, have realized that his appointed ghostwriter had views on animal magnetism far less conventional than his own. As Bertrand wrote in the preface to a book on which he was working at about the same time as the Leroux case: "I find myself in a rather singular position with respect to both the adversaries and the partisans of animal magnetism. While among the adversaries I pass for a believer of the most exaggerated sort, in the eyes of the partisans I am nothing but a heretic, a hundred times more blameworthy than the most inveterate unbeliever" (Bertrand 1826a, p. i).

Before turning to an analysis of the Leroux case, a plot summary is in order. Nanette Leroux was an 18-year-old Savoyard village girl, "red-haired, freckled, bright-eyed." She had received an education a bit above her social stature, having spent a year with the nuns learning to read and write. Her health had always been sound until the summer of 1823, when she fell ill with a variety of nervous symptoms, including convulsions, lethargy, and the statue-like immobility known as hysterical catalepsy.

---

5. Some of the story behind the manuscript is told by Despine in the introduction to an omnibus work that he published late in his life. Despine depicts himself as a practitioner in need of a ghostwriter, or at least a more conceptually minded collaborator, who could impose order on the mass of observations that he had collected during a long career of treating nervous ailments in Aix-les-Bains by means of magnetism and hydrotherapy. After approaching a number of physicians in such urban centers as Paris, Lyons, and Geneva, he finally found his man in Alexandre Bertrand. Accordingly, he sent him the "totality of my notes," which Bertrand planned to use "in a large work devoted to the comparative study of catalepsy, ecstasy, magnetism and various kinds of somnambulism." Six volumes of this magnum opus were planned, but Bertrand died suddenly and prematurely before any could be published. Despine "subsequently offered these same materials to other physicians that I knew were involved in magnetism, but these gentlemen failed to respond to my appeal" (Despine 1840, pp. xliii-xlv).

There was no mystery in Nanette's mind about the precipitating cause of her illness, and her doctors were inclined to agree with her assessment of the matter. As Bertrand puts it (ms. pp. 1/143–2/144), "the patient attributed the onset of her malady, not without reason, to the repeated frights caused her by an evil person, a field warden (*garde champêtre*), who on several occasions subjected her to indecent exposure."[6] Medical personnel were not called until November, when a local practitioner, Dr. Vidal, prescribed a "calming potion." By this time the patient believed herself in such grave danger that a priest was also summoned to hear her confession and administer extreme unction. Nanette did not, however, die. Instead, her malady persisted and, in the protean manner of hysteria, continued to generate new symptoms, most notably at this point loss of the capacity to speak and episodes of the *transport des sens*, a migration of sensory capability from the organs in which it is physiologically grounded to other parts of the body.

The first therapeutic breakthrough occurred in January 1824 and was due to the interventions not of Dr. Vidal but of a layman in the household named Mailland. ("This Mailland," Bertrand informs us with anticipatory excitement upon first introducing him, "is going to play a major role in the history of our ecstatic" [ms. p. 4/146].) As Bertrand tells it, Mailland so succeeded in "reassur-

---

6. Two terms in this passage require explication. A *garde champêtre*, which I have here translated as field warden, was a government-appointed rural policeman entrusted with protecting agricultural property, especially pastures and harvested crops. The French original describes the warden's action by saying that he had wanted to "attenter à sa pudeur." *Attentat à la pudeur*, literally an offense against (or attack on) modesty, is a technical legal term employed in the Napoleonic Code. It is, however, ambiguous in its referent, covering a range of sexual acts, from exhibitionism at one end of the spectrum to attempted rape at the other. While textual evidence in the manuscript seems to support the view that the *attentat* to which Nanette was subjected was of the milder sort—and hence I have translated *attentat à la pudeur* as indecent exposure—we can never be sure of the precise nature of the policeman's impropriety, save for the fact that it fell short of rape.

ing" the patient simply "by the force of his homespun, folksy eloquence" that her speech came back. But the cure proved ephemeral, and at the beginning of March 1824, Dr. Despine visited the
patient. Finding Nanette in the throes both of mutism and the *transport des sens*—he spoke to her through the nape of her neck and
she replied in sign language—Despine wasted no time in advising
that she be brought to his establishment in Aix-les-Bains for a bat-
tery of therapies, including baths, showers and electro-magnetism.
Upon receiving her first hot bath at Aix a week later, Nanette manifested the *transport des sens* in florid form: "Her ears lost their capacity to hear and that sense moved successively to her elbows,
breasts, abdomen and fingertips" (ms. p. 7/142). Nanette would
experience the *transport des sens* repeatedly, and its bizarre anatomical displacements give rise to poetic turns of phrase in the text
of the case study—for example, "They tried in vain to make the
patient hear them by touching her" (ms. p. 202).

For most of 1824, Nanette's life adhered to a distinct geographi-
cal and temporal pattern: periods of convalescence in her native
village, where she was supervised by Mailland, alternated with
periods of aggressive treatment at Aix. Her symptoms continued
to mutate. She began, for example, to issue prescriptions about what
she required in order to be cured, and when the designated items
or series of procedures—jokingly called "amulets" by her doctors—
were furnished, her condition momentarily improved.

The turning point in Nanette's case occurred in September 1824.
Announcing to Despine that "she no longer [had] anything to fear
from her illness," she was eventually cajoled by him into reporting the "strange" incident that had altered her "manner of being"
and definitively released her from her suffering. Two weeks before, while comfortably settled in a lukewarm bath that she had
drawn herself, she had placed a baton of Spanish wax (one of the
standard accoutrements of Despine's magnetic experiments) across
her lower abdomen and pubic area. She then took a drinking glass
and marched it over various parts of her body. When she placed
the glass, mouth down, like a cupping glass (*ventouse*) over the
nipple of her left breast, she experienced a kind of "overall shudder" (*frémissement universel*) accompanied by an "electric fire" that
passed through her insides (ms. p. 6/179). Once these violent

movements had subsided, she found her nervous ailments gone. From that day forth, she was happy, active, and hard-working. By Christmas, several suitors had declared their wish to marry Nanette. Some consulted Dr. Despine about the state of their prospective bride's health; he pronounced her fundamentally cured and fit for marriage as long as her husband treated her with "gentleness and consideration" (ms. p. 242).

Nanette was married in January 1825. The picture begins to darken just as Despine's journal, and the case study, close. Nanette, we are told, would not "long enjoy the health that she had with such difficulty recovered" (ms. p. 9/182). She became pregnant in July and by November was continually distraught and quarreling frequently with her husband; ominously, the *clou hystérique*—the hysterical pain that feels like a nail in the head—had reappeared.

In analyzing this case, it is important to distinguish the various levels of that analysis: what the participants thought was happening and what we, reading the text in light of Freudian and other theories, might surmise. Let me begin by teasing out the participants' views.

The striking fact is the general agreement of all the participants about the cause of Nanette's illness. The case study mentions the indecent exposure of the *garde champêtre* at least five times, each time in a different context. A fresh glimpse of the offender or an overheard account of the offense suffices to provoke a relapse in Nanette; and even after her recovery in the lukewarm bath, she acknowledges the "extreme repugnance" that she still feels whenever she sees a chestnut tree because "a chestnut grove was the scene of the event that first made her sick" (ms. p. 247). While the field warden incident might seem, in classical Freudian terms, to be the sexual trauma at the root of Nanette's hysteria, the participants do not construe it in that fashion. In the first place, the incident is always consciously available to Nanette; she does not have to struggle against repression in order to remember it, nor does she derive any therapeutic benefit from that remembrance—quite the contrary. Secondly, while the participants seem to assume the broadly traumatic nature of the incident, no one defines that trauma as sexual or speculates about the sexual feelings that it

may have elicited in this young Catholic virgin.[7] Instead, everyone seems to believe that Nanette simply felt "fright" (*frayeur*) when
the field warden exhibited his genitals to her, and that this "fright"
served as the pathogenic agent.[8]

Since the traumatic etiology of Nanette's hysteria was already
on the surface from the beginning, Despine (unlike Freud in the
1890s) had no need to uncover it, and we can assume that he enlisted magnetism for other ends. If I have thus far refrained from
broaching the magnetic treatment of Nanette, that is because I have
been frankly daunted by its often weird paraphernalia and procedures: for example, rubbing the fur of an alley cat and channeling
the current to Nanette through a human chain made up of her
neighbors. But the Leroux case and the stake of the two principal
doctors in it are largely incomprehensible if the arcane intellectual world of early nineteenth-century French magnetism is ignored. Indeed the very prolixity of the case seems driven by the
singularly puzzling nature of magnetic phenomena in the 1820s
and by the two doctors' desire to amass and set forth as many data
as possible to explain those phenomena in a way philosophically
congenial to them. Despine and Bertrand had, moreover, opposite
philosophical allegiances, making the case that much more ver-
bose and producing the internal tension that runs through it.

Despine subscribed philosophically to the late eighteenth-
century tradition of Franz Anton Mesmer, who cured his patients

---

7. Nanette's virginity is, at least, assumed by the doctors in the case.
When Despine chats with her three months after her wedding, she as-
sures him (apparently in response to his pointed question) that "coitus
had no [adverse] effect on her, in terms of [reactivating] her nervous illness" (ms. p. 242). Implicit in Despine's report is his assumption that
sexual intercourse was a factor in Nanette's life only after she became a
married woman.

8. For use of the word *frayeur* in connection with Nanette's response
to the field warden's actions, see ms. p. 1/143 ("*frayeurs répétées* qui lui
avait causé un mauvais sujet, un garde champêtre"); ms. p. 5/147 ("dans
son délire elle répète toute la scène dont elle avait été *si effrayée*"); ms.
p. 30/172 verso ("ce fut par suite du récit qui fit aux assistans Mr Despine
le père *de la grande frayeur* qu'on regardait comme ayant été la cause
première de la maladie de cette fille"); my italics.

by seating them together around large tubs, or *baquets*, from which protruded metal rods, and the Marquis de Puységur, who staged his cures as bucolic pageants, with his peasants connected by a rope to a great magnetized elm near his chateau. Like Mesmer and Puységur, Despine believed that the therapeutic agent in these cures was a physical one: an invisible magnetic fluid emanating from an external source that worked upon the complement of magnetic fluid in the patient's body, redistributing it so as to restore health. While Mesmer's technique required a crisis, or convulsion, in the patient, Puységur (and Despine) required only the gentler response of artificially provoked somnambulism; but for both Mesmer and Puységur, as well as the vast majority of their followers, the magnetic cure worked by palpably physical means.

Despine's physicalistic stance pervades the Leroux case. It can be seen, for example, in his avowal that his main scientific aim in bringing Nanette to Aix was to verify the hypothesis and experimental findings of a certain Dr. Petetin. In the 1820s, the late Lyonnais physician Petetin was well known among French magnetizers for having singled out the *transport des sens* as the hallmark of hysterical catalepsy. He had explained it as a compression of the nerves in the patient's sensory organs that squeezed the fluid contained in those nerves elsewhere, thus endowing unaccustomed body parts with transient sensory capacities.[9] Committed to the thesis of Petetin, Despine frequently measured Nanette's electrical properties, expecting to find them altered at times of nervous crisis. In fact, Despine tended to believe in the literal, flat-footed physicality of all the phenomena in the case. When Nanette, in a variation on the *transport des sens*, was viewing her interior organs and claimed, at Despine's prodding, to see worms in her intestines—five of them, to be exact, all whitish in color and the fifth with a long yellow spot on its back—Despine noted wistfully, "Had the patient been obliged to stay with me a few days longer, I

---

9. The available neural pathways generally guided it to such loci as the epigastrium, fingertips, and toes; hence the prominence of those body parts in manifestations of the symptom. On the theories of Jacques-Henri-Désiré Petetin (1744–1808), see Petetin 1787, Petetin 1805, Petroz 1813, Virey 1818, pp. 499–501, and Shorter 1992, pp. 137–139.

would have administered a purgative agent to her in order to [ex-pel the worms] and verify the fact"[10] (ms. p. 8/190 verso). Simi-larly, when Nanette described her self-administered cure in the lukewarm bath, complete with its phallic baton and orgasmic shudder, Despine, trying to understand why the cure had worked, pressed her to tell him the precise temperature of the bath water![11]

Despine's title for the case, "History of the *Catalepsy* of Nanette Roux of Trévigny" (ms. p. 248, my italics), underscores the cen-trality for him of the diagnostic category catalepsy and of Petetin's gloss on it. Bertrand's alteration of the title, replacing "catalepsy" with "ecstasy," likewise betrays *his* theoretical leanings. Indeed the first time that Bertrand speaks in the first person in this case, and thus inserts himself into the proceedings as something more than a scribe, is when he introduces the term "ecstasy" (ms. p. 8/150).[12]

As his published writings indicate, Bertrand (1826b) regarded ecstasy as synonymous with, and a preferable label for, the state identified by magnetizers as somnambulism. He was well aware that he had chosen an attention-getting term. Derived from Greek roots meaning the state of being outside oneself, ecstasy had long been associated in the Christian tradition with such intense spiri-tual experiences as divine inspiration and mystical union with a transcendent object. Bertrand wanted to exploit the term's religious connotations to argue for the compatibility of science and religion. He took ecstasy to refer, all-inclusively, to the whole gamut of experiences of "being outside oneself," whether joyous or not, whether or not perceived by the person involved as having a reli-

---

10. On this same page of the manuscript, Nanette describes the phe-nomenology of viewing one's insides. "Asked if she saw herself illumi-nated from behind by lights, she replied in the negative, saying that she saw herself as one sees in broad daylight when the sun is hidden behind clouds."

11. Ms. p. 241: "J'ai insisté pour savoir ce qui s'est passé dans ce bain, sa température, enfin toutes les circonstances concomitantes."

12. Despine's case notes here discuss a technique of hydrotherapy called the Scottish shower, which left Nanette in a state of weakness, or as Bertrand puts it, "a nervous condition designated by Monsieur Despine by the name lethargy (and which *for me* is only a modification of the state of ecstasy)"; my italics.

gious significance. In making ecstasy a medical category, he intended to affirm simultaneously, first, the subjective authenticity of ecstatic phenomena, second, any religious meaning that the ecstatic might impute to them, and, finally, their completely naturalistic underpinnings.

For Bertrand (1823, pp. 462–482), the ecstatic/somnambulic condition of being outside oneself was a point along the continuum of states of human consciousness. Employing the typology of the French physiologist Xavier Bichat (Bichat 1800, Haigh 1984, ch. 6), he laid out a series of correspondences. Death corresponded to the brute material aspect of our being, to that which we share with inert objects. Sleep corresponded to the continuous "organic" or "interior life" of circulation, respiration, digestion, and the like that sustains us as living beings. Wakefulness corresponded to the "animal life" that we carry on by fits and starts in perceptual relation to the external world. Now ecstasy was an intermediate conditon between sleep and wakefulness. It consisted in a radically heightened awareness of all the movements and rhythms of our internal organs, of perception trained not outward (the ordinary mode of animal life) but upon the organic life. The inward-turning, corporeal hypersensitivity of ecstasy explained the ecstatic's sense of being in an altered state. It also explained the unusual abilities these individuals demonstrated: to view their internal organs, to predict the vicissitudes of their health, to prescribe appropriate remedies for their own intractable diseases. Paradoxically, then, the total corporeal absorption of ecstasy, which cut the ecstatic off from the external perceptual field, made possible in persons with a religious sensibility a connection with the transcendent. Bertrand stressed repeatedly that entrance into ecstasy or somnambulism was achieved by mental rather than physical means. That is to say, he denied the efficacy of a putative magnetic fluid to bring about this change and placed the causal burden solely on the mental state of the somnambulist. In sum, ecstasy stood both for Bertrand's belief in the harmony of religion and science *and* for the power of psyche over soma.

Hence Bertrand's interjections into the narrative of the Leroux case were for the most part argumentative attempts to correct Despine's physicalistic view of magnetism and to assert a mentalist alternative. Take, for example, his comments about the acoustical phenomenon, a term coined by Despine to refer to Nanette's ability to hear, even through walls and closed doors, certain barely audible sounds. Despine considered the acoustical phenomenon "entirely physical," dependent upon the patient's "exquisite sensibility." Bertrand rejoined (ms. p. 10/152) that "what we have here is, in a word, a purely psychological phenomenon, whose cause ought not be sought outside the patient herself." Later he added sardonically: "I am making use here of the term [acoustical phenomenon] employed by Monsieur Despine although I am persuaded that there is nothing at all 'acoustical' in this whole business and that the ideas of the patient as influenced by the people surrounding her played an almost exclusive role."

Bertrand made similar anti-physicalist comments about the nature of Nanette's strong attachment to Mailland. At numerous points in the case, Nanette is loath to quit the company of this middle-aged man whom she calls by the pet name *mon petit* ("my little one"). Most poignant are those scenes in which, at her express entreaty, Mailland touches her left breast to alleviate her symptoms; but even after the therapeutic work has been accomplished, she wants the intimate contact to continue and refuses to allow him to remove his hand. Sometimes she attaches herself to Mailland's father, whom she calls, continuing her reversal of generational chronology, *le petit du petit* ("the little one's little one") ms. p. 21/163 verso). At one point she obliges the old man to sleep in her room and prevents him from leaving in the early morning to attend to his tasks. "The partisans of animal magnetism," Bertrand writes disdainfully (ms. p. 21/163 verso), "will doubtless see in the need that Nanette felt for Mailland's presence the proof of a magnetic influence that he exercised over her." (Elsewhere in the text [ms. p. 24/166] he wryly opines that the magnetizers would no doubt explain her attachment to both Mailland *père* and *fils* in terms of the similarities in "organization"—that is, physiology—of two men so closely tied by heredity.) But, Bertrand continues, not only were Despine's attempts to test Nanette's electrical properties in the proximity of Mailland inconclusive, Nanette's own statements were "completely unfavorable to this way of seeing." Nanette repeatedly said that she needed Mailland around so that she could confide in him the "curative recipes" that she was devising for her own condition. As Bertrand quotes her directly, "'When Mailland is near me, he asks me what will relieve me, and then I don't suffer as much or for as long a time'" (ms. p. 174 verso).

Bertrand's jabs at a physicalist interpretation of magnetic and ecstatic phenomena and his proposals for an alternate interpretation employ a range of vocabulary. At times he designates the phenomena in question as "psychological" and at other times traces them to Nanette's "ideas" or to her "imagination." The overarching concept that seems to join these terms for Bertrand is *confiance*: "confidence" or "trust." The powers over the patient attributed by magnetizers to fluid are for Bertrand acquired by the patient *over herself*, though in a mediated and disclaimed fashion, through her trust in some thing or person; and that sentiment of trust can so act on her physiology as to move her across the threshold into ecstasy or modify her nervous symptoms.

Hence Bertrand chalks up to Nanette's *confiance* the two transitory cures carried out on her during the earliest phase of her illness. The first, already mentioned, was the reassuring "folksy eloquence" of Mailland, which restored Nanette's power of speech. In an important marginal note (ms. p. 4/146), Bertrand remarks that this cure was "produced by the *conviction* that this man communicated to her," susceptibility to the convictions of others being "a feature characteristic of [this] malady." Nanette is just as susceptible to the blandishments of a more opportunistic healer: a "country charlatan" or "village Asclepius" who (probably for a fee) applied a blistering agent (*vésicatoire*) to all the places on her body where muscular palpitations had occurred. His remedy, though "absurd" and painful, nonetheless eradicated her symptoms for over two weeks simply because, according to Bertrand (ms. p. 5/147), the healer had inspired "confidence" in Nanette. Bertrand makes the same point when discussing the singular efficacy to improve Nanette's condition exhibited by her so-called amulets. "These [cures] are the effects of *confiance*"—here Nanette's confidence in techniques of her own devising—"effects that are very powerful and, I will volunteer, infallible where ecstatics are concerned" (ms. p. 30/172 verso).

The Leroux case thus functions as a textual battleground on which Bertrand's psychologistic assumptions confront Despine's physicalistic ones. In fact, Bertrand may even have taken on the task of writing up Despine's case notes just to demonstrate that his colleague's data could be marshalled in support of the opposing explanatory thesis. While Bertrand's mode of explanation, with its emphasis on and respect for the subjective experience of the patient, may seem to prefigure Freud's, the two positions bore radically different meanings within their respective historical milieux. Freud saw the kind of psychological interpretation that he advanced as antithetical to religious interpretation; in the course of elaborating his psychoanalytic theory, he attacked the religious worldview as if the eighteenth-century Enlightenment had never occurred. Bertrand, by contrast, intended his insistence on psychological causation as a corrective to the Enlightenment and as a gesture friendly to religion. He wanted to draw from the healing power of *confiance* a lesson about the health-giving nature of traditional Christianity as well as its compatibility with a posture of scientific rigor. As he wrote in the preface to one of his published works, "the discovery of the beneficent effects, of the regular and almost constant effects on man of hope, *of faith in a salutary power*, . . . is equivalent to the discovery of an entirely new truth" (1826a, p. xxix, my italics).

In the 1820s, when the memory of the upheavals of the 1789 Revolution colored everything in France, Bertrand's position on the power of psyche over soma would not be read by his contemporaries as a stance in favor of the psychotherapeutics of empathy. It would instead be read as a way to integrate science into a nonrevolutionary politics, one that steered a safe course between anticlericalism and Catholic orthodoxy, between excesses of liberty and authority. Hence the importance of Bertrand's friendship with the future prime minister Guizot. It is easy to understand why Guizot, who in the 1830s and 1840s would become the most important architect of the middle-of-the-road political position he called the *juste milieu*, found a congenial spirit in Bertrand, the medical architect of ecstasy.

But the data amassed by Despine and narratively ordered by Bertrand can, of course, also allow us to draw our own conclusions about what occurred in the Leroux case. Let me cite some of my tentative conclusions, which are variously of a historical, anthropological, and psychological nature.

CULTURAL BLUEPRINTS FOR MENTAL ILLNESS

From our late twentieth-century vantage point, many of Nanette's symptoms, especially the *transport des sens* and the capacity to view one's own interior organs, seem extremely unusual, to say the least. Yet the case makes clear that appropriately trained contemporaries were quite familiar with these symptoms and took them in their stride. The role of Dr. Vidal, the first physician to see Nanette, stands out in this regard. Although he initially functioned with respect to Nanette as an ordinary country doctor, Vidal in fact had a close working relationship with the specialist Despine as well as a post on the medical staff of the thermal baths. It was he who brought Despine into the case, and when Nanette went to Aix, he went with her, collaborating with Despine on his various treatments and experiments. Hence it is significant that Nanette first exhibited the *transport des sens* in the presence of the knowledgeable Vidal (who, we are told, promptly "recognized" it), and that her manifestations of that symptom intensified in the presence of the still more knowledgeable Despine. Through their expectation that they would see such "standard" symptomatology, Vidal and Despine probably subtly elicited it from their patient.[13] As the

---

13. Indeed Despine's establishment at Aix-les-Bains may have served as a hatchery for this array of symptoms. We know from the manuscript that Despine brought Nanette into the company of Micheline, another so-called cataleptic under his care, and that he was in the habit of subjecting the two young peasant girls, individually, to the same experiments. Interestingly, Bertrand made a similar point about the large number of cataleptics treated by Petetin. "Two things in the works of Petetin are surprising even to those who do not call into doubt the reality of his singular experiments. One might wonder: (1) how it happened that he had occasion to encounter, in his practice alone, eight patients afflicted with a malady as rare as catalepsy; (2) how it happened that these eight persons all presented the incomprehensible phenomenon of the *transport des sens*." Bertrand goes on to answer his own question: Petetin "created around himself . . . an epidemic of catalepsy." He probably did not act singlehandedly but was aided by the existence in Lyon at the end of the eighteenth century of a magnetic treatment frequented daily by numerous patients who could propagate symptoms by "imitation" to other similarly nervous persons (Bertrand 1826, pp. 254–255).

ethnopsychiatrist George Devereux (1980, p. 37) has remarked,
"cultural preconceptions of 'how to act when insane'" help to determine the psychopathologies which proliferate in any given society. In other words, if you were a troubled Francophone peasant
girl in Restoration Savoy, the prevailing medical culture would
likely lead you to manifest your emotional distress by hearing with
your knees and seeing your intestines as if they were spread out
before you.

THE QUASI-PUBLIC NATURE OF MAGNETIC TREATMENT

One of the most striking features of the Leroux case, never remarked upon by Bertrand because he takes it so much for granted,
is the large number of spectators who generally congregate whenever Despine is at work on his hysteric[14]—a far cry from the private treatment that Freud and Breuer gave their patients.

That the Leroux case begins amidst a crowd of onlookers is
purely accidental: when Dr. Vidal first speaks to Nanette by means
of her fingertips, and she replies, the numerous spectators who
register their "astonishment" had come to her bedside because
Nanette's last moments were expected to be imminent. But as
Nanette embarks on the career of a nervous patient, 1820s style, a
crowd of onlookers invariably assembles even though she is no
longer considered on the verge of death. One such incident of
spectatorship is especially telling. When a completely immobile
Nanette is magnetized and induced to get up after a mere "two
passes," the speedy success produces "general astonishment in all
the people present." Yet, Despine suspects, this turn of events has
also disappointed the audience: "they would have wanted the spectacle to last a longer time" (ms. p. 29/171 verso). Thus Despine
observes that the spectators to these rituals of healing come at least
in part for the titillation and theatricality rather than with a sober
scientific curiosity or an exclusively benevolent wish to see the

---

14. In fact, Bertrand often uses the word "scene" in his narrative, a
theatrical metaphor that implicitly recognizes that the treatment is enacted or played out before an audience.

patient cured. That he makes this observation without a hint of indignation or protest indicates his full acceptance of the spectators as a fixed element on the landscape of healing.

The unquestioned public nature of the treatment of Nanette's nervous illness is no doubt a direct legacy of the public sessions around the mesmeric tub in the 1780s or, later, around Puységur's magnetized tree. The timing and meaning of the shift in the treatment of nervous illness from a public to a private venue needs to be investigated. Does the shift reflect a reconceptualization of such treatment from a practice akin to exorcism to one akin to confession? That is, communal witness to the priestly power of exorcising *objectively* evil spirits is entirely fitting, while privacy is necessary to protect the shamefully *personal* nature of the information revealed in the confessional and to demarcate individual spiritual growth as a distinct and privileged realm. Does the publicity of Nanette's illness function additionally as a kind of communal safety measure—for example, by ensuring that prospective suitors can, as they actually did, find out about the nervous health of a would-be spouse by consulting her physician?

THE PLACE OF SEXUALITY

From the vantage point of the late twentieth-century reader, the Leroux case seems curiously filled with sexual references that are not categorized as such. The text plunges us into a clinical world whose details readily lend themselves to Freudian interpretation, but the people invested with the interpretive power—that is, Despine and Bertrand—seem not to see what is, in our view at least, under their noses. Thus the field warden's exposing himself to Nanette in the chestnut grove inspires only "fright" in the nubile, inexperienced young woman. Thus, while immersed in the "famous bath," Nanette derives enormous relief from an orgasm-like shudder after she positions Despine's waxen stick on her pubic area and uses a glass to simulate a sucking action on her nipple; yet neither Bertrand nor Despine thinks to describe that shudder as orgasm-like.

What are we to make of these omissions, these peculiar silences? Perhaps, given their historical milieu and the scientific framework in which they are considering this case, the physicians Despine and Bertrand perceive most strongly the analogy of Nanette's shudder to the therapeutic convulsions at the mesmeric *baquet*. A Freudian explication of their worldview, on the other hand, would see them as stolid bourgeoisie repressing the plainly sexual significance of the episodes they recount. But in some ways this aspect of the Leroux case seems most amenable to a Foucauldian reading. To Despine and Bertrand's way of thinking, the sexual may simply be too ordinary, too quotidian, to possess the kind of hidden significance that can be revealed only by an exegetical operation, by a peeling off of layers of manifest meaning. Put differently, the early nineteenth-century rural world of Nanette Leroux and her doctors, as conjured up in the pages of this manuscript, may be the world that Foucault (1978) has told us we have lost: the world before sexuality was invented as a discursive category and posited as the concealed and underlying "truth" of human beings—the locus of authenticity about which they must be made to speak, thus generating the thick web of discourse that would both create and constrain them as subjects.[15]

WHAT WAS TROUBLING NANETTE LEROUX? OR GENDER DEFINITION AND THE ISSUE OF "REGULARITY"

The distinctive clinical feature of hysteria is its rapidly shifting physical symptoms coupled with the impossibility of pinning those symptoms to demonstrable physical lesions. Hence one of the standard ways of making sense of hysteria in the twentieth century, a way pioneered by Freud and later adopted by social historians, has been to view it as a somatic language that conveys in covert form what the patient cannot bring herself to say in the more readily decipherable language of words (Goldstein 1982, pp. 211–213). This approach to hysteria is bolstered by the fact that the disease frequently focuses on and interferes with the organs of verbal expres-

---

15. Foucault argues in this work that sexuality, in his particular sense of the term, was invented in the late nineteenth century and was given one of its purest expressions in the psychoanalytic theory of Freud.

sion: certainly that is true of the key symptom, the hysterical ball rising in the throat and threatening to suffocate the patient.[16] Coupled with these symbolic properties, the remarkable epidemiological flowering of hysteria among the female populations of nineteenth-century Western Europe and America suggests that the hysteric may not only be engaged in the simultaneous disguise-and-revelation of a personal message but may also be ambivalently protesting some of the shared features of women's lot. Does the Leroux case fit this model? Or put differently, what was troubling the Nanette Leroux?

Nanette's hysteria (like that of Emmy von N.) obviously entails the requisite blockage and deformation of verbal expression. Emmy's "clacking" has its counterpart not only in Nanette's bouts of mutism but in her periods of speaking in falsetto and in her occasional recourse to nonsense syllables. But what is Nanette "saying" by means of her symptoms?

Let me skip over the messages in the case that appear to be largely personal to Nanette and turn to one of a more general character. Typically for nineteenth-century physicians, Despine and Bertrand demonstrate an unflagging interest in Nanette's menstrual cycle, which they apparently regard as an infallible index of her state of health. The almost obsessive texture of this interest can be seen in the opening pages of the case, where we learn that Nanette menstruated for the first time at the age of 15½; that her periods have always been somewhat irregular; that she had good coloring, except for her pre-menstrual pallor; that her encounter with the *garde champêtre* immediately suppressed a period in progress; that her first consultation with Despine took place on the morning after she had begun to menstruate for the first time since the onset of her malady. And so on.

The French word for menstrual period is *règles*, which is also the word for "rules." To have one's menstrual period is to be *réglée* or, literally, regulated.[17] There is no overt indication that Nanette

---

16. Nanette had "frequently experienced the hysterical ball ever since the onset of her malady"; see ms. p. 5/147.

17. Freud, who evinces a passing interest in Emmy von N.'s menstrual cycle, also employs the language of regulation in discussing it. He re-

regarded the doctor's preoccupation with her menstrual cycle as intrusive, but the dynamics of the case make that point, I think, in veiled form. When Nanette, following the standard scenario for hysterical cataleptics, began to issue prescriptions about what would cure her, the first object she named was a small gold watch.[18] Nanette in other words announced with great flourish before her usual spectatorial entourage that she had to be the keeper of her own clock. And the French vocabulary for clocks is virtually identical to that for menstrual periods. At one point, Nanette succumbs to lethargy, and she tells Despine that her crisis was provoked by the fact that her watch had stopped. Despine then removes the watch, winds it and places the hour and minute hands on the correct numbers. Pronouncing the watch *réglée*—that is, regulated, in good order—he restores it to Nanette, who immediately wakes up, her attack of lethargy over (ms. p. 212). Despine surmises that Nanette had forgotten to wind the watch, that it had run out. The French word he employs for run out, *écoulée*, is a cognate of the word used for menstrual flow, as in another passage of the case: "Since her last trip, Nanette has felt very well. Her periods have flowed (*coulés*) rather abundantly" (ms. p. 240).

I would hazard that the regularity of her menstrual periods, as well the doctor's constant inquiry into them, represent to Nanette society's expectations of her. Indeed, to be *réglée* in French is also to have paid one's bill, to be squared away. As a lowborn young woman living in a rural setting in early nineteenth-century Europe, Nanette is supposed above all to be reliable and predictable in a

---

marks: "[Emmy's] period began again today after an interval of scarcely a fortnight. I promised to regulate this by hypnotic suggestion and, under hypnosis, set the interval at 28 days." Breuer and Freud, 1893–95, p. 57. Freud added a footnote (57n1) indicating that the suggestion was in fact carried out.

18. Indeed the watch was the only discrete object she named. The other "amulets" were complex sets of instructions—for example, take two five-franc pieces, place one on Nanette's left ear, the other on her right breast, and press forcefully on each; or separate an egg, putting the white in one bowl and the yolk in other, and then put a little of the white on Nanette's left breast, cook the rest and give it to her to eat.

procreative capacity; her biological cycle defines her social being. It is noteworthy in this regard that as soon as Nanette marries, Despine becomes just as fixated on the continued presence of her menstrual periods as he was previously fixated on their worrisome absence: "Nanette has been married for three months. She is not yet pregnant. Her periods have appeared at the usual times" (ms. p. 242).

That Nanette uses the conventions of cataleptic symptomatology to demand a watch of her own, surely speaks of her desire—articulated through the medium of symptom rather than in plain language—for some measure of autonomy, some freedom from society's demands on and close scrutiny of her biological performance, some self-regulation. (That this rebellious desire is also fraught with ambivalence is seen in her recourse to Dr. Despine to set the watch for her when she has failed to attend to it responsibly herself.) Indeed the whole story of Nanette's illness is in some sense a story of Nanette's self-regulation: after all it is she who announces to Despine that she has been cured, and she who engineers that cure by giving herself a bath and manipulating Despine's stick of Spanish wax and a cupping glass on her body. Perhaps not coincidentally, this reading of the case is in tune with Bertrand's theory of ecstasy/somnambulism: that all the phenomena in the case, whether pathological or therapeutic, occur neither as a result of some physical power of magnetic fluid nor of the charismatic power of another person over the patient, but through the emotions of the patient herself.

REFERENCES

Bertrand, A. (1823). *Traité du somnambulisme et des différentes modifications qu'il présente*. Paris: Dentu.
—— (1826a). *Du magnétisme animal en France et des jugemens qu'en ont portés les sociétés savantes*. Paris: J.-B. Baillière.
—— (1826b). Extase. *Encyclopédie progressive*: 337–392. Paris: Bureau de l'encyclopédie progressive.
Bichat, X. (1800). *Recherches physiologiques sur la vie et la mort*. Paris: Brosson.
Breuer, J. and Freud, S. (1893–1895). Studies on hysteria. *Standard Edition* 2:3–335.

Despine, A. (1840). *De l'emploi du magnétisme animal et des eaux minérales dans le traitement des maladies nerveuses.* Paris: Germer Baillière.

Devereux, G. (1980). *Basic Problems in Ethnopsychiatry.* Trans. B. M. Gulati and G. Devereux. Chicago, IL: University of Chicago Press.

Foucault, M. (1978). *The History of Sexuality, Volume 1: An Introduction.* Trans. R. Hurley. New York: Random House.

Goldstein, J. (1982). The hysteria diagnosis and the politics of anticlericalism in late nineteenth-century France. *Journal of Modern History* 54:209–239.

—— (1987). *Console and Classify: The French Psychiatric Profession in the Nineteenth Century.* New York and Cambridge, MA: Cambridge University Press.

Haigh, E. (1984). *Xavier Bichat and the Medical Theory of the Eighteenth Century.* London: Wellcome Institute for the History of Medicine.

Janet, P. (1894). *Etat mental des hystériques,* 2 vols. Paris: Rueff.

Petetin, J.-H.-D. (1787). *Mémoire sur la découverte des phenomènes que présentent la catalepsie et le somnambulisme.* n.p.

—— (1805). *Electricité animale, prouvée par la découverte des phénoménes physiques et moraux de la catalepsie hystérique.* Lyons: Bruyset and Buynaud.

Petroz, A. (1813). Catalepsie. *Dictionaire des sciences médicales,* 4:280–84. Paris: C.L.F. Panckoucke.

Pinel, P. (1801). *Traité médico-philosophique sur l'aliénation mentale, ou la manie.* Paris: Richard, Caille and Rivier.

Shorter, E. (1992). *From Paralysis to Fatigue: A History of Psychosomatic Illness in the Modern Era.* New York: Free Press.

Tissié, P. (1887). *Les aliénés voyageurs: Essai médico-psychologique.* Paris: O. Doin.

Virey, J. (1818). Magnétisme animal. *Dictionaire des sciences médicales,* 29:463–558. Paris: C.L.F. Panckoucke.

7

Falling into History: Freud's Case of Frau Emmy von N.

Michael S. Roth

I made it impossible for her to see any of these melancholy things again, not only by wiping out her memories of them in their *plastic* form but by removing her whole recollection of them, as though they had never been present in her mind.

Sigmund Freud, "The Case of Frau Emmy von N."

Studies on Hysteria (Breuer and Freud 1893–1895) is a curiously hybrid text. It belongs to the prehistory of psychoanalysis, and one of the interests it has for us is that in it we can see Freud in the process of breaking away from, even as he is nourished by a variety of influences: Meynert, Charcot, Breuer, and Bernheim, to name just a few. We can also see Freud staking out a terrain for psychoanalysis: the effects of the remembered past, mediated through desire, on the present.

The effects of the past that concerned Freud and Breuer were, of course, the symptoms of hysteria. Hysteric patients suffer mainly from reminiscences, they wrote, and their investigations in the 1890s were aimed at removing the potency of the past. Breuer and Freud were committed to the view that the reminiscences that caused hysterical suffering were historical in the sense that they were linked to actual past traumas in the patient's life. The affect associated with the past trauma provokes no balancing reaction, and it remains unacknowledged; the amnesia (or paramnesia) results from the force of that affect being dammed up. "The injured person's reaction to the trauma only exercises a completely cathartic effect if it is an *adequate* reaction," they wrote (p. 8). The past that continues to wound is the past that originally found no outlet. Denied an appropriate response, the ghost of past experience continues to haunt the hysteric: "*The ideas which have become pathological have persisted with such freshness and affective strength because they have been denied the normal wearing-away process by means of abreaction and reproduction in states of uninhibited association*" (p. 11, italicized in original).

In the whiggish histories usually written by partisans of psychoanalysis, *Studies on Hysteria* is read as Freud's recognition of the value of "uninhibited association" for coming to terms with the past, and especially of the role of sexuality in that past and our present relation to it. The uninhibited Freud, the conquistador as he liked to say, was ready to go where no one had gone before—or at least where very few doctors were willing to linger. Where abreaction was, there association would come to be. In the demonic accounts of Freud's nefarious effects on our century, *Studies on Hysteria* is read as the tale of the psychoanalyst's first learning to listen to his female patients, but also of his coming to ignore the realities of what they were telling him. According to this account, in *Studies on Hysteria* the patriarchal, authoritarian Freud was about to lose his nerve when confronted with the testimonies of women who were often the victims of male sexual violence.

The whiggish and demonic emplotments of the history of psychoanalysis neglect Freud's precursors in this terrain of release/ understanding through association, just as they simplify Freud's own reluctance to move onto what was for him frighteningly uncertain ground. Conquistadors are not supposed to be dragged into the new territory by the natives. But in Freud's case, the natives of neurosis were the ones who best knew the terrain of dammed desire, and he had to learn to follow them. But, like his patients, Freud was full of resistances. Doctors were not supposed to learn from their patients, they were supposed to *make them better.* The doctor was the scientist, the man of reason: his neurotic patient had to be brought onto *his* terrain, and it should be firm ground in contrast to the swamp of (feminine) hysterical desire. But who would conquer whom?

The case of Emmy von N. presents a complex Freud, neither hero nor villain, a theorist undecided about the relation of memory to real events, and a doctor not yet convinced that the "normal wearing-away process" is best achieved through a talking cure that allowed the patient to acknowledge the past as a way to escape its domination. When Freud began treating Fanny Moser (Emmy von N.'s real name) in 1889, he was intrigued by the possibility of simply removing the reminiscence that caused the hysterical suffering. Hypnosis, Freud had learned in France, could be used as an amnesic technique, a tool for removing the past from patients so that they could get on with their lives. Amnesic techniques gave the doctor enormous authority, the possibility of remaking the identity of the patient. But in order to become a real Freudian, Freud would have to dispense with the dream of removing the past in favor of a model of recollection, of constructing a past with which one could live.

In this paper I will discuss the school of forgetting against which Freud would define psychoanalysis. This school is most familiar to us as the group of researchers and clinicians around Charcot. Although Charcot and his colleagues at the Salpêtrière were locked in an intense rivalry with Bernheim and his students at Nancy, for Freud their use of hypnotism and suggestion linked them as a common temptation and as an Other against whom he would define himself. In the case of Emmy von N., Freud was still trying out his French lessons as he attempted to assume the authority of suggestion and to wield the power of erasing the past. In this case study we see him working through the French forgetters, as he began to make the problem of suggestion an issue for any attempt to make sense of the past, not just a tool for erasing it. This issue—how can we actively recover the past for the present without simply inventing the past?—would remain at the core of psychoanalysis and of modern historical thinking generally. It is not an issue that can be driven away through suggestion or through the attack on suggestion. Modern historical thinking and psychoanalysis acknowledge the problem of suggestion, which is a version of the problem of epistemological contamination: there is no pure place from which one can know the past. Though they acknowledge suggestion as a possibility, neither psychoanalysis nor historical thinking claims this possibility as a reason for embracing the position of the skeptic, of the person who would reduce insight to imitation, knowledge to persuasion. Whether the position of the skeptic is ultimately a hysterical position is a question beyond the scope of this essay.

For Charcot and his school, hysteria could often be traced back to a shock to the nervous system that disrupted subsequent memory. An original trauma continued to produce a psychic piercing, or a dynamic lesion of the nervous system, and could be healed through forgetting. A good example of this psychic piercing can be found in the strange case of Mme. D.'s hysterical amnesia, which was discussed by Charcot, Janet, and other physicians of the 1880s (Charcot 1892, P. Janet 1893, Souques 1892; cf. Roth 1996). Mme. D.

was told by a stranger that her husband had been killed on the job, and that she should prepare a bed, for they would soon be bringing back the body. Since the initial shock of this odd practical joke, she did not remember anything back to the previous July 14, nor did she seem to have any new memories. The trauma, when combined with a predisposition to hysteria, led to hysterical "retro-anterograde" amnesia. Charcot used the word *elaboration* to describe the process through which an idea or remembered event acquired hysterical potency over time. Through elaboration or autosuggestion the trauma accumulated force and became the root of the hysterical symptoms. Like hypnotic suggestion, elaboration was a process that took place in the brain but not one that involved any conscious awareness. In the case of Mme. D., the shock of hearing of her husband's death and then seeing him alive continued to block her capacity to remember (and thus to experience) any new events.

The concept of elaboration depended on a new and complex notion of the brain and of memory. An original event is remembered by the subject in ways that are independent of consciousness. The subject, or perhaps we can say "part of the subject," registers the event neurologically and its representation is stored in the brain. That stored event continues to have effects on the workings of the nervous system, even if the event itself cannot be recalled consciously by the subject. This process, of course, is very familiar (if still controversial) for us, but in the late nineteenth century the idea of memories having effects independently of consciousness was new and disturbing. Curiously, Charcot paid almost no attention to the significance of the stored event. The initial experience was treated as an electrical charge that continued to have consequences on the nervous system, not as an event that was cognitively or emotionally unbearable for the conscious subject.

He saw the phenomenon under what he imagined as controlled conditions in hypnosis. Under hypnotism, subjects are given access to a different set of memories from those they would recall in their normal personalities. This access can itself often be remembered, with the proper hypnotic suggestion, so as to integrate the different faculties of memory. In other words, once a forgotten event is remembered under hypnosis, it can often be opened to the normal faculties of recollection. Paradoxically, once it is part of these normal faculties of recollection, it can be forgotten—the normal wearing-away process, as Freud put it. Alternatively, that which happens during the hypnotic trance can, through suggestion, be closed off from remembrance in the normal state: "You will remember nothing of what has happened here after I awaken you."

These techniques were long familiar to mesmerists and more mainstream scientific investigators by the time Charcot announced his serious interest in hypnosis in 1882.[1] But when Charcot lent his prestige to the study of hypnosis and related states, it seemed to make new phenomena visible and old explanations suddenly worth taking seriously. Charcot took a narrow view of his subject, one that legitimated his own expertise. There was nothing mysterious about the phenomena, no invisible fluids or forces from the beyond. Hypnotism was a series of several "nervous states" that like the stages of hysteria, could be isolated and described in detail. As Anne Harrington (1988) notes, "Charcot manages, in one fell swoop, both to give an aura of medical respectability to a formerly shunned and suspect subject, and simultaneously to stake a clear claim to the medical profession's exclusive competency to deal with this subject" (p. 227). For him, hypnotism was an artificially created hysteria and thus could be used to investigate cases of the spontaneously generated disease. One of the ways the master did this was by hypnotizing female hysterics and suggesting to them that they mimic the symptoms of male hysterics. His best patients performed splendidly.

In the case of Mme. D., hypnosis proved very valuable indeed. First, it allowed Charcot (1892) to determine that the woman was indeed registering her experiences, even though she could not recall them:

> This woman, whom we have been able to hypnotize, rediscovers in her hypnotic sleep the memory of all the facts that have transpired until the present, and all these memories thus uncon-

---

1. Adam Crabtree (1994) regards Charcot's paper delivered to the Académie des Sciences on February 13, 1882 as decisive (Charcot 1882; cf. Carcot 1881).

sciously recorded are revived in hypnosis, associated, uninter-
rupted, so as to form a continuous course and as a second self,
but a latent, unconscious self, which strangely contrasts with the
official self with whose profound amnesia you are acquainted.
[p. 85]

Hypnosis thus revealed a second self that did not suffer the effects
of the trauma afflicting the patient's conscious self. The traumatic
idea, the false report of her husband's death, had acted as a form
of suggestion, cutting off a faculty of memory as did hypnotic sleep.
For Charcot, the nervous system of the traumatized subject functioned much like the nervous system of the hypnotized subject.
They were hysterical. The task for Charcot in the case of Mme. D.
was to use hypnotism to overcome the disjunction between the first
and second selves. Hypnosis functioned both as the sign of the
pathology and as the possibility of curing it. If the patient was
willing to follow the hypnotic suggestion to remember, then the
wound of the trauma could be healed.

But remembering, for Charcot, did not have any of the connotations of integrating the self or facing one's desires that it would
come to have in the twentieth century. Remembering was a behavior that Charcot wanted to promote, a behavior currently inhibited by a (probably degenerate) nervous system that had not
recovered from a shock, a trauma, it had received. Marcel Gauchet
(1992) has emphasized Charcot's indebtedness to the neurophysi-
ologists who by 1870 had established that "the totality of the nervous system can and should be analyzed in terms of unities similar
in structure and function; that is to say, in terms of sensori-motor
connections and reflex processes" (p. 65). The reflexive reactions
of a degenerate nervous system following a trauma leave it vulnerable to suggestion; that is one of the key reasons for the production of symptoms. Suggestion can be used to get the system back
on track.

From Pierre Janet's perspective, elaboration led to what he saw
as the root of hysteria: the dissociation—the breaking apart into
isolated fragments—of the personality. But how was the doctor to
provide the hysteric with renewed capacities for psychological synthesis? One of the chief obstacles was the now elaborated memory
of the trauma. Thus forgetting was essential to cure: "One of the
most precious discoveries of pathological psychology would be that

which would give us the certain means to provoke the forgetting of a specific psychological phenomenon" (Janet 1925, p. 404). Since Janet regarded the memory of the report of her husband's death as Mme. D.'s idée fixe, after some months of failing to get her to make it a conscious memory, he concentrated his efforts on "suppressing" it, or at least reducing its potency. The strength of the memory was such that it could not be removed, so Janet "modified" it by "transforming" the idea to make it less frightening. Instead of a stranger entering the house, during hypnosis Janet "modified his features" so that it was the psychologist himself who knocked at Mme. D.'s door! And instead of announcing the terrifying news, Janet's image said only: "Mme D., prepare a bed because I would like to sleep at your house in M." (Janet 1925, p. 146). Now when Mme. D. had the recurrent dream about the incident, it aroused much less emotion, thus allowing her personality to integrate the various segments of the past into her personal memory. Janet de-elaborates the memory and thus removes its potency. In Charcot's terms, by manipulating the image he destroys its ability to continue to affect the nervous system. The past is in the way. By changing the past, the psychologist opens the possibilities of new memory for Mme. D.: "In a word, after the disappearance of the obsessional idea (idée fixe), the unity of the spirit us reconstituted" (Janet 1925, p. 405).

The problem with hysterics, it seems, was that they neither remembered nor forgot. That is, they could not bring to mind consciously (by an act of will) the element in their past that disturbed them, or when they did so it was without any of the affect that seemed to have been linked to the memory. But the therapeutic task was not simply to help the patient forget or ignore the pathogenic past. Hypnotism was thought to be a way of giving the hysteric access to this past, but whatever happens during the hypnosis was often forgotten upon awakening. Thus only during hypnotism did some of Janet's patients feel connected with the past that otherwise haunted the present. As a result, a dependence on hypnotism and on the hypnotist often developed. Janet's patient Marceline would need to be hypnotized every two to three weeks (in secret, since her employers knew nothing about this) in order to avoid a relapse into a catatonic, anorectic state. Blanche Witt, a severely hysteric patient from the Salpêtrière, grew even more

dependent on her physician, Jules Janet: "Blanche will now speak
only to me, will be touched only by me. She does not pay any attention to the words addressed to her by the other people present"
(J. Janet 1888, p. 618). The hypno-psychologist might complain
about dependence (or *électivité*, as Jules Janet called the attraction
to the doctor), but this did not stop him from remaking the personality of his patient. In Blanche's case, he even named his
new creation!

> If I asked her what she thought of this new state [of hypnosis],
> she would tell me that she still feels herself to be Blanche Witt;
> but, on the other hand, she discovers a personality, inclinations,
> and properties so different that she has difficulty believing that
> she is still the same. She accepts, therefore, very willingly the
> name "Louise" that I propose that she take. [Janet 1888, p. 618]

Finding the right balance between memory and forgetting was
very difficult. Who would define what the balance should be? In
the case of the hysteric patient Irène, she remembered the *fact* of
her mother's death, but displayed none of the affect "appropriate"
to the event. But in this age of mediums and spiritist reconnections
with the dead, what *should* she have felt? How could the memory
be brought into relation with the emotions "proper" to it? In the
end, when Pierre Janet considered the great body of his own and
his colleagues' cases, he chose another solution. The final sentence
of his weighty *L'Etat Mental des Hystériques* (1911) runs as follows:
"In conclusion, the biggest favor that the doctor can do for an hysteric is to direct his mind"[2] (p. 618).

If some form of autosuggestion or hypnoid state is at the root
of hysteria, then a cure would be to replace the poisonous claim of
the traumatic past with the hygienic claim of the benign physician.
Suggestion through reason, or reason through suggestion, but if the
idea of reason includes the independence of mind, how can it be
achieved through suggestion? The replacement of *elaboration* by
the direction of the physician would not cure hysterics of their vulnerability to suggestion. Indeed the need for, demand for, suggestion was one of the byproducts of the treatment. Janet called this

---

2. "*En résumé, le meileur service que le médecin puisse rendre à un
hystérique, c'est de diriger son esprit.*"

the *passion somnambulique:* "The hysteric who awaits somnambulism resembles in many ways the morphine addict who awaits his shot, even though his anxiety has perhaps a more moral and less physical character" (P. Janet 1911, p. 429). Although Janet seemed uneasy at times with the power these patients were willing to give him, as he wondered what it said about "the dependence that exists naturally among people" (p. 423), he did not think through what it would mean to "cure" the hysteric of his or her need for suggestion, direction, or authority. After all, hysteria was an ancient illness perhaps always triggered by the power of suggestion, and hypnosis seemed to put this power into the (well scrubbed) hands of the physician. The authority was immense, but in the hands of a truly scientific doctor it need not be infallible, only self-correcting. Pontalis (1973) quotes Charcot as saying: "What one does one can always undo" (p. 236). Suggestion from the past was malignant; suggestion from the doctor as the voice of Reason and Progress was benign. Janet (P. Janet 1911) put the well-worn appeal to the weak predisposition of the patient in a new form: "some minds, more than others, have the need for perpetual imitation" (p. 479). The problem was a technical one. How could the physician be present enough for the hysteric in constant need of direction? "The true treatment of hysteria, Briquait said, is happiness. I have tried to understand what was this happiness that is proper to hysterics; it is, in my view, simplicity, almost the monotony of a simple existence that reduces the effort at adaptation" (p. 478). The monotony of a simple existence would mean that hysterics would have less need for suggestion; little variety would mean they could continue imitating the tried-and-true models provided by the physician. Reason, when imitated, created normality: this happiness that is proper to hysterics, what Freud called "common unhappiness."

In addition to Bernheim's hypnotic techniques, Charcot's and Janet's views on suggestion and hysteria had a decisive impact on Freud's understanding of the etiology of hysteria and of the possibilities for cure. Freud, like Charcot, was intensely concerned with the process through which a memory could become a psychological wound, that is, a trauma. In his early work (writings that precede, roughly, *The Interpretation of Dreams*) Freud strove to remove the memory's potency, not through forgetting, as Janet had done, but through the discharge of energy through a particular form of recollection. Freud came to develop psychoanalysis as a mode of interpretation that would create a past with which one could live. Psychoanalysis emerged out of mourning, out of the work that enables a person to detach him- or herself from the past even while retaining some (narrative) connection to it. The talking cure demands that one situate oneself (or one's desires) in relation to the past, not that one reconstruct the actual past in the present. The role of trauma has been of decisive significance in the history of psychoanalysis, and as Freud emerged from mourning for his father he also radically altered the place of childhood trauma in the theory of hysteria. This has led some writers to claim that Freud was fleeing from an insight into the persecution of (especially female) children, or that he was covering over his and his friend Fliess's gross incompetence, or that he was protecting his own abusive father. I shall not discuss these claims here, but I want to emphasize that Freud created psychoanalysis as a mode for connecting with and representing the past that has important affinities to mourning, in contradistinction to neurosis. He developed a hermeneutics of memory rather than a tool for some unmediated expression of the past (whatever that might be) that would pretend to get free of it. That is, Freud developed psychoanalysis as a way of using the past rather than revolting against it (see Roth 1987, 1995).

But in *Studies on Hysteria* psychoanalysis had yet to emerge, or rather its early modes of inquiry and application are in competition with other approaches to dynamic psychology. One of the most fascinating aspects of Freud's treatment of Emmy is his attempt to play the role of the powerful physician wielding the latest tool of science, hypnosis, to direct the mind of his patient, who happened to be one of the richest women in Europe. And when hypnosis didn't work, he fell back on overt command: "If you don't accept my explanation for your stomach pains by tomorrow, I will ask you to leave. You'll be on your own and in need of another doctor." The normally independent woman returned docile and submissive, we are told. Freud is clearly pleased with what he seems able to do (for a change), but he is also uncomfortable with the feeling, the illusion of power and authority. He is at best awkward in making his patient forget too much, and at worst irresponsible as he gives her a suggestion as a joke. Freud, who has great ambition for but little confidence in what he is doing, always feels about to be judged, perhaps dismissed by this "normally independent" and abnormally powerful woman. His authority, when he has it, is hysterical, a symptom of the patient's inability to live with the powers of the past. How to use this authority without merely producing new symptoms or acting out his own and the patient's fantasies?

Under hypnosis, Emmy describes scenes from her past, and after she does so, Freud removes the fear or the visions associated with them: "My therapy consists in wiping away these pictures [of frightening episodes from the past], so that she is no longer able to see them before her. To give support to my suggestion I stroked her several times over the eye" (p. 53). The therapy goes well as the patient "unburdens herself without being asked to. It is as though she had adopted my procedure and was making use of our conversation, apparently unconstrained and guided by chance, as a supplement to her hypnosis" (p.56). While in hypnotic sleep, she punctuates her stories of frightening memories with the "protective formula": "Keep still!—Don't say anything!—Don't touch me!" Emmy is afraid, she explains, that if her reminiscence is interrupted, then "everything would get confused and things would be even worse" (p. 56).

Freud listens to these stories and tries to piece together their significance. At the same time, he used the power of hypnotic suggestion to change the content of the memories that had given rise to the stories in the first place. Thus there is a deep tension in the case between Freud's aggressive use of his authority, through hypnosis, to change his patient's relation to her past, and his recognition that before the memory of the past can be successfully altered it has to be constructed in a conscious, possibly narrative form. "I cannot," Freud complains, "evade listening to her stories in every detail to the very end" (p. 61). This tension is most evident when Emmy complains about Freud's eagerness to erase her memories before she has had the chance to recount them for him: "Her answer, which she gave rather grudingly, was that she did not know. I requested her to remember by tomorrow. She then said in a definitely grumbling tone that I was not to keep on asking her where this and that came from, but to let her tell me what she had to say. I fell in with his, and she went on ..." (p. 63). In this passage we can see the conquistator stopped (at least for a moment) in his tracks. It is the patient who sets a limit, or at least a context, for his authority: "Let me speak these memories before you try to explain them or wipe them away with the tool of hypnotic suggestion. Fall in with me before you use that authority to which I am supposedly so susceptible." Freud describes himself not as giving definitive explanations nor as wiping away the past with the tool of hypnotic suggestion, but as "falling in" with the patient's chosen procedure [*Ich gehe daruf ein*]. Like Anna O. (at least in the stories told about her), Emmy teaches her doctor to listen.

By "falling in" with Emmy's stories, Freud was falling into psychoanalysis and falling away from Charcot, Bernheim, and the road taken from them by Janet. What is the significance of this fall, for psychoanalysis and for thinking about history generally?

The significance for psychoanalysis is well known, if still controversial. By falling in with the patient's stories, the analyst becomes part of a relationship, a component in a process in which he or she has only limited (albeit important) control. Freud certainly recognized the phenomenon that so impressed the Janets: patients make an enormous, sometimes bottomless, investment in the relationship to the doctor; they reproduce their illnesses in this relationship. But whereas this phenomenon contributed to therapeutic pessimism about the capacities of the hysteric to lead a normal life, it also became a therapeutic opportunity for the psychoanalyst. That is, the "need for suggestion" and the "perpetual imitation" evinced by patients within the therapeutic process was an exposure of the history of the illness, a revelation of the etiology of its symptoms, if only the analyst were prepared to read it properly. Freud would later understand this exposure through the concept of transference, and the psychoanalytic investigation of the therapeutic relationship itself as a tool for theory and treatment became one of the defining elements of this new approach to the mind and to mental illness.

The concept of the transference also describes the power of the analyst in treatment. This power is a function of the unconsciously repetitive elements of the transference itself. How to use this power without sinking patients further into the dynamic that is itself at the root of their problems? How to use one's authority to expose one's authority as neurotic? These questions were already apparent in *Studies on Hysteria* and would remain crucial for the criticism and defense of psychoanalysis as a clinical enterprise. By falling into Emmy's stories, Freud was falling into the domain demarcated by these questions.

Since Freud's time, psychiatrists and therapists have tried to escape this domain in two very general ways: (1) by denying they really have authority; (2) by denying that the basis of their authority is neurotic. Those who favor the first option often underline the *relational* aspects of the psychotherapeutic situation (as if these were not always present in Freud's work), apparently with the happy thought that by telling clients they are in an equal relationship they suddenly acquire equality. The power of suggestion obviously remains strong. The second option assumes that the legitimacy of the therapeutic practice (whether analytic, psychopharmacological, or both) somehow naturalizes and neutralizes the dependence that the client comes to have on the doctor (after all, so this reasoning goes, they *should* be dependent!). This was the route Janet himself took when he defined the kind of happiness appropriate to the hysteric and attempted to provide that kind of happiness. Since the dependence is on a reasonable person—a source of Reason and Progress—it is suddenly no longer a symptom.

The domain demarcated by the transference is dangerous ground on which to stand because it is always in danger of shifting under one's feet. As critics of psychotherapy regularly remind us, there is no firm (epistemologically clean) place to stand in this domain. The analysand makes multiple investments in the possibilities for insight through the analytic relationship, and doing so is part of the conflicted history that leads the person to desire change; yet doing so is also part of that history which in the present makes any change extremely difficult. The conflicted history of the person *is* the present, and any change that can occur must occur *through* that history. The French theorists of amnesiacs whom Freud was still trying to follow in the case of Emmy von N. were developing techniques that would remove the troublesome parts of the patient's history, or that would transform the reminiscences causing suffering in the present. They wanted to act on the person's contaminated past *from outside that past,* thereby protecting their intervention (and themselves) from contamination. In falling into Emmy's stories, Freud was falling into her history; there was no longer an intervention possible from a point outside it.

Freud's fall has been suggestive, if I may use that word, for theorists of history trying to understand the stories that are left to us from the past. Since the professionalization of history writing in the mid-nineteenth century, there has been an effort to ensure that historians stand outside of, or at a distance from, the events that they are attempting to explain or interpret. The standpoint of objectivity was to ensure that the authority of the historian was derived from established scientific criteria in the present, not from some personal, biased connection to the material from the past being described.

Recent theorists of history have called into question the picture of the neutral, disconnected historian relating past events from the outside. The point of this questioning is not that all interpretations of the past are equally valid, but that it is important to interpret the complex ways historians establish connections between their own present and the past they are bringing to it. Some of these connections can, as Dominck LaCapra (e.g., 1994) has stressed, be usefully described as transferential, since they facilitate the unconscious repetition of past patterns in the present. Historians re-present the past, and often in doing so also act out their unconscious or hidden investments in the objects of their research, which are often objects of complex longing and loathing. An acknowledgement of the transferential relations between historians and the pasts we construct enables us to attend to the processes of mediation and unconscious repetition that contribute to any historical representation.

By falling in with Emmy's stories, Freud was beginning to develop psychoanalysis as a form of historical consciousness that focused on the role of desire vis-à-vis the past. How does our relationship to a remembered past, or to the past that we imagine is inaccessible to us, serve particular desires in the present? And how does serving *those* desires make it impossible to serve others? These are questions Freud was already beginning to pose in *Studies on Hysteria*, and they would become crucial to the domain of psychoanalysis as a theoretical and clinical enterprise. I have argued in *The Ironist's Cage* (1995) that they are also central to the construction of history as a theoretical and practical enterprise. Historical representations attempt to satisfy or stimulate certain desires, and it is usually impossible for them to do so without denying others.

Recent controversies surrounding the commemorations of World War II provide many examples in this regard. But the retreat from the transferential, and attempts to have uncontroversial museum exhibits, cool detached histories, or neat little positive therapeutic experiences, are merely denials, not solutions, of the problem. One can hope to make the workings of transference in historical representation more apparent, but one cannot avoid this dynamic through some properly hygienic stance towards the past.

How does the remembered or imagined past draw one to it? How does the traumatic past compel our attention, care, or obsession even as it seems to demand acknowledgement that one can never comprehend what happened there? These questions are as important for psychoanalysts as they are for historians. The models of Charcot and Janet pointed in a different direction. They are alien to modern historical discourse and to psychoanalysis, because they are unconcerned with the investment that one has in the past. Charcot and Janet employ technologies of memory or forgetting but neither has conceptual space for the desire that one has for the past, a desire that results in an effort to link present and past narratively.

This conceptual space was what Fanny Moser opened up for Freud in the case of Emmy von N. It remains the space of modern historical consciousness, which understands freedom as the result of acknowledging one's past in a present containing possibilities for change. It is the space into which Freud was beginning to fall in *Studies on Hystera.*

REFERENCES

Breuer, J. and Freud, S. (1893–1895). Studies on hysteria. *Standard Edition* 2.

Bynum, W. F., Porter, R., and Shepherd, M., eds. (1988). Hysteria, hypnosis, and the lure of the invisible: the rise of new-mesmerism in *fin-de-siècle* French psychiatry. In *The Anatomy of Madness: Essays in the History of Psychiatry*, vol. III. London and New York: Routledge.

Charcot, J. M. (1881). *Contribution a l'étude de l'hypnotisme chez les hystériques.* Paris: Progrés médical.

—— (1882). Sur les divers états nerveux déterminé par l'hypnotisation chez les hystiques. *Comptes-rendus hebdomadaires de Séances de l'Acadamie des Sciences.*

—— (1892). Sur un cas d'amnésie rétro-antérograde: Probablement d'origine hysterique. *Revue de médecine.*

Crabtree, A. (1994). *From Mesmer to Freud: Magnetic Sleep and the Roots of Psychological Healing.* New Haven, CT: Yale University Press.

Gauchet, M. (1992). *L'Inconscient Cérébral.* Paris: Seuil.

Harrington, A. (1988). Hysteria, hypnosis, and the lure of the invisible: the rise of neo-mesmerism in fin-de-siècle French psychiatry. In *The Anatomy of Madness: Essays in the History of Psychiatiy.* London and New York: Routledge.

Janet, J. (1888). L'hystérie et l'hypnotisme, d'aprés la theorie de la double personnalité. *Revue Scientifique,* no. 20.

Janet, P. (1893). L'Amnesie continue. *Revue générale des sciences* (30 Mars).

—— (1911). *L'Etat Mental des Hystériques,* 2nd edition. Paris: Felix Alcan.

—— (1925). *Névroses et idées fixes: Etudes expérimentales sur les troubles de la volunté, de l'attention, de la memoire, sur les émotions, les idées obsedantes et leur traitement,* 4th edition. Paris: Felix Alcan.

LaCapra, D. (1994). *Representing the Holocaust: History, Theory, Trauma.* Ithaca, NY: Cornell University Press.

Pontalis, J.-B. (1973). Le Séjour de Freud a Paris. *Nouvelle Revue de psychanalyse,* 8.

Roth, M. S. (1987). *Psycho-Analysis As History: Negation and Freedom in Freud.* Ithaca, NY: Cornell University Press.

—— (1995). *The Ironist's Cage: Memory, Trauma and the Construction of History.* New York: Columbia University Press.

—— 1996. Hysterical remembering. *MODERNISM/modernity,* 3, no. 2.

Souques, A. (1892). Essai sur l'amnésie rétro-antérograde dans l'hysterie, les traumatismes cérébraux et l'alcoolisme chronique. *Revue de médecine.*

8

Eroticism and Representation: The Epistemology of Sex in Light of the Case of Frau Emmy von N.

David Schwartz

While historians of psychoanalytic thought will find much of interest in the details of the case of Frau Emmy von N. (Breuer and Freud 1893–1895), my own intent is to use this case as an early instance of a particular problem in contemporary psychoanalysis. The case of Emmy reveals a conflicted attitude toward what constitutes psychoanalytic knowledge. It is the very same epistemological conflict that I believe to be central to psychoanalysis' problems in the area that interests me most, that of sexuality. Therefore my discussion of Freud's case will serve to introduce my particular concern with sexuality.

The case of Frau Emmy von N. presents the reader with a quandary, for it contains two texts at odds with one another. The first text is a clinical one, in which Freud furnishes the details of his observations of Emmy and of his activities with her. Here, presenting himself as a psychological innovator, Freud shows us how it is possible to understand the patient's bizarre suffering by persistently uncovering the environmental traumata to which she was exposed.

In his description of the patient and of his therapeutic interventions, Freud implicitly replaces the old theories of neurological degeneracy and uterine mobility with a theory that takes the cause of the patient's misery—then labeled "hysteria"—to be external trauma mediated by ideation. Freud engages in an indefatigable pursuit of relations between events and their representations, Emmy's symptoms. The modernity and radical potential in psychoanalysis are evident as Freud begins a more general process of relocating the source of human suffering from the body to the mind. With painstaking empathy, Freud works with Emmy to reveal the sources of her strange behavior. He thus recognizes the immense power of representation in human life, the power that fantasies, attributions, images, and beliefs have in the process of making meaning of the events that befall us. Beyond this broad recognition and the display of his new clinical technique, Freud's offers few, if any, theoretical assertions.

A second text emerges in the last quarter of the case presentation. Freud's optimistic delight in the psychoanalytic method, his emphasis on psyche over soma, is subtly undermined as another mentality emerges. Freud now asserts that "Frau von N. was undoubtedly a personality with a severe neuropathic heredity [and that it] seems likely that there can be no hysteria apart from a disposition of this kind" (p. 102). In contrast to the psychological explanations offered until this point, which included Emmy's social isolation, her actual persecution by her malevolent in-laws, the large number of obligations she shouldered, her conscientiousness, and her status as a woman, Freud now underscores Emmy's "hereditary disposition, . . . her *natural* disposition" (p. 102, emphasis added). This is an attitude that appears to foreclose further clinical work.

In these last pages the aspects of Emmy that were not accounted for in the treatment—the disappointing transience of her cure, the impressively large number of traumatic events she retained as unconscious memories—are spoken of as if their mystery is understood: they flow from her essential nature, her "neuropathic heredity" (p. 102), something in her physical body. The picture of Emmy that Freud now paints is changed. Circumstances and life's actions are not sufficient to explain her and her illness; she also has an essential nature, reified and unarticulated, that accounts for who she is. She becomes part of a system of types, in which there are those who have the disposition, and those who do not. When Freud speaks of the hereditary disposition, the word *hysteria* is no longer just a shorthand way of naming a collection of like phenomena; it becomes the name of a naturally unified physiological condition, a knowable entity. Who Emmy is now includes, if it is not dominated by, her hysteria.

Of course it is hard to know how the reader of one hundred years ago experienced this shift in emphasis. To me, the effect is jarring and initially puzzling. The case that was sounding so modern, so psychological, and so *psychoanalytic,* suddenly sounds antiquated, like a Victorian medical text. The Freud who daringly and fruitfully intruded into the actualities of Emmy's life and social milieu, who painted a portrait of Emmy that was so respectful, even admiring, reassumes the position of the medical researcher, outside the patient, imagining a hypothetical structure within her: "a severe neuropathic heredity" (p.102).

This ending of Freud's narration of Emmy's treatment suggests that at precisely the point where he encountered the insufficiency of his knowledge, Freud leans on the presumption of such underlying essences to gain closure. He makes his bows to heredity just as he is acknowledging the transience of Emmy's cure.

To the extent that Freud's discursive shift was replicated in future psychoanalytic texts, the shape of psychoanalytic treatment and understanding was changed. No longer concerned only with its method and explaining particular symptoms and feelings, psychoanalysis also undertook to describe human nature, believing that such a thing can be known and conceiving itself as instrumental in knowing it.[1] Thus the case of Emmy provides us with an example of an important discursive move in psychoanalytic writing: a shift from viewing psychoanalysis as a therapeutic method interested in decoding and thereby understanding individual systems of representation, to viewing it as a way of gaining and deploying knowledge about the human species, its limitations, and its afflictions.[2] It moves from persistent questioning of the other and the self to reifying concepts and theorizing nature, sometimes importing such concepts from very unpsychoanalytic, or prepsychoanalytic disciplines. It goes from psyche and uncertainty to soma and science, from expanding complexity and detail to the condensation that categorization offers, and from Emmy's life to her hysterical body.

This discursive shift (which of course was more widespread than in just the Emmy case) may have provided fertile ground for various positivist tendencies in psychoanalysis that persist today.

---

1. I don't mean to imply here that there was a point in psychoanalytic history when psychoanalysis was purely concerned with promoting its method; I am employing a temporal metaphor to describe what I assume was relatively jagged oscillation between different epistemological emphases.

2. In calling this a shift I am referring to changes that may take place both within a given psychoanalytic text and across texts in psychoanalytic history.

Among the more important of these is the invasion of psycho-analysis' dialectical practice by theory in the way that Spence (1982) has described. In his or her zeal to see psychoanalytic theory about human nature illustrated (or perhaps in an anxious response to the inevitable uncertainties that arise in every analysis), an ana-lyst may feel pressured to "uncover" material and may even sug-gestively apply transferential influence to that end, albeit unwit-tingly; the "new material" makes him or her imagine that the theory has been confirmed. Worse still, the patient may be subtly pres-sured to collude.

A second, and related, consequence of this discursive move toward positivism, is the importation of concepts, especially body-related concepts, from other, usually more scientific disciplines as aces-in-the-hole when psychological explanation and analytic deconstruction are insufficiently satisfying. Instead of granting the necessity (or even value) of living with some ignorance, this prac-tice implies that biological explanations offer the real solutions and can explain away uncomfortable uncertainties.

The effect of shifting psychoanalytic discourse toward the dis-course of physical science may be to diminish the vigor of the ana-lytic dialectic: the frustrated analyst can attribute some of the in-trinsic inertia in the analytic situation to essential, and therefore unanalyzable, natures.

Explanation for the occurrence of the discursive compromise displayed in the case of Emmy undoubtedly lies in the interplay of several historical, political, and psychological forces (see Sullo-way [1983] for various possibilities). The explanation I would em-phasize is psychological. I wonder whether Freud did not begin to experience the anxiety that was destined to be associated with psy-choanalysis, the anxiety that accompanies uncertainty and the awareness of the limitations of our ability to know ourselves, to know or be known by an other; and whether this experience mo-tivated him to turn away from the innovative hermeneutic dis-course he was constructing and back toward the biological positiv-ism that was then in full gear elsewhere.

Because I am more interested in exploring how the discursive practice described above may have influenced psychoanalytic theo-rizing in a particular area of inquiry, namely that of sexuality, I will not speculate further on that psychohistorical problem. I suggest there is a similarity, or even a continuity, between the discursive device I am emphasizing in Emmy, and what we find in psychoanalytic writing about sexuality.

Taken literally, the majority of the theoretical assertions, images, metaphors, and speech-styles of psychoanalytic writing about sexuality seem to inhabit an ambiguous epistemological realm that straddles physiological and psychological discourses. Theoretical assertions about sexuality in classical psychoanalysis are quite wide-ranging. Sexuality is: present from birth; pressing for discharge; pressing for union; capable of being perverse, flexible, displaceable, mobile, bisexual, polymorphous; coming under the sway of desires to reproduce when mature; dependent on anatomy; mostly unconscious; psychically incestuous; normally including masturbation for children but not for adults; tied to gender; possibly conflicting with gender; making us beasts; producing great art when sublimated; instinctual; and so forth.

But underneath the majority of these concepts there is the taken-for-granted assumption that this is a domain the fundamental nature of which is physical. In the emphasis on sexuality's evolutionary purpose, on its "actual" mechanics (including the developmental progression through the psychosexual stages), and its "true" nature (libido theory), sexuality's representational nature and the range of its idiosyncratic meanings are undermined. That is to say, these concepts link sexuality much less to the interplay between individual and culture (including family), and more to an acultural body.[3] If eroticism is grounded in a physiological nature, then the range and quality of its representations—linguistic, symbolic or behavioral—are perforce limited and to some degree emptied of strength. For example, if we believe that eroticism originates in endogenous stimulation of the genitals, and in the sway of a reproductive purpose, what implicit categorization and evalu-

---

3. In effect, such a discourse positions the *scientific* knowing of sexuality above a psychoanalytic, deconstructive, or symbolic interactive apprehension of sexuality.

ation are we then prompted to make of nongenital sexual desire, such as the appeal of breasts or erotic language?

In what follows, I argue that the dominance of a body or bio-physical discourse is influential in the production of psychoanalytic writing on sexuality that is antithetical to some of the fundamental aims of psychoanalysis. I will explore some concrete illustrations of the operation of body-talk and its derivatives in psychoanalytic sexuality theory, and offer an alternative conceptualization. The branch of sexuality theory that will serve as my touchstone is the theorization of same-sex desire. This subcategory of sexuality theory is especially useful because the history of its theorization shows clearly how the physicalizing (including medicalizing) of a culturally contingent category can shape its functioning within psychoanalysis.[4]

Until recently, most psychoanalytic theories of same-sex desire appeared to be psychological theories. They tried to show that same-sex desire becomes predominant in an individual as the result of various circumstances of development, including fixations and the adoption of particular defensive configurations, both of which could be fostered by certain congenial family constellations. (Although the details of this varied, depending on the theorist, the favored family constellation has consistently been too much mother and too little father.) However, when those theories, including the technical recommendations that accompanied them, are examined carefully, their essentialism and reliance on a notion of a disturbed homosexual *body* become clearer.

Virtually all psychoanalytic writing on same-sex desire prior to 1972 took as its point of departure the idea that it was theorizing a particularly serious form of psychopathology. This, in turn, rested on two interlocking ideas: first, adult sexuality emerges out of a sequence of psychosexual stages, the nature of each being

---

4. In celling same-sex desire "culturally contingent" I mean to say that it is a social construction the characteristics of which depend on historical conditions, not on any intrinsic characteristic of the category "homosexuality" itself. I am not naive, regarding the controversial nature of this assertion; its justification is beyond the scope of this paper.

determined by a preprogrammed sensitization and arousal of a body area, an erogenous zone. Second, if the progressive integration of the events of the psychosexual stages goes properly, a healthy individual's psychoerotic system will be dominated by an evolutionarily determined desire to reproduce. Freud (1935) summed it up powerfully when he wrote in his "Letter to an American mother" (freely quoted): "Homosexuality is an arrest of sexual development [in which] the germs of heterosexual tendencies [are] blighted" (p. 786).

What did Freud mean when he referred to blighting the germs of heterosexual tendencies? Did he mean that a part of the homosexual's representational system, a psychological thing only, was arrested? Or did he mean something about biology? In what sense is the classical psychoanalytic homosexual "stunted"? There is no way to *demonstrate* what Freud meant here, but these images appear to contain a good deal more than psychological description. There is a sense, in particular, that something in the growth mechanism ("blighted germs") of the homosexual body is damaged, immature, ungrown, something that flourishes and reproduces in the normal heterosexual body.

The technical recommendations advanced by psychoanalytic theorizers of same-sex desire who followed Freud (and who characterized themselves as Freudians) offers some validation of my reading of him. (For a detailed presentation of this material see Mitchell [1981].) The technical deviations they advocated are consistent with the sense that they, too, at least unconsciously, imagined a homosexual body, not merely a psychology, as the impediment to mature development and heterosexuality.

Such writers argued that an effective treatment of a homosexual (which at its best, from their point of view, meant conversion to heterosexuality) required prohibition of homosexual behavior supplemented by timely exhortations and encouragements to compliance. What did they think they were up against so that the usual psychoanalytic procedures were likely to be insufficient? Psychoanalysis deals with ideas, affects, and their symbols. The lives of homosexual patients as seen by these writers must be determined by something beyond that representational realm; they will not respond to interpretations like normal patients; they require prohibitions and cheerleading.[5] The implication is that homosexuality is an especially stubborn problem, and in that sense not merely mental. Needless to say, to have *openly* theorized homosexuality as a bodily event would have created still more difficult technical problems for these writers. (It would certainly have diminished the plausibility of psychoanalysis' claim to be the treatment of choice for homosexuals.) The contrasting images of homosexual and heterosexual bodies concealed within the psychoanalytic theorizations of same-sex desire had to remain unarticulated.

Psychoanalytic writing about sexuality has changed somewhat in the past twenty years. Interestingly, changes in the psychoanalytic theory of sexuality are particularly evident in writing about same-sex desire. Many psychoanalysts have self-consciously and publicly relinquished the view that homosexuality is a psychopathological condition; some advocates of conversion therapy have narrowed the scope of their claims. But there is a sense in which these changes are superficial and even consistent with an enhanced physicalization of sexuality. This is illustrated in the readiness of some analysts, such as Isay (1991) and Friedman (1988), to accept the poorly founded reports of the heritability of sexual orientation. (See Byne and Parsons [1993] for a rigorous review of the scientific literature on various biological aspects of sexual orientation.)

What I am suggesting will become clearer if we examine the work of writers who specifically advocate a psychoanalysis that is solely about personal meanings, and who derive their stated concern with respecting patients' autonomy and individuality from that epistemology. In a case presentation that generated substantial controversy with respect to its discussion of same-sex desire, Trop and Stolorow (1992) described a patient who sought treatment because he "felt . . . depressed . . . and did not know whether he was homosexual or heterosexual" (p. 429). Three of the five com-

---

5. For reasons of time I am neglecting another sense of the homosexual patient that lay buried, albeit not too deeply, in these writers' texts. This is the sense of the homosexual's moral inferiority that is embedded in the exhortational treatment recommendation, but also in certain dynamic formulations, such as the assertion that homosexuals are particularly narcissistic.

mentators on this paper (Blechner 1993, Lesser 1993, and myself, Schwartz 1993) emphasized its implicit disparagement of homosexuality; my commentary, as part of an effort to understand how that disparagement came about, highlighted the concealed presence of an idealization of heterosexuality, for which I coined the term *heterophilia*. Reconsidering that interchange in light of a rereading of the case of Emmy, I now believe that my analysis of the problem in Trop and Stolorow's text neglected a deeper level of discursive error. For I did not ask the question how their *understandable* idealization of heterosexuality—after all, these days, who does not favor their own sexual identity?—could make its way into a text and treatment apparently unanalyzed and uncriticized by themselves and editors alike, especially when the treatment is said to be dedicated to a respectful analysis of personal meanings. (I intend this question with no disingenuousness; it is too reductive and simple-minded to see Trop and Stolorow as merely biased.)

The answer may lie in their literal-minded acceptance of the patient's troubled question, "Am I homosexual or heterosexual?" In both the person who poses this question and the analyst who accepts it, is an implicit belief that there is *some* reified meaning to the idea of *being* homo- or heterosexual, in much the same way as when Freud asserts the existence of Emmy's neuropathic constitution, he grants physical existence to hysteria and hysterics. Without a hysterical *body* there can be no hysteria. Behind the idea *the patient is heterosexual* lurks a vision of the heterosexual body, of its homologous relationship to our culturally informed images of animal behavior, of its neurohumoral substances (that used to be drives), of the perfect fit between its body parts and those of other-sexed heterosexual bodies, of its capacity to be fulfilled by the other-sexed body: in short then, of its essential biological nature. And of course there is an analogous vision of the defective homosexual body, with its corresponding imagery and the meanings it stirs. (The content of the two sets of images are of course constantly shifting with historical and cultural change.)

Trop and Stolorow, as much as their patient, believe that the patient has a sexual nature—an essence—that can be known. This is shown by their omission of a psychoanalytic inquiry into the meanings of his preoccupying desire to be one sexuality or another. Would "knowing" that he is homosexual provide the patient with

prescriptions for living, a cognitive antidote to misguided efforts
to seek the gender he is by nature not suited to? It seems quite
possible that the patient thinks so. Trop and Stolorow's avoidance
of exploring such a belief suggests that they may think so too, thus
foreclosing psychoanalytic inquiry and elevating a defensive ideational configuration—one's true nature—to the level of psychophysiological fact.

By contrast, a psychoanalytic *questioning* of the patient's stated
desire to "be" either homo- or heterosexual (or, at least as important, a questioning of the analyst's desire to know whether a patient is homo- or heterosexual) could expose the functional roots
of a naturalized view of sexual orientation and might imply another
vision of sexuality itself.

In one such alternative vision, sexuality is *only* representational: as a purely psychological phenomenon,[6] eroticism then
derives its character not from a content (a specific aim, object,
practice, or neurophysiological process), but from a formal property of experience. For the sake of my argument let us imagine
that one such formal property might be what I call a contextual
licensing of the forbidden. Any matrix of object, practice, and body
part can be mentally designated as forbidden or taboo, and simultaneously be marked with the special circumstances that permit
its enactment. For example, placing one's tongue in the mouth of
another person is, in general, strictly forbidden. However, very
clear but usually unarticulated rules tell us when this is permitted. This would mean that French kissing *is* allowed, but that even
when the rules make it situationally permissible, any given subject will tend to image that act accompanied by its remembered
transgressivity. And this may be what does the trick: the sexual is
found in the intersections of our obedience to those rules, our prox-

---

6. Someone might imagine that in my zeal I have dematerialized sexuality completely and envisioned a mental event with no physiological
correlate, in effect a disembodied spirit. This is not true; I am only denying that there are any specific, reliable physiological correlates of eroticism. For a representation to be known or experienced at all it must appear in some way; in the case of sexuality this varies greatly.

imity to violating them, what degree of consensual validation for transgression the other offers, in the face of what degree of prohibition, and, therefore, what inner experiences of forbiddenness, triumph over prohibition, and surrender to perversity are idiosyncratically stirred by a particular French kiss with a particular person. The experienced intersection of the forbidden and the licensed may superimpose on, may imbue, any material, thing, or situation with its character and energy. This, I suggest, may be a properly updated translation of "libidinal cathexis."

Now I am not specifically arguing in favor of viewing all eroticism as specifically entailing the licensed forbidden. Rather, I am suggesting that eroticism depends on *some* psychological deployment of representations: in other words, on a special manipulation of experience, of words and images, a manipulation that fosters the attachment of these representations to certain matrices of conflicting socially defined characteristics—these characteristics probably form a class, the defining features of which are as yet unknown—such as "licensed/forbidden," or "dangerous/eager," "dirty/desirable," "disgusting/compelling," and so forth. In order for a representation to become eroticized, it must be capable of plausibly carrying the meaning of the conflicting social terms.[7] Beyond that, nothing is more intrinsically eroticizable than anything else. To say that eroticism springs from a deployment of representations, not from any bodily process, and not from any evolutionary design, is to grant it the transformability and independence of physical specificity that allows for the wide range of phenomena (not to mention people) that can become eroticized or be experienced as sexual. It excludes no one and no thing. It does, for the most part, exclude the possibility of sexual psychopathology, at least as that idea has been used until now.

What are the clinical implications of a more or less complete dereification of sexuality? The obvious one is that under its influ-

---

7. What imagery is likely to do that most reliably will of course be determined by cultural and idiosyncratic conditions. Differences between cultures and between individuals with respect to how sexy body fat looks and feels, for example, can be understood in this way.

ence analysts are less likely to be judgmental about particular
sexual practices or to advance any particular sexual agenda. But
subtler and more expansive changes in countertransferential process may also be seen. I will end my paper by offering a brief vignette that illustrates such a change.

A single, middle-aged man lets me know, with a combined sense
of shame and righteous anger, that he has recently engaged in an
unsafe sexual practice with a partner with whom he was cultivating a romance. He ruefully suggests that he can have no sexual
fulfillment if he is denied this activity. At first I am sad for him,
thinking that this nascent relationship may wither in the absence
of fulfilling sex. I imagine that he needs to mourn the loss of a full
sexual relationship, an unavoidable consequence of the AIDS epidemic and his physical condition. I anticipate helping him come
to terms with the difficult reality of sexual restriction. But his
slightly angry tone suggests that a defensive process is escaping
me. It occurs to me that I am being taken in by a false vision that
only one kind of sex will do. His depressive affect hampered my
recognizing that his refusal of erotic creativity might be serving
other ends, perhaps an investment in an image of himself as sexually deprived, an image of self-degradation. When I tell him this,
he is quite angry, aggressively pressuring me to tell him what other
sexual options are open to him. I answer in some detail, worrying
the whole time that I am making things up that cannot work; he *is*
doomed to deprivation. Toward the end of the session he grants
that he feels terribly guilty, and that perhaps imagining himself
unfairly denied sexual pleasure served to distract from that feeling. For me the session ends with a strengthened sense that the
reification of sexuality—in this case, the insistence on a single type
of sex as sole gratifier—can be a powerful defense for patient and
analyst alike. As I recollect my extemporaneous sexual suggestions
to him, I am reminded that, when it is needed,[8] a new erotic may
be constructed on a moment's notice.

---

8. It should be noted that other situations besides AIDS may call for
erotic creativity: breast cancer, prostate cancer, and various phenomena
associated with aging, to name but a few.

REFERENCES

Blechner, M. (1993). Homophobia in psychoanalytic writing and practice. Commentary on Trop and Stolorow's "Defense analysis in self psychology: A developmental view" and Hanna's "False-self sensitivity to countertransference: Anatomy of a single session." *Psychoanalytic Dialogues* 3:627–637.

Breuer, J. and Freud, S. (1893–1895). Studies on hysteria. *Standard Edition* 2.

Byne, W. and Parsons, B. (1993). Human sexual orientation: The biologic theories reappraised. *Archives of General Psychiatry* 50:228–239.

Freud, S. (1935). Letter. *American Journal of Psychiatry* 107:786, 1951.

Friedman, R. (1988). *Male Homosexuality: A Contemporary Psychoanalytic Perspective*. New Haven, CT: Yale University Press.

Isay, R. (1991). The homosexual analyst. *Psychoanalytic Study of the Child* 46:199–216.

Lesser, R. (1993). A reconsideration of homosexual themes. Commentary on Trop and Stolorow's "Defense analysis in self psychology: A developmental view." *Psychoanalytic Dialogues* 3:639–641.

Mitchell, S. (1981). The psychoanalytic treatment of homosexuality: Some technical considerations. *International Review of Psycho-Analysis* 8:63–80.

Schwartz, D. (1993). Heterophilia—the love that dare not speak its aim. Commentary on Trop and Stolorow's "Defense analysis in self psychology: A developmental view." *Psychoanalytic Dialogues* 3:643–652.

Spence, D. P. (1982). *Narrative Truth and Historical Truth: Meaning and Interpretation in Psychoanalysis*. New York: Norton.

Sulloway, F. (1983). *Freud: Biologist of the Mind*. New York: Basic Books.

Trop, J. and Stolorow, R. (1992). Defense analysis in self-psychology: A developmental view. *Psychoanalytic Dialogues* 2:427–442.

9

Psychoanalysis and the Degradation of Romance

Stephen A. Mitchell

This chapter appeared as an article of the same name in *Psychoanalytic Dialogues: A Journal of Relational Perspectives* 7:1 (1997).

Romantic love has occupied a curious place within psychoanalysis throughout its development. On the one hand, psychoanalysis has concerned itself more consistently and more centrally with love and its vicissitudes than with any other emotion and motivation. Freud granted self-preservation a primary status early on, but it was relegated to a secondary position after 1920. Conversely, aggression was added to eros in 1920 but played a peripheral role until then. Only love, in various terminological guises—libido, psychosexuality, eros—was designated by Freud as foundational throughout. And, according to Erikson (1950), Freud thought of the analytic process as primarily aimed at the restoration of this capacity: to love and to work.

Yet Freud early on came to regard love with a skeptical, jaundiced eye. Although the ultimate place of love in his own life is mired in biographical controversy, the romantic passion of his love letters to his fiancée seems to have faded quickly for him. We might say that one of Freud's central projects was precisely the deconstruction of romantic love, the demonstration that it is not what we think it is, the exposure of its seamier aspects, its forbidden objects, its incestuous underpinnings. Mature love, in much of the analytic literature, the love that emerges from the analytic process, realistic love tempered by "secondary process," often seems a somber, dispassionate affair, indistinguishable from mourning.

What I want to do in this essay is to consider both the degradation of romantic love in many people's lives as well as the degradation of romantic love in traditional psychoanalysis. I also want to point to what I believe has been the reemergence of romance in some more recent developments in psychoanalytic theorizing. For our consideration of psychoanalytic understandings of love, let us take as a point of departure one of the short case histories in *Studies on Hysteria* (Breuer and Freud 1893–1895).

Miss Lucy R. was referred to Freud because she had entirely lost her sense of smell, and in its place was a persistent olfactory hallucination, the "smell of burnt pudding." She was also quite depressed. Miss Lucy was a young Englishwoman working as a

governess in the Viennese home of a rich, widowed factory director. Freud was able to solve the mystery of what he took to be an
hysterical neurosis in short order: Miss Lucy was in love with her
employer. Because of the social-class differences between the two
of them, Miss Lucy experienced her romantic longing as doomed.
An intimate conversation had aroused her hopes, but they had been
crushed by an odd scolding from her employer for her allowing
visiting adults to kiss his children. The burnt-pudding smell had
been in the air at a later moment when a letter from her mother
signaled to her the inevitability of her departure from this house
that had aroused her romantic longings. Thus Lucy's neurosis had
resulted from conflictual, repressed wishes of an erotic nature.

There is a charm to Freud's account of the case of Miss Lucy.
It is written with what, from our perspective, is a metapsychological
naiveté. The formulations are simple, close to the lived experience,
without all the complex dynamic, energic, genetic, and structural
apparatus soon to be introduced in connection with drive theory.
But the very metatheoretical innocence of the case of Miss Lucy
allows us a fresh look at two of the major issues that dominate the
lives of most people—romance and transcendence—issues that
were largely buried in the turn Freud was soon to take toward infantile sexuality as the Pandora's Box to which all forms of psychopathology can be traced.

The case of Miss Lucy is a story of love and hope, social class
and transcendence, romantic ambition and hierarchical place. In
Freud's model of neurosis at this time, the problem was conflict
not between impulse and defense, but between incompatible ideas
more broadly and loosely conceived. And the ideas that had become incompatible for Miss Lucy were her ordinary sense of herself and her place in contrast to her improbable, one might almost
say subversive, romantic longings for her employer. In some sense,
viewing the mind in terms of incompatible clusters of ideas is a
forerunner of some of the latest thinking about multiple selves
(Bromberg 1998, Davies 1996, Mitchell 1991, 1993, Ogden 1986,
1989, 1994).

We might say that in falling in love with her employer, Miss
Lucy had fallen out of her everyday sense of self, securely nestled
in its place within a well-defined socioeconomic status system.
And Miss Lucy's story serves as a springboard for us to consider

whether there is not something in the very nature of romantic passion that is destabilizing, inherently conflictual, and potentially transcendent.

Seventeen years after the publication of *Studies on Hysteria* Freud (1912) published an extraordinary paper entitled "On the Universal Tendency to Debasement in the Sphere of Love," in which he described, with crystalline clarity, what he called "psychical impotence," a widespread problem in his patients, second in frequency only to the symptom of anxiety. He noted a split between tender and sexual feelings in his patients: "Where they love, they have no desire; where they desire, they cannot love" (p. 183). By this time, Freud's theory of infantile sexuality, culminating in the Oedipus complex, was firmly in place, and he explained psychical impotence in terms of a universal incestuous fixation on the mother.

In 1912, when this paper was written, the dual instincts that fueled Freud's psychic apparatus were self-preservation and sexuality, leading to two currents of feeling in the boy toward his mother: tender, affectionate feelings and sensual feelings. It is very difficult— perhaps, Freud thought, ultimately impossible—for the boy to fully reconcile his sexual wishes toward mother as sexual object with the mother who protects and preserves him.

I find Freud's early exploration of the conflict between sexual and tender feelings, between the mother as the object of desire and the mother as the provider of safety and comfort, to be very useful. But this framework for viewing the conflicts of love and romance was lost when Freud substituted aggression for self-preservation as libido's counterpart in his always dualistic drive theory. The central conflicts in life were no longer between erotic impulses and safety, but between libido and aggression. Self-preservation was no longer assigned foundational status but became a secondary concern of the ego's adaptational functions. As a consequence, love was increasingly collapsed into sexuality; romance became a libidinal derivative. In the Freud/Abraham scheme that was consolidated in the 1920s, one loved according to one's libidinal fixation point, and mature love was an expression of what was termed "genitality."

The full absurdity of this collapse of the interpersonal dimensions of love into the concretely sexual, with the consequent loss of the tenderness that Freud had associated with the now defunct self-preservative instinct, was articulated (unknowingly) by Wilhelm Reich (1929), long before he veered off from mainstream Freudian thought into orgone theory. Here is his portrait of the fully mature, genital character:

> Since he is capable of gratification, he is capable of monogamy without compulsion or repression; but he is also capable, if a reasonable motive is given, of changing the object without suffering any injury. He does not adhere to his sexual object out of guilt feelings or out of moral considerations, but is faithful out of a healthy desire for pleasure: because it gratifies him. He can master polygamous desires if they are in conflict with his relations to the loved object without repression; but he is able also to yield to them if they overly disturb him. The resulting actual conflict he will solve in a realistic manner. There are hardly any neurotic feelings of guilt. [p.151]

(Reich seems not to consider at all the possibility of genuine guilt.)

There was clearly something important missing here, and one function of the rise of object relations theories in the 1940s and 1950s was to address this missing dimension (Spezzano 1993). It was, on the level of theory, a return of the repressed, a correction for the minimization of the importance of tenderness, affection, and security, which had lost their foundational status after 1920. Thus the object relations theorists, from Fairbairn to Bowlby, from Spitz to Mahler to Loewald, began to emphasize the role of the mother not only as the object of desire but also as the object of tenderness and attachment. Another way to describe this same movement is to say that the center of gravity of analytic theorizing shifted from the oedipal to the preoedipal.

One of the major conceptual tasks at our current stage in the development of psychoanalytic ideas is the problem of understanding the relationship between attachment and desire, preoedipal and oedipal, or, to return to the terms Freud was employing in 1912, the relationship between safety and the erotic. Fromm (1947) grappled with this problem in his discussion of primary and secondary attachments; Loewald (1978) addressed it in his extraordinary paper "The Waning of the Oedipus Complex" by defining incest as a loss of boundaries between identificatory and libidinal objects. And today's analytic clinician confronts this problem daily in his clinical work.

There are many patients today who suffer from the very same issues that Lucy and Freud's other patients struggled with: the splitting of love and desire, the longing for inaccessible objects, the numbing of passion in long-term relationships: all forms of "psychical impotence." In approaching such issues it has seemed useful to me to expand Freud's insights beyond his focus on early childhood into a broader existential perspective. As John Ross (1992) has put it:

> Psychoanalysis was designed by Freud to be a psychology of love. Yet, it has had more to say about the childish precursors of what has been called mature "genitality" than about Eros in adult life. Not all sexuality is infantile sexuality after all, yet our analytic literature almost makes it seem so. [p. 445]

Reconciling safety and passion is not only a childhood dilemma but an adult struggle as well, a problem not only for boys and girls but also for men and women.

There is a fundamental contrast between the familiar and the transcendent that runs throughout human experience, characterized in different ways depending on the discipline and interests of the characterizer. Students of comparative religion have written of the distinction between the profane and the sacred; Piaget (1937), in his theory of cognitive development, stressed the dialectic between *assimilation* of new stimuli to established schemata and *accommodation* of those schemata to new stimuli; in psychoanalysis, most recently, Jay Greenberg (1991) has proposed a dual instinct theory grounded in conflictual needs for safety and effectance. In its own way, each of these dichotomies rests on two fundamental, conflictual human needs: on the one hand, a need for a grounding that feels completely known and predictable, a reliable anchoring—a framework, as Fromm put it, for orientation and devotion—and, on the other hand, a longing to break out of established and familiar patterns, to step over boundaries and encounter something unpredictable, awe-inspiring, or, to use one of Sullivan's favorite terms for describing experiences outside the usual borders of the self, *uncanny*. Romantic love belongs in the second realm.

Although there are accounts of instances of romantic love throughout antiquity, some historians, for example, de Rougemont

(1956), date the emergence of romantic love as a universal potential and a literary genre in the institution of courtly love in the late Middle Ages, coincident with the beginnings of what would develop into the modern notion of the personal self. Whereas the classical and medieval epic portrayed life as a test of endurance, the early Renaissance romance began to portray life in terms of a personal quest. There is something at stake for the individual in leaving the security of the familial and the familiar, in overstepping established boundaries into the unknown. And romantic love became almost paradigmatic of the transcendent experience; courtly love was at once both erotic and sacred. The lady loved by the knight, like Beatrice for Dante, might be virtually unknown, glimpsed only from afar. It is her very status as beyond the ordinary that makes her extraordinary, and opens up the possibility for transcending the boundaries of the familiar.

Consider the central place of idealization in loving. In romantic passion, the lover attributes illusory value to the beloved, who becomes the embodiment of ideals of beauty, power, perfection. Traditional psychoanalytic theorizing has generally taken a dim view of the idealizing dimension of loving, understanding it as fundamentally regressive and defensive. Thus Freud (1914) regarded what he termed the overvaluation of the beloved as a consequence of the projection of a segment of primary narcissism onto the other: the beloved is loved as perfect and complete, as the very small baby loves himself. Because it depleted the ego of its own narcissism, Freud regarded idealization of the other as immature and dangerous. And idealization, particularly as developed by the Kleinians, has been regarded as fundamentally a defense against destructive aggression. Because the idealization in romantic love is a bulwark against hate, love itself is unstable and developmentally primitive, less preferable than a more mature ambivalent relationship to the object. Thus, for those who rely on Freudian and Kleinian perspectives, romantic love tends to be regarded as, at best, a brief prelude to more stable, ambivalent love; once reality intervenes and one gets to know the other as they "really" are, the idealization that fuels the illusions of romantic love are no longer possible.

According to popular cliché, consistent with the traditional psychoanalytic canon, idealization and erotic romance fade with familiarity and reality. Many feel that passion requires danger, the illicit. As Ross suggests, "when it comes to erotic love, as opposed to recreation, there is no such thing as 'safe sex.' Danger, the great love stories tell us, is an integral aspect of sexual love" (p. 454). The more known and dependable the other becomes, the less ground there is for passion to emerge: "Where they love, they do not desire and where they desire, they cannot love" (Freud 1912, p. 183).

But some of the more innovative of contemporary psychoanalytic theorists, like Loewald and Kohut, have introduced into psychoanalytic theory ways of thinking about idealization and fantasy that make it possible to consider romantic love from a perspective less dominated by Freud's dour pessimism and tragic demeanor. Whereas Freud saw fantasy as opposed to and clouding reality, Loewald and Kohut regard fantasy as enriching and enhancing reality. Consider Loewald's (1974) startling definition of reality testing:

> Reality testing is far more than an intellectual or cognitive function. It may be understood more comprehensively as the experiential testing of fantasy—its potential and suitability for actualization—and the testing of actuality—its potential for encompassing it in, and penetrating it with, one's fantasy life. We deal with the task of a reciprocal transposition. [p. 368]

For Loewald, the rational, objective perspective we normally consider "reality" has no superior epistemological status; it is, rather, a devitalized shadow of the fuller reality that is made possible when the actual can be animated and brought alive through fantasy. And Kohut (1977), in arguing against the "developmental morality" of traditional Freudian ego psychology, regarded the capacity to sustain and actualize ideals to be a central component of mental health. Thus contemporary psychoanalytic theorists, in contrast to their classical forbears, have begun to prepare the ground for the reintroduction of romance as a credible adult experience. Nowadays some mainstream contemporary Freudians (like John Ross) write somewhat favorably of romantic passion as a late-adolescent phenomenon, which is at least two steps up from early childhood!

In the customary approach to clinical situations involving splitting and psychic impotence, the illicit sexuality and the danger in romance is seen as requiring explanation. Why does the woman feel sexual excitement only in transient situations with threatening men? Why does the man feel someone else's wife is endlessly fascinating? When psychoanalysts try to explain something they do not understand, we often reduce it to a childhood precursor. Thus danger, the illicit, the crossing of boundaries, the lust for adventure are all generally understood as recreations of oedipal longings and fantasized transgressions. The customary psychoanalytic understanding often matches well the patient's subjective experience: there is a conflict between the drabness of the known and familiar and the excitement of the unknown, which provides room for idealization and childhood oedipal fantasies to emerge. The obvious solution seems renunciatory: the rationality of secondary process must triumph over the illusions of infantile fantasy.

But I have found it useful in these kinds of clinical situations to reverse the question and ask, instead: How is it that in their primary relationship this man or woman manages to feel so safe? With such patients, it is as if the available is assumed to be completely known, always accessible, wholly predictable. Safety is presumed. But in exploring in detail the textures of such an established relationship, I have invariably discovered that the sense of safety is not a given but a construction, the familiarity based not on deep mutual knowledge but on collusive contrivance, the predictability not an actuality but an elaborate fantasy. So often, in long-standing relationships that break apart, one or both partners discover with a shock that the assumptions they made about the other's experience, the very convictions that made the other both safe and dull, were inventions, often collusively agreed upon. They often discover that their dull "partner" has had all sorts of secrets, very private thoughts and feelings, and, perhaps, a secret relationship to express them in. "She is not the person I thought she was," is the lament of the betrayed. Precisely.

A central feature of the inherent instability of passionate love is the aggression that is always the close companion of dependency. The Kleinians have shed enormous light on this dynamic in their study of depressive anxiety. Desire is risky and dangerous. The unresponsive, ungratifying object is infuriating. To want something important from someone important is inevitably to place oneself at risk. One solution to this problem is the retreat to the paranoid-schizoid position: the object that disappoints was rotten all along. There is a really good object out there somewhere that will not disappoint. Another solution is manic reversal: it is not that I want an other, but that others want me. And so on. So aggression is a perpetual threat to security in love relationships (Jessica Benjamin, personal communication). The most common way for lovers to reduce the threat of aggression is to collapse their expectations of each other by colluding in an illusory predictability. But lowering expectations also empties out passion. No risk, no gain. Robert Stoller (1985) has argued that aggression is a central feature of the erotic, an aggression derived from childhood humiliations. If we assume, with the Kleinians, that all dependency is potentially humiliating, then all of us have known deep humiliation in childhood. This makes passionate love necessarily dangerous for everyone and establishes aggression as love's shadow, an inextricable accompaniment and necessary constituent of romantic passion.

How knowable and predictable *is* another person? How knowable and predictable are we to ourselves? Some of the major currents in traditional psychoanalytic thought suggested that the self is very knowable indeed: ego psychology portrays the self as built of stable and predictable structures; self psychology presumes a continuous core self; and some object relations theorists, like Guntrip especially, envision a singular core self, if safety is presumed, that seeks validation. But there are other currents within contemporary psychoanalytic thought that portray the self as much more inaccessible, fluid, or discontinuous: Winnicott's incommunicado, private self; Ogden's decentered subject, oscillating within dialectics between consciousness and unconsciousness, and among the autistic-contiguous paranoid-schizoid, and depressive positions; and Hoffman's perpetually constructed and co-constructed experience. If one takes these approaches to self seriously, it is not adventure and danger that need explaining, but claims to predictability and safety!

The longing for the inaccessible and the sense of possession of the known are Janus-faced illusions that function to contain risk and uncertainty. To long for the unavailable object is to segregate desire into a domain in which its fate is predetermined. Unrequited love is painful but safe. Conversely, the sense of security, possession, ownership that often attends long-term relationships is a contrivance based on fantasies of permanence.

There is a powerful motive at work in long-term relationships to establish security, a predictability over the unpredictable, a knowingness over the unknown. Adam Phillips (1994) has described this beautifully:

> Freud and Proust are alert in complementary ways to the senses in which knowing people—or certain kinds of knowledge about people—can be counter-erotic; that the unconscious intention of certain forms of familiarity is to kill desire. It is not simply that elusiveness, or jealousy, sustains desire, but that certain ways of knowing people diminish their interest for us; and that this may be their abiding wish. So we have to watch out for the ways people invite us—or allow us—to know them; and also alert ourselves to the possibility that knowing may be too tendentious, too canny, a model for loving. [p. 41]

Consider the following brief clinical vignette:

Susan is a woman in her mid-forties who seeks psychoanalytic treatment because she is confused about some of the choices she has made and is afraid that her life is in danger of becoming a sociological cliché. Her childhood had been quite impoverished, both materially and interpersonally. What shreds of security she had were imposed by her mother through a religious piety that felt contrived but sustaining. Susan had had a very bumpy adolescence and early adulthood but had managed to use her considerable intelligence and creativity to fashion a satisfying, if somewhat dull, life for herself. She shared with her husband and children a family life that felt quite rich and meaningful to her. Yet, two years prior to entering treatment, she had begun an affair with a somewhat younger man that she had been pursuing with a recklessness that both excited and frightened her. Was this a mid-life crisis? Should she renounce the excitement of the affair and settle maturely for a comfy domestic existence? Or should she abandon familiarity and conventionality and seek a more authentic if dangerous life with her lover? There was something about the very banality of the choice, as if right out of a made-for-TV movie, that both depressed and paralyzed her.

For our purposes in this volume I want to describe some of the themes of our work at a point about one year into it. One of the things that struck me about Susan was the way in which she sys-tematically undersold herself. She was a woman of great talents and appeal, but her sense of herself was always of someone living on the edge of collapse. As we came to understand the way in which her marriage was put together, it became clear that it was partly marriage, partly potential day hospital. Her husband was a caring, somewhat doting man who conveyed to her a perpetual availabil-ity and responsiveness. She complained bitterly about the anti-erotic impact of this doting, but the more closely we explored the arrangements of their lives, the clearer it became that she counted on it and in some sense insisted on it. She believed that the dull-ness of her marriage and the excitement of her affair derived from properties of the two men themselves. I pointed out ways in which she insisted on her marriage remaining dull and predictable and segregated her risk-taking into the other relationship. I suggested that, despite her successes and durability, she was always prepar-ing herself for a collapse and required her husband to be dull and dependable to take care of her. Things began to open up in differ-ent ways in both relationships as she became aware of the ways in which she orchestrated excitement in the one and dreary predict-ability in the other.

She was surprised to discover how inhibited she was in her interactions with her husband, and she began talking to him about wanting to open things up between the two of them. He began to respond, at first somewhat cautiously, and she reported one Mon-day that they had had an uncharacteristically romantic weekend away. He had even responded to her interest in moderately kinky sex in a way that had been much more exciting for her. "It was a lovely weekend," she said. "Very cozy."

I got very interested in her use of the word *cozy*. Cozy was a word she had used in relation to her husband when he was pad-ding around in slippers serving her coffee. Cozy was not a word she would ever use in relation to her lover. Cozy seemed an odd way to characterize the break in protocol that had taken place over the weekend. Susan and I came to feel that the word choice here was an important part of the way in which she processed her ex-perience to, in fact, maintain herself as a sociological cliché, to continually refurbish a familiarity and predictability that she felt she might desperately need someday, but against which she needed to continually rebel in order to find something more authentic and alive in herself.

The need to feel one knows oneself and another person is a powerful need both for children and for adults. But in human relationships safety and predictability are difficult to come by. One of the things good parents provide for their children is a partially illusory, elaborately constructed atmosphere of safety. Good-enough parents do not talk with young children about their own terrors, worries, and doubts. They construct a sense of buffered permanence in which the child can discover and explore, without any impinging vigilance, her own mind, her creativity, her joy in living. As adults, we gradually learn how illusory, effortful, and managed was that cocoon-like potential space our caregivers were able to provide (and even in the best of circumstances, this is only relative). Yet, in our relationships, we continually strive to reestablish that illusory sense of permanence and predictability. Thus, with patients who complain of dead and lifeless marriages, it is often possible to show them how precious the deadness is to them, how carefully maintained and insisted upon, how the very mechanical, totally predictable quality of lovemaking serves for them as a bulwark against the dread of surprise and unpredictability. The separateness brings about loneliness and longing and fear for the fragility of all relations; the transcendence in the couple's union brings about the sense of oneness with the world, of permanence, and new creation. Loneliness, one might say, is a precondition for transcendence.

Kernberg, who writes about love in interesting and complex ways, stresses two preconditions for the capacity to experience love deeply: "firm boundaries of the self with the constant awareness of the indissoluble separateness of individuals" (1980, p. 290). I am not so sure about the firm boundaries part, because I think we are all much more permeable than we like to think. But the ability to tolerate separateness, along with the sense of relative instability and unpredictability that accompanies it, is very important. As Kernberg notes, "the separateness brings about loneliness and longing and fear for the frailty of all relations . . . loneliness, one might say, is a precondition for transcendence" (p. 290). All of us regularly attempt to fudge both these states of separateness and connection. Both can be frightening; both are risky. The dangers inherent in each seem to be circumvented by contriving both. Thus the unconscious contract that parallels many legal marriage contracts is an agreement to pretend to be permanently, unalterably, impossibly bound, creating the necessity for a carefully guarded, perpetual, measured distance. Lacan never seems to have grasped the possibility of a genuine relatedness, but he captured vividly the mirages of degraded romance in the service of illusory security: "Love," he noted, "is giving something you don't have to someone you don't know" (quoted in Phillips 1994, p. 39).

Total safety, predictability, and oneness, permanently established, quickly become stultifying. Blake and the other romantics were the first to discern that the secret hero of Milton's *Paradise Lost* is not God but Satan. Because it is illusory and contrived, permanent safety stifles vitality and generates expressions of exuberant defiance. It is striking how frequently members of separating couples will reclaim and explore their sexuality under the banner of "giving myself the adolescence I never had." In reality, virtually no one actually had the adolescence they wish they had had, built around a vision of freely explored sexual expression, unconstrained by concerns for security or convention. This is why it is difficult for many people to find a place for adolescent versions of self in long-term relationships founded upon collusive contracts of illusory safety. Sexuality is perfectly designed for rebellion against such contracts, precisely because sexual response can be neither willed nor willfully controlled. Sexual arousal is unruly and unpredictable; it entails vulnerability and risk; it gives the lie to illusions of safety and control.

Oscar entered treatment because an increasing sense of dissatisfaction had nearly led him to end a relationship of many years. The relationship had been very gratifying to him in many ways, but Oscar had never agreed to marry, mostly because he felt his girlfriend was quite constricted sexually. He continually felt driven to flirt with other women and was adept enough at it to constantly have on hand at least several relationships that could easily have been sexually consummated. Until he fell in love with one of these other women, who he felt was clearly less desirable than his lover in many other respects, these dalliances provided him the excitement he felt he needed because of the latter's inhibitions.

Not just Oscar's behavior, but also his speech was constricted with his girlfriend, who, he was quite certain, regarded him as "goatish"; he certainly could not share with her his various sexual thoughts and fantasies, his past sexual experiences, because, he was quite sure, she would regard these as evidence of his wavering commitment to her.

Over the course of our work, we came to understand the ways in which Oscar perpetually conveyed to his girlfriend the idea that his sexuality was a great danger to their relationship. He came to understand that there was something terribly important to him about experiencing himself and being regarded by her as a wild, dangerous, pan-sexual creature who, if not for her control over him, would be ravishing every woman in the neighborhood. There was something centrally important to him, I suggested, about experiencing himself as a "goat on a leash." The leash was at least as important as the goatishness, and he was adept at luring his lover into seeming to exert an external control on what he liked to think of as his sexual voraciousness. In terms of actual sexual encounters, he was the most loyal of lovers, but, like the juggler who keeps many plates spinning concurrently, his life was exhausting.

Was this essentially a sexual conflict? I think not. We began to think of this issue in broader terms after one session that he began by reflecting on his difficulty in knowing where to begin. There were so many possible things he wanted to talk about, to consider; he pictured them laid out before him like food on a smorgasbord. He felt hesitant about choosing a starting point, for fear of losing the others. I was struck by this image and asked for his associations to smorgasbords. He had grown up in a working-class neighborhood of a big city, with few nice restaurants. At some point during his childhood, a Swedish restaurant appeared and became an instant hit. The opportunity to consume as much as one wanted for a fixed price was irresistible. He and his family would frequent this restaurant, but, they felt, with a difference from their neighbors. They saw themselves as superior to the others in terms of social-class background and moral refinement. An important part of this dining experience for them would be to watch with amusement their fellow customers return, again and again, to heap their plates full of food, while they proceeded with great restraint. If their neighbors indulged themselves in oral greediness, theirs was an orgy of righteousness.

Oscar and I came to appreciate the pervasiveness and centrality of the theme of restraint in the ways he conducted his life. One of the most important functions of the relationship with his girlfriend was that it allowed him to demonstrate his fidelity, despite continual frustration and perpetual, intense temptation. This righteousness, thereby established, preserved his sense of his own goodness, and lovability and therefore provided for him a certain sense of security. Thus in Oscar's life, and in many others, I have found it useful to understand the kind of splitting Freud termed psychical impotence not in terms of a conflict between childhood needs for self-preservation and forbidden sexual impulses, but in terms of a lifelong craving for security and the creative/disruptive nature of sexual passion.

Consider the precariousness of the intense idealization that is a central ingredient of romantic love. I am not referring to a worshipful, self-abnegating deference, but rather to the experience of being "head-over-heels" excited about another person. As Freud (1914) noted long ago, this is a dangerous state. The excitement might not be reciprocated; love might remain unrequited. It is bad enough at the beginning of a relationship, with someone you do not know well; there is so much less at stake. But falling into intense, passionate idealization with someone you count on for safety and predictability is hazardous indeed. They know *you* too well, with all your flaws and blemishes. There is too much at stake.

The romantic fervor of Freud's letters to his fiancée faded quickly, and his dour rationalism and pessimism formed the basis for the traditional psychoanalytic skepticism about the idealization of romance as a particularly dangerous form of illusion. This anti-romantic view also fit nicely with the epistemological objectivism and scientism of Freud's day. One gets to "know" another person in the same way one gets to know an inorganic object like a rock. As you find out what they are "really like," the grounds for idealization vanish. You know them too well. Familiarity dissipates passion.

But contemporary philosophers have come to regard objectivism itself as an illusion, a longing for an impossible epistemological foundational security. In this more modern (really postmodern) frame of reference, coming to the conclusion that you "really know" another person is a dangerous fiction. One knows only selected aspects of an other at any one time, in a specific context, for a specific purpose. Similarly, in a contemporary psychoanalytic perspective based on the principle of a decentered subject (Ogden, 1994), there is no way ever to "really know" oneself, to have access to one's various, multiple self-organizations simultaneously.

From this perspective, the common experience of the fading of romance over time may have less to do with the inevitable undercutting of idealization by reality and familiarity than with the increasing danger of allowing oneself episodic, passionate idealization in a relationship that one depends on for security and predictability. Kohut demonstrated that narcissistic excitement about oneself is, for many people, highly anxiety-provoking and destabilizing. Similarly, intense excitement about another is dangerous business; it often is much safer to surrender to it with someone you cannot possibly spend much time with or will never see again.

It is not that romance fades over time; it becomes riskier. Love is sometimes described as being "crazy" about another. To become crazy about someone you actually depend on for a variety of security needs, real and illusory, can feel crazed indeed. Thus many couples come to inhibit the appreciation and excitement they felt about each other earlier on in the relationship. Each tells themselves they know the other better now. What they know now is that the idealizable features of the other are not *all* there is to them, that they are also disappointing, that their passion cannot be a steady state. So they use what they know of the other as a defense against the surrender of idealization. The idealizable features of the other may not have been illusory at all; what was illusory was the guarantee they sought against disappointment and perpetually regenerated solitude.

George sought treatment because of intense unhappiness in his marriage of ten years. Although he loved his wife and young child, he had increasingly come to regard his wife as unbearably controlling and to experience himself as claustrophobically trapped. Her various demands, like an insistence on his calling her to inform her that he would be late coming home for dinner, had come to feel intolerably coercive. He found sexual liaisons with other women irresistible and felt increasingly disaffected from his wife.

With some embarrassment George eventually revealed that among the most intense of his sexual adventures were regular visits to several madams who played the role of dominatrix with him. In these encounters, he would place himself totally in the woman's hands. She could order him around, tie him up, do anything she wanted to him. He would beg and plead for mercy and release, to no avail. Although there was rarely any actual genital contact or orgasm George found these encounters extraordinarily thrilling. I was of course struck by the odd irony of a man who found oppressive his wife's demand for common courtesy placing himself under the total control of a virtual stranger. George explained that the woman's control was a dramatic fiction. The way it worked was that they would establish a code word before beginning. He could beg and scream for mercy to no avail, but if he said the code word, the play would stop instantly. He was really in total control, and it was that complete power that made it possible for him to pretend that she was in control.

As we came to understand it, the control George objected to from his wife was a control he longed for and was terrified he would surrender himself to. Because he actually depended on so much from his wife, even minor concessions like a phone call seemed too dangerous. He could let himself yield, in a perversely contrived scenario, only to someone with whom he had nothing at all at stake. Much later on I asked him how he was so sure that the dominatrix would, in fact, comply with the code word. Of course, there was economic power as a background factor. But there seemed to be a leap of faith that was essential for him not to notice. Once again, this suggests that actual, as opposed to fantasized, control is difficult to come by. He believed he was in control, imagining himself under her control. But from another perspective, he *was* in her control, imagining himself to be in control in order to pretend that he was surrendering. Because human relationships are built around such complex interdependencies, control and predictability often take on this sort of nesting-doll quality.

Later in our work another feature of George's relationship with his wife emerged. He began to reconnect with memories of their early years together, which were very exciting and passionate. As he spoke of their romance, his eyes would fill with tears at the thought of what a remarkable woman she had been and still was. We began to explore why it was possible for him to tell me about his memories and his admiration for her, but not possible for him to tell her. To speak to her about his appreciation, past and present, felt to him like a form of pandering. To romance her, so to speak, would be to put himself in the position of asking for something, perhaps begging. To allow himself to crave her would make him seem craven to her and himself. He had come to feel that his stalwart performances as husband had earned him the right to her love. To approach her appreciatively or seductively would be to renounce those claims. There was, of course, a long family history around this worldview. His father had been a high-ranking army officer whose career had been cut short because he believed his advancement should have been secured on the basis of his achievements on the field of battle, with no need to pay his dues through administrative and social participation at the Pentagon. He felt, as George and I came to talk of it, above "romancing" his superiors. Thus, for George, desire had become synonymous with begging and humiliation, appreciation with a self-demeaning pandering. The only love worth having was earned through virtuous deeds. The anti-erotic fallout of that worldview became increasingly apparent to him.

In many cultures, and at earlier points in Western cultural history, there is a separation between marriage and romance. Marital "rights" are legally established, as they often are unofficially in the power negotiations of relationships. Eros is sought elsewhere, on terrain that, ultimately, seems safer. It is interesting to note how much romance is sold in a degraded form in popular culture: soap operas, romance novels, fascination with the lives of celebrities. Once deadness is established as a requirement for security in actual relationships, passion is sought vicariously in distant, safer realms.

Authentic romance, in contrast to its degraded forms, is not split off from a longing for security and predictability but is in a continual dialectical relationship with it. Authentic romance cannot arise in a world in which there is a willed, contrived separation between safety and desire, just as authentic spirituality cannot emerge in the context of a willed, contrived separation between the sacred and the profane.

For us today, the ending of Freud's case report of Miss Lucy is quite unsatisfying. The evaporation of her symptoms with the interpretation of the forbidden love for her employer seems hard to believe. (Interestingly, in terms of our current ideas of transference, her olfactory hallucination of burnt pudding was replaced for a time with the hallucination of the smell of cigars. And we all know who smoked cigars. Perhaps with Miss Lucy, as with many patients, her passion moved from her symptoms to the analysis itself.) But most importantly, from our current vantage point, we would hope that whatever depths of passion and search for transcendence erupted in Miss Lucy's romantic longing would not simply be renounced as neither sensible nor practical. We would hope that Miss Lucy would not simply return to her "place," rather that she would find other channels for development and self-exploration.

REFERENCES

Breuer, J. and Freud, S. (1893–1895). Studies on hysteria. *Standard Edition* 2.

Bromberg, P. (1998). *Standing in the Spaces: Essays on Clinical Process, Trauma, and Dissociation*. Hillsdale, NJ: Analytic Press.

Davies, J. M. (1996). Linking the "pre-analytic" with the post-classical: integration, dissociation, and the multiplicity of unconscious process. *Contemporary Psychoanalysis* 32:553–576.

De Rougemont, D. (1956). *Love in the Western World*. New York: Pantheon.

Erikson, E. (1950). *Childhood and Society*. New York: Norton.

Freud, S. (1912). On the universal tendency to debasement in the sphere of love. *Standard Edition* 11:177–190.

—— (1914). On narcissism: an introduction. *Standard Edition* 14:67–102.

Fromm, E. (1947). *Man for Himself*. Greenwich, CT: Fawcett.

Greenberg, J. (1991). *Oedipus and Beyond: A Clinical Theory*. Cambridge, MA: Harvard University Press.

Kernberg, O. (1980). *Internal World and External Reality*. New York: Aronson.

Kohut, H. (1977). *The Restoration of the Self*. New York: International Universities Press.

Loewald, H. (1974). Psychoanalysis as art and the fantasy nature of the psychoanalytic situation. In *Papers on Psychoanalysis*, New Haven, CT: Yale University Press, 1980.

—— (1978). The waning of the Oedipus complex. In *Papers on Psychoanalysis*, pp. 384–404. New Haven, CT: Yale University Press.

Mitchell, S. A. (1991). Contemporary perspectives on self: toward an integration. *Pychoanalytic Dialogues* 1:121–147.

—— (1993). *Hope and Dread in Psychoanalysis*. New York: Basic Books.

Ogden, T. H. (1986). *The Matrix of the Mind*. Northvale, NJ: Aronson.

—— (1989). *The Primitive Edge of Experience*. Northvale, NJ: Aronson.

—— (1994). *Subjects of Analysis*. Northvale, NJ: Aronson.

Phillips, A. (1994). *On Flirtation*. Cambridge, MA: Harvard University Press.

Piaget, J. (1937). *The Construction of Reality in the Child*. New York: Basic Books.

Reich, W. (1929). The genital character and the neurotic character. In *The Psychoanalytic Reader*, ed. R. Fliess. New York: International Universities Press, 1948.

Ross, J. (1992). A psychoanalytic essay on romantic, erotic love. In *Affect: Psychoanalytic Perspectives*, ed. T. Shapiro and R. Emde.

Spezzano, C. (1993). *Affect in Psychoanalytic Theory and Therapy: Towards a New Synthesis*. Hillsdale, NJ: Analytic Press.

Stoller, R. (1985). *Observing the Erotic Imagination*. New Haven, CT: Yale University Press.

10

From Hypnotic Suggestion to Free Association: Freud as a Psychotherapist, circa 1892–1893

Lewis Aron

An earlier version of this article was presented at New York University Postdoctoral Program Conference, "The Psychoanalytic Century: Psyche, Soma, Gender, Word," May 6, 1995. In its present form, this article was first published in *Contemporary Psychoanalysis* 32:99–114 and is reprinted by permission.

In this article, I want to celebrate one aspect of Freud's creative genius, and in doing so, I want to make use of Freud as a model for contemporary students of psychotherapy and psychoanalysis. My use of Freud in this way will ironically have subversive implications for psychoanalytic practice. The facet of Freud's originality that I will focus on was his unsurpassed ability and determination to develop a way of working as a psychotherapist that was uniquely his own and that best expressed his own character. Freud believed that he was discovering a scientific method, an instrument that to a great extent eliminated or minimized what he called "the subjective factor." Nevertheless, he recognized that to work as a psychotherapist different people were likely need varying procedures. In the third chapter of *Studies on Hysteria* (Breuer and Freud 1893–1895), the case of Miss Lucy R., Freud wrote, perhaps a bit sarcastically, in regard to the practice of clinical hypnosis, that he was sure that many other physicians who practice psychotherapy could deal with certain technical difficulties with more skill that he could. "If so," he went on, "they may adopt some procedure other than mine" (p. 109). This comment foreshadows his later remark, in the opening paragraph of his (1912) "Recommendations for physicians on the psycho-analytic method of treatment," that "I must, however, expressly state that this technique has proved to be the only method suited to my individuality; I do not venture to deny that a physician quite differently constitute might feel impelled to adopt a different attitude to his patients and to the task before him" (p. 111). Indeed, Freud was relatively open-minded and even encouraging of experiments with psychoanalytic technique as long as they did not directly challenge his theoretical beliefs or risk endangering the reputation of the psychoanalytic movement.[1] Ironically, by taking Freud as a model of a clinician

---

1. An excellent example of his liberal attitude concerning technical innovation is reflected in his tolerant stance toward Ferenczi's clinical experiments over many years, especially in the 1920s. It was only when

who was insistent upon working in a way that was personally satisfying, some of us may find ourselves working in ways very different from Freud's, using clinical techniques that are perhaps
better adapted to our own characters. (It must also be remembered
in this context that Freud never seems to have practiced as he
preached in his technical papers.) It is in this spirit that I wish to
celebrate Freud as a model of a creative psychotherapist.

Freud himself, in a letter to Jung of February 17, 1908, declared
that the "case histories in the *Studies* are no less antiquated than
Breuer's theories and are not worth translating" (1974, p. 120).
Luckily for us, in spite of Freud's 1908 retrospection, these early
cases have been translated and preserved so that we may celebrate
them now, one hundred years later. I will focus here on Freud's
development as a psychotherapist up to and during the years 1892–
1893, when he treated Lucy. Lucy came to Freud toward the end
of 1892 and her treatment continued until early 1893. Freud probably wrote the case history in 1893. I center my study on these
years because they marked a turning point in the development of
Freud's practice, in that it was at this time that he shifted from hypnotism to a rudimentary form of free association. In his description of Lucy's consultation hours, Freud indicates that in his work
with her, by the end of 1892, he still tried to induce hypnosis, settled
for a nonsomnabulistic state, but did have her lie on the couch,
eyes closed. He says she was in a state that may have differed very
little from the normal one.

While the story of Freud's abandonment of hypnotism has been
told innumerable times before, I would like to tell it yet again with
the benefit of the availability of recent historical scholarship, focusing on Freud's struggles at the very time he was treating Lucy.[2]
At the onset I want to acknowledge my indebtedness to the ground-

---

Ferenczi challenged Freud's clinical and developmental theories, and
when Freud heard reports of Ferenczi's allowing his patients to kiss him,
that Freud voiced any objection to Ferenczi's clinical experimentation.

2. It may be helpful for me at this point to clarify my usage of the
terms *hypnosis* and *hypnotism*. Following Weitzenhoffer (1989), I will use
hypnosis to mean an inferred psychophysiological state, an altered state
of consciousness, and I will use the term *hypnotism* to refer to its study,
production, and utilization.

breaking work of Henri Ellenberger, Peter Swales, and Albrecht Hirschmüller. Much of what I have to say is taken directly from their work, and Peter Swales, in particular, has most generously guided my understanding of this period.[3]

To anticipate my broadest conclusions, I will say that I believe that Freud's creation of the psychoanalytic method was a unique, revolutionary, and personally expressive development, and that by 1893 he had evolved a distinctly psychoanalytic brand of psychotherapy, *but also* that the development of this form of psychotherapy was a product of its time and a logical outgrowth of the *Zeitgeist*. Looking at Freud's discoveries in historical context does not diminish our appreciation of his achievements but rather enhances our awareness of his unique contributions.

Other accounts of Freud's abandonment of hypnotism have tended to blame Freud for the general decline in the use of hypnotism. That is, they have suggested that hypnotism became less popular because psychoanalysis became the dominant form of treatment.[4] I will be suggesting that the causal flow was more complicated, moving in both directions, that psychoanalysis itself came about because of a more general trend away from hypnotism and toward verbal psychotherapy conducted in the awake state.

Writing in 1923, Freud observed, "It is not easy to overestimate the importance of the part played by hypnotism in the history of the origins of psycho-analysis. From a theoretical as well as from a therapeutic point of view, psycho-analysis has at its command a legacy which it has inherited from hypnotism" (p. 192).

---

3. My thanks as well to John Kerr for sharing with me his insight into this early phase of psychoanalytic history.

4. See, for example, the highly polemical *Freud and Hypnosis* by Kline, 1958. But even the most authoratative reviews of the history of hypnotism have taken this stand. For example, Wolberg (1948), in his comprehensive textbook *Medical Hypnosis*, asserts that "the growth of the psychoanalytic movement and the development of other forms of psychotherapy reduced hypnosis to a place of relatively minor importance" (p. 12). More recently, in their introduction to the *Handbook of Clinical Hypnosis*, Rhue, Lynn, and Kirsch (1993) similarly suggest that "after the abandonment of hypnosis by Freud, its clinical use virtually vanished for decades" (pp. 6–7).

Here to go back in time: between 1860 and 1882 hypnotism had fallen into disrepute. This was a period of heavily organic psychiatry that placed a strong emphasis on neuroanatomy and neurophysiology, on heredity on theories of degeneration, and in which there was little room for mental events and for psychology. Remember, after all, that it is not as if these psychiatrists held any real keys in their hands, and attitudes of pessimism and therapeutic nihilism dominated the psychiatric teaching hospitals of the time. But then, during the 1860s and 1870s, the Danish hypnotist Carl Hansen stirred up a great deal of popular and scientific interest in hypnotism by traveling from city to city performing public demonstrations. In his autobiographical study, Freud (1925) remembers that as a student he had seen one of Hansen's performances and "was convinced of the genuineness of the phenomena" (p. 16). Freud is referring to demonstrations of hypnotism given by Hansen in Vienna in 1880.[5]

Up to and around 1880 clinical hypnotism had still not become widespread. Two unrelated occurred in 1882 that were to quickly raise hypnotism into something of a fad in European medical circles. First, Jean Martin Charcot, who had an international reputation as the greatest neurologist of his time, had begun to experiment with hypnotism in 1878, and on February 13, 1882 he read a paper to the Academy of Sciences in Paris that was to establish hypnotism as a legitimate subject of scientific study. Freud (1886) was to write regarding Charcot that he had made a scientific study of hypnotism "a region of neuropathology which had to be wrung on the one side from skepticism and on the other from fraud" (p. 11). Second, it was in 1882 that Hippolyte Bernheim, a professor with an excellent reputation in the faculty of medicine at Nancy, visited the country doctor and hypnotist A. A. Liebault and became a disciple and proselytizer of clinical hypnotism and the founder of the so-called Nancy school of hypnotism. Freud was soon to be directly influenced by both of these leading pioneers.[6]

---

5. See Freud's letter to Eduard Silberstein, February 3, 1880.

6. Space does not permit me to discuss the differences between the views of the so-called Paris and Nancy schools or to reflect on Freud's position on these differences. However, Freud clearly summarizes his

In Vienna, Moritz Benedikt, a neuropathologist, had experimented with hypnotism a neuropathologist, had experimented with hypnotism from the late 1860s. Breuer, who was at that time his assistant, warned Benedikt to discontinue these experiments because he was practicing a form of animal magnetism (Chertok and De Saussure 1979, p. 115). Benedikt vacillated in his opinions regarding hypnotism. After meeting Charcot he spoke in favor of hypnotism, but at other times he opposed the practice of hypnotism and even its investigation. I will return to Benedikt later, because in his own opposition to hypnotism, he was moving in a direction that anticipates where Freud would ultimately go. With the help of some intervention by his teachers Brücke and Meynert, Freud was to be awarded a travel grant from the University of Vienna to go and study with Charcot in Paris, which he did from late 1885 to early 1886. It was Benedikt who wrote a letter of introduction for Freud to Charcot.

Freud had seen hypnotism being practiced in Obersteiner's private sanitorium for three weeks prior to his visit to Paris, and Jones (cited in Chertok and De Saussure 1979, p. 116) believes that he may have first tried it at that time. Nevertheless, when Freud left Vienna to go to study with Charcot, his intention was to study neuroanatomy, but by the time he left Paris a few months later, his mind was filled with thoughts regarding hypnosis, hysteria, and the neuroses. Undoubtedly, Freud's meeting with Charcot had a profound effect on him in spite of the fact that, as Ellenberger (1970) has demonstrated, he actually studied with Charcot only for a few weeks. The meeting, in Ellenberger's account, took the form of an "existential encounter" (p. 436), and Charcot remained so important in Freud's estimation that in December of 1889, when Freud's first son was born, Freud named him Jean Martin after his teacher.

Upon his return to Vienna, Freud was singing the praises of Charcot, so much so that this idealization of Charcot contributed to getting him into some trouble with his colleagues. I am referring to the infamous episode of Freud's reading his paper on male

---

understanding of the differences in his (1889) review of Forel's book (p. 97), as well as in other places.

hysteria to the Society of Physicians in October 1886. Freud's colleagues were offended by the credit that Freud attributed to Charcot and to the way in which he consequently devalued their own contributions and understandings (see Ellenberger 1970).

Freud opened his own private practice as a nerve specialist on Easter, 1886 and was married that September. In that same year he translated a volume of Charcot's lectures. Hysteria and hypnosis dominated Freud's imagination, yet in his practice he relied on the then traditional techniques of electrotherapy, hydrotherapy, massage, rest cures, and perhaps most importantly suggestion and manipulation. In a letter to Fliess of December 28, 1887, Freud writes that "During the last few weeks, I have taken up hypnosis and have had all sorts of small but remarkable successes" (quoted in Breuer and Freud 1893–1895, p. xi). Given Freud's enthusiasm about hypnotism, why did he wait almost a year and a half after opening his practice before beginning to use the method?

It needs to be remembered that Freud was just beginning his practice, had just gotten married, and would have been reluctant to do anything overly controversial, particularly because he had already been involved in two controversies, one about his use of cocaine and the other regarding his 1886 paper on male hysteria, which had offended some of his colleagues. Remember too that the clinical use of hypnotism still had very strong opponents in Vienna, including Freud's teacher Meynert as well as Benedikt. Furthermore, it must be understood that even Charcot had *not* been enthusiastically advocating hypnotism as a treatment procedure; rather he only cautiously endorsed hypnotism for therapeutic purposes. For Charcot, hypnosis was important mostly as a means of demonstration and experimentation, because through the use of hypnotism he could stimulate through suggestion in hysterical patients the same somatic symptoms typical of traumatic hysteria. In our efforts to understand Freud's fledgling efforts at utilizing hypnosis, it should not be forgotten that at this time therapeutic treatment for nervous and mental disorders was still dominated by degenerationist thinking, and even Charcot's views on hysteria were quite strictly neurological. As Micale (1995) writes concerning the clinics of Charcot and Bernheim during this period, they were "above all sites for medical observation and experimentation. Generally speaking, the second half of the nineteenth century, while a major period of advancement in the etiological understanding of disease, was not a great age of healing" (p. 268). So Freud's therapeutic use of hypnotism could not have come about under the influence of Charcot. As both Hirschmüller (1978) and Swales (1988) conclude, in spite of the fact that he was lecturing on hypnosis by 1886, having been influenced by his trip to Paris, it seems evident that his clinical use of hypnotism did not occur for another eighteen months, and, we are about to see, it was more the result of the influence of Bernheim.

In any event, Freud began to experiment with clinical hypnotism beginning in December 1887, and he later wrote (Breuer and Freud, 1893-1895) that he began to use Breuer's cathartic method combined with direct hypnotic suggestion in May 1889 in the case of Emmy von N. Again we must ask, now that Freud was using hypnotism with his patients, why the long delay of another year and a half before he would shift from pure hypnotic suggestion to catharsis with suggestion? Contradicting his earlier remark, Freud later wrote in his *Autobiographical Study* that "from the very first I made use of hypnosis in *another* manner, apart from hypnotic suggestion" (1925, p. 19). This would imply that he had been using the cathartic method from the time he began using hypnotism. Swales concluded that Freud probably had been using Breuer's cathartic method along with suggestion even before May 1889 and certainly by that summer. But again the question arises, why would Freud have waited so long to use either hypnotism with suggestion alone or hypnotism with catharsis, when Breuer had treated Anna O. during the years 1881–1882 and had described the case to him as early as November 1882 and throughout 1883? Presumably, by the time Freud opened his practice he had been familiar with the idea of the cathartic method for a few years and would have been eager to try it for himself. I cannot develop this line of thought further here, except to say that a reading of Hirschmüller (1978) leads one to question how much the story that we have come to know of Anna O. was not the end result of much retroactive reconstruction by Freud and Breuer that occurred years after the actual treatment of Bertha Pappenheim.

But let's look even more carefully at the state of hypnotism at this time and at the chronology of Freud's use of hypnotism. In Germany, in 1888 and 1889, hypnotism gained momentum through the work of Moll and Forel, and in 1889 Krafft-Ebing emphasized the medical and therapeutic aim of hypnotism. By 1888–1889, the center of serious work in hypnotism had shifted from France to German-speaking countries, and furthermore it was now largely dominated by the influence of Bernheim.

In an article on "Hysteria" in 1886, Freud is already able to write that in the direct method of treating hysteria we look for the causes of hysteria in "unconscious ideational life" (p. 56), and he credits Breuer with the method of leading patients under hypnosis back to the psychic origins of their symptoms. He writes that once Bernheim's ideas concerning the use of suggestion had more deeply penetrated medical circles, direct suggestion would turn out to be the best method for treating hysteria. It is completely unclear from reading Freud's paper of 1888 how he reconciled his understanding of Breuer's ideas and method with those of Bernheim and the Nancy school.

Freud never regarded himself as particularly adept at hypnotism, and he tells us that he went to Bernheim in Nancy to perfect his hypnotic technique (1925, p. 17). During the years 1888 and 1889 he translated Bernheim's first book. He had contact with August Forel, a well-known Swiss psychiatrist, and in July and November of 1889 he wrote a review of Forel's work on hypnotism. It was Forel who introduced him to Bernheim. By 1889, in his review of Forel's *Hypnotism*, about a year and a half after beginning to experiment with the clinical use of hypnotism, Freud would write quite authoritatively that he himself had "reached an independent judgement in matters relating to hypnosis" (p. 93), and he asserts that his own patients improve through hypnosis.

If Freud was just beginning to use catharsis at this time, then what else had he been doing with his hypnotized patients? Using hypnotic suggestion, he would emphatically deny the patients' symptoms, giving patients assurances, commands, explanations, and posthypnotic suggestions. In an 1891 article on hypnosis, Freud adds that he would question his patients about the origins of their symptoms, but to answer they must be somnambulistic, otherwise they should not talk (p. 112). This is a critical point for us to understand. It was believed that a hypnotized patient's talking would be likely to lessen the depth of the trance, and therefore Freud could not use the cathartic method with patients unless they were somnambulistic.[7] Freud correctly realized that most patients were not this hypnotizable. This would have meant that catharsis, or any talking therapy, would be useful only with very few exceptionally hypnotizable patients. As long as Freud was relying on direct suggestion, the depth of the patient's trance did not matter very much because the patient did not have to talk, but with the cathartic method patients had to be verbally, cognitively, and affectively active, and so if hypnosis was necessary then they needed to be in a very deep or somnambulistic trance. In practice, Freud would not always get a deep trance. This is what drove him to go to Bernheim to learn to perfect his hypnotic technique in 1889. Freud's dissatisfaction with his skill as a hypnotist and his ultimate shift away from hypnotism were both due in part to his requirement that his patients be more verbally active. Freud did not want to be the one doing all of the talking; he wanted to listen to his patient so that he himself could learn. This represents a major turning point in his use of the method, and we shall return to this shortly.

What did Freud actually learn from his visit to Bernheim? Freud (1925) later wrote that his visit to Bernheim in 1889 taught him the limitations of hypnotic suggestion (p. 21). I think that the visit to Nancy was pivotal because Freud clearly got the idea from Bernheim, although Bernheim had not yet articulated it in this way, that he could do psychotherapy, which was at the time synonymous with hypnotherapy, without inducing formal hypnosis. A number of things point in this direction. Freud had brought a patient of his (Anna von Lieben) with him to Nancy for Bernheim to hypnotize, and Bernheim failed to hypnotize her and told Freud that he had his greatest success with hospitalized patients. Bernheim taught that hypnosis was easier to induce in people accustomed to passive obedience, and he had poor results with people in the higher and wealthier classes. It must be considered that the working class and peasantry tended to be in far greater awe vis-à-vis physicians and educated people generally, Liebault, from whom Bernheim had learned hypnotism, was a country doctor whose patients were largely poor city people and local peasants who paid

---

7. Somnambulism refers to a very deep state of hypnosis whose chief feature is spontaneous amnesia.

only what they could afford or nothing at all. Keeping in mind that Freud was in private practice and that his clientele came predominantly from the upper and upper-middle classes, we can see that Freud would have had to modify his approach to make it more useful with these patients. On his visit to Nancy, Freud was impressed with Bernheim's contention that posthypnotic amnesia, the sine qua non of somnambulism, was not complete, that with concentration, the pressure technique, and skillful questioning, the patient could remember what had occurred even while in hypnosis. It struck Freud that one could access the unconscious directly through consciousness, without bypassing consciousness through hypnosis.

Bernheim's theory that hypnotism was nothing other than suggestion led the way for the abandonment of the need to formally induce an hypnotic trance. If hypnosis was not a special altered state, but was rather just the product of suggestion, than the possibility was opened not to induce a formal state that mimicked sleep, but rather to attempt to use suggestion directly. This was the path that Bernheim was ultimately to take, making less and less use of hypnotism. By 1892 Bernheim suggested that the word *hypnosis* be dropped in favor of speaking of the *state of suggestion*. Years later, Bernheim would write that "modern psychotherapy, emancipated from hypnotism, is the creation of the Nancy school" (quoted in Ellenberger 1970, pp. 804–805).

By the time of his next book in 1891, which Freud translated in 1892, Bernheim maintained that therapeutic success was not directly related to the depth of hypnotic sleep. Most subjects, he now taught, remain partially conscious during hypnosis, and most hypnotic phenomena can be obtained with the subject awake. Ultimately, Bernheim's position led him to conclude that hypnosis was not a special state and that all of the phenomena described by the term hypnotism could have been discovered in the waking state.

In a lecture of April 27, 1892 to the Viennese Medical Club, Freud espoused Bernheim's view of hypnotism and advised physicians to go to Nancy to learn it (Ellenberger 1970, p. 485, n. 288). And as late as in his 1892–1893 paper on clinical hypnotism, Freud used Bernheim's method and not catharsis.

Let me put forth my own reconstruction, then, of Freud's development as a hypnotist thus far. Having begun with a strong neurological and somaticist approach to hysteria and hypnosis, Freud started using hypnotism cautiously along with the standard and more acceptable methods of treatment of the day. He soon felt increasingly frustrated with these methods, and bored by them as well, since they did not shed any light on the origins or meanings of hysterical symptoms. While it was under Charcot's influence that he became seriously interested in the phenomenon of hypnosis and the descriptive diagnosis of hysteria, it was under the influence of Bernheim that Freud began to think psychologically about the dynamics of hypnotism.[8] Once Freud was able to see that hypnosis was largely a psychological phenomenon, he was able to begin to move beyond the formalistic induction of trance. Freud, I believe, was mostly interested in investigating the psychological origins of his patients' symptoms, their memories. Breuer had been lucky in his work with Bertha Pappenheim because she went into deep trance states spontaneously. As a matter of fact, as Hirschmüller (1978) emphasizes, it was only after she went into trances by herself, spontaneously, that Breuer began to induce hypnosis in her. Freud went to Bernheim in the hope that he would learn to deepen his patient's trance states in order to be able to allow the patients to talk to him, so that he could investigate the origins of their symptoms and then eliminate the symptoms through suggestion. Instead, Freud learned that he could have his patients talk with him directly, while awake, and accomplish as much.

Freud was not alone in coming to these conclusions following his exposure to Bernheim. He was among a number of leading hypnotherapists who were attempting to develop methods of psychotherapy that did not rely upon formal hypnotic induction. Bernheim, by showing that hypnotism was a psychological phenomenon, namely that it was a form of interpersonal suggestion, created

---

8. This is so in spite of the fact that, as Gauld (1992) points out, it is an oversimplification to describe Bernheim's theory as "psychological" since his early speculations as to the nature of the hypnotic state were neurophysiological.

the possibility for the shift from hypnotic suggestion to verbal psy-chotherapy in the waking state. Bernheim showed that the distinc-tion between states of consciousness was not absolute, and that through an act of will patients could recall what happened in hyp-notic amnesia.

From 1889 to 1892, following his experience with Bernheim and coinciding with his treatment of Anna von Lieben, who Peter Swales (1986) has documented was the patient whom Freud brought with him to Nancy, Freud would place less and less emphasis on hyp-notic trance and more and more on understanding the meaning of symptoms and tracing their origins. Freud may have stopped try-ing to hypnotize her, or perhaps he just stopped worrying about the depth of her trance state. If patients could overcome hypnotic amnesia while awake, then they could overcome other motivated forgetting or repression while awake as well. As Swales has docu-mented, Freud used the pressure technique that he learned from observing Bernheim: he questioned and probed relentlessly, and free association asserted itself more or less spontaneously in Freud's attempt to unravel the most intricate threads of his patients' memory.

The claim that I am making is that by the early 1890s, largely because of the impact of Bernheim's teachings, a number of lead-ing hypnotherapists were quickly abandoning the hypnotic proce-dure and evolving a variety of forms of talking therapies that were conducted in the waking state. These practitioners were, each in their own way, evolving from hypnotherapists to psychotherapists. To some degree we must take into consideration here that hypno-tism had indeed attracted a lot of quacks who tended to bring it into disrepute or at least to foster suspicions and mistrust among the public and among the medical community. As Swales remarks, by the early 1890s hypnotism was far from being à la mode. Freud's development of the free association method and of psychoanaly-sis was a part of this trend in the late 1880s and 1890s, and in this respect it was absolutely a part of the Zeitgeist. However, Freud was eager to substitute for hypnotic suggestion something that was more his own, and the very specific form that Freud's psycho-therapy was to take was highly distinctive and reflected his own personal, complex synthesis.

Let me give a few examples to document this trend that I am describing of hypnotherapists who were evolving into psychotherapists, largely under the influence of Bernheim, during the early 1890s. Following his brief visit to Nancy in 1889, Freud came to Paris in the company of Bernheim and Liebault to attend the first International Congress on Hypnotism. It is unclear whether Freud was in attendance when H. Bourru and P. Burot presented a joint paper. However, these authors had published their ideas in a book the year before, and what is most important is that these ideas were in wide circulation at the time. Bourru and Burot proposed that the retrieval of traumatic memories and the relieving of the associated memories, both within and outside of hypnosis, was curative. These authors emphasized the return to origins as well as the necessity for a kind of discharge or explosion (see Ellenberger, p. 760).

At the same congress, A. W. van Renterghem and F. van Eeden described their Clinic of Suggestive Psychotherapy. Ellenberger observes that this may have been the first time that the word psychotherapy was used in a congress (p. 760). These two Dutchmen were under the influence of Bernheim and established their clinic in 1887. Van Eeden preferred not to put his patients into a deep or somnambulistic state because he believed that this interfered in furthering his aim of enlarging the sphere of effectiveness of the patient's will. Instead he developed the method of having patients "passive; lying still with closed eyes." and he avoided using the terms hypnosis or hypnotism and preferred the term "psychotherapy" (quoted in Gauld 1992, p. 340). Van Renterghem, while still using hypnotism, taught that hypnotic suggestion was not enough. He emphasized that one must locate the underlying causes of the problem and try to alleviate it. Van Renterghem and van Eeden's work was well known among their contemporaries because of the detailed statistics that they published regarding their success rate.

Earlier I mentioned the work of Benedikt in Vienna and his ambivalence regarding hypnotism. Benedikt had been attracted to hypnotism following his exposure to Charcot, but he was concerned about the deep, almost mystical dependency of the patient on the hypnotist. By 1891, Benedikt argued vehemently against hypnotism and in favor of psychotherapy on a conscious verbal level. Interestingly as well, Benedikt suggested that, the actual cause of hysteria was either a psychic trauma or a functional disturbance of the genital system or the sexual life, and he emphasized the extreme importance of the patient's fantasy life (see Ellenberger, p. 764).

As further evidence of how prevalent was the trend away from trance induction, consider this statement by Strumpell in his inaugural lecture as vice-rector of the University of Erlangen in November of 1892, titled "On the origin and healing of diseases through mental representations." He said, "No healing occurs through hypnosis that could not have been caused by other means" (quoted in Ellenberger, p. 766, n. 73). Ellenberger concludes, "Thus we can see that in 1892 there was a choice of psychotherapies ranging from hypnotic suggestion and catharsis to the combination of supportive, expressive, and directive therapy" (p. 767).

By reducing hypnotism to suggestion, Bernheim made hypnotism less appealing to those physicians trained in a somaticist tradition who might have been more attracted to it as a method of exploiting a neuropathological condition, as it had been presented by the Paris school. On the other hand, by eliminating the need for a formal hypnotic induction, and by pointing out the lack of correlation between hypnotic depth and effectiveness of suggestion, Bernheim made possible the more direct application of verbal psychotherapy in the awake state. By explaining hypnotism in terms of suggestion, a vague phenomenon itself not much understood, Bernheim inadvertently brought the focus of attention onto a psychological and interpersonal phenomenon. In his preface to the translation of Bernheim's first book, entitled *Suggestion*, Freud (1888a) presents a penetrating critique of the idea of suggestion. At the end of 1892 when he is treating Lucy, and still in 1893 when he is writing the case history, Freud moves back and forth between his use of suggestion to eliminate symptoms following Bernheim, his remaining loyalties to Charcot who dies in 1893, and his own development of Breuer's cathartic method. It is only by the end of 1892 that Freud largely gives up direct suggestion under Breuer's influence, and even following this Freud publishes a case in which he relied on direct suggestion. Gradually, Freud relies more on "concentration" and the pressure technique, and then directed and increasingly free association.[9] Each step in this development leads to increased activity on the part of the patient and to the furtherance of the patient's autonomy. To review: from Charcot, Freud took his interest in hysteria and hypnosis; from Bernheim, he took the recognition that hypnotism was unnecessary and that he could look to the psychological to explain the apparent phenomenon of somnambulism; and from Breuer he took the idea of catharsis and its implication that he should listen at length to his patients.

By 1892 a number of the leading practitioners of hypnotism, following Bernheim, were experimenting with conducting psychotherapy with patients awake. Freud was the most important of these pioneers. What Freud did in essence was to take the freedom offered by Bernheim's elimination of the need for a somnambulistic patient and to construct a method that allowed him to listen to his patients, to all of them whether somnamulistic or not, for an extended period of time. From a hypnotic technique that was first thought to be important because of its neuroanatomical and neurophysiological underpinnings, Freud developed a method that would ultimately turn out to be important because it allowed one person to understand and influence another psychologically. With the abandonment of hypnotism and the shift in interest away from the depths of trance and the forms of consciousness, and toward the contents of the patient's history and dynamics, much was gained, but there was also much lost. It is only now, a century later, that as analysts we have once again become quite interested in our patients' states of consciousness. For example, witness the rising interest in the phenomenon of dissociation. In a recent ar-

---

9. Space does not permit a discussion of the widespread popularity of the notion of catharsis in the 1880s following the republication of Bernay's book on catharsis in 1880. Clearly, this played a key role in the development of Breuer's cathartic technique. For more on this, and for a better understanding of Breuer's influence on Freud, see Hirschmüller (1978) and Swales (1986, 1988). I have likewise not discussed the similarities to Freud's work in the approach of Pierre Janet. This is because my focus here has been on the move away from hypnotism, and while Janet's work overlaps with Freud's in a number of ways, Janet continued to rely on hypnotism as a method, although by the turn of the century he was using a wide assortment of therapeutic techniques.

ticle, cowritten with Annabella Bushra (Aron and Bushra 1995), we have examined this resurgence of interest by contemporary psychoanalysts in states of consciousness. There we concluded that one important contribution of the psychoanalytic setting, as developed by Freud, was that it created the conditions wherein both patient and analyst could move freely back and forth among a wide variety of mental and behavioral states; that is, the analytic situation allows for mutual and optimal levels of regression within the analytic dyad.

With the shift from hypnotism to free association, the change was not only from neurology to psychology: in effect, Freud's work reversed the general flow of the conversation between the patient and the doctor. Instead of using hypnotism to put the patient into a passive, sleeplike state in which *she* was to listen to the doctor as *he* told her what she felt and what to do about it, Freud (following Breuer) developed a method in which the doctor was to listen to the patient as she told him about her life. Thus, as Jessica Benjamin (1995) has described, patients were transformed from passive objects of his investigations to become speaking subjects. Of course, as John Forrester (1990) points out, Freud maintained his authority in that it was he who decided what the patient's stories meant; nevertheless, a crucial step had been taken in destabilizing the structure of authority relations between doctor and patient.

Freud's method permitted him to be very much himself as a therapist. His tendency was to be an explorer, an investigator, an archeologist, a puzzle solver, and the traditional methods of his day not only did not work, but he frankly admitted that they bored him because they did not permit him to use these aspects of himself fully. The method that he developed had the distinct advantage, as he pointed out repeatedly, that it was at one and the same time a method of treatment and of investigation and research. To put this differently, Freud was comfortable with the fact that the method met his own needs as well as the needs of his patients. The method of psychoanalysis, the free association method even in its rudimentary form, and its accompanying theory of neurosis, particularly the emphasis on defense, was uniquely Freud's own. While very much a part of the *Zeitgeist*, by 1892–1893 Freud evolved a way of working that met his own needs, interests, and personal requirements. These conditions included that the work he was conducting be interesting and challenging to him and that it allow him to utilize his considerable investigative and analytic talents. Freud wrote in an 1897 letter to Fliess, "one always remains a child of his age, even in what one deems one's very own" (in Freud 1985, p. 277). By 1893, when he writes the case history of Lucy, Freud is well on his way to developing his very own method of psychotherapy—psychoanalysis. A century later, we celebrate that achievement.

REFERENCES

Aron, L. and Bushra, A. (1995). The mutual regulation of regression in psychoanalysis. Presented at the Division of Psychoanalysis (39), Spring Meeting, Santa Monica, CA, April.

Benjamin, J. (1995). Between body and speech: The primal leap. Keynote Address, New York University Postdoctoral Program Conference, The psychoanalytic century: psyche, soma, gender, word. New York, May.

Breuer, J. and Freud, S. (1893–1895). Studies on hysteria. *Standard Edition* 2.

Chertok, L. and De Saussure, R. (1979). *The Therapeutic Revolution: From Mesmer to Freud.* New York: Brunner/Mazel.

Ellenberger, H. (1970). *The Discovery of the Unconscious.* New York: Basic Books.

Forrester, J. (1990). *The Seductions of Psychoanalysis.* Cambridge, MA: Cambridge University Press.

Freud, S. (1886). Report on my studies in Paris and Berlin. *Standard Edition* 5:3–18.

———(1888a). Preface to the translation of Bernheim's *Suggestion. Standard Edition* 12:73–88.

———(1888b). Hysteria. *Standard Edition* 1:39–62.

———(1889). Review of August Forel's *Hypnotism. Standard Edition* 1:89–102.

———(1891). Hypnosis. *Standard Edition* 1:103–114.

———(1892–1893). A case of successful treatment by hypnotism. *Standard Edition* 12:115–128.

———(1912). Recommendations to physicians practicing psychoanalysis. *Standard Edition* 12:109–120.

—— (1923). A short account of psycho-analysis. *Standard Edition* 19:191–212.

—— (1925). An autobiographical study. *Standard Edition* 20:3–76.

—— (1974). *The Freud/Jung Letters: The Correspondence between Sigmund Freud and C. G. Jung*, ed. W. McGuire, trans. R. Mannheim and R.F.C. Hall. Princeton, NJ: Princeton University Press.

—— (1985). *The Complete Letters of Sigmund Freud to Wilhelm Fliess: 1887–1904*, ed. J. M. Masson. Cambridge, MA: Harvard University Press.

Gauld, A. (1992). *A History of Hypnotism*. Cambridge, MA: Cambridge University Press.

Hirschmüller, A. (1978). *The Life and Work of Joseph Breuer*. New York: New York University Press.

Kline, M. V. (1958). *Freud and Hypnosis*. New York: Agora (reprinted 1966).

Micale, M. S. (1995). *Approaching Hysteria*. Princeton, NJ: Princeton University Press.

Rhue, J. W., Lynn, S. J., and Kirsch, I. (1993). *Handbook of Clinical Hypnosis*. Washington, DC: American Psychological Association.

Swales, P. (1986). Freud, his teacher, and the birth of psychoanalysis. In *Freud Appraisals and Reappraisals: Contributions to Freud Studies*, ed. P. E. Stepansky, pp. 3–82. Hillsdale, NJ: Analytic Press.

—— (1988). Freud, Katharina, and the first "wild analysis." In *Freud: Appraisals and Reappraisals: Contributions to Freud Studies*, ed. P. E. Stepansky, pp. 81–166. Hillsdale, NJ: Analytic Press.

Weitzenhoffer, A. M. (1989). *The Practice of Hypnotism*. New York: John Wiley.

Wolberg, L. R. (1948). *Medical Hypnosis: Volume 1: The Principles of Hypnotherapy*. New York: Grune & Straton.

11

Back to the Future in Psychoanalysis: Trauma, Dissociation, and the Nature of Unconscious Processes

Jody Messler Davies

The poet, T. S. Eliot wrote:

We shall not cease from exploration
And the end of all our exploring
Will be to arrive where we started
And know the place for the first time.

So it is, in large measure, the contention of this paper, that at the end of the first century of psychoanalytic thought, theorizing, and practice, we have implicitly returned to many of the technically "pre-analytic" writings of Sigmund Freud, and to the wealth of clinical investigations in dynamic psychiatry that marked this period at the end of the late nineteenth century. In fact, in devoting an entire three-day conference to this remarkably fertile period in psychoanalytic thought, we must ask ourselves what knowledge from this period should be brought with us into the next century, as well as what contemporary psychological and psychoanalytic conceptualizations can be used to illuminate controversies that were irresolvable at that time and at the level of clinical sophistication then available.

In examining this question I will suggest that much of what we now know about the psychological difficulties of those who have suffered physically and sexually abusive childhoods was well known, at least in a rudimentary sense, one hundred years ago. Indeed I will suggest that the ways in which we understood trauma one hundred years ago were not only more in keeping with current trauma theories but suggest the nascent beginnings of a model of mind more in keeping with contemporary psychoanalytic practice, most particularly with relational psychoanalysis.

In order to illustrate my points, I will refer to Freud's case history of Katharina (Breuer and Freud 1893–1895). This is in actuality not a case history of a patient treated by Freud, but a description of a series of conversations Freud conducted with Katharina, a young girl who approached him while he was on vacation in the eastern Alps. It can be regarded as a schematic rendering of the way in which Freud was conceptualizing hysterical neurosis, at this point in the late nineteenth century, when he still believed neurosis to be caused by the premature sexual overstimulation of children. Indeed Freud's later emendations to the case history will also shed light on the ways in which he came to alter his initial views. The schematic nature of the case may well lend itself to the questions I wish to pose. What was known about the etiology of hysteria, and its particular relationship to sexual trauma, before Freud? What did Freud himself add to these early conceptualizations? What effect did Freud's later rejection of the seduction hypothesis have on our understanding of psychic trauma in particular, and on our way of viewing unconscious processes, more specifically? And finally, what exciting new theoretical and clinical insights can be attained by returning to the pre-Freudian conceptualizations of trauma and psychic structure and attempting to integrate these with the more postmodern renderings of multiple self-organizations implicit in relational theories of psychoanalysis?

For those unfamiliar with the case history of Katharina, let me briefly describe the facts of its narrative.

Freud described Katharina as an unhappy-looking, yet healthy and robust young girl who described to him the sudden onset of a series of symptoms—extreme breathlessness, dizziness, and intense nausea—for which no known physiological determinants could be discovered. As Freud questioned the girl about the incidents surrounding the onset of her symptoms, she began to recall that they followed almost directly upon her discovering her uncle and her cousin alone in bed together: "he was lying on her" (p. 128). In a 1928 note to the original case, Freud reveals that indeed it was Katharina's father who had been discovered, not her uncle. Though Freud claims he changed the man's identity to preserve confidentiality, the actual paternal identity becomes necessary within the revised structural view of hysterical neurosis.

Freud comments: "Fräulein Katharina, if you could remember now what was happening in you at that time, when you had your first attack, what you thought about it—it would help you."

Katharina: "Yes, if I could. But I was so frightened that I've forgotten everything."

Freud here explains to the reader that "[t]he affect itself created a hypnoid state, whose products were then cut off from associative connection with the ego-consciousness" (p. 128). As I hope to show later, this is indeed an explanation of traumatic dissociation much more in keeping with contemporary explanations of the neurobiology of trauma than are Freud's later changes.

It was only in later discussion with Freud, when Katharina was able to connect up her experience of discovering father and cousin together in intercourse with earlier memories of being sexually approached by father herself, that her physical symptoms appeared to abate; she was in essence cured. Freud states:

> At the end of these two sets of memories she came to a stop. She was like someone transformed. The sulky, unhappy face had grown lively, her eyes were bright, she was lightened and exalted. Meanwhile the understanding of her case had become clear to me. The later part of what she had told me, in an apparently aimless fashion, provided an admirable explanation of her behaviour at the scene of the discovery. At that time she had carried about with her two sets of experiences which she remembered but did not understand, and from which she drew no inferences. When she caught sight of the couple in intercourse, she at once established a connection between the new impression and these two sets of recollections, she began to understand them and at the same time to fend them off. [p. 131]

At this point in time Freud's understanding of the mechanism of hysteria presupposed some necessary incompatibility between the conscious, unconflicted prepubescent experience of the patient (in Katharina's case her memories of father climbing into bed with her, of feeling his body against hers) and a precociously sexual, overstimulating idea that forced itself upon the mind at some later point in time (perhaps father had been trying to involve Katharina in the same kind of sexual intercourse that she now understood him to be having with her young cousin). The actual traumatic moment involved the repudiation of the incompatible idea, the conversion of overstimulating excitation into somatic symptomatology, and the setting up of independent, incompatible psychic centers of activity.

As I hope will become clear, these theories are considerably less original than we have grown used to consider and draw in very large measure from the earlier work of Charcot, Richer, and most specifically the very detailed clinical account of childhood trauma articulated by Pierre Janet. Though Freud uses the word *repres-*

sion to describe this process of psychic incompatability and splitting, it is clear that his description of the process is more in keeping with Janet's descriptions of "traumatic dissociation" than with
our later understanding of repression as a defensive manifestation
within the topographical model of unconscious, preconscious, and
conscious and the later structural model of id, ego, and superego.
Repression implies a hierarchical structuring of consciousness and
unconsciousness, with the goal of keeping certain experiences
entirely and permanently out of awareness, while dissociation
implies the failure to integrate certain fundamentally incompatible experiences and the vertical splitting of consciousness into
independent centers of awareness and activity.

Freud states:

> When this process occurs for the first time there comes into be-
> ing a nucleus and centre of crystallization for the formation of a
> psychical group divorced from the ego—a group around which
> everything which would imply an acceptance of the incompat-
> ible idea subsequently collects. The splitting of consciousness in
> these cases of acquired hysteria is accordingly a deliberate and
> intentional one. At least it is often *introduced* by an act of voli-
> tion; for the actual outcome is something different from what the
> subject intended. What he wanted was to do away with an idea,
> as though it had never appeared, but all he succeeds in doing is
> to isolate it psychically. [p. 123]

Ten years prior to *Studies on Hysteria,* Janet (1887) began working with hysterical patients, attempting to make sense of their puzzling symptomatology. His conclusions, which began appearing in
print seven years prior to Freud's and Breuer's *Studies on Hysteria,* bear a startling similarity to the latter. Janet came to believe
that the memory processes, the usual typical schemas for integrating new incoming information, provided the essential organizing
mental systems. When operating smoothly, most of these processes
went on out of awareness. These schemas are flexible, and there
is a constant oscillation between the effect of new information in
changing the internal structure of organizing schemas, and the
individual's reliance on these schemas in order to create mental
order and internal organization. Thus schemas affect the way in
which each individual views reality, and reality affects the ongoing structural nuances of schemas (Janet 1889). It is interesting

here to consider the Piagetian notions of accomodation and assimilation (cf. Piaget 1962) and to keep in mind that Piaget himself was one of Janet's most influential pupils. It is also, I believe, extraordinary to appreciate the prescience of these ideas, to compare them to current theories of the constructed nature of memory in the empirical work of people like Daniel Schacter (1987), and to note their application to clinical psychoanalysis in work by Irwin Hoffman (1983, 1991, 1998) and their application to such contemporary theories of consciousness as those of Donnel Stern (1997) on unformulated experience.

True psychic trauma, in Janet's terms, occurs when the integration of particularly overstimulating, intensely affective, uncharacteristic events cannot be incorporated into pre-existing schemas and indeed overwhelm the mental resiliency to accomodate such schemas to ongoing experience. Where such unintegrated traumatic events occur, Janet (1894) posited the establishment of what he termed "subconscious fixed ideas," believed by Ellenberger (1970) to be the first mention of a subconscious process in the history of clinical literature. Because of this basic incompatibility between traumatic events and pre-existing cognitive schemas, Janet maintained that hysterical symptoms are related to these split-off aspects of personality that come to operate and develop as autonomous centers of awareness and activity. He posited that curing hysterical symptoms would necessitate understanding the roots of these subconscious fixed ideas and reintegrating such experiences within the operative organizing schemas of meaning. We can compare these formulations to Freud's later writings, as described above.

Janet experimented with both hypnosis and "automatic talking," his own model of free association, in attempting such integration. Indeed, Henri Ellenberger (1970), who along with Bessel van der Kolk (van der Kolk and van der Hart 1989) has been most responsible for reintroducing Janet's work to contemporary clinical dialogue, observes that "it is difficult to study the initial periods of Janet's psychological analysis and of Freud's psychoanalysis without coming to the conclusion expressed by Regis and Hesnard, that . . . the methods and concepts of Freud were modeled after those of Janet, of whom he seems to have inspired himself constantly . . . until the paths of the two diverged" (p. 540).

The divergence here referred to, the divergence that led Freud on to the discovery of psychoanalysis and left Janet's work all but forgotten, was Freud's ultimate turning away from his work in *Studies on Hysteria,* his abandonment of the seduction hypothesis, and his formulation instead of a new model for understanding neurosogenesis. In 1944, Fairbairn made an interesting observation on the direction of Freud's work, noting that:

> it was upon a study of hysteria that Freud originally based the concept of repression; and it was only when he turned his attention from the nature of the repressed to that of the agency of repression that he became preoccupied with melancholia. In my opinion it is a matter of regret that he did not pursue his study of the agency of repression within the same field as his study of the repressed and thus did not make the phenomena of hysteria the basis of his theory of the mental apparatus. Had he done so, I feel convinced that his conception of repression would have been based, not upon what Melanie Klein subsequently described as "the depressive position," but upon what may be described as "the schizoid position," that his conception would have been based upon recognition of the fact that repression implies a splitting of the ego. [p. 169]

Freud's new theory turned the clinican's attention away from the realities of childhood trauma and abuse to a highly elaborated developmental schema of endogenously organized instinctual wishes and phase-specific object-related fantasies, out of which internal conflict and the division between conscious and unconscious processes was derived: a hierarchical rendering of conscious and unconscious processes, with vastly different theoretical implications and clinical applications from those of the model of vertical splits, organizing schemata, and multiple self-states described by Janet and the young Freud and later alluded to in the passage from Fairbairn. Indeed, suggested in the Fairbairnian quote is an interpretation of Kleinian theory, particularly when regarded in the dialectic style of Ogden (1986) rather than in its original hierarchic developmental mode, that suggests that development implies a movement to states of increasingly elaborated multiple self-experiences.

In a 1993 paper, Lewis Aron reconfigures the depressive position in Piagetian terms as the capacity for operational thought: the ability to tolerate the simultaneous awareness of two entirely different representational schemas of self and other. Likewise, Irene Fast's *Event Theory* (1985) offers an integration of Piaget and psychoanalytic thought by positing that the movement from part-object relationships to whole-object relationships, that is, the ability to hold good and bad aspects of the same representation in mind simultaneously, emerges out of the child's growing capacity to perceive and tolerate contradictory action schemas of self-other affect and action. It is my position that, in turning to Piaget, both Fast and Aron implicitly bring together the poststructural emphasis on multiple self-states and internalized object relations with the pre-Freudian writings on organizing mental schemas first conceptualized by Janet. I believe that by returning to these fundamental organizing schemas, but suggesting from our position one hundred years later, (based on our enhanced understanding of object-relational and self-psychological theories) that they are essentially organizing interpersonal schemas, we have in fact created a separate line for the development of a new psychoanalytic model of mind. I believe that such a model is more in keeping with a relational approach to psychoanalytic work and, because it contains cognitive, representational, and psychodynamic aspects, is more conducive to an integration of psychoanalytic theory with other branches of academic psychology.

The second major premise of this paper is that another essential difference between classical and post-classical psychoanalytic theories dates back to the point at which Pierre Janet and Sigmund Freud parted paths over the nature of hysterical disorders. This distinction has to do with fundamental differences in the nature of conscious and unconscious processes, the development of mental structures and the processes of psychic elaboration and differentiation that divide the two systems of thought. I will suggest that relational theories of mind are much more essentially tied to the pre-Freudian theories of Janet and the pre-analytic versions of Janet's theories articulated by Freud in *Studies on Hysteria*. Here we find the roots of dissociation, multiple self-states, and organizing cognitive and emotional schemas, as well as a very modern notion of constructed memory and meaning. In the remainder of this paper, I will attempt to articulate certain essential differences between what I will henceforth call the classical unconscious and

model of mind, the model articulated by Freud following his repudiation of *Studies on Hysteria,* and the very different structure of a
relational unconscious and model of mind, based in large measure
on these early writings of Janet.

A contemporary classical view holds to the underlying assumption that the individual unconscious is a compilation of psychically
dangerous object-related wishes, awareness of which threatens to
flood the person with all forms of unwelcome, even overwhelming, anxiety and/or depressive affect. It is these sexually and aggressively driven wishes themselves, as well as the elaborate system of defenses used to keep them out of awareness, that form
the substance of the classical unconscious. The symptom arises
as a compromise between the wish and the defense. The mode
of therapeutic action is then to help the patient uncover what it
is that he really wants from the important people in his life, via
the reactivation of such wishes in the transference relationship
to the analyst.

The classical unconscious is, therefore, a repression-based
model, organized around a developmental layering of fixed structures denoting the history of endogenously organized, phase-specific, object-related drives and drive derivatives. The very nature
of the significant objects toward whom these unconscious wishes
are directed is overwhelmingly determined by the developmental
progression of phase-specific drive derivatives instead of the actual qualities and textures of self–object interactions. Enhanced
psychic development implies a progressive distanciation from the
real, the primitive, the unneutralized passions of infancy and childhood that denote the substance and essence of this form of unconsciousness. The direction of therapeutic action has always been
from the surface inward or downward, starting with the defense
and the resistance and moving ultimately closer to the real wish.
Such a process has been alternatively described as the peeling of
an onion or as the progressive excavation of archeologically preserved layers of civilization permanently preserved yet fixed and
encrusted in primitive internalized structures. In an appropriately
neutral and non-gratifying atmosphere such unconscious wishes,
as well as the elaborate system of conscious and unconscious defenses against the emergence of these desires, would find their way
into the patient's transference relationship to the analyst. It there-

fore becomes incumbent upon the analyst to, essentially, stay out of the analytic process, providing a sterile non-contaminating medium within which the carefully reconstructed past can be meticulously resurrected.

It is my belief that the emerging relational paradigm within psychoanalysis makes it increasingly difficult to maintain such a static and unitary notion of unconsciousness. If indeed the internal integrity of experience evolves out of an ever present yet constantly changing system of affective, cognitive, and physiologically based self-experiences in ongoing interactive and dialogic discourse with a host of significant internally and externally derived objects, would it not be more reasonable to assume that what is conscious and what is unconscious at any particular point in time, rather than being carved in stone, emerge more fluidly out of the particular constellation of self- and object-related experience that crystallizes in the foreground of interpersonal experience at any given moment? Not one unconscious, not the unconscious, but multiple levels of consciousness and unconsciousness, in an ongoing state of interactive articulation as past experience infuses the present and present experience evokes state-dependent memories of formative interactive representations. Not an onion or an archeological site, but a child's kaleidoscope in which each glance through the pinhole of a moment in time provides a unique view: a complex organization in which a fixed set of colored, shaped, and textured components rearrange themselves in unique crystalline structures determined via infinite pathways of interconnectedness. Even the slightest movement to the left or to the right will precipitate a complete conflation and almost instantaneous reconfiguration of these structures into an entirely new pattern, a pattern whose components, though recognizable, will come to light in different constellations of prominence and obfuscation based on their positions relative to each other and to the observer.

It is my contention that such a relational unconscious is organized around a set of fluid yet finite representational systems, each of which includes a self representation, an object representation, a predominant affective tone, an experience of the body-self, and a level of cognitive organization in keeping with the age and developmental sophistication of the internalized dyad. Such representational schemas, developmentally structured, become the filters through which all new experience is viewed, the system via which it will be organized and the pre-existing structure into which it must ultimately be integrated. Such integration must proceed via a continuous, moment-to-moment oscillation between the Piagetian processes of assimilation and accomodation. In other words, new information can be understood only in terms of pre-existing schemas, although incoming new experience will have a subtle, ongoing, shaping influence on the evolutionary track of these malleable schemas. In more psychoanalytic terms, the organizing potential of unconscious fantasy infuses all emotional self-object schemas; however, within relational theory, new interpersonal experience, along with insight into old maladaptive schemas, carries the potential to change the nature of unconscious fantasy via which experience is interpreted. This is an invitation to sustain two contradictory schemas of self- and object-representation simultaneously: one anticipated, one enacted and actualized that disembeds the therapist and the patient from the experience of the moment alone and creates the potential for previously unavailable insight.

The relational unconscious is, as I view it, a dissociatively based system of averageable and irreconcilable mental representations of self in ongoing relationship to a complementary system of averageable and irreconcilable representations of significant others. Those experiences that can be averaged, generalized, affectively modulated, and ultimately encoded linguistically within memory systems and subsystems will essentially come to form the "glue" of psychic integrity: a sense of identity and continuity over time, an experience of character, order, and agency. But what of those representations of self and other that elude codification: unencoded, irretrievable, yet ever present, experiences of self with other that feel irreconcilably different, strangely incompatible, linguistically inexplicable, or affectively uncontainable? In a fanciful use of metaphor I like to think of these unformulated dyadic representations as the free radicals of the relational unconscious, roaming the mind in a hungry search for vulnerable moments, using their magnetic charge to disrupt the established order, to pull the patient into all forms of mystifying, inexplicable reenactment. Though such a system encompasses repressive defenses, particularly where the affective connection between self and other overwhemingly threatens the psychic continuity of either (as in Fairbairn's notion of the repression of bad objects), I believe that the overarching organizational structures of the relational mind are integrative and dissociative rather than repressive in nature. It is my contention that such self-states contain individualized definitions of conscious and unconscious material that are dependent upon an understanding of the particular vicissitudes of what was acceptable and unacceptable within the confines of that object or part-object relationship. It seems perfectly reasonable to presume that such multiple states of consciousness and unconsciousness will vary according to the particular demands and dictates of specific object-related experiences, most particularly those between patient and analyst.

The relational unconscious will be composed, then, of three categories of experience: (1) object-related wishes or fantasies that become unacceptable within the context of a particular internalized, real or fantasized self-object dyad (this aspect is closest to the classical unconscious, with the exception that what is conscious or unconscious at any given instant will vary in accordance with what internalized self–other dyad is being evoked by the interpersonal present; (2) mutually incompatible experiences of self in relationship to irreconcilable aspects of the other that cannot be maintained in simultaneous awareness (the kind of dissociation that occurs in cases of traumatic abuse might well be the prototype for this aspect of unconscious experience), and finally (3) aspects of self-experience that, because of their idiosyncratic or extreme nature become dropped from the linguistic categorization of generalizable experience (here I refer to the role of unformulated aspects of experience [Stern 1983]) in both the symbolization of experience and the subsequent organization of memory).

Such a model of dissociated unconscious subsystems and nonlinear forms of consciousness finds its roots in the pre-Freudian writings of Janet and Charcot and owes its ongoing influence on relational theory to the maintenance of divergent assumptions about the multiplicity of self-states found in the recent writings of Bromberg (1998), Davies (1996a, 1998), Davies and Frawley (1992, 1994), Mitchell (1991), and Rivera (1989). I would suggest that such formulations of psychic structure are not only in keeping with contemporary psychoanalytic process, but also consistent with empirical research and theoretical writings in the areas of trauma (Davies and Frawley 1992, 1994, Herman 1993, van der Kolk 1987, 1994, van der Kolk et al. 1996), infant research (Fast 1985, Beebe and Lachmann 1993), and the constructed nature of memory (Schachter and Tulving 1994). I would further suggest that so reconfiguring psychic structure and the nature of unconscious processes has the potential to reopen a more meaningful dialogue among psychoanalysis, trauma research, infant research, cognitive psychology, and neurobiology.

The theoretical underpinnings for such a reformulation of psychic structure come, I believe, from the intellectual confluence of three disparate areas of interest: infant research, trauma theory, and the neuroscience of memory storage and retrieval. From the developmental infant research of Daniel Stern (1985), Fast (1985, 1997), and Beebe and Lachman (1991, 1993) comes growing evidence that the early representational world of the child involves the internalization, encoding, and organization of endless numbers of interactive images: a representation of self, a representation of other, and an important affective tone that unites them. Fast's "events," Stern's "RIGs" (representations of interactions that become generalized), and Beebe and Lachmann's "dyadic systems view," though different in detail, are all organized around such an interactive tripartite model. From Stern's (1985) work we learn that infants tend to average their experiences with significant others in order to form recognizable categories of interpersonal events. Within such a model, what happens to the interpersonal extremes, those interactions that cannot be averaged and therefore integrated because they are in some way irreconcilable with the more characteristic patterns? Might these extremes not fall away into the nascent underpinnings of unconscious experience?

A partial understanding of this question can be garnered from our knowledge of the most extreme cases of interpersonal contradiction, namely our knowledge of the psychological sequelae of traumatic childhood abuse. From the research of van der Kolk (1987), Briere and Runtz (1988), and Spiegel (1990), as well as a host of others, comes the inevitable connection between dissociative disorders and histories of severe parental abuse, histories characterized by such disparate contradictory attachments to early significant others. In earlier work coauthored with Mary Gail Frawley, we (1992, 1994) have suggested that such dissociation represents more than a defensive disavowal of the abusive situation and the related conflictual fantasies. We suggest that such dissociation grows, in fact, from an alteration of psychic structure made unavoidable by the need to integrate irreconcilable images of the other and contradictory images of self that become organized around concordant and complementary identifications with abusive and "otherwise loving" parents. This model represents our attempt to integrate the early theories of traumatic dissociation espoused by Janet, and their later neurobiological modernization by theorists such as van der Kolk (1987, van der Kolk et al. 1996), with contemporary psychoanalytic object relations theory.

In this paper I wish to go one step further and suggest that this aberration of psychic structure that reveals itself so clearly in true cases of multiple personality disorder and severe dissociative pathology is, in fact, only the severe, pathologically induced exageration of what I believe to be a more accurate rendering of unconscious psychic structure. If we begin with the presumption that the unconscious structure of mind is fundamentally dissociative rather than repressive in nature, and that the present interpersonal interaction heralds an evocation of significant past relationships, part-object relationships, and specific systems of fantasy organization encapsulated within each unique self–object system, then the current fascination with multiple self-states, multiple ego-states, and multiple personality disorders becomes a natural extension. Within such a system any psychic distress, be it internally or externally derived, can potentiate a fracturing of integrative processes, splitting apart along what might be considered more structurally normal stress points or fault lines, such lines, here, being based upon the internalization of early dyadic representations. If we choose to make such a shift in our conceptual rendering of psychic structure, then it seems inevitable that our understanding of the therapeutic process will shift from that of fixed unconscious conflict made unavailable by repressive barriers to that of a more fluid, interactively derived pastiche of self- and object-related experience, organized cognitively and affectively, called forth in the transference–countertransference constellations by instances of state-dependent memory, existing in an ongoing state of tension between averaging and irreconcilability, between integration and dissociation. Our notion of analytic success would therefore change from an emphasis on greater experiences of psychic integration and conflict resolution to a model that stresses an enhanced capacity to move fluidly between the more idiosyncratic, affectively intense, object-specific experiences of self in relation to other and the more generalizable, less specific, emotionally modulated composite experiences in which a multitude of internalized dyadic representations can be averaged and experienced as one.

An unexpected benefit of so reconfiguring psychic structure is that it obviates the need to question whether the current fascination with multiple personality and dissociative pathology reflects a change in the epidemiological prevalence of such disorders, or the iatrogenically stimulated suggestion of a therapeutic field gone astray. For if we understand the essential processes of mind as a continuous interplay of associative and dissociative trends, as a striving toward integrative conceptualization and a fending off of regressive, disintegrative forces, the common appearance of what appear to be dissociative states in the course of intensive psychoanalytic work would not be surprising. Not unlike the X-ray of a broken bone improperly set, intensive psychoanalytic work will reveal the points of developmental fracture and incomplete fusion even years after the fact. Though the patient can walk, it is not unusual for him to experience pain, particularly when the climate changes, and for us to continue to regard the leg as particularly suceptible to subsequent vulnerability and/or injury.

Such a model of multiple, interpersonally derived "unconsciouses" is further supported, I believe, by current trends in cognitive neuroscience, particularly the study of memory and mind-body interaction. One thinks here of such models as Bucci's (1985) multiple coding theory, which postulates separate memory subsystems for verbal and nonverbal experience, or Dennett's (1991) multiple draft model, which posits "that all varieties of thought or mental activity are accomplished in the brain by parallel, multitrack processes of interpretation and elaboration" (p. 111). Also of interest in this regard is Candace Pert's (in Meyers 1993) work on endogenous morphines and other identifiable neuropeptides as the biochemical correlates of emotion and of a psychosomatic communication network in which mind and body exist in a constantly fluctuating state of interaction.

Bessel van der Kolk's most recent (1994) research has stressed a belief in the state dependency of memory, and his work with traumatic memory, in particular, focuses on the difference between the taxon system, which encodes memory according to quality and remains verbally irretrievable and context free, and the hippocampal system, which encodes information verbally along a space–time dimension and can be re-engaged via the verbal exchange between patient and therapist within a traditionally organized psychoanalytic process. Contemporary research (see Bremner 1995) reveals that chronic severe stress can suppress hippocampal functioning, creating fearful associations that are hard to locate in space and time. This results in amnesia for the specifics of traumatic experiences but not the feelings associated with them. Such a process is not unlike infantile amnesia, not coincidentally caused by the developmentally incomplete myelinization of the very same hippocampus. Surely infantile memories cannot be verbalized, but I dare say that few among us would want to argue for anything other than their fundamental centrality to early emotional and interpersonal development. Herein lies the therapeutic necessity to work through all aspects of the multiple self- and object-representations that volley back and forth in expressions of concordant and complementary identifications, within the transference–countertransference matrix.

When regarded as a body of work, all the research would suggest that memory may or may not be context dependent, according to the individual's state of emotional arousal; that it is organized with particular regard to intense emotional states; that it can be selectively recalled under circumstances that recapture the original emotional tone; and that multiple versions of the same event can coexist in different brain systems, averaged and linguistically encoded in ways that both integrate and obfuscate the essentially irretrievable particulars of early life.

CONCLUSION

If we return to Katharina, what can she tell us about the evolution of psychoanalytic theory and our changing notions of unconscious process and psychic structure? For Freud, Katharina's "cure" surely lay in recovering the unconscious, repressed memories of her father's sexual overtures to her, and integrating those with the rest of her conscious ego. In this way the horrifying nature of the traumatic incident—finding cousin with father—could be fully explained and brought to light. A post-seduction-hypothesis model would call into question Katharina's actual memories of sexual overtures on her father's part, attributing these instead to fantasies growing out of the young girl's unconscious incestuous wishes. The nature of the trauma came when the actual vision of father with cousin, threatened the emergence into consciousness of these unaceptable thoughts. Treatment in this light would involve bringing the unconscious wishes into awareness so that the nature of the fantasies could be examined, particularly in the transference relationship to the analyst.

What of the second main artery of psychoanalytic thought? Janet would look at Katharina not so much in terms of what ideation or event had been pushed out of awareness, but rather in terms of what independent centers of self-organization had been necessitated by the traumatic betrayal by her father. He would ultimately attempt to identify what aspects of the personality had been dissociated and set up as independent centers of awareness, what functions each maintained, what traumatic memories each held.

Janet would attempt to define the environmental and interpersonal triggers for the somatic manifestations of the traumatic situation, Katharina's dizziness, nausea, breathlessness. He would consider such psychosomatic manifestations as actual sensorimotor memories of the traumatic events, much as current trauma theorists would. For Janet these early abusive experiences would form the template through which all subsequent experience would be viewed. It would be up to the therapy and a more gentle future to try and change these essential organizing schemas.

Finally, how would a relational analyst, building on the mental model first set forth by Janet, interpret Katharina's plight? She would certainly wonder about different centers of self-organization and awareness, different centers of initiative and action. What dynamic function does each self-organization serve? What significant object-related memories and fantasied elaborations of those memories coalesced in the internalized self- and object-representations that belong within each dissociated state? What traumatic events?

Clinically, one could surely wonder who followed Freud up the lonely mountain path. What aspect of this traumatized young woman so boldly and pleadingly approached the strange, handsome young doctor? Surely not the frightened and traumatized Katharina? Where was she? How could one reach her clinically? What could she add, what emotional potency could she bring to this rather matter-of-fact rendition of a childhood seduction? What would be the therapeutic efficacy of a reported insight so split off from any affective dimension? Was Katharina's excited and flushed face a result of the insight garnered from Freud's interpretation, or was there a more powerful and mutually seductive unconscious force in operation? Was a traumatic reenactment in the making? How did Katharina, whose father had ultimately turned to her cousin, interpret the undivided attention of the young doctor? What did Freud himself think of interviewing this young girl about such intimate matters in this lonely and isolated place? What were his fantasies? Where was Katharina's mother in this scenario? She had, after all, believed the girl and rescued her from further abuse. Would the scene have been different had mother not responded so decisively? Ultimately, the relational analyst would look to answer all of these questions, would eschew the possibility that a linear transference neurosis organized around predominantly oedipal material could account for all aspects of these split-off, projected, and introjected self- and object-representations, would regard as impossible the likelihood that such dissociated aspects of experience could be recaptured in a purely insight-oriented, verbal exchange of ideas, would seek or at least be prepared for the fact that triggers to these otherwise dissociated aspects of self and other are to be found in the infinite nuance of the interpersonal moments: reenacted, experienced, put into words, and explored, perhaps for the first time, in the transference–countertransference matrices that define the particular psychoanalytic encounter.

So we have returned together to the beginning, and in so doing come, perhaps, to see that some of our most heated psychoanalytic debates are embedded in very different models of mind, models that began to part ways in our very earliest writings one hundred years ago.

REFERENCES

Aron, L. (1993). Working toward operational thought: Piagetian theory and psychoanalytic. *Contemporary Psychoanalysis* 29:289–313.

Beebe, B., Jaffe, J., and Lachman, F. (1992). A dyadic systems view of communication. In *Relational Perspectives in Psychoanalysis,* ed. N. Skolnick and S. Warshaw. Hillsdale, NJ: Analytic Press.

Bremner, D. J., Krystal, J. H., Southwick, S. M., and Charney, D. S. (1995). Functional neuroanatomical correlates of the effects of stress on memory. *Journal of Traumatic Stress* 8(4):527–554.

Briere, J. and Runtz, M. (1988). Symptomotology associated with childhood sexual victimization in a non-clinical adult sample. *Child Abuse and Neglect* 12:51–59.

Breuer, J. and Freud, S. (1893–1895). Studies on hysteria. *Standard Edition* 2.

Bromberg, P. (1998). Standing in the Spaces: Essays on Clinical Process, Trauma and Dissociation. Hillsdale, NJ: Analytic Press.

Bucci, W. (1985). Dual coding: a cognitive model for psychoanalytic research. *Journal of the American Psychoanalytic Association* 33:571–607.

Davies, J. M. (1996a). Linking the pre-analytic with the post-classical: integragion, dissociation and the multiplicity of unconscious process. *Contemporary Psychoanalysis* 32(4):553–572.

—— (1996b). Dissociation, repression, and reality testing in the countertransference: the controversy over memory and false memory in the psychoanalytic treatment of adult survivors of childhood sexual abuse. *Psychoanalytic Dialogues* 6(2):189–218.

—— (1998). The multiple aspects of multiplicity: symposium on clinical judgments in psychoanalysis. *Psychoanalytic Dialogues* 8(2):195–206.

Davies, J. M. and Frawley, M. G. (1992). Dissociative processes and transference-countertransference paradigms in the psychoanalytically oriented treatment of adult survivors of childhood sexual abuse. *Psychoanalytic Dialogues* 2(1):5–36.

—— (1994). *Treating the Adult Survivor of Childhood Sexual Abuse: A Psychoanalytic Perspective.* New York: Basic Books.

Dennett, D. (1991). *Consciousness Explained*. Boston, MA: Little Brown.

Ellenberger, H. F. (1970). *The Discovery of the Unconscious*. New York: Basic Books.

Fairbairn, W.R.D. (1944). Endopsychic structure considered in terms of object relationships. In *Psychoanalytic Studies of the Personality*. London: Routledge and Kegan Paul, 1952.

—— (1951). A synopsis of the development of the author's views regarding the structure of the personality. In *Psychoanalytic Studies of the Personality*. London: Routledge and Kegan Paul, 1952.

—— (1954). Observations on the nature of hysterical states. *British Journal of Medical Psychology* 27:105–125.

Fast, I. (1985). *Event Theory: A Piaget–Freud Integration*. Hillsdale, NJ: Lawrence Erlbaum.

—— (1997). *Selving: A Relational Approach to the Development of Self*. Hillsdale, NJ: Analytic Press.

Herman, J. (1993). *Trauma and Recovery*. New York: Basic Books.

Hoffman, I. Z. (1983). The patient as interpreter of the analyst's experience. *Contemporary Psychoanalysis* 19:389–422.

—— (1991). Discussion: Toward a social-constructivist view of the psychoanalytic situation. *Psychoanalytic Dialogues* 1:74–105.

—— (1992). Some practical implications of a social-constructivist view of the analytic situation. *Psychoanalytic Dialogues* 2:287–304.

—— (1998). *Ritual and Spontaneity in the Psychoanalytic Process*. Hillsdale, NJ: Analytic Press.

Janet, P. (1887). L'anesthésie systématisée et la dissciationdes phénomenès psychologiques. *Revue Philosophique* 23(1):449–472.

—— (1889). L'automatisme psychologique. Paris: Alcan.

—— (1894). Histoire d'une idée fixe. *Revue Philosophique* 37:121–163.

Mitchell, S. A. (1993) *Hope and Dread in Psychoanalysis*. New York: Basic Books.

Moyers, B. (1993). *Healing and the Mind*. New York: Doubleday.

Ogden, T. (1986). *The Matrix of the Mind*. Northvale, NJ: Jason Aronson.

Piaget, J. (1962). *Play, Dreams and Imitation in Childhood*. New York: Norton.

Pizer, S. (1996). Negotiating potential space: illusion, play, metaphor and the subjunctive. *Psychoanalytic Dialogues* 6(5):689–712.

Rivera, M. (1989). Linking the psychological and the social: feminism, poststructuralism and multiple personality. *Dissociation* 2:24–31.

Schacter, D. (1987). Implicit memory: history and current status. *Journal of Experimental Psychology* 13:501–518.

Schacter, D. and Tulving, E. (1994). *Memory Systems 1994*. Cambridge, MA: MIT Press.

Spiegel, D. (1990). Trauma, dissociation and hypnosis. In *Incest Related Syndromes of Adult Psychopathology*, ed. R. Kluft. Washington, DC: American Psychiatric Press.

Stern, D. B. (1983). Unformulated experience. *Contemporary Psychoanalysis* 19:71–99.

——— (1997). *Unformulated Experience: From Dissociation to Imagination in Psychoanalysis*. Hillsdale, NJ: Analytic Press.

Stern, D. N. (1985). *The Interpersonal World of the Infant*. New York: Basic Books.

Van der Kolk, B. A. (1987). *Psychological Trauma*. Washington, DC: American Psychiatric Press.

——— (1994). The body keeps the score: memory and the evolving biology of post-traumatic stress. *Harvard Review of Psychiatry* 1:253–265.

Van der Kolk, B. A. and van der Hart, O. (1989). Pierre Janet and the breakdown of adaptation in psychological trauma. *American Journal of Psychiatry* 146:1530–1540.

Van der Kolk, B. A., McFarlane, A. C., and Weisraeth, L., eds. (1996). *Traumatic Stress*. New York and London: Guilford.

12

On Trauma: A Freudian Perspective

Paola Mieli

An earlier version of the present paper was published as "Traumatisme et fascination: une perspective freudienne." *Che vuoi?*, n.5, Paris, 1996.

In 1938 Freud returns to a point he made on several occasions: "No human individual is spared . . . traumatic experiences; none escapes the repressions to which they give rise" (p. 185). Traumatic experiences form the basis not only of neurosis but of subjectivity in general. In the United States the debate surrounding the role played by reality and fantasy in trauma ends up in court; summons to parents and teachers for abuses allegedly committed twenty or thirty years before are now common results of therapy, results of revelations of the unconscious and the business of analysis. Here the response to a Recovered Memory Movement is the creation of a False Memory Syndrome Foundation. It is imperative for psychoanalysts to question their own responsibility in this farce, where the stakes still remain a subjective suffering that receives no adequate hearing. Within analytic circles and the theoretical eclecticism that derives from them, the great confusion around the notion of trauma is one of the reasons for a misunderstanding that in fact calls into question the very specificity of psychoanalysis and its entire history. It is worth our while to step back in time and return to founding principles, to Freud's teachings.

According to Freud, the notion of trauma is structurally connected to the prematuration of the human offspring, to the nature of the libido, to the double-phased development of human sexuality, to sexual difference, to the assumption of oedipal prohibition, and to primary repression as a constitutive mechanism of psychic structure. This is why it is redundant to speak, for instance, of "countertransference issues in work with patients with histories of trauma." All patients have had histories of trauma.

My goal here is to try to put the question of trauma back into a Freudian perspective. This does not mean that I want to diminish the role played by the violence of certain traumatic events, such as sexual or physical abuses, medical traumas, and the like, much less that I want to deny the specificity of their consequences. It is important, however, to recall that these traumatic events are a part of the category of trauma mapped out by Freud. It is useful for the analyst to lead his/her own observation back into a more general conception of the role played by trauma in transference. This broader picture can in fact help the analyst gain a better understanding of what is at stake when working with patients who have been the object of serious physical and moral abuses.

The time of an analysis is by definition that in which trauma is brought to evidence; it is the time of the production of the trauma and consequently of its symbolic construction. The relation between trauma and transference is thus structural.

For Freud the notion of trauma implies the elaboration of a particular concept of psychic time. In his early seduction theory, Freud (1895) shows how trauma is based upon two events separated in time: the first takes the form of a sexual scene (passively experienced by the subject). The second takes the form of an event that, by means of associations, retroactively evokes the first event, the original scene. In this second moment, this after-beat, the ego is caught off guard, insofar as it is unable to mobilize its defenses against the amount of libido discharged. The repression of the recollection is eventually accompanied by the appearance of symptoms. Through the discharge of libido, the second event retroactively imposes a traumatic effect upon the first scene.

The trauma constitutes itself in a temporal scansion that involves a *Nachträglichkeit*, literally an *après-coup*, an *a posteriori*, an *afterward*. It is unfortunate that the Standard Edition translates *Nachträglichkeit* as "deferred action," generating a series of misunderstandings. Deferred action conveys the notion of a psychic determinism, of a time lag between a certain stimulus and a certain response, suggesting the idea of a delayed discharge. The Freudian concept of *Nachträglichkeit*, in fact, points in the opposite direction. It does not signal a delay in action or in reaction, but rather an event that in the very act of positing itself, reinvests a past inscription and takes on the status of a revelation. That which occurs "after" turns what has preceded it into an occasion—and here the word "occasion" must be appreciated in both its etymological senses of *opportunity* and *fall*. In implying the notion of a linear, developmental time, the expression "deferred action" misses a fundamental aspect of the psychic mechanism involved in the constitution of trauma, which is logical and not linear, structural and not developmental.

With the abandonment of his seduction theory, Freud maintains the notion of trauma together with its temporal scansion at the core of the psychogenesis of neurosis. The role played by fantasies in psychic reality expands with the discovery of children's sexuality (Freud 1905, 1908). The change does not mean a denial of the pathogenic value inherent in certain episodes actually experienced in childhood. It is rather the acknowledgement of the role that fantasies play in sexuality. Fantasies and sexuality are structurally related.

Traumatic experiences, paradoxically, reveal themselves as a kind of necessity:

> The only impression we gain is that these events of childhood are somehow demanded as a necessity, that they are among the essential elements of neurosis. If they have occurred in reality, so much to the good; but if they have been withheld by reality, they are put together from hints and supplemented by fantasy. The outcome is the same, and up to the present we have not succeeded in pointing to any difference in the consequences, whether fantasy or reality has had the greater share in these events of childhood. [Freud 1916–1917, p. 370]

Freud does not question the reality of certain traumas, but he recognizes the role played by fantasies. Moreover, he postulates the structural function played by *Urphantasien*, primal fantasies, in the activation of trauma (Freud 1914, 1915–1917). According to Freud these fantasies—primal scene, seduction fantasy, castration fantasy—substantiate the infantile sexual theories and answer fundamental enigmas concerning origins (the origin of the individual, of sexuality, and of sexual difference). Like myths, they are constructions that later offer a content to an earlier moment, an explanation of an enigmatic prior cause that eludes symbolization.

Freud's introduction of the notion of *historical truth* (1934–1938, 1937b) in its differentiation and dialectical relation with historical reality emphasizes, if anything, the hypothesis made at the time of the seduction theory: the actualization of trauma involves a timing that retroactively invests a past inscription; the advent of sexuality is structurally related to what is experienced as traumatic, such an experience being necessary for the sexuation of the human being; the very constitution of trauma involves repression and thus the persistence of the return of the repressed.

With his myth of the murder of the primordial father, with the construction of the scene of the primal trauma of humankind, Freud (1913) indicates how the relation between law and desire sets up prohibition (and consequently loss) as the *condition* for symbolization and civilization (Mieli 2000). The barrier against incest and the Oedipus complex are two sides of the same coin; it is insofar as the object is unattainable that it can be desired. If the father is an obstacle to the attainment of satisfaction, murdering him doesn't open the way to satisfaction but rather strengthens its prohibition. From *Totem and Taboo* to *Moses and Monotheism*, the myth of the murder of the primordial father represents the precedence of the law over subjectivity; human beings are borned into a symbolic context, into a social order, that imposes restrictions on the fulfillment of the drives. At the same time, the myth of the murder of the primordial father illustrates the fact that the inscription of trauma crosses generations.

A third moment completes the tempo of trauma, that of the return of the repressed, of repetition; what is inscribed and obliterated is condemned to return in different guises. And it is precisely the time of this return, of its insistence, that permits the reconstruction of trauma, the unfolding of the sequence of individual traumas.

From a clinical point of view, analysis is the time of the construction of the individual myth. It is the time when the subjective truth finds its articulation in a history that traverses generations. It is the moment of reckoning with the limits of symbolization, with the real—the "impossible"—that cannot be symbolized. Within this framework Freud (1937a) indicates that the culminating point of an analysis, of every analysis, is the encounter with the trauma of castration.

The notion of historical truth does not overshadow that of material truth. On the contrary. It indicates the registering of psychic events that, in their specificity, concern the truth of the subject, the singularity of individual history within material reality. With his concept of historical truth, the insistent core of truth in the return of the repressed, in the manifestations of the symptom or in the constructions of delusions, Freud shows how negligible the philosophical opposition of true and false is to the domain of psychoanalysis. For the subject of psychoanalysis, a subject divided by the presence of the unconscious, the notion of falseness is of relative value: Falseness may speak the truth. Truth and falsity emerge in the constructions of conscious thoughts of the secondary process, in the causal logic that is the product of censorship. Rather, with the universe of myth, psychoanalysis shares another opposition: like myth, it counters truth with obliviousness.

The advent of sexuality is experienced as structurally related to what befalls the subject from without. In his early theory of seduction, in the notion that trauma follows upon subjection to adult sexuality, Freud points out how sexuality is first encountered in the Other. Seduction prompts an incursion of the real from the external world; in this context, the registration of the traumatic event cannot be assimilated into the network of representations of the psychic apparatus, since its presence provokes a heightening of tension that cannot find a proper discharge. From the standpoint of the pleasure principle the traumatic recollection is inadmissible; it functions as an external body threatening the entire psychic system (Freud 1895, Braunstein 1990). Through the mechanism of repression the psychic apparatus isolates and excludes the inadmissible memory; yet at the same time, in repressing it, it endows it with eternal life in the unconscious. What once came from without, from the overwhelming external world, now is lastingly encapsulated from within. The defense mechanisms generated by its presence maintain "a State within the State" (Freud 1934–1937, p. 76). The repressed is condemned to return.

As early as his first seduction theory Freud lays the groundwork for what will be his future elaboration of the relation between the pleasure principle and its "beyond." Trauma is by definition an occurrence that exceeds the limits of the pleasure principle. It is precisely from the clinical data on the repetition of painful experiences, associated with an increase of stimulation, that Freud (1920) introduces the notion of a "beyond" of the pleasure principle, one that works independently of the pleasure principle itself and to some extent in disregard of it. Such a mode of satisfaction evinces the more "intimate" character of the drive. In order to understand the effects of traumatic experiences and deal with their clinical incidence, it is therefore necessary to take into account the death drive that animates repetition.

In traumatic experiences, repetition brings along the insistence of the real, of that which cannot be symbolized (and which, in Freudian terms, needs to be bound and worked through); it brings along the insistence of *jouissance*. The word *jouissance*, used in place of "pleasure" or "enjoyment," accounts for the fulfillment of the drive according to the pleasure principle *and* its beyond. It reckons with the relation existing between erotic and death drives in the libidinal economy. Trauma inscribes *jouissance* in the body and condemns it as intolerable. Its repressed engraving constitutes a crystalization subject to the law of the primary process, capable of attracting other intolerable representations.

In response to the notion of dissociation, opposed to that of repression, currently used in the United States to describe the specific dynamic of the defense mechanism operative in trauma, it is useful to reexamine certain aspects of Freud's concept of repression. It will then become apparent that the notion of dissociation does not add a new understanding to the defense mechanism involved in traumatic experiences. As early as the *Studies on Hysteria* Freud indicates how the mechanism of repression operates, isolating a specific ideational group in the psyche. The very "splitting of consciousness," as he calls it there, the "peculiar situation of knowing and at the same time not knowing" characteristic of subjective division, is a direct *result* of repression (1893–1895, p. 165).

Repression acts upon neither the drive nor the affect, but rather on the psychical (ideational) representatives of the drive (*Vorstellungsrepräsentanz,* Freud 1915, p. 148), upon what we might define as markings, traces of traumatic experience, or various somatic memories. Repression does not refer exclusively to experiences that are encoded in language and then forgotten, as the notion of primal repression demonstrates. In striking the representatives of the drive, repression perpetuates into fixation an unconscious inscription that the formations of the primary process will attempt to decode.

It is essential to recall that Freud, to the very end of his life, upholds a specific relation between sexuality and seduction: he never tires of repeating that the mother, the original Other, is the first seducer. "By the care of the child's body she becomes its first seducer" (1938, p. 188). As Freud shows in the *Three Essays*, sexuality is first organized around erotogenic zones, erogenous borders of the body where a privileged exchange with the mother or caretaker occurs. Seduction is inescapable; it is the means through which the body becomes an erotogenic locus. At the same time, it is the means through which the desire of the Other is manifested in the subject. And this desire orients the child's desire. Seduction turns the child's body into an object of *jouissance*. Thus, in elaborating the notion of trauma, it is fundamental to bear in mind the effects of such *jouissance*, and the place the subject occupies in the fantasy of the seducer.

Trauma involves *the realization of the fantasy*. It is no accident that Freud introduces the idea that certain primal fantasies may be the motor forces of trauma. The essential discovery of "A child is being beaten" (1919) cannot be overlooked. The fact, moreover, that in the permutations of the subject's grammar (the father is beating a child, my father is beating me, a child is being beaten), the repressed link, the one that is untraceable, ties *jouissance* to the invocation of trauma. This occurs precisely because trauma enacts a *transmission* between the Other and the subject, a transfusion of *jouissance* that is also an inscription. The repressed moment—my father is beating me, (my father loves me)—designates the place occupied by the subject in the fantasy of the Other; it is the proof of his desire, on which the recognition of the subject depends.

Repetition in the treatment, that compulsion to repeat that "evidently disregards the pleasure principle in every way" (Freud 1920, p. 36), is a part of the transference. The time of analysis, therefore, is invariably the time of trauma production. Within the picture rapidly sketched here, we can mention some of the problems raised by clinical work with patients who have been subjected to exceptional traumatic experiences. In this framework, though, it is important to underline that "the term 'traumatic' has no other sense than an economic one" (Freud 1915–1917, p. 275).

> If we may assume that the experience acquires its traumatic character only as a result of a quantitative factor—that is to say, that in every case it is an excess in demand that is responsible for an

experience evoking unusual pathological reactions—then we can easily arrive at the expedient of saying that something acts as a trauma in the case of one constitution but in the case of another would have no such effect. [1934–1937, p. 73]

In notes added in 1924 to the *Studies on Hysteria*, Freud reveals that in two instances, in the case of Katharina and in the case of Rosalie, the seducer is the father of the patient, not the uncle, as he had originally written for matters of confidentiality, a distortion of some consequence for the understanding of the cases (p.134).

Rosalie, who is training to be a singer, is in treatment with Freud because of a feeling of choking and constriction in her throat that prevents her from performing in public. Such a retention hysteria, Freud remarks, manifests the repression of her unexpressed contempt for her father's brutal behavior toward his family. Yet it is only the manifestation in the course of the treatment of a specific, new symptom that reveals the different layers of the trauma. One day she comes to her session with a symptom formed just the day before: a disagreeable prickling sensation in the tips of her fingers that forces her to make a peculiar kind of twitching movement with her hands. Various associations bring about a number of childhood memories, which seem to have in common her suffering some injury. But the recollections lead to a specific scene in her girlhood, when she gave a massage to her father, who suffered from rheumatism: "He was lying in bed at the time, and suddenly threw off the bed-clothes, sprang up and tried to catch hold of her and throw her down" (p. 172). Only *after* relating this scene does Rosalie relate the previous day's event, which triggered the new symptom in her fingers. She is living in Vienna as guest of an uncle of hers, whose friendliness toward her causes her aunt suspicion. The previous day, at her uncle's request, she played the piano and accompanied herself in a song. Unexpectedly, her aunt appeared at the door: "Rosalie jumped up, slammed the lid of the piano and threw the music away" (p. 172).

In the *Studies*, Freud remarks that Rosalie's new symptom is the outcome of her violent resentment at the unjust suspicion to which she is subjected, an observation that appears reductive on the ground of Freud's later elaboration on the nature of the symptom as a compromise formation that entails, always, the satisfaction of a fantasy. The proclamation of innocence is not without relation to a sense of guilt.

Rosalie is caught in the position of being the object of her uncle's attentions. Her aunt's suspicion confirms, if anything, the special place she occupies in the household. It is not by chance that this scene can be told of only after Rosalie recalled the father's sexual aggression; its postponement signals how charged the scene still is with affects. It is also not by chance that the prickling sensation in her fingertips appears then and there, to condense in the present emotion, in the realization of the fantasy, the power of the trauma. The same fingers that massage the back of her father play the piano; they reach the other, they have something to offer him. The trauma paradoxically marks a moment of extrordinary intimacy. And, in its brutality, the incestuous aggression confirms the special interest, the sudden attention received from a father usually too busy pursuing other women.

In the case of Katharina, the anxiety attack develops after a "discovery": she witnesses the embrace between her father and Franziska, who, in the case report, is described as a cousin. Again, the present event involves the actualization of the trauma, disclosing a series of associations that lead to a prior scene of seduction: years before, one night, her father had approached her sexually. The scene of discovery that inaugurated the symptom deserves to be called traumatic, Freud remarks. It is operative on account of its own content and not merely as something that revived previous traumatic experiences. It combines "the characteristics of an auxiliary and a traumatic moment" (p. 134). Its psychic value manifests the confrontation with a repressed truth.

Katharina spies, and from being the active witness now of her father's secret, she is brought back to that time when she was the object of her father's desire. Katharina was then in the place of Franziska, the pursued object. A second series of associations brings about episodes that she couldn't understand where, in fact, she already witnessed her father's fondness toward Franziska. If the present scene offends her, exposing the truth of the trauma and making her "understand," it is also because, in actualizing her fantasy, it suddenly confronts her with a place now occupied by another woman. At the same time, the scene of the discovery reveals the role Katharina plays in her father's scheme. Only now will she speak up and become very active, breaking up at once her parents' marriage and the complicity that had tied her to her father. The sense of guilt that follows, represented in the persecuting vision of her father's angry face during her panic attacks, will speak less of her responsibility for the broken marriage than of her complicity in the traumatic plot.

Clinical work shows how often abused patients express their belief in having occupied a special place in the life of their abuser, an idea that occasionally allows them to maintain certain ties with the aggressor. The victim's expressed or unexpressed conviction of being special deserves particular attention: it manifests the dynamic of the subject's relation to the Other, the certainty with which he/she feels caught in the adult's fantasy. Receiving the marking of the abuse on his or her own flesh, the child knows that he/she occupies a precise place in the adult's desire—a desire that the child desires. The violence of the aggression is at once a recognition and an initiation, a trace that does not cease to produce *jouissance*. If the work of mourning is imposed in the analytic experience of working through trauma, it is precisely because the trauma has inaugurated a mode of fulfillment of the drive that is continually summoned up and satisfied. The patient's attachment to his/ her own symptoms, as Freud soon recognized, becomes a main obstacle for the production of a new subjective position.

It may be argued that the victim's conviction of being special in the eye of the aggressor permits a redemption from a submissive, passive position. Yet, in "A child is being beaten," Freud remarks that a person's shift from a passive to an active position in the fantasy is one way of masking the *jouissance* associated with the subject's passive position. Such a shift is accompanied by repression and generates a sense of guilt that is derived from unconscious desires and legitimated by their endurance. The abused child's sense of guilt is to be related above all to the *jouissance* generated by the traumatic situation, to what is unconsciously experienced as the realization of a fantasy. In Freud's view such a sense of guilt also feeds the desire for punishment generated by the superego. Ferenczi (1932) observed that this sense of guilt equally expresses the introjection of the adult's sense of guilt. The paralyzing fear that forces the child to submit to the aggressor's will, to guess that aggressor's impulses of desire, forces him/her "to follow those desires by totally identifying with the aggressor" (p. 421). If such a mimetic process in fact allows for active appropriation, and the transvaluing of an intolerable passivity, this also empha-sizes the intimacy, the exchange with the *jouissance* of the aggres-sor, the interiorizations of the traits that characterize it.

The fact that trauma, its silence and its guilt, its persistence, should function as a pole of attraction, an inextinguishable source of seduction in the patient's life, is borne out by the whole history of psychoanalysis. The manner in which seduction concerns the analyst is another matter. Today, in light of a renewed interest in the technical problems raised by the analytic work with victims of abuses, some professionals remark that when faced with such patients, the therapist is seduced into the position of the "inter-ested bystander," the witness of the abuse. "I have come to see the experience of being 'fascinated' by a patient as an alarm bell that raises a question for me of whether in fact the patient has a his-tory of abuse" (Thomas 1995, p. 3). The fascination of the analyst is depicted as the outcome of the "special" position shared with the patient, sole recipient of a secret, hitherto unexpressed truth; it would function as the signal of a narcissistic impulse on the part of the analyst as savior.

It is worth reflecting upon these remarks, especially since they indicate a transference/countertransference conception that dis-tances itself from Freud's still original and fertile ideas on the di-rection of the treatment. When in the countertransference rela-tion the analyst confuses her position with the one that is attributed to her by the analysand's projections, this is the signal of an imagi-nary identification with the patient: the analyst, here, is caught in the analysand's fantasy, which encloses the treatment in a dead-lock. To say that in the transferential reactivation of the trauma the analyst becomes the abuser, or the silent witness, is to con-fuse the position of the analyst with those of the imagos attributed to her. It is to take oneself as the recipient of a discourse of which in fact the analyst is and must be only the *function*.

According to Freud, the transference does not lead back to an empathic, binary exchange between two subjects, in which the analyst "feels" in the place of the patient, as many analysts put it. The idea of the transference/countertransference relation as a dy-adic exchange rules out the possibility for the analyst to hold the proper place: that is, *a third place*, that of the Other, of the uncon-scious. Only this place permits the recognition of the series of projective identifications that invest the analyst and accompany the unfolding of the transference process; it permits the recognition of the unconscious drives that find in the symptom their own satisfaction.

To avoid the empathic error of the analyst's imaginary identification with the analysand's projections is one of the conditions that enables the self-destructive compulsion of symptom repetition to be interrupted, traumatic experiences to be articulated into language, and the emergence of a true speech to usher in the new. It is the condition enabling the subject to reckon with his/her complicity in events of which he/she was the victim, to recognize the *jouissance* that marked them. Freud's notion of psychic causality specifically indicates how, in the process of a cure, a human being must assume the subjective responsibility for the very events of which his life is the effect.

But the notion of a fascination experienced while working with abused patients may be interesting from another standpoint. I wonder, that is, to what extent, if fascination emerges in the work with severly traumatized patients, it signals the fact that the abuse in question *conceals another abuse*. As Blevis noticed, the child's silence about a father's incestuous abuse may be a way of distancing the mother from the incest scene, insofar as the child thinks "that the mother participates in it unconsciously" (1987, p. 33). We cannot break the spell that scenes of incest exert upon the subject "without considering the solidarities that weave them together" (p. 33).

Something similar can be said for other experiences of childhood abuse as well. Often, in clinical practice, the persistence with which a trauma magnetizes the subject in its opacity and its silence veils another abuse logically associated with it. I am thinking, for instance, of the case of the child repeatedly seduced by an uncle during his mother's bouts with alcoholism, or that of the boy tortured in order to divulge his father's movements as a political activist, or again that of the little girl savagely beaten by the grandmother who raised her—the mother had no room at home for this child who, as it turns out, had been born out of wedlock.

The invisible traces of the uncle's hands, the unspeakable scars of physical torture, the bones broken by the grandmother, veil and in their silence distance another injury: the position occupied by the desire of the one who didn't prevent the abuse. What is the desire of the absent father, what is the desire of the alcoholic or neglectful mother, in the dynamics of which the abuse proves to be the effect? Another *jouissance* is at stake behind the *jouissance* of the abuser, a *jouissance* with which the abused is condemned to reckon. And when, as often happens, the revelation of the child's secret is met with a refusal to hear, this new abuse added to the old one reveals the role played by the confidant in the plot he/she participates in. In this framework, the fascination exerted during treatment by a certain abuse can be considered the sign of a stagnation of the work on a trauma, whose spell dazzles precisely to hide another trauma.

Confirming Freud's early hypothesis of the "summation of traumas" (1893–1895, p.173), clinical experience demonstrates that trauma is never isolated, that it is always associated with a set of other traumas that go all the way back to birth and often earlier, traversing generations—as, for instance, clinical work with the grandchildren of the *Shoah* shows. And it is precisely in taking into account this set of traumas, the place occupied by the individual in the web of relations that define the uniqueness of his/her truth, that the fascination exerted by one particular trauma can cease. As the so-called traumatic neuroses illustrate (neurosis caused in adulthood by shocks of various kinds), the trauma that sets off the symptoms gives voice *nachträglich*, a posteriori, to the traumatic experiences of the past; it condenses and subsumes them, restoring in the present their disruptive potential. Last and logically first in the sequence of traumas, the current trauma becomes an opportunity, the first step in a construction.

REFERENCES

Blevis, M. (1987). Un inceste peut en cacher un autre. *Patio* 7:27–38.
Breuer, J. and Freud, S. (1893–1895). Studies on hysteria. *Standard Edition* 2.
Braunstein, N. (1990). *Goce*. Siglo Ventiuno Editores.
Ferenczi, S. (1932). Confusion of tongues between adults and the

child. In *Final Contributions to the Problems and Methods of Psychoanalysis*, ed. M. Balint. London: Karnac (1980).

Freud, S. (1895). Project for a scientific psychology. *Standard Edition* 1.

—— (1905). Three essays on the theory of sexuality. *Standard Edition* 7:125–245.

—— (1908). On the sexual theories of children. *Standard Edition* 9:205–226.

—— (1913). Totem and taboo. *Standard Edition* 13:1–162.

—— (1915). Papers on metapsychology. *Standard Edition* 14:105–235.

—— (1916–1917). Introductory lectures on psychoanalysis. *Standard Edition* 16.

—— (1918). From the history of an infantile neurosis. *Standard Edition* 17:7–123.

—— (1919). A child is being beaten: a contribution to the study of the origin of sexual perversion. *Standard Edition* 17:175–204.

—— (1920). Beyond the pleasure principle. *Standard Edition* 18:3–64.

—— (1925). Inhibitions, symptoms and anxiety. *Standard Edition* 20:77–175.

—— (1934–1938). Moses and monotheism: three essays. *Standard Edition* 23:6–137.

—— (1937). Analysis terminable and interminable. *Standard Edition* 23:209–253.

—— (1937). Constructions in analysis. *Standard Edition* 23:255–269.

—— (1940). An outline of psychoanalysis. *Standard Edition* 23:141–207.

Mieli, P. (2000). Femininity and the limits of theory. In *The Subject of Lacan*, ed. K. Malone and S. Friedlander, pp. 265–278. New York: SUNY Press.

Thomas, N. K. (1995). Beware fascination: countertransference in the treatment of trauma and dissociative disorders. Paper delivered at the colloquium *Revisiting Sex and Gender at the Threshold of the 21st Century*, Paris, June.

13

The Physicality
of the Gaze

Teresa Brennan

A version of this paper served as the conclusion to
Brennan and Jay 1996.

Anna O.'s talking cure released ideas that had been imprisoned by images. This is true of those times when she would mistake one entity (a tree branch) for another (a snake); it is also true of the way her visual daydreams, in which she spent many waking hours, also predisposed her to hysterical illness. In Breuer's first theorization of Anna O's illness (and Freud concurred), daydreams paved the way for her "hypnoid states," states in which her mental energy was turned back against herself, via her inward gaze.

To see the gaze as an energetic force, as Breuer and Freud for a time surely did, is to run counter to received views on sight. In the standard positivist account, the eye is a passive organ that receives information and honorably transmits it. The contrasting view is that sight is shaped culturally and linguistically, and that there is far more to seeing than meets the eye. There are some who hold the not unreasonable belief that both are true. One such is Martin Jay.

At the beginning of his *Downcast Eyes*, Jay (1993, p. 5) suggests that some physiological explanation of human visual experience needs to sit alongside the culturalist one. In fact, everyone Jay discusses is culturalist, but some are more culturalist than others. The most culturalist of all is Marx Wartosfsky, who believes that all perception is shaped by historical changes. Jay opts for the more modulated view that allows for some physiological explanation of vision within a cultural one. Still, he notes that there are difficulties in specifying the relation between the physiological and cultural accounts. I suggest that these difficulties become especially acute when it comes to the notion of the gaze.

The gaze might be a powerful force, and yet, in the positivist and culturalist accounts, it is not a force at all. It is immaterial, symbolic, indeed "metaphorical." There has been no physical account of the gaze, in the West at any rate, since the theory of extramission was set aside. This was the idea that rays were emitted from the eyes: the eye did not only receive light rays; it gave them out. Jay, in his encyclopedic study, notes that while the theory "has long since been discredited, it expressed a symbolic truth. For the eye . . . can clearly project, signal, and emit emotions with remarkable power. Common phrases such as 'a piercing or penetrating gaze,' 'melting eyes,' 'a come-hither look,' or 'casting a cold eye,' all capture this ability with striking vividness (pp. 9–10).

But how is it that only a symbolic truth is expressed here? Precisely how does the eye convey what it conveys if it does not do so by active physical means? My interest here lies not in defending the theory of extramission, but in suggesting, as I shall below, that it was dismissed on grounds that were far too thin. Moreover, the theory of extramission (and with it notions of an active eye) was dropped at a specific historical moment, although, as we shall see it resurfaces in a different guise in Freud's discussion of sight in hysteria, and in Lacan's of the gaze. It was the demands of the moment as much as the rigors of experimentation that decided the fate of extramission. My main concern is with situating this historical moment in a broader process whose contours I have tried to explain elsewhere (Brennan 1993). And from that standpoint, modern Western history has profound consequences for how we view the physical, energetic existence of things.

In the modern era, psychic and social processes, by some strange alchemy, have an immaterial existence. If one mentions the material or physical force of psychic or social processes, one is assumed to be some kind of reductionist who thinks that the "biological" or the "physical" determine said processes. The fact that psychic and social processes also shape more overtly physical ones is neglected.

The theory of extramission might have been a lousy theory. But in some of its manifestations, it was also a theory that did not split psychic and physical effects, as we shall see in the next section. After that, we turn, through Freud, to how visual matters have come to be treated metaphorically rather than physically. Freud is relevant here because he also disputes that the eye is a passive receiver, and he effectively credits the active eye, in hysteria, with a physical force. But he, like Lacan, does not see the cultural eye as an active transmitter of light; it is more an agent of darkness. The eye, or one side of the eye, to be precise, becomes something that stops us from seeing. It does not, as in the extramission theory, enable us to see. In the last part of this paper, I shall situate this shift in the historical terms mentioned above. As Jay (1993) shows us, the denigration of vision means that other perspectives on sight have faded. But the paradox may be that the denigrated vision of twentieth century thought is no metaphor, but a reflection of a physical, historical reality in which we see less, and disavow more.

THE THEORY OF EXTRAMISSION

The idea that there are two sides to sight is as ancient as extramission. In fact, it was a weighing up of these two sides that predisposed Galen, the best known of the extramissionists, toward that theory rather than toward intromission or reception. For Galen, either what we see transmits to us, or we know it "because our sensory power extends towards the perceived object." In his excellent discussion, Meyering (1989) goes on to note that, as the former alternative was untenable, Galen opted for extramission. Galen's elaboration of it:

> involves the Stoic conception of *pneuma*, an all-pervasive agent composed of a mixture of air and fire. The optical pneuma flows from the seat of consciousness, the *hegemonikon*, through the (hollow!) *nervus opticus* (or optical nerve) to the eye. Upon its emergence from the eye, it immediately combines with the adjacent air and assimilates it instantaneously (just as sunlight only has to touch the upper limit of the air in order to transmit its power directly to the whole). This double instantaneous assimilation of the air to the sensitive pneuma as well as to the light from the sun transforms the air itself into a homogenous instrument of perception for the eye (just as the nerve is for the brain). ... [p. 26]

Galen was building on the Stoical tradition. He was also, despite the fact that Aristotle had founded a rival school of vision (according to Meyering), building on Plato.[1] Extramission, light from the eyes, was believed in for almost two thousand years.

---

1. The theory of reception opposed to the theory of extramission also had to deal with the mechanism for the transmission of the visual image. One of the most imaginative solutions was that of Lucretius. He posited an "onion-skin" theory of perception in which the object's "skins" floated towards the subject. See Lucretius 1951, pp. 131, 137.

In the seventeenth century, extramission became absurd. The key event here was Johannes Kepler's 1604 analogy between the eye and the camera obscura.[2] Now the camera obscura had been around since at least 1521 (see the discussion of Leonardo da Vinci's use of the device in Jay 1993), and a few words on it are in order. It is the simplest image-forming system, an enclosed empty space with a small opening through which light enters. Such devices form an inverted image of relevant external objects on the internal surface opposite the opening. Relevant objects are those whose image is refracted by the light as it enters.

Until Kepler made the analogy, it was unclear whether the eye was an emitter or a receiver. But the balance of public opinion was in favor of extramission. According to Smith (1970), "The sixteenth-century inventor of the camera obscura had to defy current opinion and state that the eye was always a receiver, never a transmitter, of rays. Ever since then the science of optics and an understanding of the eye have run parallel" (p. 385).

Kepler recognized that inverted vision held for both eye and camera obscura, and he then assumed that both operated on the same receptive principle. In fact, as Gillian Beer (1996) shows, the eye fell well short of the actual camera, or at least had radical differences from as well as major similarities with it. But for this knowledge, we have to wait for the nineteenth-century invention of the camera proper, together with the "great advances in microscopes [and] telescopes. . . . Even as the domain of sight advanced by means of such instruments, the evidence was mounting that the eye was an uncertain instrument and men of science insecure observers" (p. 88).

In the seventeenth century, however, before Helmholtz's evidence (which Beer dissects) showed that visual perception was inherently unreliable, the purity of the passive eye was accepted. It was thought that light, to vary Krauss's metaphor, "passes to the human brain as if it were transparent as a window pane" (1985, p. 15). In one of those shifts that characterize the evolution of normal science together with conventional wisdom, extramission

---

2. See the discussion in Wade and Swanston (1991, p. 42). The best source on the decline of the camera obscura model is Crary 1990.

was rejected, and it was taken for granted that eye and camera obscura were the same: passive receivers alike.

As if it were sensed that an analogy was not really enough to dispense with the theory of extramission, an experiment "disproving" it would occasionally be invoked. Jay (1993) mentions this experiment in a footnote, suggesting that the belief in extramission was due to the way light shines off the eyes: "This is especially evident in certain animals. Descartes, as late as *La Dioptrique*, credited the cat with extramission for this reason. In 1704, however, an experiment showed that if a cat is immersed in water, the lack of corneal refraction prevents the eye from shinning" (p. 9, note 26). Unfortunately, while the experiment is mentioned in the literature, it is difficult to find any details of it. Anthony Smith, to whom Jay refers, is typical. Smith (1970) says that he too was unable to find a source for the experiment but regards it as significant, although he gives us no more information than that the cat's eyes did not shine when it was immersed because there was no corneal refraction (p. 387). So we do not know whether the cat was alive or dead, swimming or scratching; just that it was put in water, its eyes did not shine, and the theory of extramission was polished off accordingly. Like the conviction that the eye was a camera, the willingness to believe that the immersion of the cat simultaneously doused the theory of extramission owes something, probably everything, to the historical dynamics, the contextual shifts under discussion here. We shall come back to this.

SEEING AND NOT SEEING

No sooner had extramission hit the bucket than it resurfaced in theories that emphasized the worrisome side of it (Mesmer's rays from the eyes, the anthropologist's relocation of the evil eye) and neglected the theory's concern with how perception is shaped. For, as we have seen, part of Galen's point was that the light from the eyes joins with *and shapes* the view we have of reality. This notion of perceptual modulation (which is what I think it is) of course stayed with us in various forms, but it was no longer thought of in active physical terms. The irony here is that by the mid-nineteenth century, as Beer (1996) tells us, "[t]he invisible, instead of being placidly held just beyond the scope of sight, was newly understood as an energetic system out of which fitfully emerges that which is visible" (p. 85).

Now Beer concludes her analysis of the nineteenth-century world of the invisible, and of the climate in which the human being was discovered to be "unbounded because pulsed through by process," with a prescient note on Freud's positive response to the great physicist Helmholtz. In the context of Beer's analyses of "energetics" and wave-theory ". . . Freud's response becomes evidence of his capacity to catch the reverberations that sound most intimately in many lives of his time" (p. 95). And in this context, we might allow that Freud's account of sight repeats something of the logic of extramission, a logic of waves and rays and invisible energetic forces that reemerges in the left field of psychoanalysis (good psychoanalysis is always in left field). Paradoxically, sight was the one field excluded from the nineteenth-century recuperation of waves and rays.

In Freud's account, and Lacan's after him, there are literal blind spots, things that we refuse to register on our retina, or that, having registered them, we refuse to receive consciously. We disavow or scotomize them. How exactly do we do this? For Freud, seeing was an activity "that ultimately derived from touching" (1915). This meant that sight was an active sense. It reached out and followed the contours of its objects. It penetrated (on occasion). In Freud's writings on hysteria, the implications of this view are extended.

Freud always saw hysteria as a physical problem. The body expressed a symbolic truth in an hysterical symptom, but the symptom was precisely a physical expression. The question that initially fascinated Freud (and prompted his *Project for a Scientific Psychology* [1895]) was the mechanism of this physical expression. To say the same thing, he was fascinated by the mechanism of repression in hysteria, for this mechanism expressed itself in a physical turning back against the subject's own body.

In Freud's early published work on hysteria (Breuer and Freud 1893–1895) he pursued the physical path of hysteria through the mechanism of the daydream. It was the *images* of the daydream, as well as the drowsy affective state that accompanied it, that so often paved the way for the symptom. As everyone knows, he also pursued hysteria through the release of the image of the symptom into language. But let us stay for a little with the role of the image in symptom-formation.

I have argued elsewhere (Brennan 1992) that there is a necessary relation between the inward-turning imagery of hysteria (the archetype of femininity) and the aggressiveness of the gaze. In the first case, a fantasy is held before one's own eyes; it is one's own product, and it is turned inwards against the self. In the case of the gaze, the fantasy is projected onto the other. It is an aggressive projection because, in Freud's terms, active seeing, the type of projective, external focusing Lacan was to call the gaze, is an expression of the drive for mastery. The drive for mastery, in turn intertwined with sadism, is also constitutive of the drive for knowledge, which Freud mentioned occasionally. Mastery, knowledge, and seeing are all grouped together by Freud. He terms them the "less organic" partial drives, as distinct from the more organic and more familiar oral, anal, and phallic drives.

These less organic drives constitute a problem for Freud's view of reality. For, on the one hand, they are properties of the ego, part of the ego drives. Seeing is especially critical in perception and reality-testing, and these pertain to the ego. On the other hand, the theory of the less organic drives was first propounded in the *Three Essays* on sexuality of 1905. Like all the sexual drives, seeing, knowledge, and mastery are thus fantasy-imbued. We see what we desire (hope and fear) to see, as much as what is there. Freud of course wished to keep the ego and reality testing clean of fantasy. As is well known, he did not succeed. What is less well known is that he first introduced the distinction between the ego drives and the sexual drives in an article on hysterical blindness. In a letter to Ferenazi (12/4/1920) Freud writes dismissively of this paper: it was no more than a contribution to a *Festschrift* (Jones 1955, p. 274).[3]

---

3. But this *pièce d'occasion*, "On the Psychogenic Disturbances of Vision" (1910), tries to blame hysterical blindness on the sexual drives, thus keeping the ego clean. However the same article will, on examination, reveal that it is also the ego that withholds visual information from consciousness. This means that in hysteria the ego and the sexual drives are in some way intertwined. Obviously this article predates Freud's eventual theory of the common origin of ego libido and object libido, in that it tries to separate the ego and sexual drives for the first time.

But our immediate interest lies in the inescapable energetic aspect of the less organic drives. For while they are less organic, they are no less energetic. They are precisely *drives.* Like all drives, they are also directional. They have an aim. Still, the idea that the projected gaze is an energetic force is one thing. It is another to really think of it in physical terms. It is easier somehow to do this in the case of the inward-turning gaze. It is easier because we can see the physical results of the inward-turning gaze taken to an extreme in hysterical symptoms of paralysis. When the capacity for fantasmatic visualization, for projected gazing, is turned back against the self it can, quite literally, hold one still.

The inward turning, or turning back against the self, of the drives for mastery, knowledge, and seeing is constitutive of femininity. It is a turning back that overlays an earlier one, when the ego is first formed. Lacan (1953) termed this process *passification*, understood in terms of a mirror stage. In more detail: my argument is that the ego is first formed at the hands of the other, through taking her imagined capacities (mastery, knowledge, and seeing) as one's own. But precisely because they are her capacities, they are not directed outwards, but inwards against the self. Just as the other looks at one, so one looks at oneself. One does not look out, actively. The reversal of passivity into activity occurs when one does look out. This reversal characterizes the latency period and continues to characterize masculinity. In femininity, one looks back, yet again. From this standpoint femininity is a passification that overlays an earlier passive state; masculinity is the active state in between.

But the very stillness, this constructed passivity, which marks hysteria in an extreme form and femininity in a more diluted dose, means that it would be well here to qualify the notion that Freud picks up on a Galenic, extramissionist thread dropped in the seventeenth century. Freud, or rather Freud's theory, does indeed imply that a physical light of perception comes from within and shapes what we see. It implies this insofar as it implies that we see everything through constructed realities, realities that are colored by the fantasies that construct us in turn. But his theory also implies that this physical, perceptual force can curtail our active agency in the world as much as it can extend it. For the extramissionists, the emphasis was on the vision that comes from within.

Galen himself did not have it both ways; he did not believe that the eye was passive. The light from within took us out and up to the unending stars.

What I want to propose now is that there is something else that lives alongside these historical shifts, an alternative vision altogether. Freud (1910) directs us to it in a remarkable observation:

Appropriate experiments have shown that people who are hysterically blind do nevertheless see in some sense, though not in the full sense. Excitations of the blind eye may have certain psychical consequences (for instance, they may produce affects) even though they do not become conscious. Thus hysterically blind people are only blind as far as consciousness is concerned; in their unconscious they can see [*Die hysterisch Blinden sind also nur fürs Bewusstsein blind, im Unbewussten sind sie sehend*]. [p. 212]

Once the ego is implicated in the withholding of sight, the idea that hysterically blind people still see "in their unconscious" can be explained only if an alternative source of information about reality coexists with the information the ego receives through reality testing. We have to remember here that Freud was writing in German. Strictly, "in their unconscious" means "in that which is unconscious." It is not that we have an unconscious. Rather, we are unconscious of what we have. And "it" can be busily registering another reality, a reality other than the constructed one. It is this other reality I want to propose as the alternative vision that is overlayed by a constructed, fantasy-imbued, sight.

This other reality has been observed across time. Freud was part of a fine tradition in outlining his two simultaneous sets of vision. Kant (1790), in that wildest of books, *The Critique of Judgement*, said that we observe the world through imposed categories most of the time. But sometimes, for some reason, the categories are suspended. When they are, we have an experience of the "super-sensible," a perspective that is not confined to a personal standpoint. This other perspective is receptive, but it is not passive. The passive and the receptive may sound the same, but they do not look alike. The heart of the difference is that the passive is historically constructed, while the receptive is not. By this account, the other, receptive, vision becomes a symptom of another reality, a point of connection with it. It is in all of us, but we resist it. It is outside time and therefore the only thing that can disrupt time and timeliness. It is in us as an alternative to our egocentric, categorizing visual standpoint. (Today we call this standpoint the subject-centered position.)

THE VISUAL TURN (AGAIN)

If we survey the various turns in the fortunes of constructed vision, a survey prompted by Jay's own book (1993) and the articles in Brennan and Jay (1996), a fairly clear pattern emerges. When the notion of the active eye went underground, it was replaced, in the seventeenth and eighteenth centuries, by the eye as passive receiver. This passive eye was not meant to be constructing anything; it received nothing less than the virtual truth. Thereafter, the predominance of this passive eye was disputed by the power of the invisible in the nineteenth century (Beer 1996) and by the power of construction, understood by some in the nineteenth century (Crary 1990) and stressed in the twentieth.

Eventually, we arrived at a position where we could recognize once more that vision was constructed, but the construction was now an inward-turning one as well as a projected gaze. This was an advance, but its cost was the rejection of any notion of *constructed* physicality. Together with this rejection, I will suggest, goes a loss of the other reality, the alternative receptiveness manifest in another way of seeing. These things go together because the power of the constructed fantasy, the projected gaze, becomes stronger and covers over that other reality.

It remains to trace these turns in more detail. Everyone seems to agree that the seventeenth century marks a new turn. Lacan (1953) describes it as the shift from self-definition based on identification with the other: "that is I," to a definition based on assimilating all that is other to oneself: "that is me." That assimilation included the visual world. The subject did not go to visual objects. Visual objects came to it. The subject did not emanate to the object. The object performed this service for the subject. I am putting things this way because, in the seventeenth and eighteenth centuries, there is a visual turn from active to passive seeing. On the face of it, it can seem that this is a move away from subject-centeredness, that it is an abdication of the subject's power if the subject no longer imposes its view, but rather humbly receives it. However, this passive move makes the subject the center of the world; however passively it sees, it does so from its own standpoint, which also happens to be the world's center.

As Conley (1996) shows us, this passive centrality is not without its critics. By building anamorphosis into his painting *The Ambassadors*, Holbein mounted his own critique of the new subject-centered perspective. Anamorphosis means having to abandon the central position in order to see something else altogether. From the central position, the subject's standpoint, *The Ambassadors* looks like two ambassadors. From the side, crouched down a little, the mysterious object in the foreground becomes a skull. Conley draws this out in a discussion of Holbein, Lacan, and the famous Renaissance discovery or rediscovery of three-dimensional perspective. On the one hand, Conley suggests that the subject-centered fixed point is born in the Renaissance with Brunelleschi's and Alberti's discovery of perspective, and that we have been trying to stand out of our own light ever since. On the other, there was the practical anamorphic critique of the idea that the subject's standpoint revealed all there was to be seen.

Conley uses my argument in *History After Lacan* (Brennan 1993), as well as mounting a fine critique of it. He points out that I had underestimated the complexities of visualization (which I had; I am trying to redress the balance here by looking at the other "unconscious" vision, which sits alongside the constructed one). I had considered only the vision involved in fantasy, and how passivity is constructed in the first place. I call this construction the foundational fantasy. At the risk of presuming on the reader's patience with more summary, I will outline this theory briefly, as it is relevant to the visual turn under discussion.

The construction of passivity depends on the construction of fixed points. The first fixed point is brought into being by the repression of the first hallucination. On this repression depends one's sense of oneself as a subject with one's own standpoint. This repression and any subsequent repression constitute a fixed point, because repression runs counter to the hypothetical flow of energy into which we are born and of which we remain a part.[4] It is essential to the birth of a subject not only because it constitutes a fixed, still point, but because of the contents of the hallucination that is first repressed. This first hallucination is that of commanding the breast (or the mother attached to it), and from this fantasy comes the foundations of our being. When we imagine that we command the breast, we arrogate to ourselves the functions of intelligence, planning, calculation, and imagine the other as dumb, passive matter, an object to be directed and patronized by the subject, oneself. In other words, the foundational fantasy is also the occasion whereby ideas and matter, or (subjective) mind and (maternal, objective) body, are split. This split, paradoxically, is the reason we think of fantasy or any thought process as immaterial. Any visual fantasy of course involves images, and therefore a distribution of light. That one thinks of an image in the mind's eye as somehow immaterial reflects the very prejudice I am attempting to analyze. The tendency to think of mental processes (fantasies or pure thought) as immaterial increases over time, by this argument. It remains to see why.

The foundational fantasy is not only a subjective, psychic affair, it is also an historical, monolithic, or totalizing force. To say this more clearly: as a subjective, psychic event, the foundational fantasy is ancient, in the West at least. But there are other psychic possibilities. Until the visual turn or thereabouts, the foundational fantasy is not dominant as a belief system, because its pretensions to direction and control are held in check by religious and political forms. It becomes dominant psychically only when human beings begin to deny their indebtedness in various forms: one was born free and equal in the marketplace, one owes nothing to nature or to the other, occasionally to one's father but most certainly not to one's mother. With these denials is born the illusion of autonomy. In this context, perhaps the most significant thing about the dematerialization of the active eye is that it makes

---

4. The theory of fixed points was already in the air in the Renaissance. For Dante, the still point of the universe was Satan's anus. Presumably, this held in what it had and refused to give anything out, as well as refusing to let anything in.

us really separate from one another. If the way we see one another is no longer a way of touching, it makes us truly independent and alone.

Janet Soskice (1996), in discussing the shift from the late medieval period to early modernism, notes Eco's argument on the move from Albertus Magnus to St. Thomas Aquinas. For Albertus, beauty is there regardless of whether people exist or not. For Aquinas, the object's beauty is constituted in relation to a knowing subject. While the relevant mindset (one's subjective standpoint is all) is critically reinforced in the Renaissance, the foundational fantasy, as a force in human affairs gathers steam only when it has the technological means to make itself come true. It is then that it really pays out. The actual means to the domination of nature (as object) are necessary before the fantasy can act itself out on the larger scale, replicating and reinforcing the microcosmic version that governs our individual, highly competitive psyches.

The parallel extends to the construction of fixed points. Just as fixed points are constructed psychically through the repression of energy, so they are constructed technologically through the repression of nature. By this I mean that, when nature is bound into technological forms (commodities) that cannot reenter reproduction, it is bound into fixed points. Critical for our purposes is the idea that the proliferation of fixed points on the outside, in the built environment, reinforces the fixed points, and the need for fixed points, in the psyche. Thus this is a dialectical argument. On the one hand, the subject's psyche is altered by its physical environment. On the other hand, the subject's imposition of a foundational psychic fantasy alters that environment.

But let us back up a little to Conley. Conley discusses Lacan's theory of the fixing of the letter, how we need to be tied to a certain word or sound in order to stop language perpetually sliding (and our self concept along with it). Lacan's theory of the anchoring point, *point de capiton*, says nothing of fixed visual points in the psyche (as in the energetic repression of hallucination) or the parallel fixed points of technology that are constructed out of and against the reproducible flow of nature. Nonetheless, the desire to fix the sliding of the signifier is symptomatic of a broader social process, to which Holbein was superbly sensitive. After the seventeenth century, the new perspective was more or less fixed, so to speak, and for a time any notion of a constructed vision disappeared.

In that most visual of centuries, the eighteenth, seeing was thought of as mainly passive. This not only contrasted with the position of the extramissionists; it also conflicted with the rationalist insistence (Descartes was preeminent here) on the importance of innate intuitions, and of course reasonable deductions. In other words, while Descartes may have limited responsibility for the dualism of consciousness and matter, he at least retained an active consciousness that could construct ideas. They were not all the result of perceptions imposed on the passive receiver. This is what they were for Francis Bacon, Locke, and Newton, and it was their sensationalist perspective that gained the ascendancy in the eighteenth century:

> What we have called the visual tradition of observation thus largely replaced that of speculation, once the residual active functions of the mind assigned by Locke to reflection were diminished, as they were by David Hume, Etienne Bonnet de Condillac, and other *philosophes*. Although all elements of the Cartesian attitude toward vision were not abandoned in eighteenth-century France . . . they were fighting a losing battle with the more uncompromising sensationalism that gained ascendancy in the late Enlightenment. [Jay 1993, pp. 84–85]

Peter de Bolla (1996), in his article on the *Siècle des Lumières*, shows that there was nonetheless a reflective notion of the gaze operating in that key philosopher of the Enlightenment, Adam Smith, who possessed a sense of positioning and perspective that parallels that of Lacan. While one sees, one is aware of oneself being seen. This awareness acts as a guarantor of one's existence, a hidden guarantee that makes it possible to occupy the fantasmatic objective standpoint. Otherwise, we might add, the weight of passive reception might be altogether too much for the active subject. From the time of the eighteenth century especially, this newly born narcissistic subject needs to control the action, at the same time as he insists that he knows the object as it really is. He knows it because he passively receives information from it. He does not try to impose his own view upon it. As we have suggested, he manages these apparently contradictory things by passively receiving from his own standpoint. This is reflected in the new obsession with landscaping, and other devices that enable him to shape and enlarge the parameters of what he sees from that standpoint. From his enlarged and dominant perspective, accepting that his actual mechanism of sight is passive is not so hard, especially when he is the center of the sardine-can's attention (cf. Lacan 1953).

At the same time, knowing that the object is *watching* him encourages his paranoia. Bryson's (1983) observation on the essentially paranoid nature of some Enlightenment painting is relevant here. It is especially relevant when one recalls the dialectic engendered by passification. When one is the recipient of the gaze, and rendered passive by it, one feels trapped and confined. One is also anxious about the intentions of the image-giver, the watcher. This anxiety is the wellspring of aggressiveness (Lacan's *aggressivité*) that relieves the subject of anxiety by projecting the affect of fear outwards, onto another. In this manner we go from the inversion of capacities and drives (mastery, knowledge, seeing) to the claiming of them as our own, unless we are corralled into the feminine position, in which case they are once more inverted.

It would seem that by the beginning of the nineteenth century, the subject had had enough of the pressure of visual passification, never mind it had made him the center of the world. In the context of charting the waning of the Enlightenment trust in sight at the end of the eighteenth century, Jay (1993) observes: "One mark of the change was the replacement of passive sensation by a more active will as the mark of subjectivity in the philosophies dominating the early nineteenth century" (p. 107).

This dialectic of passification and aggression intensifies as the foundational psychic fantasy makes itself materially true. As it makes itself come true, it physically alters how we perceive ourselves and the environment we are in. It does so because the physical environment we inhabit is also, quite literally, changed by our technological interactions with it. Our need to project outwards changes the environment, which increases the objectifying pressure on us and in turn increases the paranoid need to control an environment that is felt as more and more threatening. What can be visually identified can be most readily controlled (cf. Burgin 1994). This is Heidegger's point, and it is developed by Lacan and Foucault alike.

Part of the nineteenth-century fascination with the invisible is, I suggest, a desire to increase the sphere of control. Part of the anxiety about the invisible is that it cannot be controlled. Part of what gives a theory like extramission its paranoid feel is that it purports to describe something that cannot be seen or identified, and that might even, as in the case of the "evil eye," be out to get us. The trend is always to insist that whatever cannot be seen and controlled is not real. The idea that the instrument for seeing, the eye itself, has invisible properties is beyond bearing. The idea that the eye *touches* others threatens autonomy and atomism alike.[5]

The truth about paranoia is and always will be that it is prompted by the projection of one's own aggressive desires. Our paranoia increases, together with our need for visual control (of all those invisible rays), as our real aggression toward the other, and the natural world, increases. The unconscious fear is that one will be *touched* by what one has harmed. The passification dialectic has real effects on us, just as we have effects on others and on the *physis*, the natural world.

Vision is denigrated in the twentieth-century thought under discussion in Jay's (1993) book. As Jay shows us, the denigration is unjust: sight has not been universally privileged. But if I am right about the effects of the dialectic on the *physis*, and the related tendency to think in terms that split mind and matter, it may be that we are looking past what the denigration of vision really entails. In other words, if the gaze has a physical component, if the aggression in the gaze increases in circumstances such as these in which we live, then vision has been physically affected and deserves its denigration. In other words, how we see changes over time. Different theories of perception and of sight may be more true for their times than they appear with hindsight.

The idea that we see the same way at all historical points is of course untenable. Even so, we persist in thinking that, say, the Egyptians painted the eye that way because they were a bit thick, or the medievalists showed perspective the way they did because they were a bit slow (cf. Rawson 1983 and Dubery and Willats 1983).

---

5. It is, I would suggest, exactly because of this atomism that the idea that the eye touches can also be felt as reassuring (cf. Merleau-Ponty 1969).

We do not credit them with their own critiques of a subject-centered perspective, even though we are quick to spot, say, Cubism's relation to subjectivity. Is it a critique? Or is it a revealing of the object to the subject in all its aspects—a revealing that saves the subject the work of walking around to look at the object's other side?

It is plain enough that the dominance of the vision that would subordinate everything to one's own standpoint is recent. Still, there is more than one vision. Freud's unconscious vision is there as an alternative to the passive ins and active outs of constructed vision. It is worth reiterating that this receptive vision is not the same as a constructed passive one. This can be a difficult point to grasp. For instance, when Heidegger eulogizes the receptive passive relation to Being over the activity that rules in the West, he often conflates two senses of the word *receptive* (cf. Scheibler 1993). Once a distinction between these two forms of receptiveness or passivity is made, it becomes easier to grasp both the nature of the passification dialectic and the source of the alternative to it.

Human beings did not and do not always see out of self-centered eyes. There is another receptive vision, whose very existence disrupts the subject-centered perspective. The point here is that this other vision is at risk. For this other vision depends on unbound energy. It becomes less the more that energy is bound in a proliferation of fixed points, within and without the psyche. The more that is bound, the less we receive of that which disrupts. Somewhere we know this, so we denigrate the constructed vision that blinds us but mistake it for all there is to sight.

One can read Jay's (1993) book overall, and some of the articles I have discussed here, as mappers or markers of how a different, receptive vision was lost, covered over by a dominating gaze, yet resurfacing in hysteria. In an earlier essay of Jay's (1986), he suggests an alternative positive vision to that described in negative panopticism. But in accord with the anti-dualist temperament of the times, he backs away from the implied dualism in *Downcast Eyes*. By the end of that fine book, Jay has enjoined a plurality of vision, a mixed bag with some goodies as well as rotten eggs. He enjoins this as an alternative to the negative notion of the gaze, the denigrated vision of twentieth-century French thought.

Of course, I have nothing against pluralities. I am prepared to say *feminisms, masculinities,* and even *contexts.* However, the theme of the duality of vision warrants more investigation. The wish to go beyond dualities does not stop a given duality from existing as a fact. Moreover, the duality, let alone plurality, of vision is something of an endangered species. One of its poles is in danger of disappearing, leaving us with a monolithic vision that is precisely negative. We no longer receive much that disrupts, so we denigrate the vision that stops us from receiving but mistake it for all there is to vision. For, if I am right, the disjunction between a receptive and a constructed vision (active or passive) is the source of all disruption of received views, hysterical or otherwise. It is the condition of pluralities. But it is a condition that depends on the existence of things that are beyond our control.

REFERENCES

Beer, G. (1996). Authentic tidings of invisible things: vision and the invisible in the later nineteenth century. In *Vision in Context*, ed. T. Brennan and M. Jay. New York: Routledge.
Brennan, T. (1992). *Interpretation of the Flesh: Freud and Femininity.* London: Routledge.
———(1993). *History after Lacan.* London: Routledge.
Bryson, N. (1983). *Vision and Painting: The Logic of the Gaze.* New Haven, CT: Yale University Press.
Breuer, J. and Freud, S. (1893–1895). Studies on hysteria. *Standard Edition* 2.
Burgin, V. (1994). Paranoic space. In *Visualizing Theory: Selected Essays from V.A.R. 1990–1994*, ed. L. Taylor. New York: Routledge.
Conley, T. (1996). The wit of the letter: Holbein's Lacan. In *Vision in Context*, ed. T. Brennan and M. Jay. New York: Routledge.
Crary, J. (1990). *Techniques of the Observer: On Vision and Modernity in the Nineteenth Century.* Cambridge, MA: MIT Press.
de Bolla, P. (1996). The visibility of visuality. In *Vision in Context*, ed. T. Brennan and M. Jay. New York: Routledge
Duberty, F. and Willats, J. (1983). *Perspective and Other Drawing Systems.* London: Herbert.

Freud, S. (1905). Three essays on the theory of sexuality. *Standard Edition* 7:123–243.

——(1910). The psychoanalytic view of psychogenic disturbance of vision. *Standard Edition* 11:209–218.

——(1915). Instincts and their vicissitudes. *Standard Edition* 14: 109–140.

Jay, M. (1986). In the empire of the gaze: Foucault and the denigration of vision in twentieth century French thought. In *Foucault: A Critical Reader*, ed. D. Couzins. London: Blackwell.

——(1993). *Downcast Eyes: The Denigration of Vision in Twentieth-Century French Thought*. Berkeley, CA: University of California Press.

Jones, E. (1955). *Sigmund Freud: Life and Work*, vol. 2. London: Hogarth Press.

Kant, I. (1790). *The Critique of Judgment*, tr. James Creed Meredith. London: Oxford University Press, 1990.

Krauss, R. (1985). *The Originality of the Avant-Garde and Other Modernist Myths*. Cambridge, MA: MIT Press.

Lacan, J. (1953). The function and field of speech and language in psychoanalysis. In *Ecrits: A Selection*, tr. Alan Sheridan. London: Tavistock.

Lucretius. (1951). *On the Nature of Things*, tr. R. Latham. Harmondsworth, UK: Penguin.

Merleau-Ponty, M. (1969). *The Visible and the Invisible*, tr. A. Lingis. Evanston, IL: Northwestern University Press.

Meyering, T. (1989). *Historical Roots of Cognitive Science: The Rise of a Cognitive Theory of Perception from Antiquity to the Nineteenth Century*. Dordrecht: Kluwer Academic Publishers.

Rawson, P. (1983). *The Art of Drawing: An Instructional Guide*. London: McDonald.

Scheibler, I. (1993). Heidegger and the rhetoric of submission: technology and passivity. In *Questioning Technology*, ed. V. Conley. Minneapolis, MN: University of Minnesota Press.

Smith, A. (1970). *The Body*. London: George Allen and Unwin.

Soskice, J. M. (1996). Sight and vision in medieval Christian thought. In *Vision in Context*, ed. T. Brennan and M. Jay. New York: Routledge.

Wade, N. and Swanston, M. (1991). *Visual Perception: An Introduction*. London and New York: Routledge.

14

Beyond the
Feminine Ideal:
The Body Speaks

Ann D'Ercole and

Barbara Waxenberg

Historically, psychoanalysis has characterized a woman's body as overflowing with symptoms and neuroses. Freud, in particular, saw her body as a landscape on which the conflict between what was desired and what was forbidden was waged. For Freud, the task of the psychoanalyst was to bring into conscious awareness what had been repressed, transformed, and ultimately converted into physical symptoms. *Studies on Hysteria* (Breuer and Freud 1893–1895) draws on the case material of five women whose physical symptoms were manifest in body parts that would not or could not move. From this material, a psychoanalytic theory was generated that ultimately became the bedrock for future psychoanalytic formulations.

Freud and Breuer believed the complaints of their patients were hysterical symptoms that had to be decoded. They were seen as signs that contained clues to lost cultures, to the unconscious mind and as the domain of repressed desire and experiences (Young-Bruehl 1990). This material provides a rich primary source from which to trace the beginnings of psychoanalysis and serves as a guide to the limitations of Freud's ideas about the sex/gender system and to the ways in which these limitations have impeded psychoanalytic progress.

Freud recognized the position of sexuality in his Viennese society and the profound differences in the social experiences of, and expectations for, men and women. Grounded in a modernist tradition, he viewed femininity and masculinity as acquired characteristics and correlates of the structural differences in the bodies of men and women. But his constructs were often ambiguous, and the confusing gaps have fueled current gender-revisionist efforts (Benjamin 1991, Dimen 1991, 1995, Goldner 1991, Harris 1991, Kiersky in press).

THE CASE OF ELISABETH VON R.

An examination of Freud's account of his treatment of Elisabeth von R., the last reported of the five studies, reveals more than a story of gender, love and desire, and their twisted interconnections. This narrative also discloses the original site of the material body in a psychoanalytic method that relies predominantly on language. Clearly, much remains to be known about how the body and self inform and create one another in a psychoanalytic encounter. Reviewing this case material from two mutually informing perspectives: 1) a dilemma of gender, sexuality, and role ascription, and 2) a contextualizing of issues of gender and sexuality within a particular family constellation, a particular society, and a particular young woman's experiences, conflicts, and attempts at resolution, provides an opportunity to revisit these fundamental issues.

The 24-year-old Elisabeth von R., as Ilona Weiss was pseudonymously named, was the youngest of three daughters born to a prominent Hungarian family. She was the liveliest and probably the most intelligent and ambitious of the sisters, possessed of "an independence of her nature which went beyond the feminine ideal" (p. 161). She shared a particularly close relationship with her father, since her mother suffered bouts of illness and seemed unavailable to be either his companion or hers. Her father's view of his devoted daughter was complicated and ambivalent. He admired her intelligence, regarding her as the substitute for the son he never had, and as such cultivated their close relationship. At the same time, he was disturbed by her deviation from what society expected of a young woman and by her ambition—by what he semi-facetiously referred to as her "cheeky" and "cocksure" nature—and by her bold forthrightness. He warned her not to be so truthful and feared that her nonconformist behavior would make it difficult for her to find a husband. However, the quest for a suitable mate was not as primary in importance to Elisabeth as it was to her parents. She viewed marriage as an act of subjugation in which her will would be sacrificed. She planned to study and perhaps pursue musical training instead.

These plans were aborted by her father's long and painful illness. It was Elisabeth the renegade who ultimately sacrificed her own desires and nursed her father dutifully and uncomplainingly through his illness, sleeping in his room to be available to him. After her father's death from the complications of chronic heart disease, she became fiercely protective of her family. She was seen as nurturing herself on "her pride in her father and in the prestige social position of her family" (p. 140), and set herself the task of holding the family together and guarding it against the attacks of outside predators.

But the shadows continued to gather. A year after her father's death, Elisabeth's oldest sister married a man whom she regarded as selfish, rude, and generally unacceptable, an outsider whose plans for the future collided with hers. Her second sister, in a marriage arranged by the family, happily found a mate more agreeable to Elisabeth, a man whom she regarded as considerate of the desires of his wife and the needs of the family. But another problem arose. Elisabeth's mother required eye surgery and had to be kept in a dark room for several weeks. Endlessly protective, Elisabeth remained by her side throughout her recovery. It was at this time that her much disliked brother-in-law struck another blow by relocating his family to a remote part of Austria, a move that heightened her mother's sense of isolation.

In what seems to have been a peaceful interlude during a family holiday, Elisabeth's symptoms aggressively appeared. Her incapacitation marked a reversal in the roles formerly played by family members. Elisabeth, the fierce protector of the family, had become the invalid. As she struggled with her pain, another tragedy occurred. She learned that her second sister was in the throes of a difficult pregnancy, making Elisabeth's return home imperative. But she arrived too late; her beloved sister had already died of heart disease. The family recognized that this particular form of heart ailment was probably inherited and blamed themselves, her husband, and the doctors for endangering her life by allowing the two closely spaced pregnancies that ultimately led to her death. The inconsolable grief and guilt devastated the family. Elisabeth accused the once favored brother-in-law of financial mismanagement and the two brothers-in-law fell out over money. Not only did Elisabeth lose her sister to death and her brother-in-law to rancor, but her sister's child was also lost to her.

These are recognizably painful events. But they leave unanswered the question of why Elisabeth developed the chronic pains in her legs and attendant difficulty in walking that Freud was eventually called upon to understand and cure. Was it, as he hypothesized, that she "formed an association between her painful mental impressions and the bodily pains which she happened to be experiencing at the same time, and that now, in her life memories, she was using her physical feelings as a symbol of her mental ones" (p. 144)? If we take that as fact, guilt and memory are implicated in the etiology of the hysterical disorder. Phelan (1997), a dancer who favors somatic utterances over language, has advanced performance theory's conversation with queer theory and psychoanalysis. Her reflections on this case lead her to understand hysteria as the public performance of memory, concretized in the bodies of women to help process grief. But that was not how Freud saw it.

Elisabeth became a patient of the young Freud, a patient who seemed to have less investment in the alleviation of her pain than he: "Her face assumed a peculiar expression, one of pleasure rather than of pain" (p. 137). When she described her symptoms to Freud, she showed little anxiety about their chronicity or curiosity about their etiology, which appeared to have no organic basis. It is interesting to note that Freud's objective at this period was symptom relief, and when that was accomplished, roughly eight months after treatment began, the analysis was regarded as complete. Still, certain questions must be asked.

Some of those questions concern Elisabeth's relationship with her mother. Did she sleep in her room too? How involved in nursing her mother did Elisabeth become? Did this nursing experience contribute to her symptoms? Why didn't Freud build that experience into his theory? The questions that are not asked are always as important as the ones asked (Bader 1998). And so, how can we understand Freud's failure to explore in greater depth Elisabeth's relationship with her mother? Why was this once lively, active, and ambitious young woman so willing to accept passively the immobility of her legs? What role did disability and invalidism play in this family constellation? Would she have continued her life with pain and restricted movement without Freud's intervention? What elements were unrecognized by the patient and by Freud in this psychoanalytic encounter?

BODY TALK AND THE TALKING CURE

Freud's first full treatment of a case of hysteria provides us with the opportunity to explore a family matrix in which the patient's body expresses what the self cannot speak. A revisiting of these early psychoanalytic sessions reveals a treatment heavily invested in the performative aspects of the patient's symptom, as her body parts engage in an ongoing dialogue with the physician. Freud reports: "Her painful legs began to join in the conversation during our analyses. If by a question or by pressure upon her head I called up a memory, a sensation of pain would make its first appearance" (p. 148). The body discloses a truth that the patient cannot utter. This performance provides a way to express feelings that would otherwise be confined to the dark archives of memory (Phelan 1997). In addition, this recherché affords us an entrance into the overt and covert messages about gender and sexuality in Freud's work.

PRESCRIPTIONS OF THE CULTURE

Any analysis must be viewed in terms of the cultural context in which it is enacted, the extent to which it conforms to prevalent values—with adjustment and acceptance of cultural norms as implicit goals—and the degree to which it strikes new ground. Both Freud and Elisabeth von R. were embedded in beliefs about the culturally prescribed behavior for a young woman in the late nineteenth century in Austria and Hungary, she with some degree of resistance, he with greater acceptance. Freud's writings on this case, while empathic, seem ambivalent; he appears to applaud her directness, but when it is turned on him, he labels her, as her father had, cheeky and rebellious.

Elisabeth was in the habit of telling people the truth as she saw it and was warned by her father that her forthrightness would drive away potential suitors. Her father seems to have been saying, in effect, "It is all right for you to have your thoughts but not all right for you to speak them publicly." Freud viewed her directness as unfeminine behavior and concluded that Elisabeth was "greatly discontented with being a girl" (p. 140). While he recognized that she had ambitious life plans, this desire to study and the frustration she experienced in sacrificing her desire were never focused upon in treatment and certainly never recognized or supported as a valid pursuit for a young woman.

Like many women of her generation and those that followed, Elisabeth must have faced the dilemma of doing "girl." How was she to continue to hold her place in the family, remain a woman, and not conform to social prescriptions? Could she retain values and ambitions that were seen as being at odds with her gender assignment? In this context, the symptoms that impeded movement can be conceptualized as an attempted resolution to a dilemma of direction. These symptoms represent a partial solution to a conflict-laden and psychologically immobilized state, as well as an accommodation to the prevailing mode of illness in this particular family and an accepted mode of being for women of her time. Thus Elisabeth played dutiful daughter, a role that received considerable parental support and certainly had its satisfactions, but one that encouraged masquerade.

ELISABETH'S MASQUERADE

Elisabeth, we are told at the outset, *masks* her troubles with a cheerful air" (p. 135, emphasis added) and later that "her mask reveals a hidden sense," implying that she had some notion of the basis of her illness, "that what she had in her consciousness was only a secret and not a foreign body." Freud assumed that Elisabeth kept a part of herself frozen until the stirrings of erotic feelings led to the melting away of "her frozen nature" (p. 155). In this manner, Elisabeth appears to have retired her independent ambitions with the alleged discovery that the presence of a man in her life was essential. Freud concluded that hidden beneath her independent exterior was her true, dependent self.

However, we consider Elisabeth's emerging dependency as a form of miming, her valiant effort to participate in the culture in a way that was deemed acceptable. The ideas reflected in Rivière's (1929) essay on the conflict women experience with achievement and aggression are echoed throughout this case. Rivière, struggling herself with negotiating the gender and sex matrix, presented the notion of gender as masquerade and suggested that "womanliness therefore could be assumed and worn as a mask, both to hide the possession of masculinity and to avert the reprisals expected if [a woman] was found to possess it" (p. 306). She introduced into psychoanalytic thinking the experiences, dilemmas, and solutions that she herself must have faced. Rivière, fourteen years younger than Elisabeth von R., seems to have benefited from the maturing of psychoanalysis over that short period of time. To quote her thinking as expressed in "Womanliness as a Masquerade":

> Not long ago intellectual pursuits for women were associated almost exclusively with an overtly masculine type of woman who in pronounced cases made no secret of her wish or claim to be a man. This has now changed. Of all the women engaged in professional life today, it would be hard to say whether the greater number are more feminine than masculine in their mode of life and character. In University life, in scientific professions and in business, one constantly meets women who seem to fulfill every criterion of complete feminine development. They are excellent wives and mothers, capable housewives; they maintain social life and assist culture; they have no lack of feminine interests, e.g. in their personal appearance, and when called upon they can still find time to play the part of devoted and interested mother-substitutes among a wide circle of relatives and friends. At the same time they fulfill the duties of their profession at least as well as the average man. It is really a puzzle to know how to classify this type psychologically. [p. 303]

Puzzled as she was by a woman's ability to shift between expected and nonexpected gendered behaviors, Rivière struggled to fit her experience alongside psychoanalytic theory. But her conceptualizations of sex and gender, though they have made a formidable contribution to psychoanalysis, sometimes seem conflated or not clearly defined. She does, however, elucidate the conflicts of a woman who, despite her success and ability, continues to need reassurance from men and who compulsively seeks sexual and professional admiration. Consequently, she must mask any evidence of rivalry or of sadistic castration wishes. Her views seem to translate into, "I must not take; I must not even ask; it must be given to me." Through behavior that elicits male approval, she wards off any possible retribution for possession of power while, at the same time, the man's acceptance reassures her that she has effectively performed the masquerade of innocence that insures safety. For Rivière, the woman's self is not masquerading; it *is* the masquerade. This sentiment is at the forefront of postmodern conceptions of the self. Butler (1990, 1993, 1995), arguing that gender is inherently imitation and a split-off site of love and loss, has built upon the concept of masquerade and shaped the discourse on gender.

Rivière, like other women of her generation, fathomed the politics of the self (Cushman 1995). She knew how exposing the so-called "masculine" characteristics of ambition, desire, jealousy, rage, and aggression could threaten a woman's existence. This was particularly true in Vienna at the turn of the century, when few women could successfully negotiate the distance between cultural norms of femininity and individual ambition and achievement (Harris 1997).

This struggle to understand the contradiction between what women did and what was expected of them can be seen as well in the work of Annie Reich (1953), another of Freud's loyal psychoanalytic daughters. While maintaining her allegiance to Freud's tripartite developmental theory, she simultaneously recognized the many ways women struggle with unrealizable ambitions and dreams, and the consequent sense of inferiority that arises. In her patients, she often saw that the solution to such conflicted ways of being lay in the choice of a love object who represents what the woman hoped to become, a man whom she could love as a way to complete herself, a vicarious satisfaction of foreclosed ambitions.

Many of the women who did accomplish this blending of desires did so under the protective umbrella of a prominent man. Like Anna Freud, they played "daughter" well. Others, such as George Eliot, George Sand, Vita Sackville-West, and Virginia Woolf, defied gender-specific behaviors, sometimes as artistic license but always courageously, both encouraging and enduring the inevitable suspicion and ghosting that accompanies living as a gender outlaw (Kiersky, in press).

Reading the case of Elisabeth von R. from the perspective of masquerade, we see her hide from Freud in a manner that permits her to "pass," less consciously gendered perhaps but no less a gender production. She mourns not only the loss of her father, but also the loss of any opportunity to satisfy her ambitions and her dreams of an autonomous existence.

Perhaps if there were a time machine that could whisk her into the consultation room of an analyst of today, she might be invited to deconstruct the narratives of her experience and to reconstruct them in a manner that would allow her greater flexibility in her productions of gender and sexuality. Because she was unaided in this way, we see Elisabeth engage in "passing" as a kind of complex sociological trick that lets a rebellious identity survive even if it is compromised and silent (Butler 1993).

Freud's constructions of identity tie sex to gender, with masculinity allied with activity and femininity equated with passivity. Not surprisingly, in the course of treatment Elisabeth appeared to become more passive, less "cheeky." But she did not surrender all; rather she demonstrated independence in some of her choices. Her conflict over ambition and aggression went into hiding. There was no chance of change. Instead, the dangerous and unacceptable feelings were masked. This gave her an opportunity to vent her anger over the way her older sister's husband treated her aging mother, in contrast to the other women in the family who ignored his temperamental outburst, and she found it difficult to forgive her sister for her "feminine" compliance and refusal to support her mother in this conflict. For Freud, this reflected her obstinate, pugnacious, and yet, paradoxically, her reserved character.

Freud constructed his theory of the genesis of hysteria while painstakingly reconstructing the development of Elisabeth's symptoms, always questioning what was indicated and wondering what was hidden from him. His conclusion: the patient suffered from the painful memory of unacceptable and consequently repressed erotic thoughts that ultimately formed a separate psychic group. An idea or memory too hideous to contemplate was rendered "like a foreign body, without having entered into relationship with the rest of her ideational life" (p. 165).

When Elisabeth was unaware of the content of her feelings, she felt only physical pain; when she was made aware of her thoughts, she felt great psychic pain. For example, Freud tells us that while standing by her dead sister's bed, she fleetingly thought, "Now he [her brother-in-law] is free again and I can be his wife" (p. 156). He suggested that these guilty feelings arose several times, once when Elisabeth enjoyed the company of a young man only to return home and find her father sicker than when she had left, again when she failed to reach her sister's bedside before the latter's death, and once more while walking with her favored brother-in-law. These conflicts were seen as the source of her conversions. It was this last event that Freud found most salient, for it was here that "the coldness of her nature began to yield and she admitted to herself her need for a man's love" (p. 165). In this way, Freud framed his story of sexuality and gender where development is *genderized* and results in prescribed sexual categories.

Others (Kiceluk 1992) have read this case as the interweaving of the body's semiotics with the narratives constructed by the mind. Kiceluk describes Freud's puzzled state as he labored over the question of why Elisabeth's symptoms took the specific form they did and why her body spoke in this way of her memories. Why was she using her physical feelings as a symbol of her mental ones, and what was her motivation for doing so? Kiceluk argues that what Freud came to know is how patients resist telling their stories. But this is a one-sided reading of resistance, one that eliminates the participation of the other person in the dyad. Freud canceled himself out of the equation and postulated the tripartite structure of the psyche, a phallocentric theory of sexuality and a concept of transference that failed to consider his own impact on the patient.

CLINICAL IMPLICATIONS FOR PSYCHOANALYSIS

In his work with Elisabeth von R., Freud developed some of the principals that ultimately formed the bedrock of the practice of psychoanalysis: the role of unconscious processes in the formation of symptoms, the interplay of defense and resistance, the injunction to suspend judgment and present whatever comes to mind, the ascetic role of the analyst, and the method of psychoanalytic inquiry. He divided this analysis into three periods: a four-week period of "pretense treatment" (p. 138) that consisted of kneading and electrically stimulating the patient's muscles; an extended period of psychic treatment in which her symptoms were evoked through pressure on her forehead and directives to describe in detail what came to mind as a consequence, but which did not yield up her most unacceptable feelings behind the mask; and the third period of scrupulous detective work that he felt led to the ultimate uncovering of her disavowed love for her brother-in-law, her envy of and rivalry with her sister, and the hideous thought that if her sister were to die, she and this man might marry.

Elisabeth is described as obstinate, pugnacious, and reserved, and variably compliant with Freud, at times earnestly trying to divine what material was required of her and joining in the search with what appears to be some interest and enthusiasm. But when the images summoned seemed morally abhorrent or shameful to her, she became silent, implicitly refusing to obey the rules and to communicate what she had imaged. This was Freud's first encounter with the phenomenon later to be termed resistance. We can only imagine what she was silently thinking as he laboriously interpreted the linkage between her physical symptoms and her painful thoughts, or how she felt about Freud and this mysterious endeavor. But since so much was conceptualized in terms of the patient's expressing in nonverbal ways what was unavailable to her elsewhere, one cannot help wondering how being ministered to, as she had ministered to others, and by a young physician, was interpreted and assimilated by the patient. For once, Elisabeth claimed center stage, not as the caretaker, but as the recipient. For once she was listened to and valued. We have only her later recollections and reflections cited by her daughter on this period of her life, in which she described Freud dismissively as "just a young, bearded, nerve specialist they sent me to who had tried to persuade me that I was in love with my brother-in-law, but that really wasn't so" (Appignanesi and Forrester 1992, p. 113).

The past is always being rewritten in the light of the present and with private agendas, so we cannot determine whose interpretation of what transpired (Freud's or Elisabeth's) is more valid. But one fact remains clear. The symptoms vanished and the patient was able to move physically and to move on in her life, eventually marrying a man of her own choosing rather than an arranged bridegroom as her sister had. In so deciding, she retained some aspects of her independent self. And she did not become a member of the Freud circle as many of his patients ultimately did. If one reads between the lines, Elisabeth von R. moved: she moved from being enmeshed in the fate of her family of origin to forming a family of her own design. And Freud, too, moved on.

Freud's objectives were fulfilled in that the symptoms disappeared. But what were the mutative factors in the treatment that led to this outcome? Was it, as he believed, his linking of physical pain and immobility to their underlying existing psychological conflicts—the giving of words to the unexpressed—that achieved this resolution? What role did the relationship Freud formed with Elisabeth play in ultimately offering her relief? What part did nineteenth-century culture and restricted choices available to women play in determining her presenting symptoms? It may well be that the nature of this particular psychoanalytic relationship overcame the structured hierarchical doctor–patient and male–female positions and allowed the previously unspoken and masked thoughts to be brought into conscious awareness. But it is more likely that, because of these factors, a good deal in the treatment remained unvoiced.

For Freud, the task was to grasp the connections between the events of Elisabeth's life, both real and fantasized, and her symptoms. In his words: "I arrived at a procedure which I later developed into a regular method and employed deliberately. This procedure was one of clearing away the pathogenic psychical material layer by layer" (p. 139), a technique he likened to an archeologist's excavation of a buried city that had remained essentially intact until exposed to light. Interpretation, the naming with increased precision of that which has been disavowed, defended against, and transmuted, was foremost in the curative process. This is the analyst as archeologist, surgeon, and detective. But it omits from consideration important elements in the story. How can we factor in the body-to-body contact, his tacit approval of her, and her feelings?

The humaneness and empathic understanding of this narrative is apparent and reflected in Freud's words: "The gap that was caused in the life of this family of four women by her father's death, their social isolation, the breaking-off of so many connections that had promised to bring her interest and enjoyment, her mother's ill health which was now becoming more marked—all this cast a shadow over the patient's state of feeling" (p. 144). And again: "Unreconciled to her fate, embittered by the failure of all her little schemes for reestablishing the family's former glories, with those she loved dead or gone away or estranged, unready to take refuge in the love of some unknown man, she had lived for eighteen months in almost complete seclusion, with nothing to occupy her but the care of her mother and her own pains" (p. 144). Such words belie attempts at analytic neutrality, and their empathic understanding must have been communicated to the patient. Looking at the treatment as a landscape artist might instead of as an archeological dig, one sees a young Freud, deeply invested in proving his theories and in expanding his professional practice, closeted daily with an intelligent and attractive young woman, with no literature on countertransference to guide him and only Breuer's disastrous experience with Anna O. to serve as a warning. And for her, his presence replaced her embittered isolation, the loss of companionship, and the special position that she had held in her family both before and after the death of her father. We see her attempting to supply the material that Freud sought, much as she must have played the admiring and admired daughter to her father. That "more" transpired than was discussed can be assumed from Freud's rueful account of his last sight of her whirling past him at a private ball to which, knowing she would be there, he had wangled an invitation, and from her teasing notes, in which she wrote that she planned to come and see him. But she never did, and perhaps his consultation and involvement with her mother, in which he acted as paterfamilias and colluded with Frau von R. to find a suitable husband for her daughter, played a prominent role in her angry rejection. This may have seemed to Elisabeth as a betrayal of their special private relationship and of her secrets at a time when she was trying to separate from her family while remaining special to him.

This is the context in which the therapeutic relationship evolved. Each participant brought to this encounter his or her own personal history. Each had a personal agenda (recognized or unrecognized) about the purpose of this particular endeavor. Each developed certain visions of the other and a sense of what was expected. Each had his or her own values, optimism or pessimism about the future, and perspectives on gender possibilities in the culture in which they lived. Within this subjectivity lives the primacy of gender in culture, and our psychic ills then and now are a refraction of the place accorded gender. Instead of the symptoms Elisabeth and the other female patients in the *Studies* suffered at the turn of the century, women who enter treatment today, for example, struggle with eating disorders or are compulsively overworked and over-exercised. Postmodern critiques (Butler 1990, Foucault 1978) urge us to consider whether we really need to keep on doing sex and gender as we have in the past. Does gender have to be the primary category upon which culture rests? Can we forego this ritual of power?

According to Foucault (1978):

> confession is a ritual of discourse that unfolds within a power
> relationship, for one does not confess without the presence (or
> virtual presence) of a partner who is not simply the interlocutor
> but the authority who requires the confession, prescribes and ap-
> preciates it and intervenes in order to judge, punish, forgive,
> console and reconcile; a ritual in which the truth is corroborated
> by the obstacles and resistances it has had to surmount in order
> to be formulated; and finally a ritual in which the expression
> alone, independently of its external consequences, produces in-
> trinsic modifications in the person who articulates it. [pp. 61–62]

We can certainly relate these words to the gendered confessional, hierarchical relationship that existed between Freud and Elisabeth. Freud quotes her as having said, when pressured to elaborate on the response she had given, "I thought of that but I didn't think it was what you wanted" (p. 154). What is confessed might never have even occurred, since the act is so linked to suggestion, the power of the accuser, the desire to please by yielding up one's secrets—real or imagined—and the arena in which the confession takes place. This is as patently true today as it was at the time of the Salem witch trials, and it divides the proponents of recovered memories and skeptics into warring camps. How many analysands, given the unequal distri-bution of power, have even today digested material as Elisabeth ultim-ately did, transformed events, circumvented anger, all in the service of maintaining the connectedness and retaining the benevolent image at painful cost to themselves and their perceptions of reality?

So how can we evaluate what happened? Was it that she spoke to a man who did not judge as she had judged, spoke of the previ-ously unspoken and, to Freud, hideously viewed private thoughts and feelings that ultimately freed Elisabeth from her constraints of movement? Was it Freud's continuous elucidation of her sup-pressed desires, which by giving them words also gave legitimacy to a woman's sexual desire? What did it mean to her to have her limbs massaged and to be cared for and listened to as she had cared for and listened to others? This is the unreferred-to mothering aspect of what transpired. Although it is impossible to separate the impacts of content and context, one factor is clear: a highly charged intersubjective experience in which two people, asymmetrically positioned, explored a selected rendition of the patient's experience, highlighting certain aspects and minimizing others such as her mourning, her relationships with her mother and siblings (who fade into insignificance in the narrative), and the narrow band of choice available to women at that time. Guilt is stressed; anger is not only not expressed but is regarded as unseemly, and assertion, although ambivalently admired, is hardly encouraged.

In considering this first complete analysis, it is important to remember that Freud was coming from a medical background in which relief of symptoms was primary. That he was still straddling the world of medicine and the realm of the psyche is apparent in his labeling the period of electrical stimulation and massage as "pre-treatment," although we are all well aware that there is no "pre-" in treatment, that treatment begins with the engagement of patient and therapist beginning, at times, before their meeting. But all this occurred long before Freud was to write, in 1937, "Experience has taught us that psycho-analytic therapy—the liberation of a human being from his neurotic symptoms, inhibitions and abnormalities of character—is a lengthy business" (p. 316). He goes on to state that for an analysis to be considered complete, not only must the patient be free of his or her former symptoms and have overcome his or her various anxieties and inhibitions, but the analyst must deem that so much repressed material has been brought into consciousness, so much elucidated and so much resistance overcome, that no repetition of the patient's specific pathological processes need be feared. And in these terms, the first complete analysis is barely a beginning.

Much has been made of the wrong turn Freud took when he abandoned the seduction theory in favor of fantasies governed by oedipal desires. Sharing the excitement of the early cases that in Freud's own words "read like short stories and lack the serious stamp of science" (1893–1895, p. 161), one can only regret that he ultimately superimposed the map of theory on what was initially "a detailed description of mental processes such as we are accustomed to find in the works of imaginative writers which enables me with the use of a few psychological formulas, to obtain at least some kind of insight into the course of that affection" (pp. 161–162). As in well-written narratives, the end is not signaled at the onset, and we don't know where we are going until we arrive. Later, this sense of individual uniqueness became mired in developmental formulae, the case studies unfold with the inexorability of Greek tragedy, and we know from the onset how the story will inevitably be told and which landmarks will be passed on the way.

Serious questions are currently being raised concerning the relationship between metapsychology and psychoanalytic exploration. Spence (1989), in particular, observes that metapsychological assumptions define the inquiry and separate, from the sometimes rich but often amorphous and confusing detail, that which confirms the guiding hypothesis. Not only is the search for a particular construct inevitably successful, but the more strongly a theory appears to be confirmed by apparent congruence, the less likely will be a search for alternative constructions.

Freud's values cast a shadow over his analysis of Elisabeth von R. Appignanesi and Forrester (1992, p. 3) report that during the 1906 Vienna Psycho-Analytic Society's discussion of the "Natural Position of Women," Freud is reported to have said, "A woman cannot earn a living and raise children at the same time. Women as a group profit nothing by the modern femininist movement." We see Elisabeth as having become more acquiescent, more conforming, and more accepting of the prevailing views on proper behavior for a young woman of her class as a consequence of her treatment. However, it is also clear that she moved from her paralyzed state, both physically and psychically. Did she move beyond the feminine ideal? No, it does not appear that she did. However, she did move, and so did a remarkable theory and process from one culturally embedded era to another.

REFERENCES

Appignanesi, L. and Forrester, J. (1992). *Freud's Women*. New York: Basic Books.
Bader, M. J. (1998). Postmodern epistemology: the problem of validation and the retreat from therapeutics in psychoanalysis. *Psychoanalytic Dialogues* 8:1–32.
Benjamin, J. (1991). In defense of gender ambiguity. *Psychoanalytic Dialogues* 1:27–44.
Breuer, J. and Freud, S. (1893–1895). Studies on hysteria. *Standard Edition* 2.
Butler, J. (1990). *Gender Trouble*. New York: Routledge.

——(1993). *Bodies That Matter: On the Discursive Limits of Sex.* New York: Routledge.

—— (1995). Melancholy gender: refused identifications. *Psychoanalytic Dialogues* 5:165–180.

Cushman, P. (1995). *Constructing the Self; Constructing America: Studies in the Cultural History of Psychotherapy.* New York: Addison-Wesley.

Dimen, M. (1991). Deconstructing difference: gender, splitting, and transitional space. *Psychoanalytic Dialogues* 1:335–352.

—— (1995). On our nature: prolegomenon to a relational theory of sexuality. In *Disorienting Sexuality: Psychoanalytic Reappraisals of Sexual Identities,* ed. T. Dominici and R. Lesser, pp. 129–152. New York and London: Routledge.

Freud, S. (1937). Analysis terminable and interminable. In *Collected Papers, Volume 5,* pp. 316–357. New York and London: Basic Books.

Foucault, M. (1976). *The History of Sexuality. Volume I. An Introduction.* Originally published as *Histoire de la sexualite 1: La volonte de savoir.* Paris: Gallimard, 1976; New York: Vintage, 1980.

Goldner, V. (1991). Toward a critical relational theory of gender. *Psychoanalytic Dialogues* 1:249–272.

Harris, A. (1991). Gender as contradiction. *Psychoanalytic Dialogues* 1:197–224.

—— (1997). Aggression, envy and ambition: circulating tensions in women's psychic life. *Psychoanalytic Dialogues* 2:291–325.

Kiersky, S. (in press). *Exiled Desire.* Hillsdale, NJ: Analytic Press.

Kiceluk, S. (1992). The patient as sign and story: disease pictures, life histories, and the first psychoanalytic case history. *Journal of Clinical Psychoanalysis* 1:332–368.

Phelan, P. (1997). *Mourning Sex: Performing Public Memories.* New York: Routledge.

Reich, A. (1953). Narcissistic object choice in women. *Journal of the American Psychoanalytic Association* 1:22–44.

Rivière, J. (1929). Womanliness as a masquerade. *International Journal of Psycho-analysis* 9:303–313.

Spence, D. (1989). Narrative appeal vs. historical validity. *Contemporary Psychoanalysis* 25:517–524.

Young-Bruehl, E. (1990). *Freud on Women: A Reader.* New York: Norton.

15

Conversations with Elisabeth von R.

Roy Schafer

This chapter was previously published in *Tradition and Change in Psychoanalysis*, International Universities Press, 1997. Reprinted with permission.

Breuer and Freud's (1893–1895) *Studies on Hysteria* provides us with an excellent place to begin celebrating the hundredth birthday of psychoanalysis. Nothing could be more fitting than to praise the revolutionary step Freud took in that work. If, however, it is asked in just what this revolutionary step consisted, one is confronted at once with all the complex questions of contemporary critical theory. For the Western world has been at work trying to answer that question from the time the work was published, and as we know, it has proposed answers that have changed as critical perspectives have changed.

During these hundred years, a great variety of critical perspectives have been in and out of favor both in psychoanalysis and in the humanities and sciences that surround it and nourish it. One must also take into account the fact that psychoanalysts have had one hundred years of experience working clinically with Freud's ideas and working theoretically not only with his sweeping propositions but with his highly particularized ones as well. Consequently, one can now ask questions and propose answers based on contemporary practice, our ideas about evidence and theoretical coherence, and our relations with reality, authority, and knowledge—questions and answers that were inconceivable one hundred years ago. That is to say, one can approach the inquiry into Freud's revolutionary step in a postmodern fashion (Schafer 1992). Working in this way, one finds in the *Studies on Hysteria* preconceptions and modes of thought about gender relations, clinical relations, and the goals of treatment that must be interrogated with the full force of present approaches to understanding. This I propose to do in my return to Freud's first immersion in the hot waters of clinical psychoanalysis: his report on his treatment of Elisabeth von R.

Using that report as my specimen, I shall first review critically Freud's understanding of hysteria in the period 1893 to 1895, and his correlated technical approach to its treatment. I shall pay particular attention to those aspects of Freud's early ideas and methods that I believe continued to color his later work. Second, I shall present my idea of how he might have, or could have, understood and approached this analysand some forty years later when he was concluding his world-shaking career of profound insight into the human condition. Too often, in my opinion, accounts of the early Freud are taken whole, that is, as the definitive accounts of Freud's ideas, if not as definitive accounts of all of psychoanalysis. That limited approach gives one the impression that neither he nor the discipline he created has a history—more exactly, a number of histories, depending on who is writing the history.

I share the common view that most of the best of Freud is to be found in the mature works written during the 1920s and 1930s. By then he had made new contributions of such scope and depth that, understandably, he was himself unprepared to appreciate them fully. I believe that they were far more consonant with general changes in the intellectual climate of the early decades of the twentieth century than he realized. In the concluding section of this essay, I shall touch on a few aspects of this lag in Freud's self-understanding. In the main, however, I shall develop a critique of some aspects of Freud's final position on Elisabeth (as I have constructed it), and I shall revise that hypothetical position, using for the purpose insights that I regard as among the most useful and deep that can be offered by the Freudian psychoanalysts of today.

In these *Studies on Hysteria*, Freud wrote that when symptoms intrude into the treatment situation, they are "joining in the conversation" (p. 148). What conversation can he have meant back then in the mid-1890s? On my reading, the assumptions and the resulting tone of the interchanges resemble detached medical interventions and passive responses far more than conversation or dialogue. That words are being used need not make it a true dialogue, that is, one evidently based on common understanding and with room for mutual influence. The record suggests that, for Freud, Elisabeth was a carrier of symptoms. Although he was already in a position to say that these symptoms should be regarded as voices speaking in other registers or languages, he was not acting on that understanding. Instead, he seemed to be limiting his role as psychotherapist to that of a zealous physician engaged in letting out the pus of festering traumatic experiences, as though that were the remedy for psychic pain and dysfunction. His technical concept of abreacting affects seems to have been organized around a medical metaphor.

Freud had already expressed his recognition that infections develop only in bodies and minds that make good hosts for the foreign invaders. Consequently, he did not inflate his claims; he emphasized that his therapy was aimed only at symptom cure and not, holistically, at transforming his analysands into organisms that would be well fortified against future infection. In support of this limited approach, he tended to take for granted that, in general, his analysands were mentally sound victims of traumatic circumstances. That they were not always readily or steadily collaborative in their treatments was noteworthy but another matter. Later on (Freud 1912a), he would no longer think it was another matter, and in recent decades much has been written on the complex, often seriously ill, makeup of his presumably mostly normal analysands burdened by their neurotic symptoms.

It would be wrong to fault Freud for maintaining this narrow perspective and setting only this limited goal. We have only to take into account the historical–professional setting in which he was working at that time, the extraordinary methods he was devising, and the discoveries he was making and reporting, in order to appreciate how great a change he was beginning to introduce into the understanding and the therapy of the neuroses. If, however, we look at this work from our current perspective, we will be better able to understand not merely what Freud was and was not seeing and doing back then, but also where we stand now in the development of our discipline.

The historians of the late nineteenth century would generally agree that it was an era of flourishing materialism manifest in the smokestacks of industrial capitalism and its colonialist offshoots. Determined management, efficiency, productivity, and technical control and progress were leading ideals. I propose that Freud was being consistent with this ideology when he approached the neurotic symptom as one would approach a colony of primitive natives sitting on a wealth of untapped natural resources and artifacts. In Freud's case, those resources were intertwined with the buried memories he was mining; when successful, he would reach the sources of civilized life. By these means, he could, so to say, both bring home the riches and bring to these "natives" all the taken-for-granted benefits of a rational, controlling civilization. Later (1923a), he would say that where id is, there would ego be.

Consequently, one could hardly expect these verbal inter-changes in his consulting room to amount to a "conversation." Today, they seem more like unfeeling interrogations or, in their milder versions, efficient paternalistic forms of taking control. Within its own pretty-closed system, the prevailing ideology of the times would confirm both the productivity and the benevolence of this approach. Therefore, it would be safe for us today to assume that the intrusion of symptomatic actions into the treatment set-ting was not so much their joining in an ongoing conversation, as Freud thought, as it was an attempt by the analysand to initiate a conversation, a true dialogue. Like Anna O. (Breuer and Freud 1893–1895), Elisabeth needed a "talking cure" and was doing her best to change the format accordingly. In a conflicted, delinguis-ticized way, the symptomatic actions of both women were convey-ing that there had to be two human participants in the process, each having power and each having available a variety of ways to further the dialogue. Contemporary reflection on the emotional positions and needs of both parties to clinical analytic interactions requires that transference and countertransference, broadly con-ceived, be put at the very center of things.

Where did Freud stand in relation to transference and coun-tertransference back in 1895? Of countertransference he was say-ing nothing; of transference he did have some immensely signifi-cant things to say. First of all, it is no small thing that he introduced the term. Then, in his later chapter on the psychotherapy of hys-teria, he characterized transference as a "false connection"; by that phrase he meant that analysands transfer onto the therapist dis-turbed ideas about others who then prove to be central figures in the painful memories currently being elicited by the treatment.

In this regard, his technical approach to the transference lagged behind his preliminary understanding, in that his attitude toward it remained administrative or benignly paternalistic and in some cases simply forcing. His report shows that, in general, he was aiming at managing and removing any and all expectable intru-sions of human feelings that would disturb his mining of the past. He believed that these alien elements should not be allowed to "obstruct" the treatment process. For example, he remarked on how the analysand's relation to the physician can be disturbed by erotic trains of thought—"especially in women"—and he recommended some substitute and limited gratifications, specifically "friendliness," to limit that disturbance. He realized that the disturbed woman's "cooperativeness" might turn into resistance should she experience—inappropriately, he implied—feelings of neglect, lack of appreciation, even humiliation, or a great fear of dependency and an aversion to feeling vulnerable to influence, or should she be exposed to criticism by others of the doctor or the method of treatment.

Consequently, he argued that the analyst should "remove" these false connections because they give rise to resistances. He proposed that the means to keep moving forward or, better yet, downward toward the buried traumatic memories is to make the transference "obstacle" conscious and show that the intrusion of the past in the present feeling has merely given rise to "a compulsion and an illusion." Only by that implicitly disapproving method could one hope that the obstructing transference would "melt away with the conclusion of the analysis."

Freud did not provide any adequate account of the therapeutic action of this rationalistic and judgmental approach. What he did provide, I suggest, was a clear picture of his determination to dominate the treatment. He felt justified in taking this approach because he saw himself engaged in a project of (in his memorable formulation) "transforming . . . hysterical misery into common unhappiness" (p. 305). Even though not thinking holistically, he did go so far as to state his belief that his method of symptom removal could yield prophylactic benefits, thereby broadening somewhat his claims for his new therapy. In his words, "with mental life that has been restored to health [the analysand] will be better armed against that unhappiness." But this he could not know. It is known now that *at that time,* and despite his disclaimers and cautious stance, Freud was not above making brash claims for his method. Moreover, as we now realize, it was in keeping with his patriarchal outlook that he manifested no awareness at all that he was unilaterally defining and deciding about neurotic misery and common unhappiness; specific goals were not the product of genuine dialogue with the analysand and mutual definition of results.

It was, of course, the colonialist doctor of civilization who knew best.

Freud's patriarchal stance may also be inferred from his neglect of the mother's role in Elisabeth's neurosis. Too quickly, he centered his analysis on the daughter's relationship to her father and other "strong" male figures. He seemed to be relying on the stereotypical view of women as the weaker sex; presumably, their lives made sense to them only in relation to men. Today, mature clinical analysts would not grasp so readily at the material Elisabeth pushed forward. And critical appraisers of this report would also be alert to the extent to which this one-sided development took place under Freud's active guidance.

We have learned to be skeptical of material that is, so to say, served up on a silver platter. What was on Elisabeth's (and Freud's) platter was a sick father, his leg in her lap, the mother on the sidelines, the triangular rivalry for a man with her sister, the desirable widower, and the unfulfilled romantic dreams about the potential suitor who would rescue her—and, as the final result of this traumatic onslaught, symptoms of a broken heart. It is all rather like a Victorian romance. In Freud's post-therapy conclusion of his narrative—his seeing the heroine whirling past him in a dance and he then hearing that she married—he offers the reader the conventional comfort of a happy bourgeois ending. It is as if he assumes that we will derive satisfaction from knowing that, finally, Elisabeth came to her senses and accepted the conventional feminine role happily—exactly the role she had always rebelled against. It is not going too far to surmise that Freud was eager to restrict his analysis to what was on that silver platter, for it fit in too well with two interrelated factors: his patriarchal social orientation and his therapeutic zeal. Also, to the extent that he had gone after just that material, he would have welcomed compliance.

Today's analysts would not buy it. In the contemporary analytic way of telling lives, mothers cannot be kept on the sidelines. They are central players from the first. If the analysand is simply trying to keep away from material pertaining to mother, she or he will make that obvious pretty soon, and the avoidance can then be taken up analytically.

If, on the other hand, the mother seems to have made herself peripheral in the child's life, as by invalidism or absence, she can only have come to be seen as a figure profoundly threatening and burdensome to the child; for in unconscious fantasy, the child will experience the manifestly sidelined mother partly as an abandoning figure filled with disgust or hatred and partly as a damaged figure driven away by the child's own demands and hostility. The child's sense of worth and security in the world will be undermined. Mixed-up images as victim, helpless one, and omnipotent one will develop. The girl will have no basis for any straightforward erotic development, leading to reasonably uncomplicated positive oedipal desire for the father and father surrogates, and no wholehearted wishes for the conventional feminine role defined as subordinate wife, mother, and homemaker. Yet, in the end, this development and these wishes were just what Freud imputed to Elisabeth. One can surmise that, even later in his career, he would have done the same, seeing that he continued to pay inadequate attention to mothers in his theoretical and clinical accounts. Mostly, mothers remained unarticulated oedipal–sexual fantasy objects of desire and rivalry.

By the end of his career, Freud had already written "Mourning and Melancholia" (1917a), *Beyond the Pleasure Principle* (1920a), *Group Psychology and the Analysis of the Ego* (1921), *The Ego and the Id* (1923a), *Inhibitions, Symptoms and Anxiety* (1926), and a number of papers on gender development and differentiation. He had already recognized the role of identification in ordinary development and psychopathology. He had installed destructive aggression alongside libido at the center of his metapsychological narratives. He had organized his account of development around anxiety and guilt and the various infantile danger situations, defense, and repetition. He had worked out a good deal about the interpretation of transference and acting out and their uses for the analyst's purposes of reconstruction of early development.

With regard to the results of analytic therapy, he had made his claims more modest, less symptom-oriented, and more articulated. With regard to the role played by the mother, however, I am not impressed by his effort in 1931, "Female Sexuality," to give more prominence to the infant–mother relationship, for by the time of his 1937 paper on termination (1937a) and his final "Outline of Psychoanalysis" (1940) he was showing that he had reverted to the castration complex and penis envy as "bedrocks," a conclusion that again put the actual mother on the sidelines. Apart from this major factor, his rich, complex, eye-opening advances in theory and technique could readily have led him to reformulate the case of Elisabeth. I should like next to try my hand at formulating this case in the terms available to him in the late 1930s.

I begin with what Freud called "the harsher side" of Elisabeth's character (p. 140). In the end, I suggest, he would have viewed that side as expressing primarily a dominant identification with her father, and he would have tried to account for it primarily in terms of her castration complex and penis envy as well as a heightened negative oedipal orientation. He would have regarded this "masculine" constellation as overdetermined by a defensive switch away from the positive oedipal orientation. He would have seen the necessity for including this defensive factor after surmising that the positive had been dangerously intensified by Elisabeth's having been her father's favorite and by the mother's invalidism having left a vacuum in the father's life for Elisabeth to fill. Probably, Freud would have also emphasized the likelihood that Elisabeth was struggling against a "sickly" identification with her sickly mother. However, I am inclined to think that he would have linked that struggle with the fantasy of the sick mother of the phallic period, that is, a castrated and therefore defective woman, very much as Annie Reich, for example, did in her studies of pathological self-esteem regulation (1953, 1960).

Continuing with this reanalysis, it is most likely that Freud would have also viewed Elisabeth's invalidism as, in part, her way of punishing herself for her rage against both of her parents and her sisters, for her infantile oedipal desires, and for her wish-fulfilling sexual fantasies in her present setting. Taking into account her locomotor symptom, he might well have gone on to suggest that, like the homosexual woman he had discussed in 1920 (1920b), she was unconsciously imagining herself to be, or acting out, the part of being a fallen woman, perhaps even a pregnant woman.

With regard to gender preference and love-object orientation, Freud, at the time of the *Studies*, wrote this of Elisabeth, that when she was under pressure of her feelings of desperation and helplessness in her emotionally overburdened circumstance, she began finally to yearn for a strong man to love and help her. Freud presented this switch of deep-seated attitude in a way that can be regarded now as notably matter-of-fact, for he referred to this change simply as an erotically charged desire for love that grew out of her painful situation. By the end of his prodigious career, however, he would have had to cast some doubt on the depth of this change, for he had come to appreciate the great power of what he called the character resistances, the adhesiveness of the libido to instinctual positions once adopted, the power of repetition, and other such factors. Most likely he would have emphasized the inexorable and enduring power of penis envy. Additionally, with his relatively new systematic focus on destructive aggression, he would have assumed that this shift of orientation was accomplished with a good deal of rage or bitterness toward men, and he would have linked that rage to Elisabeth's envious response to both the anatomical distinction between the sexes and her unconscious masculine identification. The turning to men would have seemed a neurotic act of desperation.

With regard, then, to gender preference and love-object orientation, Elisabeth's *astasia abasia* would or could have been viewed by him as a compromise formation that at one and the same time expressed her unconscious fantasy of castratedness, an identification with the invalided mother, a protest through weakness against being forced into the role of a homebound caretaking child, and her simultaneous struggle against and assertion of the homosexual side of her personality (see in this last regard the Dora case [1905a] and "Hysterical Phantasies and Their Relation to Bisexuality" [1908]).

In his early years, Freud's therapeutic optimism led him to take a light attitude toward the recurrence of Elisabeth's symptoms subsequent to termination. In contrast, the later Freud would have shown a good deal of skepticism with regard to any suggestion of recovery from her neurosis. Although her apparently symptom-free "whirling past" him in a dance, and reportedly having been married, would have been of interest to him, he could have surmised that these outward changes and developments had been based far more on a strengthening of defenses than on insight and structural change (see in this regard "Analysis Terminable and Interminable" [1937a]).

This skeptical conclusion would have been consistent with his dictum that neuroses can be considered cured only if their underlying unconscious dynamics have appeared in the transference and been analyzed there—analyzed, that is, in the continuous, even if only tacit, conversation that constitutes the analytic relationship. The conclusion would have been consistent, too, with his having laid out both his structural theory and the sequence of infantile danger situations from which basic transferences and major defenses issue. The later Freud no longer believed that merely the recovery of memories, especially those of recent origin, can suffice to resolve neurotic conflict. And that was all that had taken place in Elisabeth's treatment! To top it off, he would have shown his much greater respect for the power of sexual masochism in symptom formation and elsewhere, by not leaping to conclusions about "cure."

It remains now to develop my critique of what I have imagined to be Freud's much improved way of retelling the case in 1939. What could be still missing from this story, and what could be off-center or even wrong with it? I shall start with an overview before getting into the details. First of all, the foundation stones of this clinical story are poorly laid. The defining origins of Freud's narrative not being spelled out, it lacks a *developmental* foundation. His story of Elisabeth begins after the middle, that is, long after Elisabeth's early years of life, so that the "conversation" was necessarily quite limited in scope. Second, the *cultural setting* is ignored. Freud takes the mores of the time for granted. Unreflectively, he situates that young woman neither in her patriarchal society nor in her warped family setting—again, quite limited conversation. And third, the *philosophical preconceptions* regulating Freud's work are unsound, for his account rests on a naive positivism that allows him only to carry on limited conversations with himself about the questionable way he was trying to fit his interpretive work into his simple inductivist model of science (Schafer 1983, 1992).

1. *Developmental.* This "study" contains no exploration, through the transference and the reconstructions that it makes possible, of the oedipal years and especially the preoedipal years—what I would prefer to call the dyadic years. I refer to the mother–daughter relationship from the time of birth onward. I share the view that the

origin of later disturbances, including those of gender identity formation and choice of love-object, must now be located in that early dyadic period. My reformulation is limited by there being no report of when the mother became sickly. If it was early, as Freud may have been suggesting when he said that Elisabeth was thrown together with her father from early on, then it is plausible that Elisabeth's initial experiences of mothering were far from satisfactory. Probably, she did not have a "good enough mother" (Winnicott 1958). One could say so even while granting the presence of a satisfactory nanny.

On this defective dyadic basis, Elisabeth's capacity to differentiate herself from her mother would have been seriously interfered with. Her tolerance of dependency, separation, and loss would have hardly begun to develop. She would have been vulnerable to unbearable feelings of helplessness, worthlessness, and "omnipotent" guilt in relation to a mother she could only perceive both as damaged by her and rejecting of her. Accordingly, she would have been burdened with a crushing need to make reparation to this mother; indeed she seems to have tried to do just that in her adult years, especially after the death of her father. If, culturally, that was the role that everyone, including herself, would have expected of her, that cultural fit would have reinforced both her servitude and her defense against realizing how conflicted she felt about it.

It may be surmised that Elisabeth had no mother to serve as a model for an identification imbued with life, vitality, and vigorous sexuality. Support for this surmise may be derived from the impression given by Freud's narrative of the mother: a woman with few substantial social and cultural skills, interests, and pursuits; additionally, a woman quite alone in the world when Elisabeth was not there to look after her. Although it is certainly possible in this regard that Freud was both showing a customary lack of interest in noting or reporting the details of the mother's life, and, as a narrator, wanting to sharpen the drama of this story by impoverishing his account of that mother's life, it would not be straining too much to infer that, psychologically, Elisabeth's invalided mother was a relatively impoverished figure.

Enter the father—for Freud a positive oedipal figure of grand proportions, considering the father's preference for Elisabeth, her care of him, and Elisabeth's other disturbed life circumstances. But wouldn't one now have to suppose that Elisabeth would have found this man an ambiguous figure? In her psychic reality, he could well have been experienced as a combined maternal–paternal figure, a parental couple one might say, the one who provided care and concern: in some respects a strong model to identify with, in other respects an exciting person toward whom to develop sexual feelings. At the same time, however, he would have been experienced unconsciously as a powerful figure who was the object of envy and thus as a stimulus of wishes to attack, spoil, and reject (her "harsher side"). Additionally, he would have lent himself to fantasies that it was he who had damaged the mother in the primal scene, in which respect he would have come to be seen as an especially dangerous figure with whom to get close, even though she also found his closeness gratifying her needs for the care and love of a mother. And that dangerousness would have been augmented by projection into him of her anger and spoiling envy.

It is, therefore, reasonable to suppose that Elisabeth's readiness to be a caretaker of her father involved the same guilty, reparative needs that seem to have controlled her relationship with her mother once her father had died. With both parents, the "altruistic surrender" (A. Freud 1936) would have reinforced repression of her rage at these exploitative and burdensome parents who had forced on her a kind of reversal of generations and deprived her of significant elements of her youth. Those erotic feelings that would have been stimulated, especially by all the physical contact involved in taking care of the two of them, would also have been defensively useful in helping to ward off not only her destructive feelings and urges but her guilt as well. Libido camouflaging aggression is a common defense; in our culture it is quite common not only in male–female relations but in same-sex relations as well.

2. *Cultural.* The preceding remarks have already anticipated much of my critique of Freud's taken-for-granted attitude toward the mores of his time and place. I refer to his assigning narrative centrality to the father; portraying women as the weaker sex; implying that heterosexual desire, love, and marriage and motherhood are the natural culmination of women's psychosexual development; enacting the unilateral paternalistic authority of the

physician; and his generally sponsoring the values of the middle-European bourgeoisie that prescribed what is "masculine" and "feminine" and what is "rough" versus "gentle" or "agreeable." Then and there, Freud could safely assume that Elisabeth shared these values, however at odds with them some of her unconscious desires might be, so that she would rejoice in arriving finally at a conformist social role. He would have had no reason to question whether any other therapeutic goals would make sense for a young woman of her sort and with her developmental background, and so no reason to detect subtle signs that she might also be questioning his prescribing those goals.

Today's analysts are, I believe, slowly coming to realize that all such opening-up types of questions should be considered possibly valuable, even essential in psychoanalytic treatment. Feminist critics and practitioners and gay and lesbian critics and practitioners have been forcing the issue by stringent critiques of hidden bourgeois, homophobic, and otherwise closed-minded valorizations of only certain conventional therapeutic goals. Also, certain segments of our social organization have changed enough to allow any analyst who might treat an Elisabeth today to analyze her apparent lack of female friends and the supportive network they can provide; similarly, it would be essential to analyze the apparently too-tight family structure in which she was confined rather like a prisoner doing time as an aide in the prison infirmary twenty-four hours a day.

3. *Philosophical.* Freud's position in 1895 was uncompromisingly positivistic. Unreflectively, he saw himself founding a science modeled on the biological and physical sciences of his time: partly field research and partly lab research. For him, Darwin and Helmholtz were paradigmatic figures (Schafer 1983). In his accounts of it, the clinical situation he devised was partly field and partly lab; he wrote about it using both types of discourse. Occasionally, he threw in archaeology as a variant of field research. To pursue either type of research, psychoanalysis required a strictly neutral, objective, genderless, uncompromising, purely inductivist inquirer and a compliant, submissive, or passive object of research. Subjective reactions—both his and his analysand's—were to be eliminated or at least kept to an absolute mini-

mum, even though it was the analysand's subjective life that was the object of study. Further, it was necessary to develop explanatory narratives based on the "fact" of drives, especially the sexual drive that guaranteed the survival of the species. So many have already written on this subject that this portrayal of Freud's methodological and conceptual precommitments and their dominance in his self-understanding should be familiar to any audience familiar with psychoanalysis.

It can be argued now that it was not so much a case of self-understanding as self-*mis*understanding. Contrary to Freud's ideal and belief, his clinical method was thoroughly hermeneutic and, for his time, gender-specific, even in its interrogatory form, for he was guided in his explorations by the continuously interpenetrating factors of what he was looking for and what he was hearing. He could raise only certain questions about his cocreated data and he could propose only certain connections among them. This I have tried to show in sketching hypothetically his later formulation of the case of Elisabeth von R., and then adding my reformulation and some comments on the continuing influence of the cultural—historical setting in which Freud framed his master narratives and the storylines they laid down.

Self-consciously, Freud had declared early that he drew back from writing only stories. I would say that he did so once he recognized that, inevitably, case histories and treatment histories are narratives. That is to say, they are *tellings* of human events, not measurements or simple records of process and materials in the physical universe. Furthermore, he could not come close to recognizing that his narratives were about Elisabeth's narratives, themselves already a product of her peculiar interaction with him. In addition, the final summary of them that he reconstructed first in his notes and then in his writing about her in the cultural and theory-laden context of his enterprise was no more than his final narrative of all the other narratives.

Mostly unknown to Freud, he was far from trafficking in naturalistic Darwinian observation and experimentally controlled lab tests. There was no "out there" to draw conclusions about directly. There was only an "in here," in the analytic space, where two storytellers were groping toward a true dialogue about the inner and outer worlds of both (Schafer 1992). Only later in his career did

Freud occasionally write about his divergence from straightforward positivism (e.g., Freud 1937b).

In conclusion, what I have set before you was, first, my version of the version worked out by Freud and Elisabeth; second, the version of that version that Freud could have developed later on; and third, my version of the best review of both one might expect of contemporary Freudian psychoanalysis.

REFERENCES

Breuer, J. and Freud, S. (1893–1895). Studies on hysteria. *Standard Edition* 2.
Freud, A. (1936). *The Ego and the Mechanisms of Defense.* New York: International Universities Press, 1946.
Freud, S. (1905a). Fragment of an analysis of a case of hysteria. *Standard Edition* 7:1–122.
—— (1908). Hysterical phantasies and their relation to bisexuality. *Standard Edition* 9:155–166.
—— (1912). The dynamics of transference. *Standard Edition* 12:97–108.
—— (1917a). Mourning and melancholia. *Standard Edition* 14:237–258.
—— (1920a). Beyond the pleasure principle. *Standard Edition* 18:1–64.
—— (1920b). The psychogenesis of a case of homosexuality in a woman. *Standard Edition* 8:145–172.
—— (1921). Group psychology and the analysis of the ego. *Standard Edition* 18:65–143.
—— (1923). The ego and the id. *Standard Edition* 19:1–59.
—— (1926). Inhibitions, symptoms and anxiety. *Standard Edition* 20:75–172.
—— (1931). Female sexuality. *Standard Edition* 21:221–243.
—— (1937a). Analysis terminable and interminable. *Standard Edition* 23:209–253.
—— (1937b). Constructions in analysis. *Standard Edition* 23:255–269.

——(1940). An outline of psychoanalysis. *Standard Edition* 23:139–207.

Reich, A. (1953). Narcissistic object choice in women. *Journal of the American Psychoanalytical Association* 1:22–44.

——(1960). Pathological forms of self-esteem regulation. *The Psychoanalytic Study of the Child* 15:215–232.

Schafer, R. (1983). *The Analytic Attitude.* New York: Basic Books.

——(1992). *Retelling a Life: Narrative and Dialogue in Psychoanalysis.* New York: Basic Books.

Winnicott, D. W. (1958). *Collected Papers: Through Pediatrics to Psycho-Analysis.* New York: Basic Books.

16

The Leap from the *Studies on Hysteria* to *The Interpretation of Dreams*

Martin S. Bergmann

Only five years stand between the publication of Breuer and Freud's *Studies on Hysteria*, published in 1895, and Freud's *Interpretation of Dreams*, which appeared in 1900. The history of thought does not offer many examples of so profound a change taking place in one man's thinking within such a short span of time. The *Studies on Hysteria* is a book written by two neurologists, addressed to their fellow physicians who treat patients suffering from hysteria. The book takes its place comfortably beside the works of other physicians, such as Charcot, Janet, and Bernheim.

By contrast, *The Interpretation of Dreams* (1900) is one of those seminal works that differentiate the twentieth century from the nineteenth. It contains the first three of Freud's great discoveries: the discovery that dreams have meaning, and that this meaning can be discovered through the technique of free association, and that all civilized men and women carry within them repressed unconscious thoughts and wishes that influence their lives without being known to them. Man is not rational, not a master in his own house, but subject to varying degrees to forces within him that are unknown to him. As a result of these insights the absolute demarcation line between normal and neurotic lost much of its validity. It was the loss of this demarcation line that proved to have momentous consequences. The unconscious will be of interest not only to the neurotically ill, but to all those who wish to know themselves.

Noteworthy in view of subsequent developments was the confidence Breuer and Freud had in the results of their work:

> For we found to our great surprise at first, that each individual hysterical symptom immediately and permanently disappeared when we had succeeded in bringing clearly to light the memory of the event by which it was provoked and in arousing its accompanying affect and when the patient had described that event in the greatest possible detail and had put the affect into words. [p. 6]

What is still admirable in *Studies on Hysteria* is the complete harmony between theory and technique, a harmony that psy-

STORMS IN HER HEAD

choanalysis will try in vain to recapture in its subsequent development. The theory postulated that hysterics suffer from reminiscences
of a repressed psychic trauma inflicted upon them as children by
the imposed sexuality of adults. Hysterics as children were victims
of sexual abuse; as adults they suffer from strangulated affect that
cannot find discharge. Breuer and Freud offer a remedy. The hysterical patient can be hypnotized and under hypnosis abreact their
memories. Their painful memories can heal once a cathartic method
is used, allowing these repressed and sequestered memories to
emerge into consciousness with the full quantum of affect with which
they were originally repressed. I wish to draw attention to the way
Freud conceptualized repressed reminiscences. These reminiscences, while not consciously available to the patient, nevertheless
can be recalled under hypnosis. No reconstructions are necessary.

The term *catharsis* was taken over from Aristotle's statement
that tragedy on the stage evokes terror and pity and thus purges
the emotions (catharsis). The application of the Greek term to the
therapeutic procedure was not altogether felicitous for, as Jonathan
Lear (1990) observed, in literature the spectator remains aware of
the gulf that separates his life from that of the dramatic hero. The
identification is temporary and imaginative. Catharsis takes place
within a fine balance of sympathy and distance. The hysteric lacks
this balance (p. 54).

The major change that Breuer and Freud demanded from the
physician was that he listen to the patient. To convert an autocratic
physician into a person who had to learn the biography of each
patient, and discover something new in every case in which treatment was undertaken, was a major step forward. We should also
note that unlike Charcot's hospitalized patients, who came from
inarticulate farming and labor classes, the patients that Breuer and
Freud treated were middle- and upper-class patients, urban and
well-educated, mostly Jewish, who possessed a capacity to articulate what ailed them.

When in 1908 a second edition of *Studies on Hysteria* came out,
Breuer and Freud could no longer combine their views in a preface. Breuer stressed: "As I personally am concerned, I have since
the time had no active dealings with the subject; I have had no part
in its important development and I could add nothing fresh to what
was written in 1895" (p. xxxi).

Freud, on the other hand, said:

> Even to-day I regard [my initial views] not as errors but as valu-
> able first approximations to the knowledge which could only be
> fully acquired after long and continuous efforts. . . . I can give no
> better advice to anyone interested in the development of cathar-
> sis into psychoanalysis than to begin with *Studies on Hysteria* and
> thus follow that path that I myself have trodden. [p. xxxi]

In the nineteenth century, hysteria was not at the center of medical interest. It was, as Freud memorably stated in 1910, a rather despised branch of medicine:

> Thus the recognition of the illness as hysteria makes little differ-
> ence to the patient; but to the doctor quite the reverse. It is no-
> ticeable that his attitude towards hysterical patients is quite other
> than towards sufferers from organic diseases. He does not have
> the same sympathy for the former as for the latter. [p. 11]

Goldstein (1982) and McGrath (1992) have made us aware that the topic of hysteria was not, politically speaking, a neutral one. For, throughout history, or at least since the twelfth century when St. Francis of Assisi showed his stigmata, many men and women in *imitatio Christi* have bled from hands and feet in a state of trance. The Church has taken these manifestations as proof of its teaching. To unmask them as hysteria and, worse, to be able to replicate them under hypnosis, was in the religious debate of the nineteenth century a highly charged subject.

Ellenberger (1970) surveyed the contemporary literature as to how the *Studies on Hysteria* was received. He noted that on the whole, the reviews were highly favorable, although some expressed concern over the right of physicians to inquire into the most detailed sexual affairs of their patients. Others were not so sure that what emerges in hypnosis is the historical truth rather than buried fantasies. The contemporary controversy between historical and narrative truth is already present at the very birth of psychoanalysis. We may conclude, using Kuhn's (1962) language, that the *Studies on Hysteria* was a contribution to normal science, and that the authors received the expectable rewards that come to those who contribute within the confines of normal science.

The shift from the *Studies on Hysteria* to psychoanalysis proper entailed two major changes. Freud slowly replaced the hypnotic method by the technique of free association. The seduction theory as the cause of hysteria slowly gave way to the recognition of role of infantile sexuality that culminated in the Oedipus complex. In *The Interpretation of Dreams*, Freud said:

> Being in love with one parent and hating the other are among the essential constituents of the stock of psychical impulses which is formed at that time and which is of such importance in determining the symptoms of later neurosis. It is not my belief, however, that psycho-neurotics differ sharply in this respect from other human beings who remain normal. . . . [pp. 260–261]

If we ask ourselves how Freud managed to bring about so substantial a change in his theory within such a short span of years, we will find the answer in his self-analysis.

Freud's self-analysis became possible when he replaced hypnosis by free association. Systematically, Freud wrote down his dreams and wrote down every association to every item in the dream. He continued to do so until the dream yielded a meaning. Only after different schools of psychoanalysis emerged did it become clear that finding a meaning in a dream, or even in a symptom, does not guarantee that we have found the meaning. Different schools can discover different meanings in any dream reported in a psychoanalytic session. When a meaning emerged, Freud felt he had arrived at the latent content of the dream.

Freud's self-analysis enabled him to overcome the inhibition on visiting Rome (Bergmann 1976). It also enabled him to overcome his idealization of Fliess and to free himself from the bondage to him. Above all, in 1898, Freud was able to begin writing his *Interpretation of Dreams*. Freud's self-analysis continued throughout his life. There is considerable evidence, as Grubrich-Simitis (1991) has pointed out that Freud's last book, *Moses and Monotheism* (1939) becomes intelligible if we understand Freud's preoccupation with Moses as a continuation of his own self-analysis. There are two ways of looking at Freud's self-analysis. Ernst Jones (1953), Freud's authorized biographer, described it thus:

> In the summer of 1897 the spell began to break, and Freud undertook his most heroic feat—an analysis of his own unconscious. It is hard for us nowadays to imagine how momentous this achievement was, that difficulty being but the fate of most pioneering

exploits. Yet the uniqueness of the feat remains. Once done it is done forever. For no one again can be the first to explore those depths. [p. 319]

Eissler (1971) has added:

Freud discovered, from the analysis of one of his own dreams, that he was harboring a death wish toward his oldest son, who had been at the front but who was missing at that time, we can get some inkling of the shock and agitation to which his psychic apparatus was at times exposed. The courage it took to publish that dream along with its interpretation, is hardly imaginable. [p. 307]

Outside of psychoanalysis, Freud's self-analysis was not regarded with the same awe. Ellenberger (1970) classified Freud's self-analysis as a form of creative illness:

A creative illness succeeds a period of intense preoccupation with an idea and search for a certain truth. It is a polymorphous condition that can take the shape of depression, neurosis, psychosomatic ailments, or even psychosis. Whatever the symptoms, they are felt as painful, if not agonizing by the subject, with alternating periods of alleviation and worsening. Throughout the illness the subject never loses the threat of his dominating preoccupation. It is often compatible with normal professional activity and family life. But even if he keeps to his social activities, he is almost entirely absorbed with himself. He suffers from feelings of utter isolation, even when he has a mentor who guides him through the ordeal (like the shaman apprentice with his master). The termination is often rapid, marked by a phase of exhilaration. The subject emerges from his ordeal with a permanent transformation in his personality and the conviction that he has discovered a great truth or a new spiritual world. [pp. 447–448]

In Ellenberger's view Fechner, Nietzsche, and Jung, in addition to Freud, went through such a creative illness. Freud can be compared with the other three only if we believe that he emerged from his self-analysis in possession of a personal truth only. If he discovered, as psychoanalysis claims, hitherto inaccessible objective truths, then his endeavor cannot be compared with the other three. This event is unparalleled in the history of science. That introspective work of the scientist himself can bring about a substantial change in an already reasonably well-established scientific procedure is a unique feature in the history of psychoanalysis. Among Freud's contemporaries Marcel Proust can be singled out as one who underwent an analogous "creative illness," but in his case the outcome was an entirely new type of novel, *Remembrance of Things Past*. That book, like Freud's work, contributed to giving to the twentieth century its intellectual climate.

The *Interpretation of Dreams* laid the foundation for the study of culture, for now not only were hysterics suffering from excessive repression, but the culture as a whole could be seen as demanding so high a degree of instinctual renunciation as to make most of its members—particularly those not strong enough to defy its restrictions—neurotic. This insight is not as yet explicit in *The Interpretation of Dreams*, but it is expressed in "'Civilized' sexual morality and modern nervous illness" (Freud 1908a). Freud and those who followed him were attempting not only to cure neurotic patients, but to become critics of western civilization.

Three further questions have to be addressed: (1) Was Freud himself aware of the magnitude of the change between the two books? (2) Did Freud in his thinking really break with the ideas he had expressed in the *Studies on Hysteria*, or did they serve as a substratum for his psychoanalytic point of view? (3) To what extent was Freud himself aware of the role of his self-analysis in bringing about the change in his therapeutic technique and therapeutic philosophy?

As to the significant role of self-analysis, in the preface to the second edition to *The Interpretation of Dreams*, written in 1908, Freud said:

> For this book has a further subjective significance for me personally—a significance which I only grasped after I had completed it. It was, I found, a portion of my own self-analysis, my reaction to my father's death—that is to say, to the most important event, the most poignant loss, of man's life. Having discovered that this was so, I felt unable to obliterate the traces of the experience. To my readers, however, it will be a matter of indifference upon what particular material they learn to appreciate the importance of dreams and how I interpret them. [p. xxvi]

In the last remark, Freud could not have been more wrong. A whole literature has grown around Freud's self-analysis and the analysis of his dreams. His readers, far from being indifferent to the material upon which Freud built his dream interpretation, have studied these dreams and his memories from many points of view, including the limitations beyond which his self-analysis did not go.

As to the question of whether Freud was aware of the jump that took place between the two works, the answer is yes, but not immediately.

In the opening paragraph of the case of Dora (Freud 1905), we read with some astonishment:

> In 1895 and 1896 I put forward certain views upon the pathogenesis of hysterical symptoms and upon the mental processes occurring in hysteria. Since that time, several years have passed. In now proposing, therefore, to substantiate those views by giving detailed report of the history of a case and its treatment . . . [p. 7]

As late as 1905, Freud understood his work with Dora not as a new beginning, but as a confirmation of what Breuer and he had discovered.

The way Dora was interrogated and treated also shows that Freud as a therapist had not moved very far from the way patients were treated in the *Studies on Hysteria:*

> [Freud] I will explain that to you presently. Does nothing else occur to you in connection with the jewel-case? So far you have only talked about jewelry and have said nothing about a case.

> [Dora] Yes, Herr K. had made me a present of an expensive jewel-case a little time before.

> [Freud] Then a return-present would have been very appropriate. Perhaps you do not know that "jewel-case" . . . is a favorite expression . . . for the female genitals.

> [Dora] I knew you would say that.

> [Freud] That is to say you knew that it *was* so. —The meaning of the dream is now becoming even clearer. You said to yourself: "This man is persecuting me; he wants to force his way into my room. My "jewel-case" is in danger and if anything happens it will be Father's fault." [p. 69]

We learn from this exchange as well as from many others that, while Dora is no longer under hypnosis, she is still very far from a free-associating analysand.

Even in his Clark University lectures, delivered in 1909 (Freud 1910), we will note that the leap I am referring to has not yet been understood by Freud. The first two lectures summarize the work with Breuer; the third begins with the recognition of the power of resistance that was discernible only after hypnosis was given up. The chapter deals with the analysis of jokes and dreams and the mechanism of repression. There is no sharply discernible demarcation line between the two.

Even in the *Introductory Lectures* (Freud 1916–1917) we find the following statement: "An introduction to psycho-analysis is provided by the study of parapraxis and dreams; the theory of neurosis is psychoanalysis itself" (p. 379). We are entitled to conclude that up to the end of World War I psychoanalysis was to Freud primarily a theory of neurosis. By 1926, a major shift had taken place:

> There is no reason for surprise, that psycho-analysis, which was originally no more than an attempt at explaining pathological mental phenomena, should have developed into a psychology of normal mental life. The justifications for this arose with the discovery that the dreams and mistakes ("parapraxes," such as slips of the tongue, etc.) of normal men have the same mechanism as neurotic symptoms. [Freud 1926, pp. 266–267]

The major step took place in 1900, but the full significance of this step became conscious to Freud only in 1926. In the *New Introductory Lectures* (1933) the emphasis is even sharper: "We should turn our attention first to the position of the theory of dreams. It occupies a special place in the history of psycho-analysis and marks the turning point; it was with it that analysis took the step from being a psychotherapeutic procedure to being a depth psychology" (p. 7). It is evident that it took a long time for Freud to understand the full meaning of his own development. It was only after he had published a number of books dealing with the general problems of mankind that it dawned upon him that psychoanalysis contains within it two significantly different lines of development. The first is concerned primarily with the process of cure that can be brought about by Freud's technique. The other attempts to understand the profound implication that the Freudian point of view has brought about in our understanding of human culture and human nature.

On the basis of Freud's published writings, we probably would not have been able to reconstruct the transition from the *Studies on Hysteria* to *The Interpretation of Dreams*. It was only because the Princess Bonaparte refused to obey Freud's wishes and destroy the letters to his friend Fliess (Freud 1887–1904) that it is at all possible for us to learn how Freud made the transition between the two books and the enormous role that his self-analysis played in this process.

The correspondence shows that Freud's self-analysis was reported to Fliess on August 18, 1897, two years after the publication of the *Studies on Hysteria:*

> The chief patient I am preoccupied with is myself. My little hysteria, though greatly accentuated by my work, has resolved itself a bit further. The rest is still at a standstill. That is what my mood primarily depends on. The analysis is more difficult than any other. It is, in fact, what paralyzes my psychic strength for describing and communicating what I have won so far. Still I believe it must be done and is a necessary intermediate stage of my work. [p. 261]

The self-analysis becomes the main focus of interest in the correspondence of October 3, 1897, where Freud reports actually having succeeded in lifting some of his childhood amnesia as he recalled having seen his mother nude between the age of two to two and a half years. On October 15 of that year, Freud writes:

> My self-analysis is in fact the most essential thing I have at present and promises to become of greatest value to me if it reaches its end. In the middle of it, it suddenly ceased for three days during which I had the feeling of being tied up inside (which patients complain of so much) and I was really disconsolate. [p. 270]

It was in the same letter that Freud communicates to Fliess the discovery of the Oedipus complex as the universal phenomenon of childhood: "I have found in my own case too being in love with my mother and jealous of my father, and I now consider it a universal event in early childhood" (p. 272).

We should note that in his self-analysis, Freud discovered only being in love with his mother and jealousy toward the father, that is, mild and acceptable derivatives of the Oedipus complex. That Freud ever experienced in his self-analysis the full impact of his sexual desire for his mother and the full measure of murderous hatred for his father is doubtful. What probably facilitated the discovery of the Oedipus complex was Freud's reading of Sophocles' tragedy as an adolescent when he fell in love with Gisela Fluss. I consider this as a remarkable transmission of insight across two thousand years. At this crucial juncture in the history of psychoanalysis Freud's familiarity with the western literary tradition came to his aid. The discovery of the Oedipus complex was based on the recall of some childhood memories, but to these was added a major reconstruction that was possible because Freud had retained his preconscious memory of Oedipus Rex and Hamlet. This may very well be why reconstruction continued to be so central to his thinking and analyzing. Freud goes on to say:

> We can understand the gripping power of Oedipus Rex. . . . Everyone in the audience was once a budding Oedipus in fantasy and each recoils in horror from the dream fulfillment here transplanted into reality, with the full quantity of repression which separates his infantile state from his present one. [p. 272]

Everyone may have once been a budding Oedipus, and Sophocles must have aroused in his audience some of the anxiety associated with the oedipal wish, but like every great writer, Sophocles also saw to it that this arousal turned to pity rather than anxiety. Only one man, living over two thousand years later, grasped the nature of the universal component that makes this tragedy so arresting, and he was able to do so only because, in his self-analysis, he took the preliminary steps that made it possible to unravel the tragedy's secret.

Freud often wondered why a world that accepted the Sophoclean tragedy offered such a resistance to his proclamation that the Oedipus complex is the kernel of neurosis. In a paper entitled "Creative writers and day-dreaming" (1908b), he himself supplied the answer. Sophocles, being a creative writer, employs a number of strategies to make Oedipus acceptable to his audience, describing him as a highly conscientious monarch who appeals to us because he is such a relentless seeker of the truth, even if it leads to his downfall. Furthermore, strictly speaking, Oedipus is not guilty of the murder of his father and the marriage to his mother, since he killed the father and married the mother unknowingly. Add to this the fact that he owed his parents no filial devotion, since they exposed him to die on the wilderness of the mountain. Finally, whatever punitive needs are evoked in the audience, Sophocles satisfies them by letting Oedipus blind himself. But above all, Sophocles describes the fate of one man, whereas Freud proclaims the universality of the oedipal wishes.

Freud repeats the content of the letter to Fliess almost verbatim in *The Interpretation of Dreams*. But he is obviously not yet aware of the magnitude of the discovery of the Oedipus complex, for he hides it inconspicuously in a chapter called "Typical dreams" (1900, pp. 262–266), adding an optimistic note:

> King Oedipus, who slew his father Laius and married his mother Iocasta, clearly show us the fulfillment of our childhood wishes, but more fortunate than he, we have meanwhile succeeded insofar as we have not become psychoneurotic, in detaching our sexual impulses from our mothers and forgetting our jealousies of our fathers. [p. 262]

It will take another ten years for Freud to understand that this detachment of the libido in so-called normals has only rarely been achieved as successfully as he believed in 1900, and that the Oedipus complex remains a psychic constellation against which most people struggle throughout their lives.

Without missing a beat both in the letter to Fliess and in *The Interpretation of Dreams*, Freud goes from Oedipus Rex to Hamlet:

> Fleetingly the thought passed through my head that the same thing might be at the bottom of Hamlet as well. I am not thinking of Shakespeare's conscious intention, but believe rather that a real event stimulated the poet to his representation, in that his unconscious understood the unconscious of his hero. How does Hamlet the hysteric justify the words, "Thus conscience doth make cowards of us all"? [Freud 1887–1904, p. 272]

Unlike Oedipus, Hamlet had not killed his father nor married his mother. How are we to understand the phrase "fleetingly the thought occurred to me"? The expression itself suggests some ambivalence. In *The Interpretation of Dreams*, Freud writes:

Another of the great creations of tragic poetry, Shakespeare's *Hamlet*, has its roots in the same soil as Oedipus Rex. But the changed treatment of the same material reveals the whole difference in the mental life of these widely separated epochs of civilization: the secular advance of repression in the emotional life of mankind. In the *Oedipus*, the child's wishful fantasy that underlies it is brought to the open and realized as it would be in a dream. In *Hamlet* it remains repressed; and—just as in the case of neurosis—we only learn of its existence from its inhibiting consequences. [1900, p. 264]

In *Hamlet*, Freud was able to deduce the paralyzing effects of the Oedipus complex from Hamlet's symptom, the hesitation over the fulfillment of the task of revenge. It is noteworthy that before Freud no adequate explanation of Hamlet's hesitation had been offered. I would like to add that Hamlet finally commits the murder only when he himself is about to die. Oedipus pays with blindness for the parricide, even though he did not know that he was killing his father. Hamlet pays with his own death for the murder of a father substitute, the man who, according to Freud, carried out Hamlet's own parricidal wishes. The oedipal wish is more subtly presented in *Hamlet* and much better disguised than in *Oedipus Rex*. Freud attributes to Hamlet only oedipal wishes, but these wishes are strong enough to awaken in him a sense of guilt that paralyzes his actions. Freud admires the capacity of great writers to compel their readers to accept ideas they would otherwise reject as immoral.

In an earlier letter, written on October 5, 1897, Freud recalls a memory of an old woman who was his teacher in sexual matters and who "complained because I was clumsy and unable to do anything" (1887–1904, p. 268). This was a standard type of memory that patients produced under hypnosis during the Breuer period. Freud recalls further memories that the same woman washed him in reddish water, in which she had previously washed herself. He returns to the subject of his nurse in the letter of October 15, in which he reports to Fliess that he did what many analysands would do after him: ask his mother to verify his memories. The mother reported that indeed there was such an old woman who stole kreuzers (pennies) from him as a child. Her theft was discovered and she was given ten months in jail. On the basis of this communication from his mother, Freud understood for the first time a puzzling scene from his childhood, where he had asked his 20-year-old brother to unlock a cupboard, expecting that his mother was locked inside it. Disappointed, the young Sigmund had cried, and eventually his mother reappeared. Freud understood that he had heard that this nurse was "boxed-up," slang for incarcerated, and he now looked for the incarcerated mother in the cupboard. It was immediately after this recollection that Freud described to Fliess the Oedipus complex.

In the chapter, "Childhood and screen memories," Freud (1901) retells this same incident, but adds the following:

> I suspected that my naughty brother had done the same thing to her that he had done to the nurse and I forced him to open the cupboard [kasten] for me. I now understand, too, why in the translation of this visual childhood scene my mother's slimness was emphasized: it must have struck me as just having been restored to her. I am two and a half years older than the sister who was born at the time, and when I was three years old my half brother that and I ceased living in the same place. [p. 51]

In 1924, he added another footnote of considerable significance:

> The child of not yet three had understood that the little sister who had recently arrived had grown inside his mother. He was very far from approving of this addition to the family, and was full of mistrust and anxiety that his mother's inside might conceal still more children. The wardrobe or cupboard was a symbol for him for his mother's inside, so he insisted in looking into this cupboard and turned for this to his big brother who (as is clear from other material) had taken his father's place as the child's rival. [p. 51]

Freud now recognized that he as a child had wanted to enter and destroy the babies inside his mother's womb, a trend of thought we usually associate with the work of Melanie Klein. We learn from these two additions to the early memory that Freud's self-analysis was a continuous process.

Today, we surmise that the nurse must have been far more important to the child Freud than he discovered in his self-analysis. Object loss in infancy was reported without having been fully experienced. A memory of the loss of an important figure in Freud's childhood thus remained hidden behind the discovery of the Oedipus complex. Was one discovery made at the expense of the other?

In retrospect, Freud made two separate, highly significant discoveries. He discovered the Oedipus complex and almost discovered the role of the early attachment between infant and caretaker, including the traumatic effect of an early separation from the caretaker. The first finding was acknowledged, and as a result, the Oedipus complex was regarded as the nucleus of neurosis. The full significance of the second discovery was not articulated and was discovered a generation later by other analysts: Winnicott, Margaret Mahler, Anna Freud, and Melanie Klein. What matters in this historical context is that another investigator traveling the same road could have failed to discover the Oedipus complex but highlighted the significance of separation trauma. We would then have had a very different history of psychoanalysis. At this historical juncture, more than one possibility existed and another self-analyzer, undertaking the same journey that Freud did, would have come up with other conclusions. That discoveries occur at crossroads remains a permanent feature in the history of psychoanalysis. It is also repeated in every individual analysis. Indeed, it must be so when the unconscious is explored through rational means. I consider this to be a major reason why it is so difficult to convert explorations of the unconscious into a scientific discipline.

Freud was a lonely self-analyzer; ultimately the balance of inner forces determined the direction that his self-analysis took. It is even conceivable that had he not read *Oedipus Rex* or *Hamlet* he would have more easily discovered the role of object loss in early childhood rather than the Oedipus complex. In a regular analysis, at a similar juncture, the analysand is not as free as Freud was, for it will all too often happen that the therapist's philosophy and his understanding of infancy will be decisive in the direction that the associations of the analysands will take. Had Freud's wish to burn the Fliess letters succeeded, we would never have known the crucial role his self-analysis played in the sequence of what he discovered and what he failed to discover.

REFERENCES

Bergmann, M. S. (1976). Moses and the evolution of Freud's Jewish identity. In *Judaism and Psychoanalysis*, ed. M. Ostow, pp. 115–141. New York: Ktav, 1982.

Breuer, J. and Freud, S. (1893–1895). Studies on hysteria. *Standard Edition* 2.

Eissler, K. R. (1971). *Talent and Genius: The Fictitious Case of Tausk contra Freud*. New York: Quadrangle.

Ellenberger, H. (1970). *The Discovery of the Unconscious: The History and Evolution of Dynamic Psychiatry*. London: Allen Lane and Penguin.

Freud, S. (1887–1904). *The Complete Letters of Sigmund Freud to Wilhelm Fliess, 1887–1904*, ed. and trans. J. M. Masson. Cambridge, MA: Havard University Press, 1985.

—— (1900). The interpretation of dreams. *Standard Edition* 4–5.

—— (1901). The psychopathology of everyday life. *Standard Edition* 6.

—— (1905). Fragment of an analysis of a case of hysteria. *Standard Edition* 2:1–122.

—— (1908a). "Civilized" sexual morality and modern nervous illness. *Standard Edition* 9:177–204.

—— (1908b). Creative writers and day-dreaming. *Standard Edition* 9:141–153.

—— (1910). Five lectures on psycho-analysis. *Standard Edition* 11:1–55.

—— (1916–1917). Introductory lectures on psychoanalysis. *Standard Edition* 15–16.

—— (1926). The question of lay analysis. *Standard Edition* 20:177–250.

—— (1933). New introductory lectures on psycho-analysis. *Standard Edition* 22:1–182.

—— (1939). Moses and monotheism: three essays. *Standard Edition* 23:1–137.

Goldstein, J. (1982). The hysteria diagnosis and the politics of anticlericalism in late nineteenth-century France. *Journal of Modern History* 54:209–239.

Grubrich-Simitis, I. (1991). *Freuds Moses-Studie als Tagtraum*. Weinheim: Verlag Internationale Psychoanalyse.

Jones, E. (1953). *The Life and Work of Sigmund Freud*, Vol. 1. New York: Basic Books.

Kuhn, T. (1962). *The Structure of Scientific Revolutions*. Chicago, IL: University of Chicago Press.

Lear, J. (1990). *Love and Its Place in Nature: A Philosophical Interpretation of Freudian Psychoanalysis*. New York: Farrar, Straus & Giroux.

McGrath, W. J. (1992). Freud and the force of history. In *Freud and the History of Psychoanalysis*, ed. T. Gelfands and J. Kerr, pp. 79–97. Hillsdale, NJ: Analytic Press.

Contributors

Lewis Aron, Ph.D., is Director, New York University Postdoctoral Program in Psychotherapy and Psychoanalysis and former president of the Division (39) of Psychoanalysis, American Psychological Association. He is the author of *A Meeting of Minds.*

Jessica Benjamin, Ph.D., is a psychoanalyst in private practice in New York City, a faculty member and supervisor at the Postdoctoral Program in Psychotherapy and Psychoanalysis at New York University, and the author of *The Bonds of Love; Like Subjects, Love Objects;* and *The Shadow of the Other.*

Martin S. Bergmann, Ph.D., is Professor of Psychology at New York University, a member of the International Psychoanalytic Association, an honorary member of the American Psychoanalytic Association, and the author of *Anatomy of Loving* and, most recently, *The Hartmann Era.*

Teresa Brennan, Ph.D., is the Schmidt Distinguished Professor of Humanities at Florida Atlantic University where she designed the Public Intellectuals Ph.D. Program. Her most recent book is *Exhausting Modernity: Grounds for a New Economy.*

Philip M. Bromberg, Ph.D., is Training and Supervising Analyst, William Alanson White Psychoanalytic Institute; Clinical Professor of Psychology, New York University Postdoctoral Program; Associate Editor, *Psychoanalytic Dialogues;* Assistant Editor, *Contemporary Psychoanalysis;* and author of *Standing in the Spaces: Essays on Clinical Process, Trauma, and Dissociation.*

Jody Messler Davies, Ph.D., is coeditor, *Psychoanalytic Dialogues;* supervisor, New York University Postdoctoral Program in Psychotherapy and Psychoanalysis; faculty member and supervisor, National Institute for the Psychotherapies; coauthor (with Mary Gail Frawley-O'Dea) of *Treating the Adult Survivor of Childhood Sexual Abuse: A Psychoanalytic Perspective.* She is currently at work on a new book, *Relational Bonds, Dissociative Barriers: Transformations of Desire and Despair in Psychoanalysis.*

Ann D'Ercole, Ph.D., is Clinical Associate Professor of Psychology at the Postdoctoral Program in Psychotherapy and Psychoanalysis and the Graduate School of Arts and Sciences, both at New York University. She is the editor of the *Journal of Gay and Lesbian Psychotherapy* and the forthcoming *Unconventional Couples/Uncoupling Conventions: Reappraisal in Psychoanalytic Theory and Practice.*

Muriel Dimen, Ph.D., is CoChair, Relational Orientation, Postdoctoral Program in Psychotherapy and Psychoanalysis, New York University. She is the author of, most recently, *Surviving Sexual Contradictions;* coeditor (with Virginia Goldner) of *Gender in Psychoanalytic Space;* and Associate Editor of *Psychoanalytic Dialogues* and *Studies in Gender and Sexuality.*

Rita Frankiel, Ph.D., is Training and Supervising Analyst at the New York Freudian Society, Associate Clinical Professor at the New York University Postdoctoral Program in Psychotherapy and Psychoanalysis, and a member of the International Psychoanalytic Association. She is the editor of *Essential Papers on Object Loss.*

Jan Goldstein, Ph.D., is Professor of History at the University of Chicago and an editor of the *Journal of Modern History.* Her books include *Console and Classify: The French Psychiatric Profession in the Nineteenth Century* and *Foucault and the Writing of History.*

André Green, M.D., is Training Analyst for the Paris Psychoanalytic Society, former President and Director of the Paris Psychoanalytic Institute, and was Vice President of the International Psychoanalytic Society and Professor of University College London for the Freud Memorial Chair. His books include *On Private Madness, The Work of the Negative, The Fabric of Affect in the Psychoanalytic Discourse,* and *André Green at the Squiggle Foundation.*

Adrienne Harris, Ph.D., is on the faculty and supervises at the New York University Postdoctoral Program in Psychotherapy and Psychoanalysis. She is on the Editorial Boards of *Psychoanalytic Dialogues* and *Studies in Gender and Sexuality* and is the coeditor, with Lewis Aron, of *The Legacy of Sandor Ferenczi.*

Paola Mieli, Ph.D., is a psychoanalyst in New York, Founder and President of Après-Coup Psychoanalytic Association (New York City), and a member of Le Cercle Freudien (Paris). She is the author of numerous articles on psychoanalysis and culture and is the coeditor of the book *Being Human: The Technological Extensions of the Body.*

Stephen A. Mitchell, Ph.D., died Dec 21, 2000. He was a faculty member and supervisor at the New York University Postdoctoral Program in Psychoanalysis and Psychotherapy and the William Alanson White Institute. He was the Founding Editor of *Psychoanalytic Dialogues: A Journal of Relational Perspectives* and author of a number of books outlining the field of relational psychoanalysis. His most book is *Relationality: From Attachment to Intersubjectivity.* A new book, *The Degradation of Romance,* will be published by Norton Press.

Michael S. Roth, Ph.D., is President of California College of Arts and Crafts. His recent publications include *The Ironist's Cage; Memory, Trauma and the Construction of History; Freud: Conflict and Culture;* and *Psychoanalysis as History: Negation and Freedom in Freud.*

Roy Schafer, Ph.D., is a training and supervising analyst at the Columbia University Center for Psychoanalytic Training and Research. He is a Vice President of the International Psychoanalytic Association and the author of numerous books and articles, including *Tradition and Change in Psychoanalysis, The Contemporary Kleinians of London, Retelling a Life,* and *The Analytic Attitude.* He is in private practice in New York City.

David Schwartz, Ph.D., is a psychoanalyst in private practice in New York City and Westchester County, New York. He is on the editorial boards of *Studies in Gender and Sexuality* and the *Journal of Gay and Lesbian Psychotherapy.*

Barbara Waxenberg, Ph.D., is a supervisor at the New York University Postdoctoral Program in Psychoanalysis and Psychotherapy; a faculty member and supervisor at the Manhattan Institute for Psychoanalysis; and co-coordinator, Project in Family Theory and Therapy, at the New York University Postdoctoral Program.

Benjamin Wolstein, Ph.D., died October, 1998, in Manhattan. He was a training and supervising analyst at the William Alanson White Institute, and a faculty member and supervisor at the New York University Postdoctoral Program in Psychoanalysis and Psychotherapy and at the Derner Institute of Adelphi University. His books include *Transference: Theory of Psychoanalytic Therapy* and *Countertransference.* He was the author of seven books and 100 articles.

Index

Subject/object relations, 295–296, 299
complementarity, 36–41, 48
Suggestion (Bernheim), 238
Suggestions, 8. *See also* Hypnosis
Sullivan, H. S., 25, 123
Sulloway, F., 190
Swales, P., 227, 231, 236
Symbolic, the, 18
Symbolic metaphorization, 82
Symbolization, 21, 55, 68, 76, 125, 270
enabled by maternal containment, 54–55
limits of, 269–270, 272
and symptoms, 42–43
Symptoms, of hysteria, 17, 25, 162, 246, 249, 276, 290
affecting speech, 58, 162–163
attempts to understand, 111, 118, 248, 260, 305, 313–314
blindness as, 289, 291
Breuer and Freud erasing, 169, 343
characterizations of, 79, 187
as compromise, 252, 274–275, 310
conversion, 71–73, 83
formation of, 274, 307, 334
Freud using hypnosis on, 170–171, 232–233
Freud's focus on, 124, 131, 133, 235–236, 326–328
in Freud's model of neurosis, 75–76
history expressed through, 10–11, 81, 288–289
loss of will as, 133–134
modern reevaluation of, 71–73
of Nanette Leroux, 148–149, 159–160
psychical impotence as, 205, 207
recurrence of, 93, 333
removal of, 84–86, 101, 119

removal through abreaction, 96–97, 112
removal through verbalization, 42–43, 84–85
role in therapy sessions, 326, 328
structure of, 13–14
unruliness as, 133, 135, 137
vs. speech, 42–43

Talking cure, 3, 8–9, 132–133, 179–181. *See also* Psychoanalysis
Tenderness, 205–206
Theatricality, as characteristic of hysteria, 9–14
Theory of Sexuality (Freud), 69
Therapeutic relationship, 7, 39, 60, 78, 123, 190, 239. *See also* Power
Breuer's, 93, 111–118, 344
changed from traditional doctor/patient model, 9, 180–181, 240, 344
coparticipation in, 40–45, 111–118, 132–133
Freud's, 178–180, 314–318, 328–329
hysterics as in need of direction, 176–177, 180
Nanette's "prescriptions" in, 150, 156–157, 164
Therapist, 190, 267, 337. *See also* Therapeutic relationship
hysteric's dependence on, 175–176, 181
listening by, 8, 129–130, 344
patient putting as ego ideal, 46, 50–52
power of, 7, 82–83
response to victims of abuse, 277–279
role of, 75, 78, 117, 305, 316
techniques individualized by, 113, 225–226
using own subjectivity, 52–54